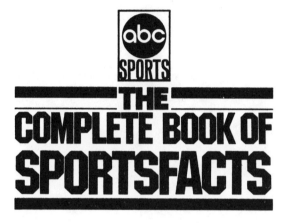

abc SPORTS
THE COMPLETE BOOK OF
SPORTSFACTS

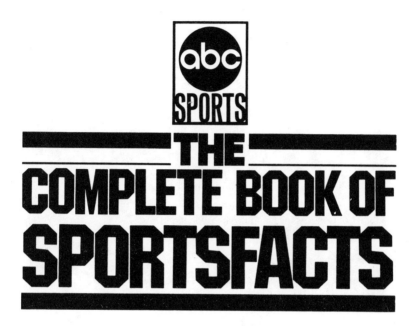

A NORBACK BOOK

 ADDISON-WESLEY PUBLISHING COMPANY
Reading, Massachusetts ● Menlo Park, California
London ● Amsterdam ● Don Mills, Ontario ● Sydney

Library of Congress Cataloging in Publication Data
Main entry under title:

ABC sports.

   1. Sports—Miscellanea.   I. Norback, Craig T.
GV704.A23   796   81-12712
ISBN 0-201-00067-9 (pbk.)   AACR2

ABC SPORTS THE COMPLETE BOOK OF SPORTSFACTS
Produced by NORBACK & COMPANY, INC.
Princeton, New Jersey

Managing Editor: Roy Winnick
Research Director: Leslie Goldwater
Art Director: Jim Bernard
Research Editors: Elizabeth Donovan, Patricia Morris
Editors: Roy A. Grisham, F. F. Phillips
Production: Betty J. Junna

Cover photo (race car) by Heinz Kluetmeier for *Sports Illustrated*; all other cover photos courtesy of ABC Sports.

Cover design by Jim Bernard and Roy Winnick.

ABCDEFGHIJ-DO-854321

ISBN 0-201-00067-9

Contents

Acknowledgments

We wish to thank the following people for their assistance in the preparation of *The Complete Book of SportsFacts:* Dale Antram, Tai Babilonia, Dave Baldridge, Stan Bergstein, Conrad Burkman, Ricky Davis, Chris Economaki, Phil Esposito, Bill Flemming, Joe Hirsch, Keith Jackson, Tom Jordan, Billy Kidd, Dr. Sammy Lee, Roger Maris, Tom McMillen, Al Michaels, Dick Mulvihill, Chuck Pezzano, Chris Schenkel, Mark Spitz, Dick Stockton, Bert Randolph Sugar, Lynn Swann, and Ed Westfall. Also, Anne Cauley, Don Suesz, Carl Berkowitz, and Pamela Long.

Special thanks to Tony Rezza of ABC Photography and Denise Shapiro of ABC Merchandising. Also, Brian Redman of ProServ, Inc., and Marilyn O'Brien.

The following organizations generously provided information and technical assistance:

AUTO RACING: International Hot Rod Association; International Motor Sports Association; International Race of Champions; Michelin Tire Corporation; NASCAR; National Hot Rod Association; Sports Car Club of America, Inc.; United States Auto Club; *BASEBALL:* American League of Professional Baseball Clubs; National Baseball Hall of Fame; National League of Professional Baseball Clubs; Office of the Baseball Commissioner; *BASKETBALL:* Naismith Memorial Basketball Hall of Fame; National Basketball Association; National Collegiate Athletic Association; *BILLIARDS:* Billiards Congress of America; *Billiards Digest;* Professional Pool Players Association; *BOWLING:* American Bowling Congress; Professional Bowlers Association of America; Women's International Bowling Congress; Women's Professional Bowlers Association; *BOXING:* Amateur Athletic Union; Golden Gloves Association of America, Inc.; *Ring* Magazine, Bert Randolph Sugar, publisher; *The Ring Record Book; FOOTBALL:* National Collegiate Athletic Association; National Football League; Pro Football Hall of Fame, Joe Horrigan, curator/historian; *GOLF:* Ladies Professional Golf Association; PGA Tour; Professional Golfers' Association of America; United States Golf Association; World Golf Hall of Fame; *GYMNASTICS:* United States Gymnastics Federation; U.S. Olympic Committee; *HOCKEY:* National Hockey League, reprinted from *National Hockey League Guide,* copyright © 1980; *HORSE RACING:* Hall of Fame of the Trotter; National Museum of Racing; Thoroughbred Racing Associations; United States Trotting Association; *ICE SKATING:* International Skating Union; United States Figure Skating Association; United States International Speedskating Association; *RODEO:* National Cowboy Hall of Fame; Professional Rodeo Cowboys Association; Professional Women's Rodeo Association; Rodeo News Bureau; *SKIING:* National Ski Hall of Fame; *Ski Racing,* Mark Gabriel, managing editor; United States Ski Association; United States Ski Team; *SOCCER:* Major Indoor Soccer League, Doug Verb, director of publicity; North American Soccer League, Mal Karwoski, director of public relations; *SWIMMING & DIVING:* Amateur Athletic Association; International Swimming Hall of Fame; National Collegiate Athletics Association; United States Diving, Inc.; United States Swimming, Inc.; *TENNIS:* Association of Tennis Professionals; International Tennis Hall of Fame; United States Tennis Association; Women's Tennis Association; *TRACK & FIELD:* Athletics Congress/USA, Pete Cava, press information director; National Track and Field Hall of Fame; *Track & Field News;* U.S. Olympic Committee.

Introduction

With this first edition of *The Complete Book of Sportsfacts*. ABC Sports is pleased to bring you nearly 400 pages of facts and figures from 18 of the most popular competitive sports in the world today: Auto racing, Baseball, Basketball, Billiards, Bowling, Boxing, Football, Golf, Gymnastics, Hockey, Horse Racing, Rodeo, Ice Skating, Skiing, Soccer, Swimming and Diving, Tennis and Track and Field.

For each of these exciting, action sports, *The Complete Book of SportsFacts* gives you a short *Overview* of the sport from its origins to the present; *Great Moments* in the sport's history; *The Setup*, listing sponsoring and sanctioning organizations, with addresses and officials' names; *The Basics*, describing the rules and how the game is played; *How to Watch*, with analyses by experts (including Lynn Swann on football, Roger Maris on baseball, Tai Babilonia on figure skating, Phil Esposito on hockey, Dick Stockton on tennis, Mark Spitz on swimming, and Billy Kidd on skiing) of how to watch their sport, what to look for, understanding style and strategy; *Main Events*, a list of major competitions and recent winners; *All-Time Greats*, listing the greatest athletes in the sport's history, with photographs and short biographies; *For the Record*, with current records in the sport's major competitions or categories; *Did You Know?*, with questions that test your knowledge of the sport's least-known facets; and *Key Words*, which defines several of the more significant and specialized terms in each sport's lexicon. In addition to all this, you'll find more than 100 action-packed or historic photographs that bring the names, the facts, and the statistics to vivid life.

Keep *The Complete Book of SportsFacts* close at hand when you watch these exciting sports on TV, or when you visit the stadiums, arenas, rinks, tracks, fields, bowling alleys, and tennis courts where competitions and events are held. *The Complete Book of SportsFacts* will give you all the facts you want about these 18 major sports. It is a book you will want to read, reread, and just have around, for a long time to come.

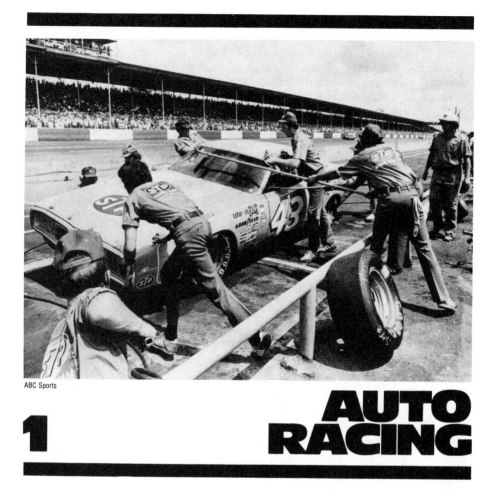

AUTO RACING

1

I f one believes that life is beautiful and fine, auto racing is irrational," declares Karl Menninger in *Man Against Himself*. "If one is full of despair, cynicism, or apathy, then racing need not be viewed as irrational." Although many people share Menninger's view that racing is a suicidal sport smacking faintly of the same mentality that produced Kamikaze fighter pilots, automobile racing nevertheless remains one of the most popular sports in the world, both to the thousands of people who participate in it and to the even more thousands of spectators.

Despite—or, perhaps, because of—its danger, racing has long intrigued people. Ancient legends are filled with accounts of races among the gods, and chariot races among the ancient Romans in the Coliseum were packed as full as today's Indianapolis Motor Speedway. The two qualities tested most rigorously by automobile racing—speed and endurance—have long been among the most favored and exciting ones in the human experience. Add to that the excitement of the search for better and better machines, and racing becomes an irresistible attraction to millions.

The first automobile races, in fact, were held not to demonstrate the skill of the driver but to promote the product of the automobile manufacturer. In the early days of automobiles, when manufacturers were many and advertising media few, races were held to demonstrate to a potential car-buying public the superiority of one brand over another. Henry Ford, the Peugeots, the Renaults, and other entrepreneurs were among the first enthusiastic participants in the early car races held in the last decade of the nineteenth century.

By 1910 or so, auto racing had become big business, as well as a big headache. To minimize the potential harm to spectators (car racing was then called the "big blood bath"), promoters began building specially designed circuits to be used exclusively by racers. Grand Prix races take place on highways and city streets, but most other races today are held on tracks. Although this minimizes the danger somewhat, the potential for harm remains—drivers, and sometimes spectators, can be killed in collisions and other accidents. Nevertheless, the idea of driver and machine united in a war against a traditional nemesis—time—continues to appeal to men and women who believe (and often prove) that it is possible to beat the odds, that one can always go a little farther or a little faster or do something a little better than it ever has been done before.

Great Moments

1894   The first recorded automobile race is held, using steam cars that race between the French cities of Paris and Rouen.

1895   *The Chicago Tribune* sponsors the first auto race held in the United States. The race, from Chicago to Evanston (Illinois), is won by the Duryea entry, which averages 7.5 miles per hour.

1902   The American Automobile Association is founded.

1903   Barney Oldfield becomes the first person to drive a car one mile in one minute. Also this year, the Firestone Tire and Rubber Company produces the first automobile tires made entirely of rubber.

1904   The first Vanderbilt Cup races are held on Long Island, with A. L. Campbell winning in his Mercedes.

1906   Races are held at the newly built Indianapolis Motor Speedway. Also in 1906, the first international Grand Prix is held, at Le Mans, France.

1909   Bert Scott and C. James Smith win the first transcontinental auto race, from New York to Seattle, and receive a prize of $2,000 donated by Robert Guggenheim.

1910   March 23: the first U.S. trial races are held, at the Los Angeles Motordrome.

1911   Ray Harroun drives a Marmon Wasp at a speed of 74.5 miles per hour to win the first Indianapolis 500 and collect $2,000 in prize money.

1925   At the Indy 500, Peter DePaolo becomes the first auto racer to average more than 100 miles per hour, with 101.13 mph.

1931   Malcolm Campbell (later knighted) sets a land-speed record of 246.575 miles per hour at Daytona Beach, Florida.

1933   Sacramento, California, is the site of the first professional midget auto races.

1946   The growing popularity of auto racing is demonstrated when a record 146,000 spectators watch the Indianapolis 500.

1947   The National Association for Stock Car Auto Racing (NASCAR) holds its first meeting, in Daytona Beach.

1948   Red Byron, driving a modified Ford, wins the first NASCAR-sponsored race, in Daytona Beach.

1952   The American Automobile Association opens an auto-racing hall of fame, which lasts until 1955. In 1956, it reemerges as the Indianapolis Motor Speedway Hall of Fame.

1957   The Automobile Competitive Committee for the United States (ACCUS) is set up to represent U.S. auto clubs in international competition.

1958   Beach racing ends as Paul Goldsmith wins the last auto race held on Daytona Beach.

1963   Twenty-seven-year-old Jimmy Clark wins Grand Prix races in France, Italy, Belgium, Mexico, the Netherlands, Great Britain, and South Africa, and comes in second in Germany.

1965   The National Stock Car Racing Hall of Fame is built.

1966   Richard Petty becomes the first driver to win a second Daytona 500.

1970   Buddy Baker, averaging 200.447 mph at Alabama International Motor Speedway, becomes the first man ever to turn a closed course at 200 mph.

1977   Janet Guthrie becomes the first woman to qualify for the Indy 500, but mechanical difficulties force her out of the race after 27 laps. She finishes twenty-ninth in a field of 33 drivers.

1979   The Daytona 500 becomes the first 500-mile auto race to be telecast in its entirety.

The
Setup

The world of professional auto racing is somewhat complex. It comprises numerous organizations that sponsor contests of both speed and endurance for cars of all different types. The complexity is deceiving, though, for only a few major organizations dominate auto racing.

Most international automobile racing is conducted under the aegis of the Paris-based Federation Internationale de l'Automobile (FIA). The FIA recognizes eight different classes of cars and awards twelve international championships, the most important of which are the Grand Prix races held throughout the world (fifteen in 1980). The FIA limits participation in the Grand Prix to qualified drivers of Formula 1 cars—open-wheeled, single-seat cars that meet rigid specifications of size, weight, power, body style, and type of tire. The World Championship of Drivers is awarded to the driver who earns the most points in Grands Prix in a given year.

The United States Auto Club (USAC), successor to the American Automobile Association's racing interests, sanctions Indy-car, stock-car, sprint-car, and midget racing in the United States. The Indianapolis 500, perhaps the best-known American auto race, is sanctioned by USAC's National Championship Division. In 1978, a group of leading Indy drivers and car owners split with the USAC and formed Championship Auto Racing Clubs, Inc. (CART). The next year, CART, in association with the Sports Car Club of America (SCCA), conducted its own Indy races and in 1980 held the PPG Indy Car World Series. CART awards an Indy Car Series Championship to the driver who accumulates the most points in a season.

Another domestic racing organization is the National Association for Stock Car Racing (NASCAR), organized in 1947. At first, the main NASCAR-sanctioned event was beach racing, usually on the wet sands of Daytona Beach, Florida; today, however, NASCAR's Grand National (GN) races are held on specially built speedways. With 39 circuits throughout the United States, NASCAR sponsors a variety of stock-car events, including the popular Daytona 500. It awards the Winston Cup Grand National Championships (open to steel-bodied, recent-model American passenger sedans) and sanctions such other events as the Late Model Sportsman races and races for convertibles, midget cars, and other stock cars.

The Sports Car Club of America (SCCA), with more than 20,000 members, is another leading U.S. racing organization. It is a member of the Automobile Competition Committee for the United States (ACCUS), the American body that establishes eligibility for the FIA and international competition. SCCA sanctions four major professional series: SCCA Budweiser Can-Am Challenge (U.S. drivers only); the CRC Chemicals Trans Am Championship; the VW Rabbit/Bilstein Cup; and the Robert Bosch/VW Super Vee series. The club also sponsors such popular, nonprofessional events as its National Club Rally Championships.

The International Motor Sports Association (IMSA), which operates in the United States and Canada, sanctions the GT series, a showcase for drivers of international caliber with cars of innovative design. The series has two championships—one in its GTO Division (for Group 4 cars with engines displacing more than 2.5 liters) and the GTU Division (for Group 4 cars of less than 2.5 liters displacement). The association also sanctions the Champion Spark Plug Challenge, for small sedans with street radial tires, and the Kellygirl Challenge, for American V-8 and six-cylinder sedans on road courses.

The International Hot Rod Association (IHRA), an organization of drag racers, divides its competitions into eight categories, depending on type of car, size of the engine, and modifications made. Cars of different classes compete on the basis of a handicap determined by computer. Among the national events sanctioned by the IHRA are the Winston Spring Nationals, the U.S. Open Nationals, the Pro-Am Nationals, and the Dixie Nationals.

The National Hot Rod Association (NHRA), with its 37,000 members, is the largest auto-racing organization in the world. The association sanctions and promotes drag racing exclusively. Although the NHRA sanctions 3,000 events during the year, it is known mainly for its Winston World Championship Series (WWCS), comprising 10 national and 34 world series races. Driving championships in 8 categories are awarded in the WWCS.

The International Race of Champions (IROC) is one of the most competitive racing series in the world. In an effort to reduce the mechanical variables of racing, and test only the skill of the driver, IROC assigns the world's top racers to drive identical cars. Presumably, the winner of the series is the best racing driver in the world.

FEDERATION INTERNATIONALE
DE L'AUTOMOBILE
8 Place de la Concorde
75008 Paris
France
265.95.54
Yvon Leon, sec.-gen.

INTERNATIONAL HOT ROD
ASSOCIATION
P.O. Box 3029
Bristol, TN 37620
(615) 764-1164
Larry Carrier, pres.

INTERNATIONAL MOTOR SPORTS
ASSOCIATION
P.O. Box 3465
Bridgeport, CT 06605
(203) 336-2116
John M. Bishop, pres.

INTERNATIONAL RACE OF
CHAMPIONS
Bob Thomas & Associates, Inc.
835 Hopkins Way
Redondo Beach, CA 90277
(213) 376-6978
Roger Penske, pres.

NATIONAL ASSOCIATION FOR
STOCK CAR AUTO RACING
P.O. Box K
Daytona Beach, FL 32015
(904) 253-0611
Bill France, Jr., pres.

NATIONAL HOT ROD ASSOCIATION
10639 Riverside Dr.
North Hollywood, CA 91603
(203) 985-6472
Wally Parks, pres.

SPORTS CAR CLUB OF AMERICA
P.O. Box 22476
Denver, CO 80222
(303) 770-1044
Tom Duval, exec. officer

UNITED STATES AUTO CLUB
4910 W. 16 St.
Speedway, IN 46224
(317) 247-5151
Richard King, pres.

The Basics

GENERAL CIRCUIT RACING

Object To complete a specified course in the least time, or to cover the greatest length of track within a specified time limit.

The course The length, characteristics, and complexity of courses vary. They must, however, meet the standards of the sanctioning organization, and they must be furnished with marshals' posts, safety barriers, and fire equipment.

Vehicles Different types of cars—sports, single-seat racing, stock, and so on—compete in circuit racing. To be eligible, a car must have no more than four road wheels, have sprung suspension between the wheels and the chassis, and meet whatever other safety and construction requirements are imposed by the sanctioning body.

Officials The officials usually are: the clerk of the course, timekeepers, pit observers, road observers, handicappers, starters, flag marshals, stewards, the secretary of the meeting, and the finish judges.

A Comparison of Formula One to American Formula Racing

The Formula	Type of Car	Speed in MPH (km)	Type of Race	Engine	Chassis Body	Tires and Rims	Pit Stop for Fuel
Formula One (FISA sanctioned): Also called Grand Prix, the International Formula is primarily run in Europe, although three races are run in the U.S.	Single-seat/ open wheel	Up to 200 (320)	Road racing	3,000 cc. (1,500 cc. if turbo) power: 475 bhp and over	Minimum weight: 575 kg. (1,270 lbs.) Maximum width: 215 cm. (84.6 ins.) Skirts are allowed	Rear wheels: 13 inches maximum diameter. Wheel/tire assembly: 21 inches maximum	Fuel tank should contain enough fuel to last the race
Indy Cars (USAC and CART sanctioned): U.S. Formula, the main and world-famous event of the season is the Indy 500.	Single-seat/ open wheel	Up to 200 (320)	Oval speedway	Production 5.8 liter or turbo power: 550 bhp	Minimum weight: 648 kg. (1,430 lbs.)	Wheel diameter: 15 inches Rim width: Front (10 in.) Rear (14 in.)	Pit stop for fuel; fuel tank capacity is limited
Can-Am (SCCA sanctioned: Similar to Formula One competition, this race is a North American Formula	Single or two-seat/enclosed wheels	Up to 200 (320)	Road racing	Production-based V8 is the most common; limited to 5,000 cc. Power: 550 bhp	Bodywork is firmly fixed covering wheels and mechanical parts. Height: 45 inches Width: 87 inches Length: 195 inches	Cars can be run on any racing tire if sanctioned by SCCA	No pit stop for fuel as in F1
IMSA GT-Grand Touring: This race is an American Formula based on international rules. Cars must also be approved by FIA	Production-based sports cars	Up to 185 (300)	Road racing	No minimum or maximum displacement; turbo is allowed	External shape must be maintained. Engine and trunk lids can be modified	Cars must run on racing tires	Pit stops for fuel depend upon the length and/or type of race
RS-Racing Stock: This race is an American Formula for volume production cars available to the U.S. public	Four-seat cars sold in U.S.	Up to 155 (250)	Road racing	Maximum: 4,000 cc. push rod or 2,300 cc. overhead cam	Cars must be stock	Cars must run on commercially available radial-ply tires	Generally, no pit stop for fuel; capacity is 22 gallons
NASCAR: Stock car racing is a typical American Formula	American-built intermediate and full-size stock cars. (From 1981 on, cars will be down-sized stock cars)	Up to 185 (300)	Oval speedway	From 5,000 cc. Engine must be the same displacement as original model	Front spoilers and a rear deck lid are the only aerodynamic devices allowed	Except for tire clearance, the original dimensions of the car must be maintained	Pit stop for fuel; fuel tank capacity is limited to 22 gallons

Courtesy of Michelin Tire Corporation.

Competitors All competitors must be licensed. The number of cars in a particular race is determined by the sanctioning organization.

Driver's equipment Drivers must wear crash helmets, goggles or visors, and protective clothing.

Length of race Races are of varying length. Some, such as LeMans, are for a set period—24 hours. Others, such as the Grand Prix, are for either 2 hours or 200 miles of racing, whichever comes first. Still others, such as the Indianapolis 500, are for a set number of laps around a course.

Rule 1 *The start* The starting order is determined by the performance of cars in trials. The race begins when the flag is dropped. In some races, drivers follow a pace car around the circuit before the race begins.

Rule 2 *Bad start* A car that begins to race before the signal has committed a "bad start" and will be penalized.

Rule 3 *Flags* Drivers must obey signals given by flags. When a black flag is waved at a driver, the driver must stop the car; when a red flag is waved, all drivers must stop. A yellow flag means "caution—do not try to pass"; it is usually waved if there has been an accident on the course. A checkered flag marks the end of the race. Other signals are: a stationary blue flag (meaning, another car is following); a yellow flag with red stripes (the course is slippery); a white flag (a nonracing official vehicle is on the course).

Rule 4 *Advice and help* Drivers may receive advice and mechanical help during a race.

Rule 5 *Dangerous situations* A driver may not drive recklessly; a driver who does so may be ordered to stop or reduce speed. Also, a car may be withdrawn from competition if officials decide that it is no longer mechanically fit to race.

Rule 6 *The winner* The winner is the driver who completes the required course in the least time, or who covers the most miles in a set time period.

DRAG RACING

Object To complete a short, straight track ahead of an opponent.

The track The track is usually a one-quarter mile, straight course.

Officials The officials usually employed are judges (at the starting and finish lines), a timekeeper, a race director, and observers.

Vehicles The many classes of drag racing vehicles fall within nine basic eliminator categories—top fuel, funny car, pro stock, top alcohol dragster, top alcohol funny car, competition, modified, super stock, and stock. Top fuel dragsters are the fastest-accelerating machines in the world, capable of covering the course in 5.65 seconds from a standing start at speeds in excess of 250 mph.

Competitors The number of participants is not set, although most fields are restricted to 16 cars. Cars compete by pairs in an elimination process that eventually determines the winner.

Rule 1 *The start* The start of the race is determined by a series of yellow, green, and red lights attached to a pole in the center of the track. The race begins at the instant the green light comes on. Quick reaction to the green light is the key to winning the race.

Rule 2   Alternating lanes   Cars must alternate lanes on qualifying runs; that is, if a car's last run was in the left lane, the next run must be in the right lane.

Rule 3   Infractions   Cars violating a rule are disqualified. If both cars in a round commit an infraction, the first car to do so is disqualified and the other car is declared the winner.

Rule 4   Weighing station   All winning cars must be weighed and spot checked at the end of a round. Failure to stop at the weighing stations results in disqualification.

Rule 5   The winner   The winner of each elimination round is the racer who crosses the finish line ahead of the opponent, though not necessarily in the shortest elapsed time from the start. The winner of an entire race is the driver who eliminates opponents one at a time, until only he or she remains unbeaten.

How to watch

ABC Sports

with Chris Economaki

Over the years, the excitement of watching auto racing has been reduced somewhat by technological advances. For instance, pit crews now communicate with drivers by two-way radios instead of by pit boards, which were often good for "ten laps of fantastic interest," as ABC Sports announcer Chris Economaki puts it. "Now," he continues, "it's all a private conversation between the driver and the crew. The fans are left out."

According to Economaki, advanced technology has also tipped the human-machine balance in auto racing in favor of the machine. "No matter how good you are, if you don't have a good car, you can't win. Years ago, cars were not as sophisticated as they are today. In some ways, it has become a race of engineers and technology, not drivers."

Nevertheless, the thrill of watching two first-rate drivers in incredibly fine-tuned, multithousand-dollar machines racing side by side around a track has not disappeared altogether. (In fact, in the IROC championship, drivers in identical cars are pitted against each other, making the race entirely a contest of skill.) So there is still plenty to watch. The first thing to look for in any auto race is good weather, which usually means no sun. The reason is simple, says Economaki: "Engines work better when the air is dense. On a hot, sunny day, the air is not dense. The best conditions for a car—and for a driver's comfort—are a cool day with not too much sun. Traditionally, track records are set when it's cool. If the weather is good on the day of the race, there will be very little to see in the way of preparation. If the weather at a Grand Prix is bad, though, there might be some exciting goings-on, because they always count on good weather. If it rains, crews have to change tires and chassis settings and so forth."

What the viewer looks for once the race begins depends to a great extent on what kind of race it is. Driver strategy isn't the same in Indianapolis 500 racing—or oval racing, for that matter—as it is in road or Grand Prix racing. Drag racing is a world of its own, and so is sprint racing. For example, stock-car racers use the pits strategically; Grand Prix racers use them only when they have to. In a long-distance oval race, the start is more important psychologically than it is in reality, whereas, in Grand Prix, where passing is severely limited, the start is the key to the rest of the race. It's important for the driver to qualify strongly, so as to be in the front line of cars at the start.

THE PIT

"At Indianapolis and other oval races," Economaki says, "many races are won or lost in the pit. The amount of fuel these cars are permitted to carry is limited for safety reasons, so they must often stop for fuel. The pit crew must work fast and accurately. The pit crew can also help the driver, in terms of strategy, simply by knowing his temperament. For instance, in car racing, there are 'drivers' and there are 'racers.' A driver is a technician—a scientist at the wheel who knows how to get the most out of the car, but who doesn't have the appetite for the cut and thrust, the wheel-to-wheel competition. The technician-driver is best when he's alone on the track. A racer, on the other hand, will drive to the point where the technician-driver would let up on the pedal; but the racer looks at the guy next to him and goes another fifty feet trying to beat him.

"In a race a few years ago that required one fueling stop, a driver's pit crew recognized that they were working with a driver and not a racer. They got him in the pit as soon as possible and let the traffic go by. When he went back out, he was alone on the track, and he could drive without having to worry so much about what the others were doing. Later, when everyone else had to stop, he pulled ahead."

Another pit strategy often used in oval racing is for drivers to pull into the pit when the yellow caution flag is up. "That's just being race-wise," Economaki says. "Because everyone else has slowed down for the yellow flag, you lose only half a lap."

ABC Sports

THE START

The importance of the start and of the starting position vary according to the race. "In the Grand Prix," Economaki says, "the start is the most important part of the race. There is very little passing. So, in order to avoid having to pass someone, you qualify well, and start up front. Now, in a sprint race, which may be only 20 or 30 laps around a short track, the start is especially important. If you can make up a couple of positions there, you have a lot better chance of staying in front."

In a race such as the Indy 500, the start is less important to the outcome of a race. "People look at records, and say no one ever wins coming from back in the pack; but that's only because the best cars and the best drivers are almost always in front. There have been cars that start far back and still come close to winning."

In drag racing, obviously, the start is everything. The rest of the race is mostly spectacle. According to Economaki, "drag racing is sights; it's sounds and smells. The big thrill is the phenomenal power of those machines. Men dressed in fire suits, and looking like astronauts, are getting in dragsters with, say, a thousand horsepower. They go only a few hundred yards, but at the finish, they're traveling maybe 250 miles an hour."

One disappointing aspect of auto racing for some spectators is that, for the most part, drivers are obscured by their cars. "It's hard for the spectators to get excited about individual drivers. They all look the same in their suits, and when they get in the cars, you can't see them at all." The spectators have to identify the drivers by car or by number.

The uninitiated may wonder how important it is to watch an entire race that may continue for 400 or 500 miles around a track, rather than the last few laps only. Economaki explains that watching the come-from-behind driver make his move in the middle or near the end of the race can be more thrilling than the actual finish. "It's exciting to watch a Mario Andretti come from thirty-second position and make a challenge for the lead. You can watch a driver come down the straightaway with traffic in front of him, trying to decide whether to pass some of those guys or wait for an opening that would give him a better shot at the lead." In that sense, auto racing is much like other sports; the fun is not just in watching who crosses the finish line first and wins the race; it's also in watching the skills and strategies it takes to do so.

Main Events

INDIANAPOLIS 500 (USAC)

Year	Winner	Year	Winner
1981	Mario Andretti	1976	Johnny Rutherford
1980	Johnny Rutherford	1975	Bobby Unser
1979	Rick Mears	1974	Johnny Rutherford
1978	Al Unser	1973	Gordon Johncock
1977	A. J. Foyt	1972	Mark Donohue

DAYTONA 500 (NASCAR)

Year	Winner	Year	Winner
1981	Richard Petty	1976	David Pearson
1980	Buddy Baker	1975	Benny Parsons
1979	Richard Petty	1974	Richard Petty
1978	Bobby Allison	1973	Richard Petty
1977	Cale Yarborough	1972	A. J. Foyt

U.S. GRAND PRIX (FIA)

Year	Winner	Year	Winner
1980	Alan Jones, Australia	1975	Niki Lauda, Austria
1979	Gilles Villeneuve, Canada	1974	Carlos Reutemann, Argentina
1978	Carlos Reutemann, Argentina	1973	Ronnie Peterson, Sweden
1977	James Hunt, Great Britain	1972	Jackie Stewart, Scotland
1976	James Hunt, Great Britain	1971	Francois Cervert, France

ABC Sports

INTERNATIONAL RACE OF CHAMPIONS

Race	Year	Winner
IROC I	1973–74	Mark Donohue
IROC II	1974–75	Bobby Unser
IROC III	1975–76	A. J. Foyt
IROC IV	1976–77	A. J. Foyt
IROC V	1977–78	Al Unser
IROC VI	1978–79	Mario Andretti
IROC VII	1979–80	Bobby Allison

WORLD GRAND PRIX CHAMPIONS (FIA)

Year	Winner	Year	Winner
1980	Alan Jones, Australia	1975	Niki Lauda, Austria
1979	Jody Scheckter, South Africa	1974	Emerson Fittipaldi, Brazil
1978	Mario Andretti, USA	1973	Jackie Stewart, Scotland
1977	Niki Lauda, Austria	1972	Emerson Fittipaldi, Brazil
1976	James Hunt, Great Britain	1971	Jackie Stewart, Scotland

U.S. AUTO CLUB CHAMPIONS

Year	Winner	Year	Winner
1980	Johnny Rutherford	1975	A. J. Foyt
1979	A. J. Foyt	1974	Bobby Unser
1978	Tom Sneva	1973	Roger McCluskey
1977	Tom Sneva	1972	Joe Leonard
1976	Gordon Johncock	1971	Joe Leonard

NASCAR GRAND NATIONAL CHAMPIONS

Year	Winner	Year	Winner
1980	Dale Earnhardt	1975	Richard Petty
1979	Richard Petty	1974	Richard Petty
1978	Cale Yarborough	1973	Benny Parsons
1977	Cale Yarborough	1972	Richard Petty
1976	Cale Yarborough	1971	Richard Petty

IMSA GT OVERALL CHAMPIONS

Year	Winner	Year	Winner
1980	John Fitzpatrick	1975	Peter Gregg
1979	Peter Gregg	1974	Peter Gregg
1978	Peter Gregg	1973	Peter Gregg
1977	Al Holbert	1972	Hurley Haywood
1976	Al Holbert	1971	Peter Gregg
			Hurley Haywood

IRHA PROFESSIONAL WORLD CHAMPIONS

Pro Dragster

Year	Winner	Year	Winner
1980	Jeb Allen	1976	Don Garlits
1979	Connie Kalitta	1975	Don Garlits
1978	Clayton Harris	1974	Dale Funk
1977	Don Garlits		

Pro Funny Car

Year	Winner	Year	Winner
1980	Billy Meyer	1976	Raymond Beadle
1979	Kenny Bernstein	1975	Raymond Beadle
1978	Denny Savage	1974	Ron Colson
1977	Dale Pulde		

Pro Stock Car

Year	Winner	Year	Winner
1980	Warren Johnson	1976	Bob Glidden
1979	Warren Johnson	1975	Don Nicholson
1978	Lee Edwards	1974	Wayne Gap
1977	Lee Edwards		

SCCA CAN-AM CHAMPIONSHIP

Year	Winner	Year	Winner
1980	Patrick Tambay	1975	no races held
1979	Jacky Ickx	1974	Jackie Oliver
1978	Alan Jones	1973	Mark Donohue
1977	Patrick Tambay	1972	George Follmer
1976	no races held	1971	Peter Revson

SCCA TRANS-AM CHAMPIONSHIP

Year	Winner	Year	Winner
1980	John Bauer	1976	Jocko Maggiacomo, Category I
1979	Gene Bothello, Category I		George Follmer, Category II
	John Paul, Category II	1975	John Greenwood
1978	Bob Tullius, Category I	1974	Peter Gregg
	Greg Pickett, Category II	1973	Peter Gregg
1977	Bob Tullius, Category I	1972	George Follmer
	Ludwig Heimrath, Category II	1971	Mark Donohue

All-Time Greats

Mario Andretti
(Feb. 28, 1940–)

Born in Italy, Andretti became an American citizen when he was 19 years old. He began his professional career in 1958, racing for such companies as Dean Van Lines and The STP Corporation. In 1965 he made a name for himself in competition racing, taking the USAC national championship that year and the next. Andretti was USAC champion again in 1969, the same year he won the Indianapolis 500 and was named Athlete of the Year by ABC Sports. Andretti, who for 10 years was a member of the President's Conference on Physical Fitness and Sports, in 1978 won both the International Race of Champions and the Grand Prix championship. He has won a total of 33 championship races.

Jimmy Clark
(Mar. 4, 1936–Apr. 7, 1968)

Clark, widely considered one of the greatest all-time racing drivers, held the world title in 1963 and 1965, winning major Grand Prix races around the world. In 1964 he was awarded the Order of the British Empire. Deeply affected by the racing death of his friend Alan Stacey, Clark considered giving up racing, especially after he himself was involved in an accident in 1961 on a track in Monza, Italy, that killed 13 spectators. Because auto racing was so large a part of his life, however, he decided to continue. Clark returned to racing and, in 1965, won the Indianapolis 500. He died three years later, when, in the Hockenheim Formula 2 Race in West Germany, his car went out of control and crashed into a tree.

Ralph De Palma
(1888?–Mar. 31, 1956)

The Italian-born De Palma, who became a naturalized U.S. citizen, was a track star and bicycling champion before turning to auto racing. He won the Vanderbilt Cup in 1912, the National Championship in 1912 and 1914, and the Indianapolis 500 in 1915. Entering 10 Indy 500s, De Palma led the field for a total of 613 laps, a record that still stands. Although he led in almost every race he entered, De Palma was plagued by mechanical failures— for example, breaking a connecting rod just over one lap from the finish of an Indy 500 that he was winning. "The Hard Luck King" nevertheless won almost every racing championship available.

A. J. Foyt
(Jan. 16, 1935–)

A. J. Foyt, the USAC's all-time record winner, has won the USAC National Championship seven times and the Indianapolis 500 four times; he is a four-time Indianapolis pole winner, and has won the USAC Stock Car Championship three times. Foyt was also Dirt Track Champion in 1972 and Eastern Sprint Champion in 1960. In 1967 he and Dan Gurney won at LeMans. In addition to holding the USAC all-time championship point record (Foyt has won more money than any other USAC driver), he was the first driver to win two national championships, the National Championship and the Stock Car Division title, in the same year. All in all, A. J. Foyt has won 67 championship races.

Dan Gurney
(Apr. 13, 1931–)

Gurney's record puts him among the top five all-time American drivers in four different categories. His amazing diversity—driving everything from Grand Prix to stock cars—is superseded only by his long string of championships. Gurney won his first Grand Prix in 1962 and went on to win three more. He won the Riverside 500 four consecutive times (1963–66) and again in 1968. In 1971, Gurney, who earned seven championship wins in his career, retired to concentrate on designing and building cars.

Lee Petty
(Mar. 14, 1914–)

Petty, progenitor of a driving dynasty, became a professional racer when he was 35 years old, placing second in NASCAR standings his first year in racing. Between that time and his retirement from racing (because of injuries suffered in a Daytona 500 race, in 1962), Petty racked up a total of 54 NASCAR Grand National wins— a record exceeded only by his son, Richard. Petty also won three NASCAR championships, in 1954, 1958, and 1959.

Richard Petty
(July 2, 1937–)

The son of champion driver Lee Petty, Richard holds NASCAR records for most races started, most races won, most victories in a single season, most money won in a single season and in a career, fastest 600-mile race, and most 500-mile victories. He is the only driver to win the Daytona 500 more than twice (he has won seven times). Petty, whose son, Kyle, is a driver and a member of his father's pit crew, is one of the most popular racers in the history of the sport.

Jackie Stewart
(Nov. 6, 1939–)

ABC Sports

The Scottish racer Jackie Stewart became a professional in 1964. He spent most of his career on the Grand Prix circuit, where he won a record 27 Grand Prix races before retiring in 1973. The first year Stewart entered the Indianapolis 500, he had a clear lead when his car developed mechanical trouble and put him out of the race. He was Grand Prix World Champion three times, in 1969, 1971, and 1973. Today, Stewart is a commentator for ABC Sports.

HALLS OF FAME

Indianapolis Motor Speedway Hall of Fame
Box 24152
Indianapolis, IN 46224
(317) 241-2501

The members of the Indianapolis Motor Speedway Hall of Fame are:

1952
Louis Chevrolet
Bert Dingley
Harvey S. Firestone
Carl G. Fisher
Henry Ford
Ray Harroun
Theodore E. ("Pop") Myers
Berna E. ("Barney") Oldfield
William K. Vanderbilt
Fred J. Wagner

1953
Robert Burman
Earl Cooper
Ralph De Palma
Tommy Milton
Ralph Mulford
Dario Resta
Edward V. Rickenbacker

1962
Fred Duesenberg

1963
Peter DePaolo
August Duesenberg

Harry Hartz
Rex Mays
Louis Meyer
Harry Miller
Warren W. Shaw
Harry Stutz
Howard ("Howdy") Wilcox

1964
James A. Allison
Gaston Chevrolet
Eddie Hearne
Ted Horn
James Murphy

1965
Anton ("Tony") Hulman
Mauri Rose

1968
Melvin E. ("Tony") Bettenhausen
Frank Lockhart
Jean Marcenac

1969
Harry ("Cotton") Henning
Lou Moore

1970
Bill Cummings
Ralph Hepburn

1972
William Vukovich, Sr.

1973
James Bryan

1975
George Bignotti

1976
Cliff Bergere
Joseph Dawson

1977
Billy Arnold

1978
A. J. Foyt, Jr.
Leo Goossen

1980
David Bruce-Brown
J. Walter Christie
George Robertson

National Motorsport Press Association Stock Car Hall of Fame
Drawer 500
Darlington, SC 29532
(803) 393-4041
Bill Kiser, dir. public relations

Members of the NMPA Stock Car Hall of Fame are:

1965	1968	1972	1976
Paul McDuffy	Fonty Flock	Junior Johnson	Bill France, Sr.
"Fireball" Roberts	Marshall Teague		
Herb Thomas		**1973**	**1977**
Joe Weatherly	**1969**	Tim Flock	Jim Paschall
	Bob Colvin	Ned Jarrett	
1966	Lee Petty		**1978**
"Cannonball" Baker		**1974**	Fred Lorenzen
Red Byron	**1970**	Rex White	
	Cotton Owens		**1979**
1967		**1975**	Bobby Isaac
Billy Meyers	**1971**	Joe Littlejohn	
Pat Purcell	Curtis Turner		

Motor Vehicle Manufacturers Assn. of the United States, Inc.

Citizens Savings Hall
Automobile Racing Hall of Fame
Citizens Savings Athletic Foundation
9800 S. Sepulveda Blvd.
Los Angeles, CA 90045
(213) 670-7550
W. R. ("Bill") Schroeder, dir.

International Automobile Hall of Fame
c/o Gary P. McGehee
Highway 27 S
Sebring, FL 33870

Michael J. Trombley, sec.-treas.
329 S. Commercial Ave.
Sebring, FL 33870

S-K Mechanics Hall of Fame
c/o Tool Group
Dresser Industries, Inc.
3201 N. Wolf Rd.
Franklin Park, IL 60131
Norman Velisek, vice-pres., S-K Tools

For the Record

USAC

Most races won, career
67 A. J. Foyt

Highest point standing
45,959 A. J. Foyt

Most national championships
7 A. J. Foyt

Most championships series wins, career
67 A. J. Foyt

Most championship series wins, season
5 A. J. Foyt

Fastest Indy 500
162.962 mph   Mark Donohue
Apr. 27, 1972

Fastest Indy Speedway lap
203.620 mph   Tom Sneva
May 20, 1978

Fastest Indy Speedway, four laps
202.156 mph   Tom Sneva
May 20, 1978

Most Indy 500 wins
4 A. J. Foyt   1961, 1964, 1967, 1977

Most leading laps, 500 races
534 Al Unser

NASCAR

Most races won
192   Richard Petty

Most victories, single season
27   Richard Petty   1967

Most consecutive victories
10   Richard Petty   1967

Most superspeedway victories, single season
10   David Pearson   1973, 1976

Most superspeedway victories, career
50   David Pearson

Fastest qualifying speed
199.658 mph   Bobby Isaac   1970
Alabama International Motor Speedway

Fastest 600-mile race, average speed
145.327 mph   Richard Petty   1975
Charlotte (NC) Motor Speedway

Fastest 500-mile race, average speed
177.602 mph   Buddy Baker   1980
Daytona International Speedway

Fastest 400-mile race, average speed
173.473 mph   Bobby Allison   1980
Daytona International Speedway

Fastest race, any distance, average speed
194.384 mph   Buddy Baker   1979
Daytona International Speedway

Most 600-mile victories
4   David Pearson

Most 500-mile victories
35   Richard Petty

Most 400-mile victories
16   David Pearson

Most pole positions, season
14   Cale Yarborough   1980

IMSA

GT Category

Highest point standing
1104.5   Peter Gregg

Most races won
47   Peter Gregg

RS Category

Highest point standing
763   Amos Johnson

Most races won
12   Carson Baird
Nick Craw
Rob McFarlin

AC Category

Highest point standing
453   Gene Felton

Most races won
18   Gene Felton

IHRA

Greatest speed, pro dragster
249.30 mph   Jeb Allen   1981

Most races won, pro dragster
25   Don Garlits

Greatest speed, pro funny car
249.30 mph   Kenny Bernstein   1981

Most races won, pro funny car
15   Raymond Beadle

Greatest speed, pro stock
176.81 mph   Don Nicholson   1981

Most races won, pro stock
12   Lee Edwards

NHRA

Most victories, career
33   Bob Glidden

Most pro stock victories, career
33   Bob Glidden

Most consecutive victories
9   Bob Glidden, Pro Stock   1978–79

Most victories, single event
6   Don Prudhomme, U.S. Nationals
     1965, 1969, 1970 (Top Fuel)
     1973, 1974, 1977 (Funny Car)

Most funny car victories, career
20   Don Prudhomme

Most victories, season
7   Bob Glidden, Pro Stock
     1978–79
7   Don Prudhomme, Funny Car
     1976

Most top fuel victories, career
21   Don Garlits

ABC Sports

SCCA TRANS-AM

Most races entered, career
58   George Follmer   1967–72, 1976–79

Most victories, career
29   Mark Donohue

Most victories, season
10   Mark Donohue   1968

Most consecutive victories, career
10   Bob Tullius   1978–79

Most consecutive victories, season
8   Mark Donohue   1968

Most driver's championships
2   George Follmer   1972, 1976

Fastest race, 100 miles
100.99 mph   Greg Pickett, Riverside   1980

Fastest race, more than 100 miles, average speed
108.898 mph   Mark Donohue, Watkins Glen   1969

Fastest qualifying speed
111.695 mph   Mark Donohue, Watkins Glen   1971

Fastest race lap
111.789 mph   George Follmer, Watkins Glen   1971

SCCA CAN-AM

Fastest lap speed
132.276 mph   Denis Hulme, Watkins Glen   1971*
124.833 mph   Keke Rosberg, Riverside   1980

Fastest qualifying speed
134.244 mph   Jackie Stewart, Watkins Glen   1971*
128.940 mph   Geoff Brabham, Riverside   1980

Fastest race, less than 130 miles, average speed
120.311 mph   Mark Donohue, Riverside   1973

Fastest race, less than 150 miles, average speed
115.145 mph   Patrick Tambay, Mosport   1980

Fastest race, less than 170 miles, average speed
117.010 mph   Patrick Tambay, Riverside   1977

Fastest race, less than 200 miles, average speed
114.580 mph   Keke Rosberg, Watkins Glen   1979

Fastest race, more than 200 miles, average speed
119.137 mph   Peter Revson, Brainerd   1971

Longest race
2 hr 42 min 26 sec   Denis Hulme, Watkins Glen   1971

Shortest race
48 min 20.08 sec   Bobby Rahal, Laguna Seca   1979

*Before Can-Am engine restrictions were instituted.

Most championships
2 Bruce McLaren   1967, 1969
2 Denis Hulme   1968, 1970
2 Patrick Tambay   1977, 1980

Most consecutive victories, career
11 Patrick Tambay   1977–80

Most consecutive victories, season
6 Mark Donohue   1973
6 Patrick Tambay   1980

Most races entered, career
63 Lothar Motchenbacher 1966–74

Most victories, career
22 Denis Hulme   1967–72

Most victories, season
6 Bruce McLaren   1969
6 Denis Hulme   1970
6 Mark Donohue   1973
6 Patrick Tambay   1977, 1980

Did you know ?

1. Who was the first American to set a land-speed record?

2. Did anyone ever complete the Indy 500 without making a pit stop?

3. In what race were three generations of the same racing family on the track at the same time?

4. What two men have won the LeMans more than three times? What country are they from?

5. Who built the Indianapolis Motor Speedway? Why?

6. What is the world's fastest pit stop?

7. What famous phrase has traditionally signalled the beginning of the Indianapolis 500?

8. How does a drag racer brake a car at the end of the run?

9. Who was the first woman licensed to run Top-Fuel dragsters in the United States?

Answers: 1. Henry Ford. He drove his Ford 999 at a speed of 91.37 miles per hour on frozen Lake St. Clair. **2.** Yes. In 1931, Clessie Cummins entered a diesel-powered car in the Indianapolis race to prove the durability of the diesel engine. He finished thirteenth, at an average speed of 81.17 miles per hour, with no stops; **3.** The Talladega 500, at Alabama International Motor Speedway, in 1979. Richard Petty and his son, Kyle, raced together for the first time, while Richard's father, Lee, lapped his son; **4.** Jacky Ickx won the LeMans in 1969, 1975, 1976, and 1977; Oliver Gendebien took the title in 1958, 1960, 1961, and 1962. Both are Belgians; **5.** The industrialist Carl Fisher built the speedway in 1909 as a test facility for car manufacturers in Indianapolis; he believed that this would help make the city the foremost automobile producer in the United States; **6.** Four seconds. It took that long for the pit crew to refuel the car driven by Bobby Unser, running the tenth lap of the 1976 Indianapolis 500; **7.** "Gentlemen, start your engines," **8.** By deploying a parachute from the rear of the car; **9.** Shirley Muldowney, of Mt. Clemens, Michigan.

Key Words

bite   traction.

burnout   spinning the rear wheels of the car in water, to heat up the tires and soften the rubber, thus improving the traction just before the start of the race.

caution flag   a yellow flag used to tell drivers to slow down because of some event or obstruction on the track ahead.

checkered flag   the black-and-white, checkered flag waved first to signal the winner of the race and then to all finishers to indicate the end of the race.

Christmas tree   a set of colored lights—yellow, green, and red—mounted on a vertical pole at the center of the starting line on a drag strip; it is used to indicate the start of each race.

dragster   a car with one or two supercharged engines especially designed for drag racing; also, a drag racing driver.

Eliminator   in drag racing: (1) a car that has won a preliminary round and is eligible to complete in subsequent heats to determine a winner; (2) any of eight categories, four professional and four sports-racing, in which dragsters may compete.

ABC Sports

IHRA Photo

E.T.   elapsed time; the actual time required to complete a course or a strip.

formula car   a racing car built according to specifications set by a sanctioning body; usually designed with a single-seat, open-cockpit, tubular body, with the engine located behind the driver.

foul   any infraction of the rules that draws a penalty, for example, starting before the signal, failing to obey a signal, unauthorized refueling.

Grand National   a series of stock car races, usually 250 to 600 miles, run primarily on oval tracks; abbreviated, GN.

Grand Prix   one of a series of international races for Formula 1 cars.

GT   grand touring cars, usually two-passenger sport coupes.

handicap   the equalizing of cars from different classes so that they may race competitively.

high-speed trials   a competition over very rough track, in which cars must maintain a speed of at least five miles per hour or travel a specified distance in a specified time.

hill climb   a competition in which cars compete one at a time, each making two attempts to complete the course (a steep grade) in the least time.

nerf bar   a bumper attached to the front, back, and sides of a modified stock car to prevent the wheels from touching another car's wheels during a race.

nitromethane   a special fuel used to increase the power output and improve a car's overall performance.

ABC Sports

out of shape   momentarily losing control of a car, thus moving out of proper position for racing.

overstage   in a drag racer, to move the front wheels too close to the starting line.

pit stop   a driver pulling into a special, designated area (called "the pit") during a race, usually for fuel, new tires, emergency repairs, or a quick consultation. Pit crews assist drivers.

pole   the position on the inside of the front row before the start of a closed circuit race. The car with the fastest qualifying time is awarded the most advantageous position, the pole position, which has the shortest distance around the track. The driver is known as the "pole sitter."

rally   a competition in which the course is divided into separate stages, with point values assigned to each stage. Penalty points are subtracted at each stage, and the racer with the fewest penalties wins.

road track   a racing circuit that contains U-turns and left turns.

slicks   smooth tires, that is, with no treads.

sprint   a competition held on a flat track, in which each car is timed twice; the car with the fastest time wins.

stage   the starting line of a drag race; cars assemble in the "staging area" before a race.

stock car   a car model available to the public for everyday use, which is used for racing; modified stock cars retain only the familiar body of the car, but replace the engine and other parts.

Top Fuel   in drag racing, a category that includes the fastest-accelerating dragsters. Modifications to the engine (some cars have two) or to the overall design of the car are virtually unlimited.

ABC Sports

2 BASEBALL

lthough the popularity of baseball has spread to many other countries, it is still widely regarded as America's national pastime. Its champions are called "world" champions, although the major-league teams represent only the United States and Canada. Few would disagree, however, that baseball belongs to American sports fans.

Contrary to some theories, baseball's closest predecessors come from England. The early game adapted features of cricket and "rounders." The English game of rounders used a ball and thick sticks, with runners moving around four wooden posts. A runner was "out" when hit by a thrown ball. Records in the United States, from the late 1820s and early 1830s, refer to the game of "base," or "goal," ball, which followed the same rules as rounders.

Whether or not the game was based on rounders, early forms of baseball almost certainly appeared before 1839, the year Abner Doubleday is supposed to have invented the game, in Cooperstown, New York. The Doubleday theory is based on a report submitted by A. G. Mills in 1907. The report was discovered in the late 1930s, just when baseball needed a boost in interest. Suddenly the baseball world had a centennial to celebrate. Although subsequent research revealed information that contradicts the Doubleday theory, most scholars have given up trying to pinpoint exactly when baseball began.

Early rules allowed "plugging," or putting out a batter by striking him with a thrown ball. The practice caused many injuries, and by the 1840s it generally was not permitted. At about the same time, the stakes used until then were replaced with flat stones to mark the bases; soon thereafter, the stones were replaced by sacks filled with sand. A "Base Ball Diagram" that appeared in 1841 shows a field that differs from today's baseball diamond. It includes a "striker's box" for the batter, first, second, and third bases, and, to the left of the striker's box, a fourth base which the runner had to cross in order to score.

The first baseball club was organized in 1845. Called the Knickerbocker Baseball Club of New York, the team was composed mostly of former cricket players. Alexander Cartwright, a surveyor and sportsman, was asked to draft rules standardizing play. He presented his rules in 1846. Included with them was a diagram that represented the playing field as a baseball diamond, although it was then called a baseball "square." The new playing field had four bases, and the rules required that the batter return to the striker's box to score a run.

Cartwright's rules were first used in a game played at Elysian Fields in Hoboken, New Jersey, during the summer of 1846. The Knickerbockers met a new team, the New York Nine, and the upstarts beat the veterans 23–1. Over the next ten years, new teams were organized, and new rules were made and changed. The press discovered baseball; the first known story about baseball ran in the New York *Mercury* in 1853. Four years later, in 1857, the game's first amateur association, the National Association of Base-Ball Players, was formed. The association amended the rules so that a game would be decided in nine innings; until then, the first team to score 21 runs won the game.

Over the years, more rule changes were made, clubs came and went, and pictures of baseball stars appeared on magazine covers and, later, on television screens. In contrast to arguments today over how many millions of dollars a baseball

ABC Sports

star's contract is worth, arguments in the nineteenth century centered on whether baseball players should be paid at all. Money has been involved in other ways. For instance, a scandal erupted in the 1919 World Series concerning allegations that Chicago had thrown the series. The prestige and glory of the game were eventually restored, however, by such people as baseball's first commissioner, Judge Kenesaw Mountain Landis, and such players as Babe Ruth and Lou Gehrig.

Some say baseball is one of the great American traditions, others that the game just isn't the same anymore. Somehow, though, baseball survives. It does better than that. With each year's crop of children on playgrounds and streets, of hopefuls on the long bus rides in the minor leagues, of fresh draftees opening major-league lockers for the first time, baseball is continually reborn.

Historian Jacques Barzun once said that, to understand the American mentality, one must first understand the game of baseball. Baseball is deceptively simple; the more one learns about the game, the more there is to learn. More than power hits and pitching feats, full of nuance and subtlety, signals and psych-outs, baseball is a game whose unpredictability and complexity keep its fans fascinated.

Despite the impact of television or attendance at ball games, today there are more baseball fans, and more interest in baseball, than ever.

Great Moments

1858 March 10: 25 clubs are represented at the second baseball convention, and join to form the National Association of Base-Ball Players. July 20: for the first time, baseball fans are charged an admission fee, of 50 cents. In the game, played on Long Island, about 1,500 fans watch New York beat Brooklyn, 22–18, with the proceeds going to cover maintenance costs for the playing field.

1869 The Cincinnati Red Stockings become the first team to play openly as professionals. The team has a payroll of $9,500; admission to a game is 50 cents.

1871 Encouraged by the success of the professional Cincinnati Red Stockings, 10 club delegates meet, on March 4, and form the National Association of Professional Base-Ball Players (NA).

1876 William Hulbert, president of the Chicago White Stockings, forms the National League of Professional Base Ball Clubs (NL) as a rival of the National Association. Boston wins the first National League game, played in Philadelphia, 6–5.

1882 The American Association (AA) is formed, picking up franchises in many cities dropped by the NL. The AA cuts the admission price from 50 to 25 cents, and schedules Sunday games, which is against the rules of the National League.

1884 The Union Association is organized as a rival of the NL and AA, but is poorly financed and folds before the year is out.

1891 The American Association disbands under pressure of finances and competition.

1900 Sportswriter Byron Bancroft ("Ban") Johnson begins movement to organize yet another rival of the National League by changing the Western Association to the American League and by working to raise the clubs from minor- to major-league status.

1901 January 28: the American League, boosted by talent from the National League, is organized, with teams in the cities of Baltimore, Boston, Chicago, Cleveland, Detroit, Milwaukee, Philadelphia, and Washington.

1903 The first "World Series," played on an informal basis, marks a temporary truce in the struggle between the National League and the American League. Boston (AL) defeats Pittsburgh (NL), five games to three, in a best-of-nine series.

1905 The official World Series is born, with the New York Giants (NL) pitted against the Philadelphia Athletics (AL). The Giants emerge as the first official world champions.

1911 The leagues sanction use of a new type of ball, one with a cork center; this changes the level of offense; 35 hitters in the American League have a season batting average of at least .300.

1914 The newly formed Federal League sues to have the entire organization of professional baseball ruled invalid in the courts. The lawsuit drags on; finally, lack of experience on the part of the Federal League, together with the impending war abroad force the new league to agree to a generous settlement by the AL and the NL. The league disbands the following year.

1916 The New York Giants establish a modern record by winning 26 consecutive games, between September 7 and September 30.

1920 Sunday baseball is legalized in New York City, and crowds turn out to watch the city's teams.

1933 The first AL versus NL All-Star Game is played in Chicago; the American League wins, 4–2.

1935 In what is to become a baseball institution—nighttime baseball—Cincinnati, the home team, beats Philadelphia, 4–1. It is the majors' first night game.

1947 On April 19, Jackie Robinson, the first black man in modern professional baseball, plays for the Brooklyn Dodgers in his first National League game. He goes on to become Rookie of the Year.

1948 The first tie for first place in American League history makes a playoff game necessary. On October 3, Cleveland beats Boston, 8–3.

1953 The Boston Braves move to Milwaukee on March 18, marking the first National League franchise change in the twentieth century.

1956 October 8: the New York Yankees' Don Larsen pitches a perfect game against the Dodgers, the only one in World Series competition.

1957 The baseball world is shaken by an announcement that the New York Giants (August 19) and the Brooklyn Dodgers (October 8) will move their franchises to California.

1961 The New York Mets are granted a National League franchise. Nine years later, they work their way up from the bottom of the league to a World Series championship.

1975 Cleveland hires Frank Robinson as the first black manager in the majors.

1977 The American League expands to 14 teams with the addition of franchises in Toronto and Seattle.

Major-league baseball is divided into two leagues, the American and the National. Each league is divided into two divisions, with six or seven teams in each division. No interleague games are played until the World Series, in which the league champions vie for the title "World Champion."

MAJOR-LEAGUE BASEBALL

American

Eastern Division	Western Division
Baltimore Orioles	California Angels
Boston Red Sox	Chicago White Sox
Cleveland Indians	Kansas City Royals
Detroit Tigers	Minnesota Twins
Milwaukee Brewers	Oakland Athletics
New York Yankees	Seattle Mariners
Toronto Blue Jays	Texas Rangers

National

Eastern Division	Western Division
Chicago Cubs	Atlanta Braves
Montreal Expos	Cincinnati Reds
New York Mets	Houston Astros
Philadelphia Phillies	Los Angeles Dodgers
Pittsburgh Pirates	San Diego Padres
St. Louis Cardinals	San Francisco Giants

ORGANIZATION OF PROFESSIONAL BASEBALL

Major league baseball is organized as follows:

OFFICE OF THE COMMISSIONER
75 Rockefeller Pl.
New York, NY 10020
(212) 586-7400
Bowie Kuhn, commissioner

THE NATIONAL LEAGUE
One Rockefeller Pl.
New York, NY 10020
(212) 582-4213
Charles S. ("Chub") Feeney, pres.

THE AMERICAN LEAGUE
280 Park Ave.
New York, NY 10017
(212) 682-7000
Leland S. MacPhail, Jr., pres.

American League Clubs

BALTIMORE ORIOLES
Memorial Stadium
Baltimore, MD 21218
(301) 243-9800
Edward Bennett Williams, chairman of
board
(games played at Memorial Stadium)

BOSTON RED SOX
Fenway Park
24 Yawkey Way
Boston, MA 02215
(617) 267-9440
Jean R. Yawkey, pres.
(games played at Fenway Park)

CALIFORNIA ANGELS
Anaheim Stadium
2000 State College Blvd.
Anaheim, CA 92806
(714) 634-1002
Gene Autry, chairman of board, and pres.
(games played at Anaheim Stadium)

CHICAGO WHITE SOX
Comiskey Park
Dan Ryan at 35th St.
Chicago, IL 60616
(312) 924-1000
William O. DeWitt, chairman of board
(games played at Comiskey Park)

CLEVELAND INDIANS
Cleveland Stadium
Boudreau Blvd.
Cleveland, OH 44114
(216) 861-1200
Gabe Paul, pres. and chief exec. officer
(games played at Cleveland Stadium)

DETROIT TIGERS
Tiger Stadium
Detroit, MI 48216
(313) 962-4000
John E. Fetzer, owner and chairman of
board
(games played at Tiger Stadium)

KANSAS CITY ROYALS
P.O. Box 1969
Kansas City, MO 64141
(816) 921-8000
Ewing Kauffman, chairman of board and
pres.
(games played at Royals Stadium)

MILWAUKEE BREWERS
County Stadium
Milwaukee, WI 53214
(414) 933-1818
Allan H. Selig, pres. and chief exec. officer
(games played at County Stadium)

MINNESOTA TWINS
Metropolitan Stadium
8001 Cedar Ave. S
Bloomington, MN 55420
(612) 854-4040
Calvin R. Griffith, chairman of board and
pres.
(games played at Metropolitan Stadium)

NEW YORK YANKEES
Yankee Stadium
Bronx, NY 10451
(212) 293-4300
George M. Steinbrenner, principal owner
(games played at Yankee Stadium)

OAKLAND ATHLETICS
Oakland Coliseum
Oakland, CA 94621
(415) 638-4900
Roy Eisenhardt, pres.
(games played at Oakland Coliseum)

SEATTLE MARINERS
Second Ave. S and King St.
Seattle WA 98104
(206) 628-3555
Daniel F. O'Brien, pres. and chief exec.
officer
(games played at the Kingdome)

TEXAS RANGERS
Arlington Stadium
P.O. Box 1111
1700 Copeland Rd.
Arlington, TX 76010
(817) 273-5222
Bradford G. Corbett, chairman of board
(games played at Arlington Stadium)

TORONTO BLUE JAYS
Box 7777
Adelaide St. P.O.
Toronto, Ontario
M5C 2K7, Canada
(416) 595-0077
R. Howard Webster, chairman of board
(games played at Exhibition Stadium)

National League Clubs

ATLANTA BRAVES
P.O. Box 4064
Atlanta, GA 30302
(404) 522-7630
R. E. ("Ted") Turner, pres. and gen. mgr.
(games played at Atlanta-Fulton County
 Stadium)

CHICAGO CUBS
Clark and Addison Sts.
Chicago, IL 60613
(312) 281-5050
William Wrigley, chairman of exec. comm.
(games played at Wrigley Field)

CINCINNATI REDS
100 Riverfront Stadium
Cincinnati, OH 45202
(513) 421-4510
Louis Nippert, chairman
(games played at Riverfront Stadium)

HOUSTON ASTROS
P.O. Box 288
Houston, TX 77001
(713) 749-9500
William E. Odom, pres.
(games played at the Astrodome)

LOS ANGELES DODGERS
1000 Elysian Park Ave.
Los Angeles, CA 90012
(213) 224-1500
Peter O'Malley, pres.
(games played at Dodger Stadium)

MONTREAL EXPOS
P.O. Box 500, Station M
Montreal, Quebec
H1V 3P2, Canada
(514) 253-3434
Charles R. Bronfman, chairman of board
(games played at Olympic Stadium)

NEW YORK METS
126th St. and Roosevelt Ave.
Flushing, NY 11368
(212) 672-2000
Nelson Doubleday, chairman of board
(games played at Shea Stadium)

PHILADELPHIA PHILLIES
P.O. Box 7575
Philadelphia, PA 19101
(215) 463-6000
R.R.M. ("Bob") Carpenter, Jr., chairman of
 board
(games played at Veterans Stadium)

PITTSBURGH PIRATES
600 Stadium Circle
Pittsburgh, PA 15212
(412) 323-1000
John W. Galbreath, chairman of board
(games played at Three Rivers Stadium)

ST. LOUIS CARDINALS
250 Stadium Plaza
St. Louis, MO 63102
(314) 421-3060
August A. Busch, Jr., chairman of board,
 pres., and chief exec. officer
(games played at Busch Memorial Stadium)

SAN DIEGO PADRES
P.O. Box 2000
San Diego, CA 92120
(714) 283-4494
Ray A. Kroc, chairman of board and pres.
(games played at San Diego Stadium)

SAN FRANCISCO GIANTS
Bay Shore
San Francisco, CA 94124
(415) 468-3700
Bob Lurie and Bud Herseth, co-chairmen
(games played at Candlestick Park)

The Basics

Object of the game To score the most runs by the end of nine innings or longer,
 until any tie is broken.

Players Nine players constitute a team: a pitcher, catcher, first baseman, second
 baseman, third baseman, shortstop, left fielder, center fielder, and right fielder.

A new player may be substituted at any time; once a player leaves the game, he may not reenter it.

Equipment   Players use a round wood bat to hit a ball made of rubber and cork and covered with leather. Fielders may use a leather glove to help them catch the ball; the catcher and the first baseman may wear a thicker glove, called a mitt.

Officials   Generally, there are four umpires: a plate umpire, who stands behind the catcher and calls balls and strikes; and an umpire at each of the three bases.

Length of a game   A game lasts nine innings, with each team having at least three turns at bat per inning. If the score is tied at the end of nine innings, the game continues until the tie is broken. The plate umpire may suspend or end a game if such conditions as rain or fog make it impossible to continue play.

Rule 1   Getting on base   A batter can safely get on base in any of the following ways:

a. By hitting the ball and reaching first base before the ball gets there
b. By the pitcher throwing four pitches outside the strike zone (called "balls"), in which case the batter advances to first base unhindered
c. By being hit by a pitched ball and advancing to first base unhindered
d. By the catcher interfering with the batter's swing

Rule 2   Advancing on bases   A player on base may advance if:

a. The batter hits safely or makes a sacrifice hit
b. The fielding team makes an error
c. He "steals" the next base by running to the base, usually starting when the pitcher releases the ball but before the batter swings

Rule 3   Outs   The team at bat is retired after three outs, at which time it becomes the fielding team. A player can be put out in one of the following ways:

a. When three strikes (either pitches within the strike zone or unsuccessful swings) are called before four balls are called or before he hits the ball
b. When he hits a fly ball that is

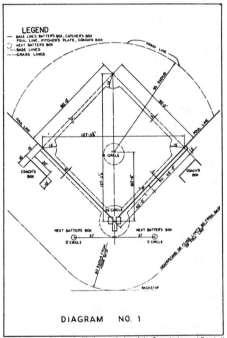

DIAGRAM   NO. 1

Reprinted with the permission of the Commissioner of Baseball

caught before it touches the ground
c. When the ball hit reaches first base before he does
d. When a base runner is tagged with the ball while off a base
e. When he is on base and is hit by a ball batted by a teammate
f. When an umpire declares a hit ball an infield fly

Rule 4   Scoring   A run is scored when an offensive player advances from batter to runner and successively touches first, second, third, and home bases.

How to watch

New York Yankees

with Roger Maris

In the view of Roger Maris, the only player to break Babe Ruth's record of home runs in a single season, there is no point in worrying about what a pitcher will hand out. "It's not the hitter's job to worry. His job is to get up there and hit, regardless of how hard the pitcher throws."

Still, if a spectator knows anything about the man up at bat, or anything about the man on the mound, he can hazard some guesses about what might happen. According to Maris, there are two kinds of hitters, basically: You got a guess hitter, or you have a zone hitter. A guess hitter is the guy who is going to look for either a fast ball or a curve ball. He will swing at one or the other A zone hitter has picked out a zone in front of him; he'll look for pitches to come in there. If a pitch comes into that zone, he will swing at it, regardless of what kind of pitch it is.

"I would say most hitters prefer to swing at a fastball," says Maris, himself a zone hitter. "If you look for a fastball, and get one, you can usually handle it. If you're looking for an off-speed pitch, and get a fastball, the ball comes by before you can handle it."

Can a hitter spot what kind of pitch he will get? "Sometimes," Maris says. "I can think of one man, in Kansas City. Whenever I could see more white on the ball before he threw, I knew he was going to throw a fastball. If I could see less white, I knew he would throw a curve ball."

Hitters are also defined according to where they tend to hit the ball. "A spray hitter can hit all over the field. Others can hit only to one corner."

What strategies are seen in a ball game depends on the clubs involved and who is managing them. For instance, when Maris played for the Yankees, stealing was rare. Some managers will let a hitter or a runner call the shots when he's up or on base; others prefer to make most of the calls. These instructions are communicated by signals known only to the players of the team, although, according to Maris, it is sometimes possible for opposing players to break the code. The players to watch for signals are the catcher, who helps the pitcher, and the third base coach. "Ninety-nine percent of the time," Maris says, "it's the third-base coach who tells runners when to steal and when to stay put."

"The catcher will study the hitter and figure out whether, for instance, he's a potential bunter. He'll also look at the hitter and try to figure out what the guy has in mind. Is he going to swing at outside pitches, or inside pitches? He signals to the pitcher."

Under certain conditions, the spectator can anticipate what a batter will do. "If you're losing, for instance, you get more picky about what to swing at," Maris says. "The idea is to get a hit and get on base. After all, you've got to get on base to score."

One type of hit a batter might use is the bunt. "Bunting is used in one of two ways—to get a base hit, or to advance a man who's already on base. This is called a sacrifice bunt." At other times, a hitter will be told to "take" a pitch, that is, not swing at it. "Most of the time, until you've taken a strike, the manager doesn't want you swinging at anything. Once you've got a strike, or a strike and some balls, you swing."

Main Events

THE WORLD SERIES

Year	Winner	Loser
1980	Philadelphia (NL) 4	Kansas City (AL) 2
1979	Pittsburgh (NL) 4	Baltimore (AL) 3
1978	New York (AL) 4	Los Angeles (NL) 2
1977	New York (AL) 4	Los Angeles (NL) 2
1976	Cincinnati (NL) 4	New York (AL) 0
1975	Cincinnati (NL) 4	Boston (AL) 3
1974	Oakland (AL) 4	Los Angeles (NL) 1
1973	Oakland (AL) 4	New York (NL) 3
1972	Oakland (AL) 4	Cincinnati (NL) 3
1971	Pittsburgh (NL) 4	Baltimore (AL) 3
1970	Baltimore (AL) 4	Cincinnati (NL) 1

League standings: American, 45; National, 32

ABC Sports

ALL-STAR GAMES

Year	Winner	Score
1980	National	4–2
1979	National	7–6
1978	National	7–3
1977	National	7–5
1976	National	7–1
1975	National	6–3
1974	National	7–2
1973	National	7–1
1972	National	4–3
1971	American	6–4
1970	National	5–4

League standings: American, 18; National, 31; 1 tie

All-Time Greats

Henry Louis ("Hank") Aaron
(Feb. 5, 1934–)

National League of Professional Baseball Clubs

Hank Aaron is perhaps best known for breaking Babe Ruth's career record of 714 home runs, although he has made numerous other contributions to professional baseball. Aaron started in the Negro American League, then moved to farm clubs, and in 1954 played his first season with the Milwaukee Braves. By the time his playing career ended in 1976, he ranked among the best, having amassed 3,771 total hits. For 21 consecutive years, from 1955 to 1975, Aaron was a member of National League All-Star teams. He holds or shares 21 major league records, including Most Games Played, Most Runs Batted In, Most At Bats, and Most Home Runs (755). He currently serves as vice-president and director of player development for the Atlanta Braves.

Tyrus Raymond ("Ty") Cobb
(Dec. 18, 1886–July 17, 1961)

Detroit Tigers

Ty Cobb ranks among the greatest baseball players of all time; many consider him *the* greatest player. Known as the "Georgia Peach," he was a great hitter and base runner, establishing numerous records during his playing career, including a .367 lifetime batting average (in 3,033 games) and 4,191 hits. Cobb spent his career with the Detroit Tigers. A ruthless competitor, he was hated by his opponents and often by his teammates. Many attribute Cobb's phenomenal success as a ballplayer to his boundless desire to win and to his unending practice and study of the game.

Joseph Paul ("Joe") DiMaggio
(Nov. 25, 1914–)

New York Yankees

DiMaggio began his career as a shortstop in the semipro Pacific Coast League. Before long, he moved to center field, eventually becoming perhaps the game's greatest player in that position. In 1935, the New York Yankees paid $25,000 for "Joltin' Joe." After a slow start, DiMaggio began to make his mark. In the summer of 1941, the "Yankee Clipper" had a 56-game hitting streak, a record that still stands. Also a great home-run hitter, he hit two home runs in one inning in 1936 and three times hit three home runs in one game.

Henry Louis ("Lou") Gehrig
(June 19, 1903–June 2, 1941)

New York Yankees

He was surely one of the most durable players, having played in 2,130 consecutive games over 14 years. He was also perhaps the most unfortunate of baseball stars, having to share the limelight with his flamboyant teammate, Babe Ruth. Gehrig's first break came in 1925, when Yankee first baseman Wally Pipp was injured. Gehrig replaced Pipp, and stayed on, setting numerous major-league records. A hard-working, consistent ball-player. Gehrig holds the record for the most grand slams (23). In May 1939, feeling his strength waning, he removed himself from the Yankee lineup. Doctors diagnosed the problem as amyotrophic lateral sclerosis ("Lou Gehrig's Disease"), a paralyzing disease that resulted in his death two years later.

Walter Perry Johnson
(Nov. 6, 1887–Dec. 10, 1946)

Minnesota Twins

Johnson is considered by many the hardest- and fastest-throwing pitcher in the history of the game. He holds career records for strikeouts, with 3,508, and shut-outs, with 113. Twelve times, Johnson recorded 20 or more wins in one season. Despite spending his career with a losing team, the Washington Senators, Johnson achieved 416 victories, including a no-hitter in 1920 and numerous one-hitters.

Christopher ("Christy") Mathewson
(July 12, 1880–Oct. 7, 1925)

National League of Professional Baseball Clubs

Christy Mathewson may have been the greatest pitcher in baseball history; he was certainly the greatest of his generation. For awhile around the turn of the century, Mathewson shuttled between semipro leagues and the majors. In his first full season with the New York Giants, in 1901, he posted 20 wins, including 5 shutouts. Teamed with manager John McGraw, Mathewson helped the Giants win numerous pennants.

Willie Howard Mays, Jr.
(May 5, 1931–)

An exciting hitter, runner, and fielder, Mays played most of his career with the Giants, first in New York and then in San Francisco.He ended his career with the Mets. May's record illustrates his versatility: third in home runs (660) and runs scored (2,062); first to exceed both 300 homers and 300 steals; first in putouts by an outfielder (7,095). In one of baseball's most memorable catches, the "Say Hey Kid," playing in the 1954 World Series against Cleveland, raced toward Vic Wertz's apparently uncatchable deep drive, pocketed the ball over his left shoulder, and fired it back to the infield.

Stanley Frank ("Stan") Musial
(Nov. 21, 1920–)

Stan "The Man" Musial started as a pitcher in the minors in 1941, and worked his way up to the majors as a slugging outfielder for St. Louis—in one season. Two years later, Stan "The Man" hit .357, for his first batting title. Musial's humpbacked, corkscrew batting stance made him easily recognized at the plate. The stance also appeared to improve his output of home runs. In six seasons during his career, Musial hit 30 homers, and once hit four in four consecutive times at bat.

George Herman ("Babe") Ruth
(Feb. 6, 1895–Aug. 16, 1948)

Babe Ruth, baseball's best-known and most popular player, began his major-league career as a pitcher with the Boston Red Sox, a position he played for three years. Before leaving Boston, Ruth switched to the outfield because of his hitting ability. His best-season (1923) batting average was .393. From 1920 to 1934, Ruth played with the New York Yankees. As the Yankees' main drawing card, he so increased the gate receipts, and thus helped finance construction of Yankee Stadium, that the new stadium was dubbed "The House that Ruth Built." The holder of many batting records, "The Babe" is often credited with helping make baseball the country's national pastime.

Theodore Samuel ("Ted") Williams
(Aug. 30, 1918–)

Ted Williams, playing with the Boston Red Sox, became one of baseball's best hitters. His keen eyesight and strong wrists helped him win two Triple Crowns during a long solid career. Known as a patient hitter, "The Kid" had only three seasons in which he struck out more than 50 times. In the 1941 season, Williams batted .406 and led the league, with 37 homers.

HALL OF FAME

National Baseball Hall of Fame
Cooperstown, NY 13326
(607) 547-9988

The members of the National Baseball Hall of Fame, by year chosen, are:

1936
Tyrus R. Cobb
Walter P. Johnson
Christopher Mathewson
George H. ("Babe") Ruth
John P. ("Honus") Wagner

1937
Morgan G. Bulkeley
Byron B. ("Ban") Johnson
Napoleon ("Larry") Lajoie
Connie Mack
John J. McGraw
Tristram E. Speaker
George Wright
Denton T. ("Cy") Young

1938
Grover C. Alexander
Alexander J. Cartwright, Jr.
Henry Chadwick

1939
Adrian C. ("Cap") Anson
Edward T. Collins
Charles A. Comiskey
William A. ("Candy") Cummings
William B. ("Buck") Ewing
H. Louis Gehrig
William H. ("Willie") Keeler
Charles G. Radbourne
George H. Sisler
Albert G. Spalding

1942
Rogers Hornsby

1944
Kenesaw Mountain Landis

1945
Roger P. Bresnahan
Dennis ("Dan") Brouthers
Frederick C. Clarke
James J. Collins
Edward J. Delahanty
Hugh Duffy
Hugh A. Jennings
Michael J. ("King") Kelly
James H. O'Rourke
Wilbert Robinson

1946
Jesse C. Burkett
Frank L. Chance
John D. Chesbro
John J. Evers
Clark C. Griffith
Thomas F. McCarthy
Joseph J. McGinnity
Edward S. Plank
Joseph B. Tinker
George E. ("Rube") Waddell
Edward A. Walsh

1947
Gordon S. ("Mickey") Cochrane
Frank F. Frisch
Robert M. ("Lefty") Grove
Carl O. Hubbell

1948
Herbert J. Pennock
Harold J. ("Pie") Traynor

1949
Mordecai P. Brown
Charles L. Gehringer
Charles A. ("Kid") Nichols

1951
James E. Foxx
Melvin T. Ott

1952
Harry E. Heilmann
Paul G. Waner

1953
Edward G. Barrow
Charles A. ("Chief") Bender
Thomas H. Connolly
Jay H. ("Dizzy") Dean
William J. Klem
Aloysius H. Simmons
Roderick J. ("Bobby") Wallace
William H. ("Harry") Wright

1954
William M. Dickey
Walter J. ("Rabbit") Maranville
William H. Terry

1955
J. Franklin Baker
Joseph P. DiMaggio
Charles L. ("Gabby") Hartnett
Theodore A. Lyons
Raymond W. Schalk
Arthur C. ("Dazzy") Vance

1956
Joseph E. Cronin
Henry B. Greenberg

1957
Samuel E. Crawford
Joseph V. McCarthy

1959
Zachariah D. Wheat

1961
Max G. Carey
William R. Hamilton

1962
Robert W. A. Feller
William B. McKechnie
Jack R. Robinson
Edd J. Roush

1963
John G. Clarkson
Elmer H. Flick
Edgar C. ("Sam") Rice
Eppa Rixey

1964
Lucius B. ("Luke") Appling
Urban C. ("Red") Faber
Burleigh A. Grimes
Miller J. Huggins
Timothy J. Keefe
Henry E. ("Heinie") Manush
John M. Ward

1965
James F. ("Pud") Galvin

1966
Charles D. ("Casey") Stengel
Theodore S. Williams

1967
W. Branch Rickey
Charles H. ("Red") Ruffing
Lloyd J. Waner

1968
Hazen S. ("Kiki") Cuyler

Leon A. ("Goose") Goslin
Joseph M. Medwick

1969
Roy Campanella
Stanley A. Coveleski
Waite C. Hoyt
Stanley F. Musial

1970
Louis Boudreau
Earle B. Combs
Ford C. Frick
Jesse J. ("Pop") Haines

1971
David J. Bancroft
Jacob P. Beckley
Charles J. ("Chick") Hafey
Harry B. Hooper
Joseph J. Kelley
Richard W. ("Rube") Marquard
Leroy R. ("Satchel") Paige
George M. Weiss

1972
Lawrence P. ("Yogi") Berra
Joshua Gibson
Vernon L. ("Lefty") Gomez
William Harridge
Sanford Koufax
Walter F. ("Buck") Leonard
Early Wynn
Ross M. Youngs

1973
Roberto W. Clemente
William G. Evans
Monford ("Monte") Irvin
George L. Kelly
Warren E. Spahn
Michael F. Welch

1974
James T. ("Cool Papa") Bell
James L. Bottomley
John B. ("Jocko") Conlan
Edward C. ("Whitey") Ford
Mickey C. Mantle
Samuel L. Thompson

1975
H. Earl Averill
Stanley R. ("Bucky") Harris
William J. Herman
William J. ("Judy") Johnson
Ralph M. Kiner

1976
Oscar M. Charleston
Roger Connor
R. Cal Hubbard
Robert G. Lemon
Frederick C. Lindstrom
Robin E. Roberts

1977
Ernest Banks
Martin Dihigo
John H. Lloyd
Alfonso R. Lopez
Amos W. Rusie
Joseph W. Sewell

1978
Adrian Joss
Leland S. ("Larry") MacPhail
Edwin L. Mathews

1979
Warren C. Giles
Willie H. Mays
Lewis R. ("Hack") Wilson

1980
Albert W. Kaline
Charles H. Klein
Edwin D. ("Duke") Snider
Thomas A. Yawkey

1981
Rube Foster
Bob Gibson
Johnny Mize

For the Record

THE CY YOUNG AWARD

The Cy Young Award, by a vote of baseball writers, is given to outstanding pitchers of the American and National leagues.

1980 **Steve Stone,** Baltimore, AL
Steve Carlton, Philadelphia, NL

1979 **Mike Flanagan,** Baltimore, AL
Bruce Sutter, Chicago, NL

1978 **Ron Guidry,** New York, AL
Gaylord Perry, San Diego, NL

1977 **Sparky Lyle,** New York, AL
Steve Carlton, Philadelphia, NL

1976 **Jim Palmer,** Baltimore, AL
Randy Jones, San Diego, NL

1975 **Jim Palmer,** Baltimore, AL
Tom Seaver, New York, NL

MOST VALUABLE PLAYER AWARD

The Most Valuable Player is chosen by a vote of baseball writers.

1980 **George Brett,** Kansas City, AL
Mike Schmidt, Philadelphia, NL

1979 **Don Baylor,** California, AL
Willie Stargell, Pittsburgh, NL
Keith Hernandez, St. Louis, NL

1978 **Jim Rice,** Boston, AL
Dave Parker, Pittsburgh, NL

1977 **Rod Carew,** Minnesota, AL
George Foster, Cincinnati, NL

1976 **Thurman Munson,** New York, AL
Joe Morgan, Cincinnati, NL

1975 **Fred Lynn,** Boston, AL
Joe Morgan, Cincinnati, NL

ROOKIE OF THE YEAR AWARD

The Rookie of the Year is chosen by a vote of baseball writers.

1980 Joe Charboneau, Cleveland, AL
Steve Howe, Los Angeles, NL

1979 John Castino, Minnesota, AL
Alfredo Griffin, Toronto, AL
Rick Sutcliffe, Los Angeles, NL

1978 Lou Whitaker, Detroit, AL
Bob Horner, Atlanta, NL

1977 Eddie Murray, Baltimore, AL
Andre Dawson, Montreal, NL

1976 Mark Fidrych, Detroit, AL
Pat Zachry, Cincinnati, NL
Butch Metzger, San Diego, NL

1975 Fred Lynn, Boston, AL
John Montefusco, San Francisco, NL

MAJOR-LEAGUE RECORDS, INDIVIDUALS

Most home runs, season
61   Roger Maris 1961 (162 games)
60   Babe Ruth 1927 (154 games)

Most home runs, career
755   Henry Aaron   1943–76

Highest batting average, season
.424   Rogers Hornsby   1924

Highest batting average, career
.367   Ty Cobb   1905–28

Most runs batted in, season
190   Hack Wilson   1930

Most runs batted in, career
2,209   Babe Ruth   1914–35

Most runs scored, season
177   Babe Ruth   1921

Most runs scored, career
2,244   Ty Cobb   1905–28

Most base hits, season
257   George Sisler   1920

Most base hits, career
4,191   Ty Cobb   1905–28

Most stolen bases, season
118   Lou Brock   1974

Most stolen bases, career
938   Lou Brock   1961–79

Most consecutive games hit safely in
56   Joe DiMaggio   1941

Most wins pitching, season
41   Jack Chesbro   1904

Most wins pitching, career
511   Cy Young   1890–1911

Most strikeouts (pitching), season
383   Nolan Ryan   1973

Most strikeouts (pitching), career
3,508   Walter Johnson   1907–27

Most shutouts, season
16   Grover Cleveland Alexander 1916

Most shutouts, career
113   Walter Johnson   1907–27

Most consecutive games played
2,130   Lou Gehrig   1925–39

MAJOR-LEAGUE RECORDS, TEAMS

Most home runs, season
240   New York Yankees   1961

Most consecutive wins, season
26   New York Giants   1916

Most World Series won
20   New York Yankees

Most games won, season
116   Chicago Cubs   1906

Most seasons, 100 or more home runs
54   New York Yankees

Most consecutive seasons, 100 or more home runs
34   Boston

Did you know ?

1. What President began the tradition of throwing out the first ball of the season?

2. Who managed the first professional baseball team?

3. What twentieth-century player hit a grand slam home run in his first major-league game?

4. Who was the first player to hit a home run in the Astrodome?

5. Who holds the career record for the most bases on balls?

6. Who is the only player voted unanimously the Most Valuable Player of the National League? When?

7. Who holds the record for the most consecutive shutout innings pitched? How many innings?

8. What pitcher was the only one to have pitched no-hit, no-run games back to back?

9. Who were the first five players inducted into the Baseball Hall of Fame?

10. Who was the first baseball commissioner?

11. Many sets of brothers have played in the majors. Name the only twins who played major league ball.

12. How many innings did the longest major-league game last? What teams played?

13. With a record of 27–9 for the 1966 season, Sandy Koufax won the Cy Young Award. Who beat him out for National League Most Valuable Player?

14. What batter holds the record for the most strikeouts in a career?

15. In the film version of pitcher Christy Mathewson's life, who plays the great baseball player and all-round athlete?

Answers: 1. William H. Taft, June 9, 1910, in Washington, DC; **2.** Harry Wright, Cincinnati Red Stockings, 1869; **3.** Bobby Bonds, San Francisco, 1968; **4.** Mickey Mantle; **5.** Babe Ruth, with 2,056; **6.** Orlando Cepeda, St. Louis Cardinals, 1967; **7.** Don Drysdale, Los Angeles Dodgers, 58 innings; **8.** Johnny Vander Meer, Cincinnati, 1938; **9.** Ty Cobb, Babe Ruth, Christy Mathewson, Honus Wagner, and Walter Johnson; **10.** Judge Kenesaw Mountain Landis; **11.** Oscar R Grimes, Sr., and A. Roy Grimes, 1920; **12.** 26 innings, Brooklyn versus Boston, 1920, ending in a 1–1 tie; **13.** Roberto Clemente, Pittsburgh Pirates; **14.** Mickey Mantle, with 1,710; **15.** Ronald Reagan.

Key Words

balk an illegal action by the pitcher, entitling each base runner to advance one base. A balk may be called in situations where the pitcher: makes any illegal pitch; throws from stretch without first coming to set position; fails to throw after making a motion commonly associated with delivery of the ball; pretends to throw to home plate or to first base; throws to a base, trying to pick off a runner, without first stepping toward that base. There are also other actions by pitchers that may result in a balk being called.

ball   a pitch in flight, which does not fall into the strike zone and that is not swung at or struck by the batter.

bases loaded   base runners occupying all three bases.

batting average   the number of times a player got base hits, expressed as a percentage. It is computed by dividing the number of hits by the number of times at bat, carried to three decimal places.

beanball   a pitch that hits a batter in the head, or that is intentionally thrown at a batter's head.

box score   tabular summary of a game, listing the players and their individual statistics for the game, as well as an inning-by-inning account of events (runs, hits, errors).

brushback   a pitch thrown high and inside, forcing the batter to move back from the plate.

bull pen   an area where relief, or substitute, pitchers can warm up before coming into the game.

bunt   a ball hit lightly into the infield near the batter. A ball thus hit is difficult for defensive players to field.

change-up   a slow pitch thrown with the same motion as a fastball, intended to deceive the batter.

curve ball   a pitch (thrown by a right-handed pitcher) that breaks sharply to the left and down as it nears the batter.

designated hitter   a player chosen at the start of a game to bat for the pitcher without causing the pitcher to be taken from the game. A designated hitter may not field, and the pitcher may not bat. The rule is currently approved by only the American League.

diamond   the portion of the playing field enclosed by base lines, although the term sometimes refers to the entire playing field.

double play   a play in which two runners are put out.

doubleheader   two games scheduled one after another for the price of one game. Also called a "twin bill."

dugout   the seating area for players and other team members in uniform when they are not batting, preparing to bat, or on the field. Also called the bench.

earned run   a run that is scored without the help of an error.

earned-run average   the average number of earned runs scored against a pitcher per nine innings. A pitcher's earned-run average is calculated by dividing the number of innings pitched by nine, then dividing the figure into the number of runs charged to the pitcher, carried to two decimal places.

fielder's choice   a situation in which a fielder makes a play to put out a runner rather than the batter. The batter is charged with a time at bat but is not credited with a base hit.

fly   a ball hit high in the air.

force play   a play in which a runner loses the right to occupy a base, and must move on to the next base because the batter has hit a fair ball and has become a base runner.

ground-rule double   a double awarded to a batter when a hit ball bounces over an outfield fence.

hit-and-run play   a situation in which the runner on first base runs toward second when the pitcher releases the ball, forcing the second baseman or the shortstop to cover second base. Meanwhile, the batter tries to hit the ball to the spot vacated by the fielder.

knuckleball   an unpredictable and difficult pitch that may break to the left or to the right, or downward. The pitcher usually grips the ball with fingernails or tips of fingers.

line drive   a ball hit hard by the batter that goes sharply and directly to a fielder without touching the ground.

on-deck circle   an area five feet in diameter between the dugout and home plate, used as a waiting area for the player who follows the batter.

pennant   winning the pennant means becoming the league champion.

pick-off   a quick throw by the pitcher or the catcher that catches a base runner off base and puts him out.

pinch hitter   a player who bats for another player. The pinch hitter may bat only once; the player replaced leaves the game.

pinch runner   a player who enters the game to run for another player. The pinch runner may be used only once, and the player replaced leaves the game.

run batted in   runs scored as a result of a batter's base hit, out (except double plays), walk, sacrifice fly, or being hit by a pitch.

sacrifice   a situation in which the batter bunts the ball and is put out, but which allows a base runner to advance. In a sacrifice fly, the batter flies out, but a runner advances after the catch.

screwball   a pitch that breaks similarly to a curve ball, but to the right, instead.

sinker   a pitch that drops sharply as it approaches home plate.

slider   a pitch similar to the curve ball, but which breaks later and less sharply.

spitter   an illegal pitch similar to a fastball, but in which the ball has been moistened with saliva or grease. The ball is released with little rotation and breaks sharply near the plate. Also called a spitball.

squeeze play   a situation in which the batter bunts in an attempt to score a runner from third base.

steal   reaching the next base safely by catching the defense off guard and running.

strike   a pitched ball swung at by the batter and missed, hit foul (except on the third strike), or that crosses home plate within the strike zone.

triple play   a play in which three runners are put out.

Courtesy NBA

3 BASKETBALL

Basketball is perhaps America's favorite sport, both to watch and to play. Millions of Americans, from grade school on up, in gymnasiums and parks, participate in or follow the sport.

Unlike most modern sports, basketball is not a game that evolved from sports played for centuries, or from the sports of ancient civilizations. Basketball was deliberately invented by a young coach, James Naismith, whose assignment it was to develop an orderly game that could be played indoors and that would hold the interest of players during the long winters between the football and baseball seasons.

In 1891, Naismith, a Canadian seminary student on leave from the seminary, worked as an instructor at the YMCA school in Springfield, Massachusetts. While there, Naismith was asked to design a game that would meet the requirements just mentioned. He decided early that a ball was necessary. Because the game would be played indoors, however, the ball should be moved by the hands rather than with a racket or bat. Naismith came up with the idea of a raised goal; on the day the game was to be tested, no cartons were available, so peach baskets were used.

Naismith outlined 13 original rules, and the first basketball game was played December 21, 1891, between two teams of nine players each. The game, quickly dubbed "basketball," was an immediate success. It spread across the United States through the YMCA network. Although colleges soon adopted the game, records indicate that there was little intercollegiate play at the time.

A new goal was introduced, which allowed the ball to drop through a net of chain rope, making it unnecessary for players to retrieve the ball after each goal. To prevent interference by overzealous fans, backboards were added in 1895, an innovation that unexpectedly brought the ricochet goal to the game. Until 1900, four different versions were played; eventually, basketball as we know it today emerged, with five players on a team and restrictions on dribbling.

The National Basketball League, basketball's first professional league, was organized in 1898 and was composed of teams from Manhattan, Brooklyn, Philadelphia, and southern New Jersey. The league lasted only two seasons, however. Other leagues were formed and dissolved. The "Original Celtics," organized in 1915, dominated the American Basketball League (formed in 1925) during the 1920s. The impact of this team was sufficient to win new fans for professional basketball, which had declined in popularity during the first two decades of the century.

The year 1934 was an important one in the development of basketball. The rules were finally standardized; now college players in one part of the country would be playing the same form of the game as players in other parts. Also in 1934, an enterprising sportswriter named Ned Irish persuaded the management of Madison Square Garden to invite major college teams to play in a tournament there. A skeptical management finally agreed, and the fans flocked to see Notre Dame and New York University play in a doubleheader. A tradition was born. The National Invitational and NCAA tournaments would become a highlight of winter sports.

Two rule changes—elimination of the center jump after a goal (1936) and, later, after a free throw—changed basketball significantly. Because the momentum of the game was no longer broken after each score, basketball became more exciting to watch. The three-second rule, introduced to prevent stalls, forced players to act, and thus made it more difficult for the team in the lead to hold that lead. Once again, the game was made more exciting. Over the years, rules have been added or revised to prevent the advantage of tall players from becoming lopsided; inevitably, however, the tall player still has a decided advantage.

After World War II, basketball, like many professional sports, increased in popularity. In a successful attempt to combine basketball crowds rather than divide them, the Basketball Association of America and the National Basketball League, in 1949, merged and formed the National Basketball Association. In the 1950s, a scandal in college basketball, involving charges of point-fixing, tarnished the image of basketball. Attendance dropped, and confidence had to be restored, just as had been necessary in professional basketball three or four decades earlier. College basketball became a training ground for professional ball as the NBA, now growing, demanded more and more good players. Weaker NBA franchises folded, the league was strengthened, and by 1970 the NBA was solidly organized, with 17 teams.

The American Basketball Association, which began playing in 1967–68, found it too difficult to compete with the established NBA, and in 1976, the two leagues merged. Four ABA teams were added to the NBA, and the remaining ABA players were absorbed by the league.

A professional basketball player's average annual salary of $85,000 is among the highest in professional sports. These salaries, however, are threatened by television, which is causing attendance to drop. Part of the problem is the tug-of-war within the sport: Is it a *team* or an *individual* sport? Although Naismith originally envisioned basketball as a team sport, it has come to be so dominated by star players that as few as one or two stars can carry a mediocre team to a championship. Perhaps it is time for a reevaluation, one that would force a shift of emphasis from individual standouts to outstanding teams.

Great Moments

PROFESSIONAL

1915 The "Original Celtics" are formed as a semipro team; they will later dominate professional basketball for many years.

1925 Stars in the American Basketball League are paid $1,500 a month over a six-month season.

1939 The all-black New York Renaissance, or "Rens," win 112 games, losing only seven, and gain the world title.

1947 George Mikan leads the Chicago Gears to a National Basketball League title for the 1946–47 season.

1953 For the first time, two division winners make it through the elimination series to the finals. Minneapolis wins four of five games against New York, to gain the title.

1959 Boston defeats Minneapolis in four straight games, for the first sweep in the history of the championship finals.

1962 In his final season, Boston's Bob Cousy caps a magnificent career by helping the Celtics win another championship.

1967 Moves and acquisitions begin to change the face of the National Basketball Association. Seattle and San Diego are granted franchises, and four teams move to new arenas.

1975 Just before the season opens, the New York Nets and the Denver Nuggets, the strongest teams in the American Basketball Association, apply for admission to the NBA.

1978 Boston's John Havlicek retires from basketball holding the record for the most seasons scoring 1,000 or more points—16.

COLLEGE

1897 On March 20, the first recognized intercollegiate game using five-man teams is played; Yale beats Pennsylvania, 32–10.

1915 The National Collegiate Athletic Association and the Amateur Athletic Union form the Joint Basketball Rules Committee in an attempt to standardize the game.

1930 All-American Johnny Wooden, "the peerless Purdue guard," leads the Boilermakers to their first undefeated season and and Big Ten championship.

1934 Ned Irish, a sportswriter, arranges a college basketball doubleheader in Madison Square Garden, and basketball soon becomes a favorite indoor attraction.

1938   The center jump after scoring is eliminated, resulting in a higher-scoring, faster-paced game.

1938   Playing in a small gym on the campus of Northwestern University, Oregon defeats Ohio State, 46–33, to become basketball's first NCAA champion.

1940   W2XMS, an experimental station, is the first to broadcast television pictures of college basketball—a doubleheader played at Madison Square Garden on February 28.

1949   College basketball changes again when a rule is introduced that allows coaches to talk to their players during time-outs without penalty.

1964   Under the direction of coach John Wooden, UCLA wins the first of what were to be many NCAA championships.

1976   Indiana goes undefeated under the leadership of controversial coach Bobby Knight, and takes its first NCAA championship in more than 20 years.

The Setup

PROFESSIONAL BASKETBALL

The National Basketball Association (NBA) governs most professional basketball competition in the United States. It comprises 22 teams, divided into two conferences subdivided into four divisions. The playoffs are held in four rounds. The first, a best-of-three series, matches eight teams with the best won-lost records (regardless of division). The four division winners meet the first-round winners in the semifinals for a best-of-seven series. The winners of the semifinals meet in the conference finals for another best-of-seven series. Finally, the conference winners play in a best-of-seven series for the world championship.

ORGANIZATION OF THE NBA

Eastern Conference

Atlantic Division	Central Division
Boston Celtics	Atlanta Hawks
Philadelphia 76ers	Houston Rockets
Washington Bullets	San Antonio Spurs
New York Knicks	Indiana Pacers
New Jersey Nets	Cleveland Cavaliers
	Detroit Pistons

Western Conference

Midwest Division	Pacific Division
Milwaukee Bucks	Los Angeles Lakers
Kansas City Kings	Seattle Supersonics
Chicago Bulls	Phoenix Suns
Denver Nuggets	Portland Trailblazers
Utah Jazz	San Diego Clippers
	Golden State Warriors

NATIONAL BASKETBALL
  ASSOCIATION
645 Fifth Ave.
New York, NY 10022
(212) 826-7000
Lawrence F. O'Brien, commissioner

ATLANTA HAWKS
100 Techwood Dr. NW
Atlanta, GA 30303
(404) 681-3600
J. Michael Gearon, pres. and gov.
(games played at The Omni)

BOSTON CELTICS
Boston Garden
North Station
Boston, MA 02114
(617) 523-6050
Harry T. Mangurian, Jr., chairman of board
(games played at Boston Garden)

CHICAGO BULLS
333 N. Michigan Ave.
Chicago, IL 60601
(312) 346-1122
Philip M. Klutznick, pres.
(games played at Chicago Stadium)

CLEVELAND CAVALIERS
2923 Streetsboro Rd.
Richfield, OH 44286
(216) 659-9100
Nick J. Mileti, pres. and treas.
(games played at the Coliseum)

DENVER NUGGETS
1635 Clay St.
Denver, CO 80204
(303) 893-6700
Carl Scheer, pres. and gen. mgr.
(games played at McNichols Sports Arena)

DETROIT PISTONS
1200 Featherstone
Pontiac, MI 48057
(313) 338-4667
William M. Davidson, mng. partner
(games played at Silverdome)

GOLDEN STATE WARRIORS
Oakland Coliseum
Oakland, CA 94621
(415) 638-6000
Franklin Mieuli, pres.
(games played at Oakland Coliseum Arena)

HOUSTON ROCKETS
Ten Greenway Plaza East
Houston, TX 77046
(713) 627-0600
George J. Maloof, pres.
(games played at Summit)

INDIANA PACERS
Market Square Center Bldg.
151 N. Delaware St.
Indianapolis, IN 46204
(317) 632-3636
Sam Nassi, chairman of board and NBA
  gov.
(games played at Market Square Arena)

KANSAS CITY KINGS
1800 Genessee, Suite 101
Kansas City, MO 64102
(816) 421-3131
H. Paul Rosenberg, pres. and mng. dir.
(games played at Municipal Auditorium)

LOS ANGELES LAKERS
3900 W. Manchester Blvd.
Inglewood, CA 90306
(213) 674-6000
Dr. Jerry Buss, chairman of board
(games played at the Forum)

MILWAUKEE BUCKS
901 N. Fourth St.
Milwaukee, WI 53203
(414) 272-6030
James F. Fitzgerald, chairman of board
  and pres.
(games played at Milwaukee Arena)

NEW JERSEY NETS
185 E. Union Ave.
East Rutherford, NJ 07073
(201) 935-8888
Alan N. Cohen, chairman
(games played at Rutgers Univ. Athletic
  Center)

NEW YORK KNICKERBOCKERS
Four Pennsylvania Plaza
New York, NY 10001
(212) 563-8000
Michael Burks, pres.
(games played at Madison Square Garden)

PHILADELPHIA 76ers
Veterans Stadium
P.O. Box 25040
Philadelphia, PA 19147
(215) 339-7600

F. Eugene Dixon, Jr., pres. and chairman of
board
(games played at The Spectrum)

PHOENIX SUNS
P.O. Box 1369
Phoenix, AZ 85001
(602) 258-5753
Richard Bloch, pres.
(games played at Veterans Memorial
Coliseum)

PORTLAND TRAILBLAZERS
Lloyd Bldg., Suite 380
700 N.E. Multnomah St.
Portland, OR 97232
(503) 234-9291
Lawrence Weinberg, pres.
(games played at Memorial Coliseum)

SAN ANTONIO SPURS
HemisFair Arena
P.O. Box 530
San Antonio, TX 78292
Angelo Drossos, pres. and chief exec.
officer
(games played at HemisFair Arena)

SAN DIEGO CLIPPERS
3500 Sports Arena Blvd.
San Diego, CA 92110
(714) 226-1275
Irving H. Levin, pres.
(games played at San Diego Sports Arena)

SEATTLE SUPERSONICS
419 Occidental South
Seattle, WA 98104
(206) 628-8400
Samuel Shulman, pres.
(games played at the Kingdome)

UTAH JAZZ
Suite 206, 100 S.W. Temple
Salt Lake City, UT 84101
(801) 355-5151
Sam D. Battistone, co-owner and pres.
(games played at the Salt Palace)

WASHINGTON BULLETS
One Harry S. Truman Dr.
Landover, MD 20786
(301) 350-3400
Abe Pollin, pres.
(games played at Capital Centre)

Los Angeles Lakers

COLLEGE BASKETBALL

College basketball, like college football, is governed by more than one organization; and, like football, it has a complicated system for determining season champions. Although most of the leading teams are members of NCAA-sanctioned athletic conferences, a few major schools remain independent. Competition is not limited to conference teams, but a conference champion is determined at the end of the season, at which time eight of the top-ranked teams are invited to compete in the NCAA playoffs. Four preliminary games are played, with the winners going on to the semifinals; eventually, two teams meet to determine the title winner.

The National Invitational Tournament (NIT), played at Madison Square Garden, competes with the NCAA tournament, inviting leading college teams of slightly lower caliber than those in NCAA tournament competition.

Whereas the NCAA champion is generally recognized as the national college champion, an NIT win is also prestigious. The team that wins the NCAA title is almost always voted the number-one team in the final polls by The Associated Press and United Press International.

The Basics

Object of the game   To score the most points by tossing a ball through a hoop mounted on a backboard 10 feet above the court.

The court   Play is on a court measured and marked according to the diagram shown, with the lane space marks and the neutral zones in a color contrasting with the boundary lines.

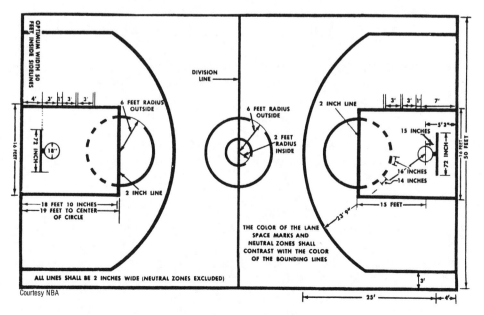

Courtesy NBA

Equipment   A round ball about 30 inches in circumference when inflated; metal-ring basket 18 inches in diameter, mounted 10 feet above the floor on a transparent, rectangular backboard.

Players   Five, usually two forwards, two guards, and one center.

Officials   In professional games, two referees; two timers, one for the game clock and one for the 24-second clock; and a statistician.

Scoring   A basket from the field (field goal) is worth two points, unless shot from beyond the three-point line, in which case it is worth three points. A basket from the free-throw line (foul shot) is worth one point.

Timing   A regulation period is 12 minutes, with four periods constituting a game. In college ball, the game is divided into two 20-minute halves. Overtime lasts five minutes, and the break between halves is 15 minutes.

Rule 1   Jump ball   The ball is put in play by a jump between two opponents in the center circle: at the start of the game and at the start of each overtime period, and in other situations requiring determination of possession.

Rule 2   Twenty-four-second clock   A team in possession of the ball must attempt to score a shot within 24 seconds after gaining possession of the ball (pro basketball only).

Rule 3   Dribble   A dribble ends when a player touches the ball with both hands simultaneously, permits the ball to come to rest while he or she is in contact with it, tries for a basket or otherwise loses control, or when the ball is dead.

Rule 4   Traveling   A player holding the ball may not move in any direction (except to pivot) without dribbling the ball.

Rule 5   Out of bounds   A player is out of bounds when he or she touches the floor or any object on or outside a boundary. The ball is out of bounds when it touches a player who is out of bounds or any other person, the floor, or any object on, above, or outside a boundary or the supports or the back of the backboard.

Rule 6   Throw-in   A player must pass the ball inbounds within five seconds of the start of the throw-in.

Rule 7   Free throw   A player fouled by an opponent is given the chance to score one point by an unhindered throw from behind the free-throw line.

Rule 8   Personal foul   A player is allowed only five personal fouls per game; on the sixth, the player is disqualified from play in that game. In college ball, a player is allowed only four fouls. The following are personal fouls, and the penalty is one or two free throws to the offended player: holding, pushing, charging, or elbowing; charging while dribbling; and illegal positioning while screening.

Rule 9   Technical fouls   The following are illegal in NBA play, and a technical foul is imposed as a penalty: zone defense (legal in college play); an excessive number of time-outs; delay of game; illegal substitution; hanging on the basket ring; and unsportsmanlike conduct.

Rule 10   Interference   A defensive player may not touch the ball or basket when the ball is on or within either basket, or when it is touching the cylinder having the ring as its base. Goaltending, or touching the ball when it is in downward flight during a try for a field goal, is illegal; in that case, the ball must be above the basket, must not have touched the ring, and, in the judgment of the official, must have a chance to score.

Rule 11   Time-outs   Each team is granted seven charged time-outs in regulation play, limited to no more than four in the fourth period and no more than three in the last two minutes of play. Each team is allowed only two time-outs in overtime.

How to watch

with Tom McMillen

One of the most important things for a person watching basketball to realize, says Rhodes scholar and Atlanta Hawks star, Tom McMillen, is the slimness of a winning margin in a college or a professional game. A seemingly insignificant factor—a missed shot or two, a play that uses up a few seconds—can make or break a game. So many strategies used, though subtle, are crucial.

Unlike the fans at a sports event, television viewers are restricted to watching what the camera sees; thus they miss much of the action outside camera range. Nevertheless, McMillen says, an alert viewer can get a good idea of what is happening on the court as a whole. A good way to better understand what you're seeing, McMillen suggests, is to watch an entire game from the vantage point of one player. If that player is on defense, you will see the many ways he or she tries to put pressure on the offensive player or players, what tactics are used to get the offense to make a mistake. In college basketball—where there is no time (24-second) clock and players can make ample use of zones—defense is more flexible than it is in pro ball. Both college and professional basketball, however, allow for creative defensive playing.

The two basic types of defense are zone-to-zone and man-to-man. Some teams, McMillen points out, use both types, which, in itself, can be a good defensive ploy, because it tends to confuse the offensive team. Man-to-man presses may consist of "passively" putting pressure on an opponent in an attempt to get that player to make a mistake—to take an extra step or move to a less favored position on the court—or to aggressively pursue an opponent and apply pressure vigorously. An aggressive defense, though a gamble (it can backfire), is sometimes useful. The aim in using a zone defense in full court is to cause a player (who must get the ball over half the court within 10 seconds) to make a mistake and throw the ball away.

When watching an offensive player, then, one of the most important things to look for is how the player breaks loose from a good defense. Although a good offensive player sometimes has to take an outside shot or maneuver to the outside of the court, that player is usually better off keeping the game on the inside. Outside games, McMillen says, look impressive—and at times spectacular—but it is very hard to maintain a game from outside positions. The chance of winning an outside game is slim, and a good team will be able to make the adjustment from an outside to an inside game fairly easily.

One of the most striking characteristics of basketball centers is the grace of their movements, especially when one considers their size; but, McMillen says, other characteristics are equally important. For example, most centers have favorite moves or favorite positions on the court. McMillen notes that even someone like Kareem Abdul-Jabbar, a player many consider unstoppable, will revert to habit based on years of experience, and that as much as 70 percent of his moves will be in certain areas, using certain types of shots. The job of the defense, therefore, consists in knowing Jabbar's "book," in trying to get him slightly off balance and make him fight, physically, for court position. A guard who is extremely mismatched physically may be forced to try to steal the ball or to lure the center outside. Whereas the tactic has certain risks (the center may simply snatch the ball away), in extreme situations, it has been used successfully.

College teams—depending, of course, on their coaches—tend to have a "set" style of play, relying less on individual players (with their own peculiar styles) and more on choreographed moves planned in advance. Professional teams are likely to be more spontaneous; but again, this depends on the coach.

A highly programmed team with many set plays tends to play with a great deal of screening. Much of the action takes place away from the ball as players try to move into predetermined positions. Teams with a freer style exhibit less action on the "weak" side (the side away from the ball); they are more likely to engage in fast breaks, running, and opening new situations. Both styles have their advantages. Structured teams, while less dependent on individual judgment, may take a beating, especially when their opponents have scouted well or when the team cannot break out of its set pattern. Looser teams depend more on the physical ability of individual players.

McMillen says that teams with highly talented players, such as the Philadelphia 76ers, can give the ball to a Julius Erving or a Darryl Dawkins and let him do something with it. Other teams, those with players of lower caliber, respond better to a systematic approach. Both types of play can be successful; it depends on how well coaches read their players.

You can get an idea of the type of play by watching the coach. When a player makes a mistake, does the coach pull him out immediately, or does the coach give the player some leeway? Sometimes only the coach spots the mistake (which may be a "mistake" only within that team's system of play).

Another suggestion of McMillen's is that the viewer watch a participant who seldom gets any attention: the referee. Some referees allow a game to become quite physical; others call fouls left and right. If fouls are called against an aggressive team starting soon after a game begins, the team may have to change its tactics, which could change the face of that particular game drastically.

In a sport as fast-paced as basketball, slight variations in play—from the mood of the referee to the spot where a center takes a shot—can make the difference between a losing season and a championship one.

Main Events

PROFESSIONAL BASKETBALL

NBA CHAMPIONSHIP

Year	Winner
1980–81	Boston Celtics
1979–80	Los Angeles Lakers
1978–79	Seattle Supersonics
1977–78	Washington Bullets
1976–77	Portland Trailblazers

NBA EAST-WEST ALL-STAR GAMES

Year	Winner	Score
1981	East	123–120
1980	East	144–136 (overtime)
1979	West	134–129
1978	East	133–125
1977	West	125–124
1976	East	123–109
1975	East	108–102

PODOLOFF TROPHY FOR MOST VALUABLE PLAYER

Award of the trophy is based on a vote of NBA players.

1979–80	Kareem Abdul-Jabbar, Los Angeles
1978–79	Moses Malone, Houston
1977–78	Bill Walton, Portland
1976–77	Kareem Abdul-Jabbar, Los Angeles
1975–76	Kareem Abdul-Jabbar, Los Angeles

COLLEGE BASKETBALL

NCAA DIVISION I CHAMPIONSHIP

Year	Winner
1980	Indiana
1979	Michigan State
1978	Kentucky
1977	Marquette
1976	Indiana
1975	UCLA

NCAA DIVISION II CHAMPIONSHIP

Year	Winner
1980	Florida Southern
1979	North Alabama
1978	Cheyney State
1977	Tennessee-Chattanooga
1976	Puget Sound
1975	Old Dominion

NAIA CHAMPIONSHIP		NIT CHAMPIONSHIP	
Year	Winner	Year	Winner
1980	Bethany Nazarene	1980	Tulsa
1979	Drury	1979	Indiana
1978	Grand Canyon	1978	Texas
1977	Texas Southern	1977	St. Bonaventure
1976	Coppin State	1976	Kentucky
1975	Grand Canyon	1975	Princeton

All-Time Greats

Kareem Abdul-Jabbar
(Apr. 16, 1947–)

Los Angeles Lakers

Abdul-Jabbar, already famous as a high school player, helped UCLA win three NCAA titles. He joined Milwaukee for the 1969–70 season and played with the Bucks until 1975, when he was traded to Los Angeles. Early in his professional career, Abdul-Jabbar joined an Islamic sect and changed his name (he was born Lew Alcindor). The elegant, smooth, versatile Jabbar, whose favorite shot is the sky hook, has been named Most Valuable Player six times. He is near the top of the list for the most field goals made, the highest scoring average, and the highest field goal percentage—and his career isn't over.

Elgin Baylor
(Sept. 16, 1934–)

Hickox Library

Baylor started in 1958 with the Minneapolis Lakers. Before long, he had brought the team up from the bottom. Baylor, always a leader in both offense and defense, moved to the West coast with the Lakers and played with Los Angeles until his retirement in 1972. Known for his grace and ability to change direction seemingly in midair, he is on the top 10 list in field goals made, free throws made, and rebounds. A member of the NBA All-Star first team for 10 consecutive seasons, Baylor was for 12 seasons the highest scoring forward in the game, and he ranks fifth on the list of all-time top scorers.

Wilt Chamberlain
(Aug. 21, 1936–)

Chamberlain left the University of Kansas after three years to join the Harlem Globetrotters and prepare for what promised to be an outstanding professional career. He let no one down. "The Stilt" (he is just over seven feet one) played center for the Philadelphia/San Francisco Warriors from 1960 to 1968 and for the Los Angeles Lakers from 1969 to 1973. Seven times he led the NBA in scoring, in addition to establishing numerous records in offense and defense. Chamberlain holds career records for the most field goals made (12,681) and the most rebounds (23,924), as well as game records for most points scored, most field goals, most free throws attempted, and most rebounds and the most minutes playing without fouling out of a game. Although controversial, Chamberlain is considered by many one of the best basketball players who ever lived.

Bob Cousy
(Aug. 9, 1928–)

Only six feet one, Cousy was the rookie nobody wanted, but the Boston Celtics got him, and they were never the same after that. Cousy helped the Celtics develop their patented long-pass-fast-break play. He had speed, and the fans loved his technique, whether he was passing, dribbling, or faking a shot. Cousy was a play-maker. He led the league in assists for eight consecutive years, he is second on the list of most assists in a game (28 in a game in 1959), and third in career assists.

George Mikan
(June 18, 1924–)

Nearsighted and outsized, Mikan became basketball's first legend. The Associated Press has named him the Greatest Player of the First Half-Century. Mikan played with the Minneapolis Lakers and helped keep the struggling new team afloat. A steady player who preferred the hook shot and other close-range shots, he also had a set shot that required merely positioning himself upcourt. In 1967, Mikan became the first commissioner of the American Basketball Association.

Willis Reed
(June 25, 1942–)

In his first year in the NBA, Reed made it to the All-Star Game as the only representative of the New York Knicks. A Rookie of the Year, he played best at center, but switched to forward for a few years and then back to center in 1968, when Dave DeBusschere arrived and Walt Bellamy went to Detroit. The shots Reed liked best were the pivot, hook, reverse layup, and short jump. In the 1969–70 season, he led the Knicks to their first championship, an achievement for which he was named Most

Valuable Player. As team captain, Reed directed plays and provided leadership and inspiration to his teammates. Injuries eventually brought his playing career to an end, although he coached the Knicks for awhile during Red Holzman's temporary retirement.

Oscar Robertson
(Nov. 24, 1938–)

Hickox Library

Robertson played forward in college; but in his first NBA season, 1960–61, he switched to guard with the Cincinnati Royals. That season, Robertson set a playmaking record, with an average 9.7 assists per game, and was named Rookie of the Year. In 1969, "The Big O" was traded to Milwaukee, where he teamed up with the young center Lew Alcindor. With a nearly flawless technique, Robertson holds career records for the most assists and the most free throws. He ranks third in career field goals and is among the top 10 in career scoring average.

Bill Russell
(Feb. 12, 1934–)

Hickox Library

Russell, a center for the Boston Celtics beginning in 1956, helped transform basketball in the late 1950s by changing the role of defense and thus giving the game a new, fast pace. He contributed greatly to the improvement of blocking shots and grabbing rebounds. One of basketball's greatest rebounders, Russell grabbed 51 rebounds in one game, a record second only to Wilt Chamberlain's 55. Five times Most Valuable Player, he was at his best in playoff situations, in the clutch, after a broken play, and at tap-ins after a missed shot. The first black to coach a major professional sports team, Russell coached the Celtics from 1965 to 1969.

Jerry West
(May 26, 1938–)

Hickox Library

Known as "Mr. Clutch," West was a player who loved pressure. He was an All-American and a member of the 1960 Olympic team. West made his reputation as a guard who could set up plays. The Los Angeles Lakers star was an aggressive defensive player, particularly in making steals. West is on the list of top 10 for field goals made, as well as for assists. He ranks second for the most free throws, with 7,160. West later coached the Lakers and now serves as special consultant to the team.

HALL OF FAME

Naismith Memorial Basketball Hall of Fame
460 Alden Avenue
Springfield, MA 01109
(413) 781-6500
Jerry Healey, dir. of public relations

In addition to the players listed below, the Hall of Fame names coaches, referees, and others who have made significant contributions to the game, as well as teams.

1959
Charles ("Chuck") Hyatt
Angelo ("Hank") Luisetti
George Mikan
John Schommer

1960
Victor Hanson
Branch McCracken
C. Edward McCauley
Charles ("Stretch") Murphy
John Wooden

1961
Bennie Borgmann
Forrest DeBernardi
Robert Kurland
Andy Phillip
John Roosma
Christian Steinmetz
Edward Wachter

1962
Jack McCracken
H.O. ("Pat") Page
Barney Sedran
John ("Cat") Thompson

1963
Robert ("Ace") Gruenig

1964
Harold ("Bud") Foster
Nat Holman
John ("Honey") Russell

1966
Joe Palchick

1968
H.G. ("Dutch") Dehnhert

1969
Bob Davies

1970
Bob Cousy
Bob Pettit

1971
Paul Endacott
Max ("Marty") Friedman

1972
John Beckman
Adolph Schayes

1973
Ernest Schmidt

1974
Joseph Brennan
William ("Bud") Russell
Robert ("Fuzzy") Vandivier

1975
Tom Gola
Edward ("Moose") Krause
Bill Sharman

1976
Elgin Baylor
Charles ("Tarzan") Cooper
Lauren ("Laddie") Gale
William C. Johnson

1977
Paul Arizin
Joseph Fulks
Clifford Hagan
James Pollard

1978
Wilt Chamberlain

1979
Jerry Lucas
Oscar Robertson
Jerry West

1980
Thomas Barlow

For the Record

NATIONAL BASKETBALL ASSOCIATION

Most field goals, career
12,681   Wilt Chamberlain   1960–73

Most points, game
100   Wilt Chamberlain   1962

Most rebounds, career
23,924   Wilt Chamberlain   1960–73

Most rebounds, game
55   Wilt Chamberlain   1960

Most free throws made, career
7,694   Oscar Robertson   1961–74

Most games played, career
1,270   John Havlicek   1963–78

Most assists, career
9,887   Oscar Robertson   1961–74

Most assists, game
29   Kevin Porter   1978

Widest winning margin
63 points   Los Angeles vs
   Golden State   1972

Longest winning streak
33   Los Angeles   1971–72

Longest losing streak
20 games   Philadelphia   1973

Highest winning percentage
.841   Los Angeles (69–13)   1971–72

Most points, game
173   Boston (vs Minneapolis)   1959

NCAA—DIVISION I

Most points, game
100   Frank Selvy   Furman
   (vs Newberry)   1954

Most points, season
1,381   Pete Maravich   LSU   1970

Most field goals made, season
522   Pete Maravich   LSU   1970

Most free throws made, season
355   Frank Selvy   1954

NCAA—DIVISIONS II AND III

Most points, game
113   Bevo Francis   Rio Grande   1954

Most points, season
1,329   Earl Monroe   Winston–Salem   1967

Most points, career
4,045   Travis Grant   Kentucky State   1968–72

Did you know ?

1. Who holds the record for the most steals in a game? How many?

2. Only one NBA player was named Most Valuable Player of the Year and Rookie of the Year in the same year. Who was he, and in what year was he named?

3. What favorite New York Knicks player also played baseball for the Chicago White Sox?

4. Who won the first Podoloff Trophy for Most Valuable Player?

5. What university has sent the most players to the NBA?

6. Who is the only man to be named twice to the Basketball Hall of Fame, once as a player and once as a coach?

7. Who is the winningest coach in professional basketball? How many victories does he have?

8. What is the NBA record for the most points scored in a quarter? What player holds that record?

9. How did Bob Cousy come to be picked by the Boston Celtics?

10. What player: is the highest scorer in Ivy League basketball history; had a fine professional basketball career; after his basketball career, entered a field far removed from basketball? What is that field?

11. What is the only team to win the NCAA and NIT basketball championships in the same season?

12. What college coach holds the record for the most victories?

13. What player holds the record for the longest field goal in college ball? What was the length of the shot?

14. What UCLA basketball player led the Pacific Coast Conference in scoring in 1940 but is better known for his contribution to professional baseball?

Answers: 1. Larry Kenon, 11, San Antonio at Kansas City, Dec. 26, 1976; 2. Wes Unseld, 1969; 3. Dave DeBusschere; 4. Bob Pettit; 5. UCLA; 6. John Wooden, an outstanding college player for Purdue and a coach for UCLA; 7. Red Auerbach, with 1,000 victories during his years with the Washington Caps, the Tri-Cities Blackhawks, and the Boston Celtics; 8. Thirty-three points, set by George Gervin, Apr. 9, 1978; 9. He had been playing for the Tri-Cities Blackhawks. When the team folded, other clubs absorbed its players. The Celtics picked Cousy's name out of a hat; 10. Bill Bradley of Princeton, who later played for the New York Knicks. He is currently U.S. Senator from New Jersey; 11. City College of New York (CCNY), in 1950; 12. Adolph Rupp of the University of Kentucky, with 874 wins and 190 losses; 13. Les Henson. The record is 89 ft 3 in, set in 1980; 14. Jackie Robinson.

Key Words

air ball an attempt to score in which the ball hits neither part of the basket nor the backboard.

assist any pass leading directly to a goal.

back court the half of the court in which a team plays defense and in which the opponent's goal is located.

bench reserve, or substitute, players; "to bench" means to remove a player from a game.

blocking personal contact that impedes the progress of an opponent.

deep bench a team that has more than one talented substitute for each position and therefore does not have to depend on a few star players.

double-team a situation in which more than one player guard an opponent.

draw a foul to act or move so as to provoke an illegal action by an opponent, thus gaining an opportunity for a free throw.

dribble to move the ball with one-handed, successive taps of the ball from hand to floor. A player must dribble while moving with the ball.

dunk a shot made leaping in the air with the hand above the rim and the ball stuffed into the basket. Also called a "stuff."

foul   an illegal action by a player, resulting in a penalty. A *technical foul* is a penalty imposed on a player or coach because of an excess number of time-outs, delay of the game, an illegal substitution, hanging on the rim, or—most often— unsportsmanlike conduct. The opposing team is awarded one free throw. Also called "T" or a "technical."

foul out   in pro ball, to be charged with six personal fouls and be disqualified from further play; in college ball, to be charged with five.

foul trouble   the situation of a player who is close to the limit for personal fouls in a game.

Courtesy NBA

free throw   an opportunity given a player to make a goal by an unimpeded throw from a position directly behind the free-throw line. Also called a "foul shot."

front court   the half of the court in which a team plays offense and that contains the basket the team shoots at. Also called "forecourt."

full court press   an attack that begins as soon as the offensive team gains possession of the ball, usually through a rebound in its back court.

give-and-go   situation in which a player fakes a run toward a stationary teammate, passes the ball, changes directions, and runs toward the basket in time to catch a return pass.

goal   two points scored by getting the ball into the basket. Also called a "basket."

goaltending   interference with a shot while the ball is on the rim of the basket or within the basket, or by touching the rim while the ball is over it. Goaltending is also called in situations where the ball is touched while in downward flight toward the basket and while, in the judgment of the referee, it has a chance of scoring.

hand-checking   continuously touching a player being guarded.

held ball   a tie ball—with two opponents having one or both hands firmly on the ball but neither player being in sole possession of it. Possession is determined by a jump ball.

hook shot   a high, one-handed arc shot toward the basket; often difficult to block, especially when used by tall players.

jump ball   a means of putting the ball in play. Two opposing players face each other while the referee tosses the ball in the air above them; each player jumps and tries to tap the ball to a teammate.

jump shot   the most common basketball shot. It is made by releasing the ball at the peak of a jump. The height from which the ball is launched makes the shot difficult to defend against. Also called a "jumper."

key   an area at each end of the court that includes the free-throw circle and the lane in front of the free-throw line.

lay-up   a shot made at the top of a jump near the basket, generally by bouncing the ball off the backboard.

loose ball   a ball in play but not in the possession of either team.

man-to-man defense   a situation in which each offensive player is guarded by a defender.

palming   a violation of dribbling rules, in which a player rests the ball for a moment in the upturned palm.

pivot   the action of a player holding the ball and stepping one or more times in any direction with the same foot—as long as the other foot remains in contact with the floor.

press   a defensive strategy calling for very close guarding and intended to make it difficult for the offense to dribble or pass.

rebound   possession of the ball gained after it hits the basket of the backboard and bounces away.

Basketball's greats are remembered in the honors court at the Naismith Memorial Basketball Hall of Fame.

screen   a tactic in which an offensive player eludes a defender by moving quickly past and close to a stationary teammate. The defender must stop and change directions because it is illegal for the defender to run into the stationary opponent. Also called a "pick."

sky hook   a high, one-handed shot made near the basket by an extremely tall player.

slam dunk   a goal made by ramming the ball through the net.

throw-in   a means of restarting play after a goal, after certain violations, or after the ball goes out of bounds. A player standing just out of bounds has five seconds in which to get the ball to a teammate inbounds.

tip-in   a goal scored by lightly pushing into the basket a rebound from the backboard or the rim.

traveling   moving with the ball in any direction without dribbling or by an illegal dribble.

turnover   loss of possession of the ball through an error.

zone defense   a situation in which each defender is assigned to cover a specific area of the court; the defender guards an opponent only when the opponent is in that particular area. The zone defense, illegal in the NBA, is used in college basketball.

4 BILLIARDS

A s anyone who has seen *The Music Man* knows, billiards, or pool, at times has been the victim of adverse publicity. Because billiard tables in the nineteenth century were most commonly located in saloons, where patrons often bet on (and fixed) their games, many potential aficionados ignored the game, and thus overlooked a sport requiring considerable skill and strategy, and offering an almost limitless number of variations.

Contrary to its somewhat clouded reputation, billiards has a quite respectable history. Shakespeare has Cleopatra playing the game, and while it is not clear that billiards ever was played in ancient Egypt, we do know that it was widely enjoyed in Shakespeare's own time. Mary, Queen of Scots, during the imprisonment that preceded her beheading, complained—among other things—about being deprived of her billiard table. Her cousin and jailer, Elizabeth I, was a skilled player. The royal physician in the court of Louis XIV recommended that the "Sun King" play billiards every day.

In the United States, billiards in its various manifestations was enjoyed by presidents Washington, Jefferson, and Grant, as well as by Mark Twain, Robert C. Ingersoll, and Henry Ward Beecher, to name just a few.

Although the game was probably brought to the New World by the Spanish, the rise to its present popularity began with the development of the plastic ball, and was almost totally the result of promotion by pool-equipment manufacturers, some of whom, reinforcing an unfortunate connection, also manufactured bar fixtures.

The most popular billiard game in the United States is pocket billiards, of which there are several variations (see "The Basics"). Other games are carom billiards (played on a table having no pockets and won by having the most cue balls carom from one object ball to another), and snooker (played on a billiard table with smaller pockets and with 21 smaller object balls; one may score both by pocketing balls and by forcing an opponent to lose points).

Each variety of billiards has its own rules, its own number of players, and sometimes even its own derivative games, making billiards one of the most varied and challenging indoor sports.

Great Moments

1571 French artist DeVigne designs the first billiard table with pockets.

1806 Players first use chalk on their cue tips, thus achieving better control over the ball.

1807 The first English-language book on billiards, by E. White, is published.

1859 The first national billiards match in the United States is held, in Detroit, Michigan.

1863 The first Championship of America tournament is held, in New York City.

1868 John and Isaiah Hyatt, of Albany, New York, develop "artificial ivory" for making billiard balls. The material, later called celluloid, is the first plastic to be widely marketed in the United States.

1906 Willie Hoppe wins the world billiards championship, in Paris.

1950 Willie Hoppe shoots a 1.33 high grand average, a record for a three-cushion tournament.

1952 Willie Hoppe retires having won 51 championship titles in three-cushion billiards.

1963 The Billiard Congress of America is founded to unite such diverse elements of the sport as players, manufacturers, retailers, and proprietors.

1965 The Billiard Congress of America founds its Hall of Fame, in Chicago, Illinois.

1966 Irving Crane sets a high-run record of 150 at the 1966 U.S. Open.

1971 Jean Balukas wins her first U.S. Pocket Billiards Championship.

1975 The Women's Professional Billiard Alliance opens its Hall of Fame, in Brooklyn, New York.

1976 The Professional Pool Players Association is formed, in Staten Island, New York.

1980 Jean Balukas wins her sixth national championship at the World Open.

The Setup

The recent history of professional pool has been marked by disputes over jurisdiction and organization, and the result has been the formation of a number of competing groups. From 1963, when it was formed, until 1976, the major governing association of professional pool was the Billiard Congress of America (BCA). The BCA still governs amateur pool and sanctions American College Unions and other nonprofessional competitions, in addition to approving billiard equipment. Its last professional tournament, however, was held in 1977, a year after many disgruntled pool players left the organization.

The players founded their own group, the Professional Pool Players of America (PPPA), based in Staten Island, New York. The PPPA sponsors an annual World Open that replaced the BCA's U.S. Open. It retains rights to and negotiates televised pool tournaments and works with promoters, manufacturers, players, retailers, and fans (all of whom are eligible for membership) to promote the sport. The PPPA also sponsors tournaments throughout the country year-round, including elimination matches through which players may qualify for participation in the world championship.

Another important group is the Women's Professional Billiard Alliance (WPBA), formed in 1975 in Brooklyn, New York, to promote the interests of professional women pool players. In 1980, the PPPA invited the WPBA to participate in its World Open tournament, running the WPBA players' matches as the women's division. The relationship between the two groups in 1981 and thereafter is as yet uncertain. The PPPA and the BCA, meanwhile, are negotiating to determine if, under their joint sponsorship, the U.S. Open might be revived.

BILLIARD CONGRESS OF AMERICA
14 S. Linn St.
Iowa City, IA 52240
(319) 351-2112
James Wilhem, pres.

PROFESSIONAL POOL PLAYERS
  ASSOCIATION
86 Vanderbilt Ave.
Staten Island, NY 10304
(212) 981-5943
Ray Martin, pres.

WOMEN'S PROFESSIONAL BILLIARD
  ALLIANCE
17 Strong Pl.
Brooklyn, NY 11231
Mrs. Billy Billing, dir.

The Basics

Object of the game To send specified balls into pockets on the sides of a billiard table with a cue ball propelled by a cue, thus scoring points up to a predetermined winning number or setting up a situation in which a game-winning shot can be made.

The table   Standard-size pool tables are either 4-by-8-foot or 4½-by-9-foot rectangles, with a playing surface (the "table bed") 29¼ inches from the bottom of the table leg. The tables have six pockets, one in each corner and one in the middle of each long side. The bed, slate-based in all quality tables, is covered with a soft fabric, usually wool felt. Raised rubber cushions, or "rails," also fabric-covered, line the bed and keep balls in play except near the pockets.

The balls   A billiard ball is a sphere of molded plastic, 2¼ inches in diameter, weighing between 5½ and 6 ounces. In full-rack games, balls used include the white cue ball, the only ball ever struck with the cue, and 15 numbered, variously colored balls. Balls 1 through 8 are (with the exception of a white numeral) of a single color (the "solids"), and balls 9 through 15 have both a color and a wide, white band (the "stripes").

Other equipment   Other equipment used in pocket billiards includes the *cue,* a long, tapered stick with a rounded leather tip at the end, used to propel the cue ball; a *rack,* the triangular wood frame used to arrange the balls at the beginning of a game; *chalk,* which is applied for increased "grip," to the tip of the cue; and a *mechanical bridge,* used to guide the cue from positions where a hand-formed bridge will not suffice; and *talcum powder,* used to absorb moisture and thus to reduce friction between hand and cue.

Officials   A referee and a scorekeeper are the officials present at billiards tournaments.

GENERAL RULES FOR TOURNAMENT PLAY

Rule 1   Acceptance of equipment   Once players begin playing, they may no longer question the legality of equipment in use.

Rule 2   Use of equipment   Players may not use any equipment for purposes other than those for which they are intended.

Rule 3   Equipment restrictions   Players may use chalk, powder, bridges, and other equipment of their choice so long as it is not damaging to house equipment or disruptive to play.

Rule 4   Marking of tables   Before competition, triangles, center spot, head spot, and foot spot must be clearly marked on the table.

Rule 5   Illegally moving ball   A player who intentionally moves a ball by illegal means (such as bumping the table) forfeits the game, the match, or both.

Rule 6   Players moving   Players must remain in the chairs designated for their use while their opponents are playing. They may not leave the playing area without permission from the referee.

Rule 7   Outside assistance   Players may not take advice, or communicate with persons other than officials, during a match.

Rule 8   Nonplayer interference   Any person who is not playing, and who interferes with or harasses the players, may be asked to leave the area.

Rule 9   Protests   A player who wishes to contest a decision or rule interpretation must do so immediately, before any other shot is taken.

Rule 10   Unsportsmanlike conduct   The referee has the authority to penalize any player who, in his judgment, is unsportsmanlike, or embarrassing, disruptive, or detrimental to the other players or to the sport.

Rule 11   Feet on floor   A player must have at least one foot on the floor while shooting the ball.

How the game is played   Pocket billiards has many variations, each with its own rules and object. All games, however, are a variation on a theme: the use of a cue to direct a cue ball toward other specified balls, which in turn are projected into the table's pockets. The way in which the cue ball is hit—the angle from which it is struck by the cue, the spot on which contact is made, the amount of force used—determines at what angle and with what force and spin the cue ball hits the object ball or balls—and, in turn, what path the struck ball or balls will take, and what speed they will have.

Following are the nine standard games played in most pocket-billiards tournaments:

Eight ball   The most popular of billiards games, this consists of a player legally sinking (pocketing) seven solid or striped balls and then legally pocketing the eight ball, or else pocketing the eight ball on the opening shot.

Rotation   This game requires that the cue ball strike the lowest numbered ball on the table first on each shot, after which any ball, including that lowest-numbered ball, may be sunk. Players continue to shoot in this manner until they fail to sink a ball. The winner is the player who has sunk balls of the greatest total point value.

Nine ball   An action game played with balls marked 1 through 9, nine ball is a variation on rotation, in which the object is to sink the 9 ball in a pocket. The lowest-numbered ball on the table must be the first ball a player's cue ball comes in contact with; that is, if a player hits the 1 ball with the cue ball, and the 1 ball knocks the 9 ball into a pocket, the game is won.

Six ball   Another variation of rotation, six ball is identical to nine ball except that only balls 1 through 6 are used, and the 6 ball must be pocketed in order to win the game.

Seven ball   Played with balls 1 through 7, with the object of pocketing the 7 ball. As in nine ball and six ball, the lowest numbered ball on the table must be hit with the cue ball first. If, on any shot, a player fails to pocket a ball or to cause either the cue ball or an object ball to hit a cushion, the player has committed a a foul, and a penalty is imposed. Games of seven ball usually last about three minutes.

14.1 Continuous   The game that requires the greatest all-round skill, 14.1 continuous requires players to call both the ball and the pocket (announce the ball to be hit and the pocket in which it is to be sunk). Players may shoot at any ball on the table at any time; they continue to play until they fail to pocket a ball as called. (Any ball sunk after the called shot is made during a given turn also counts.) A player scores one point for each legally pocketed ball and has points deducted for fouls, such as a *scratch,* and for other misconduct. The winner is the player who first achieves the predetermined number of points, usually 150 in tournament play.

Other popular pocket billiard games, although not part of tournament play, are: bottle pool, bowlliards, cowboy, cribbage, cutthroat, fifteen ball, forty-one, golf, line-up, Mr. and Mrs., one-and-nine ball, one ball, pea (Kelly) pool, and American snooker.

How to watch

with Conrad Burkman

Conrad Burkman, who, for the past 10 years, has been head referee for the Billiard Congress of America and a frequent billiards referee on ABC's *Wide World of Sports,* says that watching a game of straight pool—or 14.1 continuous, as it is more formally known—can be very boring. That, he explains, is because a good pool player, on a good day, can run dozens, even hundreds, of balls. "I appreciate the skill involved in playing straight pool," says Burkman, who is also publisher of a tabloid on pocket billiards called *The National Billiard News,* "but for you to take a friend who doesn't understand how the game works to a straight pool match and try to explain to that person what the players are doing, it's ridiculous, because it's going to take you all night. Your friend is going to think it's a stupid game."

So, says Burkman, as far as televised matches are concerned, straight pool "is almost a dead issue," and the "short-rack games," eight ball, nine ball, and, to a lesser extent, rotation, have largely taken over the tube. They make for more predictable production budgets, which television producers like, and for more excitement, which TV fans like. Burkman should know. He has refereed the finals in the U.S. Open, the principal billiards tournament, every time ABC has televised them.

"The strategy for straight pool," says Burkman, "is far different from the strategy for nine ball or eight ball. Unlike straight pool, where having to break is a disadvantage, the strategy in nine ball and eight ball centers on the break. Most professionals use what is known as a 'power break'; they strike the cue ball just over center and hit the head ball dead center, trying, in addition to sinking a ball, to pop the cue ball back to the middle of the table. This enables them to have a shot in any direction." Breaking is a disadvantage in straight pool because, if you should fail to sink any balls on the break, you could end up sitting out the rest of the game.

The ability to make shots is, of course, essential in any type of billiards, but equally important is the ability to "play position," to plan the shot and to apply english, or spin, to the cue ball in such a way as to leave it exactly where you want it after the shot. The best pool players—those of the caliber of Willie Mosconi, Steve Mizerak, Mike Siegel, Jim Rempi, and the immortal Ralph Greenleaf—know exactly what shots they will make and in what order before they begin to shoot. In straight pool, that means knowing, after the break, what your next fifteen shots are going to be, including the break shot that will start the next rack. It also means stopping the cue ball within half an inch of where you want it every time.

As anyone who has seen *The Hustler* knows, the ability to "psych out" an opponent figures prominently in billiards, as it does in so many other sports. "The psyching is done in various ways," says Burkman. "Minnesota Fats, for example, does it with his mouth, talking to you, telling you all the people he has beaten. Some players do it more subtly. They'll say, 'Oh, gee, that was a nice shot,' when you just missed it. Or you leave them a very difficult shot and they just step up and knock it in. That just does something to you mentally. Some of the lesser professionals will sit back and polish their cue stick with a white rag, and when you're getting ready to shoot, all you can see is this white thing flashing up and down in front of your eyes. Or, when you're getting ready to shoot, they will light a cigarette." It's all legal, says Burkman, "until they get caught at it." When they are caught, they are warned against such "sharking," and if they persist, the referee may call a foul. Bumping the table, moving a ball except by the shot, or, the most common foul, scratching, or sinking, the cue ball, result in "cue ball in hand" for the other player, that is, the right to place the cue ball anywhere on the table—and then shoot. "When you give your opponent the cue ball in hand," says Burkman of tournament-caliber players, "nine times out of ten that's the last time you see the table in that game."

Before the start of a tournament, players will play a few practice racks on one of the three tables generally used for tournament play. "Every table," Burkman explains, "is just like every basketball court, every football field: it's going to have its own individual characteristics. The table will roll a little bit one way or another. Or, if it's a televised match, you bring in the table today and televise—or tape—tomorrow, and the table will settle into the carpeting. Humidity will affect the play on the table; the cloth and the slate will absorb water, thereby slowing down the ball. The rubber inside the rails may be more lively or less lively on a given day because of the humidity, so humidity will make a ball come off a cushion at a different angle." Practice racks, then, enable players to "read" the table, as well as to warm up, before competition starts.

Another factor to reckon with in a televised match is the presence of the television crew itself. "The TV lights," says Burkman, "are probably the most difficult thing to compensate for. With TV you have several bright lights, which are reflected by the surfaces of the new, or highly polished, balls. It's very difficult for a player to concentrate on the spot on the object ball he has to hit—and the player who has played on television before has a decided advantage. If two players of equal skill are matched on television, and only one of them has television experience, that is the player who is going to win. He is going to obliterate the lights and the television crew from his mind, and he won't be thinking that, if he makes a mistake, millions of people are going to see it."

The physical demands on players in a billiards tournament are surprisingly rigorous. "Most people don't realize it," Burkman explains, "but in an average game of straight pool, a player will walk a mile and a half to two miles, and this is physically taxing, especially under tournament conditions. It's mentally demanding, too, and the combination of the physical and the mental stress is a very exhausting proposition for the tournament player. As a result, such players are generally in excellent physical condition."

Before a big tournament, players will have their cues reconditioned, getting all the nicks out and perhaps getting the handle rewrapped, or the tip replaced. Then they proceed to their physical conditioning, practicing for one, two, or three hours a day, and eating and sleeping regularly. "The good ones keep their minds off everything else," says Burkman. "They come to play, and when the playing is done, then they worry about the other stuff."

"Pool," Burkman explains, "has nothing to do with strength. But in pool, most of your tournament players are hardened, from a competitive standpoint, by having played on the road and played for money. This gives them that killer instinct that is necessary to win tournaments, because if you're playing for money, there's always another game. As long as you've got money in your pocket and I've got money in my pocket, we can always play. Players who only play in tournaments do not develop this ability, because there you either lose once and you're out, or you lose twice and you're out. It takes a different type of player to play well under tournament conditions. Most top-flight tournament players—though there are exceptions, like Steve Mizerak—at one time or another have played for money on the road. This gives them the cold, steel nerve that is required. Because if you come to the table, you've got to be able to have enough confidence in yourself to win the game."

Main Events

BCA U.S. OPEN, MEN'S DIVISION

14.1 Continuous

Year	Winner	Year	Winner
1977*	Tom Jennings	1972	Steve Mizerak
1976	Tom Jennings	1971	Steve Mizerak
1975	Dallas West	1970	Steve Mizerak
1974	Joe Balsis	1969	Luther Lassiter
1973	Steve Mizerak	1968	Joe Balsis

BCA U.S. OPEN, WOMEN'S DIVISION

14.1 Continuous

Year	Winner	Year	Winner
1977*	Jean Balukas	1972	Jean Balukas
1976	Jean Balukas	1971	Dorothy Wise
1975	Jean Balukas	1970	Dorothy Wise
1974	Jean Balukas	1969	Dorothy Wise
1973	Jean Balukas	1968	Dorothy Wise

*Tournament discontinued in 1977.

AMERICAN COLLEGE UNIONS CHAMPIONSHIP

Men's Division

Year	Winner	Year	Winner
1980	Peter Lhotka	1975	Robert Jewett
1979	Peter Lhotka	1974	Dan Louie
1978	Steve Cusick	1973	Dan Louie
1977	Jay Hungerford	1972	Andrew Tennent
1976	John Cianflone	1971	Keith Woestehoff

AMERICAN COLLEGE UNIONS CHAMPIONSHIP

Women's Division

Year	Winner	Year	Winner
1980	Julie Bentz Fitzpatrick	1975	Debra Bloss
1979	Julie Bentz Fitzpatrick	1974	Janis Ogawa
1978	Maridana Heydon	1973	Marcia Girolamo

| 1977 | Julie Bentz (Fitzpatrick) | 1972 | Krista Hartmann |
| 1976 | Melissa Rick | 1971 | Marcia Girolamo |

1980 PPPA Men's Pocket Billiards World Open Champion: Nick Varner

1980 PPPA Women's Pocket Billiards World Open Champion: Jean Balukas

All-Time Greats

Jimmy Caras
(1910–)

Professional Pool Players Assn.

His defeat of Ralph Greenleaf when he was only 17 years old earned Caras the title, "Boy Wonder of the World." He won his first world championship in 1936 and is still active in billiards. He set the records for most balls, most games won, and fewest innings by a champion.

Irving Crane
(Nov. 3, 1913–)

Professional Pool Players Assn.

Winning his first world tournament in 1942, Crane won almost two dozen championships, including a victory in the 1978 World Series of Billiards. His championship in the 1966 U.S. Open set a record run of 150-and-out.

Ralph Greenleaf
(Nov. 3, 1899–Mar. 14, 1950)

Fourteen times a world champion, Greenleaf and his exotic wife, Princess Nai Tai Tai, toured the vaudeville circuit in the 1920s and 30s demonstrating trick shots. Greenleaf's spectacular shots and showmanship enhanced popular interest in billiards.

William F. Hoppe
(Oct. 11, 1887–1959)

Billiards Digest

Widely considered the greatest billiards player ever, Willie Hoppe won his first international championship in 1906 when he was 18 years old. His career continued until 1952, by which time he had held the Three-Cushion Title 11 times.

Sands Hotel & Casino

Willie Mosconi
(June 21, 1913–)

A child prodigy who wielded a wicked cue when he was only seven, Mosconi went on to win the world title 15 times during the years 1940 to 1947. He began touring with Ralph Greenleaf when he was 20 years old, and set the incredible record of a 526-ball high run.

HALL OF FAME

Billiard Congress of America Hall of Fame
20 South Linn St.
Iowa City, IA 52240
(319) 351-2112

Members of the BCA Hall of Fame are:

Jimmy Caras	John Wesley Hyatt	Jake Schaefer, Sr.
Wehler Cochran	Johnny Layton	Jake Schaefer, Jr.
Irving Crane	Willie Mosconi	Frank Taberski
Alfredo DeOro	Benjamin B. Nartzik	Harold Worst
Ralph Greenleaf	Charles C. Peterson	
William F. Hoppe	Herman J. Ramow	

For the Record

U.S. OPEN, MEN'S DIVISION

Best U.S. Open winning percentage, career
.792 Steve Mizerak

Most U.S. Open games, career
77 Joe Balsis 1966–77

Most BCA championship wins, career
4 Steve Mizerak 1970–73

Most U.S. Open balls, career
10,026 Joe Balsis 1966–77

Most balls, tournament
1,788 Jimmy Caras 1967

Greatest victory margin in a 150-point match
163 Dick Baertsh 1969

Most U.S. Open appearances, career
12 Joe Balsis 1966–77
      Dallas West 1966–77

U.S. OPEN, WOMEN'S DIVISION

Most money won, career
$12,800   Jean Balukas   1972–77

Most appearances, career
10   Gerry Titcomb   1967–76

Most high-run awards
4   Jean Balukas   1972, 1973,
1975, 1977
Dorothy Wise   1967, 1968,
1970, 1971

Best winning percentage, career
.854   Jean Balukas

Most balls, career
3,583 Gerry Titcomb   1967–76

Most games, career
55   Gerry Titcomb

Most BCA championships won, career
6   Jean Balukas

Did you know ?

1. A professor of mathematics at Oxford University designed and built a circular pool table and wrote a manual for its use. The design never caught on, but the designer became famous for another achievement. Who was he, and what was it?

2. How did billiards get its name?

3. How long is the average pool cue?

4. How many balls are used in the game of bottle pool?

5. In the 1961 movie *The Hustler,* Paul Newman played the title role. Who was his technical adviser?

Answers: 1. Mathematician Charles L. Dodgson, who, under the name Lewis Carroll, wrote *Alice in Wonderland.* **2.** From the French *bille* meaning "stick"; **3.** *57 inches;* **4.** Two object balls plus the cue ball. **5.** Minnesota Fats.

Key Words

angled   also called "corner hooked," a situation in which the corner of a pocket prevents a player from shooting the cue ball directly at an object ball.

angle shot   a shot that requires the cue ball to drive the object ball in a direction other than straight ahead.

bank shot   shot in which the object ball is driven, or "banked," against one or more cushions before it is pocketed.

bed   the flat, cloth-covered surface of the table bordered by cushions; the playing area exclusive of the cushions.

bottle   a specially shaped leather or plastic container used in various games; also called the "shake bottle."

break   see *open break* and *opening break shot.*

breaking violation   a violation of special rules that apply only to the opening break shot of certain games. Unless specified in individual game rules, a breaking violation is not a foul.

bridge   the hand configuration that holds and guides the shaft-end of the cue during play; see also *mechanical bridge.*

butt   the larger end of a cue, opposite the tip. On a two-piece cue, the butt extends up to the joint.

call shot   situation in which a player is required to designate, in advance, the ball to be made and the pocket into which it will be made.

called ball   the ball the player has designated to be pocketed on a call shot.

called pocket   the pocket into which a player has designated a ball to be made.

carom   a shot in which the cue ball or an object ball glances off another ball or off a cushion before the object ball is pocketed.

carom, scoring   contact by the cue ball with object balls, the bottle, or cushions in such a way that a legal score is made, according to specific game rules.

center spot   the exact center point of a table's playing surface, marked as such.

clean bank   in bank pocket billiards, a shot in which the object ball being played does not touch any other object balls (that is, no kisses, no combinations).

combination   a shot in which the cue ball first strikes a ball other than the one pocketed, with the ball initially struck in turn striking one or more other balls in an effort to score.

contact point   the point at which the cue ball and the object ball come into contact during the shot.

corner hooked   when the corner of a pocket prevents shooting the cue ball directly at an object ball; same as *angled.*

count, the   the running score at any point during a player's inning.

cross corner shot   a shot in which the object ball banks off a side rail and then sunk in a corner pocket.

cross side shot   a shot in which the object ball banks off a side rail and then is sunk in a side pocket.

crutch   a slang term for the mechanical bridge.

cue ball in hand   a situation in which the cue ball may be put in play anywhere on the playing surface.

cue ball in hand behind the head string   a situation in which the cue ball may be put in play anywhere between the head string and the cushion on the head end of the table.

cut shot   a shot in which the cue ball comes into contact with the object ball well to one side or the other of dead center, thus driving it in a direction approaching 90 degrees from the initial path of the cue ball.

dead ball a cue ball stroked in such a manner that virtually all of the speed and/or spin of the cue ball is transferred to the object ball, the cue ball having little or no motion after contact.

dead ball shot a shot in which a "dead ball" stroke is employed; often called a "kill" shot, because of the relative lack of cue-ball motion after its contact with the object ball.

double draw shot a shot in which such extreme and effective draw stroke is employed that when the cue ball reverses direction after contact with the object ball into a cushion or rebounds, the underspin (draw) overcomes the direction and speed of the rebound, causing the cue ball to stop and reverse direction again.

double hit a shot in which the cue ball is struck twice by the cue tip on the same stroke; a foul.

draw shot a shot in which the cue ball is struck below center in such a way that it reverses direction after contact with the object ball.

drop pockets pockets from which balls must be removed manually, after each game or rack.

english a stroking influence applied to the cue ball by striking it off center; used to alter the natural roll of the cue ball and/or the object ball.

feather shot a shot in which the cue ball barely touches or grazes the object ball; an extremely thin cut.

ferrule a piece of protective material (usually white ivory or plastic) at the end of the cue shaft, to which the cue tip is attached.

follow shot a shot in which the cue ball is struck above center, resulting in the cue ball continuing in the same general direction of the stroke with the object ball. Because of the overspin applied to the cue ball, the speed of the cue ball will be faster than that of natural roll.

follow-through the movement of the cue after contact with the cue ball through the area previously occupied by the cue ball.

force draw extreme underspin applied to the cue ball; usually refers to shots in which the cue ball first travels in the direction of the stroke for a distance before the underspin takes effect and the cue ball stops and then draws back in a generally opposite direction.

free break an opening break shot in which a wide spread of the object balls may be achieved without penalty. Free breaks are detailed in individual game rules.

frozen a ball touching another ball or cushion.

game ball final ball pocketed, by which a player wins.

gully table a table with pockets and a return system that delivers the balls as they are pocketed to a collection bin at the foot of the table.

high run during a specified segment of play, the greatest number of balls scored in one turn (inning) at the table.

hold   english that stops the cue ball from continuing the course of natural roll it would take after having been driven in a certain direction.

in the rack   a situation in which a ball would interfere with the reracking of the object balls in games that extend past one rack.

jaw   the slanted part of the cushion that is cut at an angle to form the opening from the bed of the table into the pocket.

jawed ball   generally refers to a ball that fails to drop because it bounces back and forth against the jaws of a pocket.

joint   on two-piece cues, the screw-and-thread device, approximately midway in the cue, that permits it to be broken down into two separate sections.

jump shot   a shot in which the cue ball and/or an object ball is caused to rise off the bed of the table and go over another ball or balls.

jumped ball   a ball that has left and remained off of the playing surface as the result of a stroke.

key ball   the fifteenth ball of each rack in 14.1 continuous billiards; used on the break shot of the next rack.

kick shot   a shot in which the cue ball banks off a cushion or cushions before making contact with an object ball or scoring.

kiss   contact between balls.

kiss shot   a shot in which more than one contact with object balls is made by the cue ball; for example, the cue ball might kiss from one object ball into another to score the latter ball. Also, shots in which object balls carom off one or more other object balls to be pocketed. Also called a "carom shot."

kiss-out   contact between balls that causes a shot to fail.

lag for break   procedure used to determine starting player of a game. Each player shoots a ball from behind the head string to the foot cushion, attempting to return the ball as closely as possible to the head cushion without touching it.

leave   the position of the balls after a player's shot.

long   usually refers to a ball that, because of english and stroke, travels a path with wider angles than those which are standard for such a ball if struck with natural english and moderate speed.

long string   a line drawn from the center of the foot cushion to the foot spot (and beyond, if necessary) on which balls are spotted.

massé shot   a shot in which extreme english is applied to the cue ball by means of elevating the cue butt at an angle with the bed of table of anywhere between 30 and 90 degrees.

mechanical bridge   a grooved device mounted on an elongated handle and providing support for the shaft of the cue during shots difficult to reach with a normal hand bridge.

miscue   a misstroke that results from faulty cue–cue ball contact, as when the cue tip slides off the cue ball without full transmission of the desired stroke.

miss   failure to execute a shot.

natural english   moderate sidespin applied to the cue ball that favors the direction of the cue ball's path, giving the cue ball a natural roll and a bit more speed than a center hit.

natural roll   movement of the cue ball when no english has been applied.

nip draw   a short, sharp stroke, used when a normal draw stroke would result in a foul caused by a drawing of the cue ball back into the cue tip.

object ball   ball or balls to be struck by the cue ball on a given shot; usually the ball or balls to be pocketed.

open break   break shot in which a player must drive a minimum of four balls, one of which may be the cue ball, into a rail.

opening break shot   the first shot of a game.

power draw shot   extreme draw applied to the cue ball; see also "force draw."

push shot   a shot in which the cue tip maintains contact with the cue ball beyond the split second necessary for a normal stroked shot.

race   predetermined number of games necessary to win.

reverse english   sidespin applied to the cue ball that favors the opposite direction of the natural cue-ball path, which causes it to rebound from an object ball or a cushion at a slower speed than it would if struck at the same speed and direction without english.

run   the total of consecutive scores, points, or counts made by a player in one inning.

running english   sidespin applied to the cue ball that causes it to rebound from an object ball or a cushion at a more acute angle and at a faster speed than it would if struck at the same speed and direction without english.

safety   defensive positioning of the balls so as to minimize the opponent's chances of scoring. (The nature and rules concerning safety play are markedly different in specific games; see individual game rules regarding safety play.) Player's inning ends after a safety play.

scratch   predetermined position of players in a field of tournament competition. Also, the accidental sinking of the cue ball, or a similar foul resulting in loss of turn and/or point.

shaft   the thinner part of a cue, where the cue tip is located. On a two-piece cue, the shaft extends from the cue tip to the joint.

short   usually refers to a ball that, because of stroke, travels a path with more narrow angles than those which are standard for a ball struck without english.

short-rack   those games in which scoring does not extend into another rack.

spot shot   player shoots a ball on the foot spot with the cue ball in hand behind the head string.

spotting balls   replacing balls to the table in positions as dictated by specific game rules.

stop shot   a shot in which the cue ball stops immediately upon striking the object ball.

successive fouls   fouls made on consecutive strokes by the same player.

table in position   term used to indicate that the object balls remain unmoved following a shot.

throw shot   1. a cue shot that alters the path of the ball applying english. 2. a combination shot of frozen or near-frozen object balls that is struck by the cue ball left or right of center on the first object ball, thus causing the second (or player) object ball to travel in the opposite direction of the cue ball hit.

triangle   the triangular device used to place the balls in position for the start of most games.

Minnesota Fats, the world's best-known pool "hustler," lines up a shot in the corner pocket.

Professional Bowlers Association of America

5   BOWLING

For thousands of years, people have derived pleasure from knocking things down; that, perhaps, is the reason for the perennial popularity of bowling. The game is at least 7,000 years old (the tomb of an Egyptian child buried in 5200 B.C. contained a bowling ball and pins) and is still going strong, as evidenced by a 1975 national poll which indicated that more Americans participate in bowling than in any other year-round sport.

The origins of bowling are obscure; forms of the game seem to have developed independently in several different cultures. Bowling (a sport unrelated to lawn bowls, which is played on bowling greens) was known in third-century Germany (pious *Kugel* players pretended that the pins were heathens) and was popular among English nobility in the Elizabethan era. The first reference to bowling in America appears in Washington Irving's *Sketch Book*, in which Rip Van Winkle is awakened from his hundred-year sleep by the sound of falling pins.

Despite its more than respectable origin, bowling for a time fell into disrepute in this country, where it was most often played in bars (for ordering a certain number of drinks you got to play a game). Spittoons, liquor, and bookies were all part of the bowling scene during the late nineteenth century, rendering the sports unattractive to most women and to almost all people who considered themselves genteel.

In the twentieth century, bowling cleaned up its act. The first women's championships were held in 1915, and since then women have been enthusiastic players. Bowling alleys, once dank caverns next to or under bars, now sport paintings on their walls and smartly dressed waitresses in their restaurants and cocktail lounges. Bowling is a sport now enjoyed by people in all areas of the country, in all walks of life and income brackets, who appreciate playing or watching an event that requires intense concentration, coordination, and grace under pressure.

Great Moments

1875 Nine bowling clubs from New York and Brooklyn combine to form the National Bowling Association.

1895 The American Bowling Congress (ABC) is formed and holds its first convention in New York City, on September 9.

1900 The game of duckpins is introduced by baseball stars Wilbert Robinson and John McGraw, co-owners of the Diamond Bowling Alleys in Baltimore.

1901 The American Bowling Congress holds its first national tournament, in Chicago.

1907 The first recorded formalized bowling for women begins when bowling proprietor and sportswriter Dennis Sweeney organizes a women's league in St. Louis. Women accompanying their husbands to an American Bowling Congress tourney in St. Louis lay plans to hold their own tournament the following year.

1908 Russell Crable takes the men's all-events title at the ABC tournament in Cincinnati, which is followed immediately by the first women's tournament.

1913 Billy Knox sets an all-time singles-division record of most consecutive strikes, with 17. That same year, William Knox of Philadelphia becomes the first person to score 300 in an ABC tournament.

1915 Ellen Kelly forms the St. Louis Women's Bowling Association and writes to proprietors across the country for the names of women who might be interested in creating a national organization for women bowling enthusiasts.

1916 The first and only three-way tie in ABC singles division competition occurs, with Sam Schliman, B. Huesman, and E. Shaw each racking up 685 points. The first women's national tournament takes place in St. Louis after the men's ABC tourney. Eight teams enter, and champions are decided in team, doubles, singles, and all other events, with a prize of $222. After the tournament, the women meet and create the organization that will eventually become known as the Women's International Bowling Congress (WIBC).

1917 The Women's International Bowling Congress holds its first tournament, in St. Louis, Missouri, on March 17.

1920 The ABC National Tournament, with 900 team entries, takes place in Peoria, Illinois.

1941   The American Bowling Congress Hall of Fame is established, in Milwaukee. The Bowling Proprietors Association of America holds its first All-Star tournament, in Chicago, on December 7.

1943   The National Bowling Council is formed.

1950   Bowling becomes increasingly popular with the widespread introduction of automated pin-setting machines. In response to two petitions received in 1946, and after litigation costing $40,000, the American Bowling Congress changes its "white males only" rule to permit black and Hawaiian players.

1951   The first American Masters Tournament, an annual event for pros and amateurs, is held.

1954   The Federation Internationale des Quilleurs (FIQ) holds its first world tournament, in Helsinki, Finland.

1958   The Professional Bowlers Association (PBA) is formed. It soon develops a star system, and the best players (who had been semipro and had to hold other jobs) are able for the first time to make a living by bowling.

1961   The National Bowling League is formed. The British Ten Pin Bowling Association is formed, demonstrating the increasing popularity of the game outside the United States.

1963   Americans enter the FIQ world tournament for the first time.

1970   The bowling All-Stars tournament comes under the jurisdiction of the PBA. It is renamed the U.S. Open and becomes a regular part of the PBA Winter Tour.

1972   The three major professional bowling organizations (ABC, WIBC, and PBA) move to a combined national headquarters in Greendale, Wisconsin.

1973   A record 48,000 women participate in the 105-day WIBC championship in Las Vegas, Nevada.

The Setup

All professional and amateur-league bowling in the United States is conducted under the aegis of the all-male American Bowling Congress (ABC), the Women's International Bowling Congress (WIBC), or the American Junior Bowling Congress. Although these organizations share the same headquarters, they operate independently of one another.

The ABC approves and inspects alleys, lanes, and equipment and maintains an equipment-testing center near its headquarters. No ABC awards or prizes are given in competitions held in unapproved alleys.

Both the ABC and WIBC have divisions for professional bowlers, who are members of either the Professional Bowlers Association (PBA) or the Professional Women Bowlers Association (PWBA). Under the rules of bowling, players may win prize money in tournaments and still retain amateur standing; players become pros only upon joining a professional association.

Both the ABC and the WIBC run their own tournaments, the most important of which are the ABC's U.S. Masters Open and the WIBC's Queens Championship Tournament. In addition, the organizations sanction independent tournaments in which various sponsors offer prize money to winning participants, as well as sanctioning other tournaments. Some of the largest events are the PGA National, the Tournament of Champions, and the WIBC Championship Tournament.

International championships, such as the World Cup, are conducted by the Federation Internationale des Quilleurs (FIQ). As of 1977, international matches are conducted according to American rules.

The major organizations in bowling are:

AMERICAN BOWLING CONGRESS
5301 S. 76 St.
Greendale, WI 53129
(414) 421-6400
Charles J. Roesch, pres.

AMERICAN JUNIOR BOWLING
  CONGRESS
5301 S. 76 St.
Greendale, WI 53129
(414) 421-4700
William T. Hall, Sr., pres.

PROFESSIONAL BOWLERS
  ASSOCIATION
1720 Merriman Rd.
Akron, OH 44313
(216) 836-5568
John Petraglia, pres.

PROFESSIONAL WOMEN BOWLERS
  ASSOCIATION
17 E. Chestnut St., Suite 2
Chicago, IL 60611
(312) 782-0780
June Llewellyn, pres.

WOMEN'S INTERNATIONAL
  BOWLING CONGRESS
5301 S. 76 St.
Greendale, WI 53129
(414) 421-9000
Alberta E. Crowe, pres.

The Basics

Object of the game   To use a ball to knock down as many as 10 pins in each of 10 turns (frames) of two tries each, thus scoring one point per pin, plus bonus points for strikes and spares.

The Lane   A bowling lane is sloped, made of wooden planks, and measures 60 by 3½ feet. It is marked by a foul line (that players may not cross) and, seven feet from the foul line, a series of triangular guide marks set in the lane and used by the player to aim the shot.

The Pins   Ten pins are placed in a uniform triangle three feet on each side at the end of the bowling lane. These pins are made of maple, are often coated with plastic, stand 15 inches high, and are automatically reset after each frame.

Equipment   Bowlers need little special equipment beyond their bowling balls, which are 8½ inches in diameter and may not weigh more than 16 pounds. The balls are made of hard rubber or plastic and generally have three finger holes for

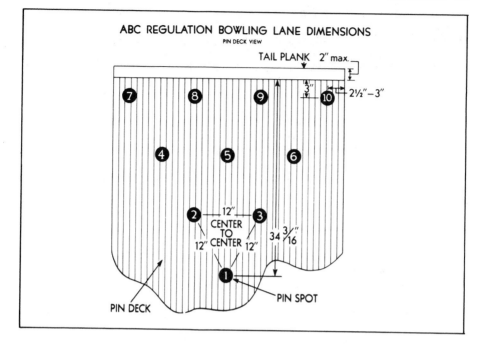

ABC REGULATION BOWLING LANE DIMENSIONS
PIN DECK VIEW

gripping. Bowlers also need soft-soled shoes with hard rubber heels, and loose, lightweight clothing.

Officials In tournaments, the only official present is a fouls judge (unless the lane has an automatic foul detector). Bowlers keep their own scores.

Rule 1   Order of play Players take turns playing. A player's turn is finished at the completion of one frame.

Rule 2   Delivery The ball must be delivered by an under-the-arm swing.

Rule 3   Fouls A bowler who crosses or touches the foul line, even if the ball has already been delivered, has committed a foul. Pins knocked down by that ball are not scored. If the foul is on the first ball, all pins are reset (if they are all knocked down on the next ball, a spare and not a strike is scored). If a foul is committed on the second ball, only the pins knocked over by the first ball are counted.

Rule 4   Scoring The winner of the game is the player with the highest score. A perfect score is 300. One point is scored for every pin knocked down. Strikes are worth 10 points plus the total of the next two balls as a bonus. Spares are worth 10 points and a bonus equal to the score of the next ball. Players who score spares or strikes in their last frames are given one or two extra balls, respectively, with which to earn their bonuses.

How to watch

with Chuck Pezzano

Bowling is one of the easiest sports to get into as a professional, and one of the toughest to succeed at once you are there. A 190 average will qualify you for membership in the Professional Bowlers Association, the major organizing body in the sport today. But, according to Chuck Pezzano, a regional director for the PBA and formerly a professional bowler, "if you only average 190, you're going to starve." A pro bowler must average 210 or 220, he says, to finish in the money.

Many players, says Pezzano, have the physical ability to execute any shot in the book. What distinguishes champions like Earl Anthony, Mark Roth, Marshall Holman, and Wayne Webb—or, among women bowlers, Donna Adamek—is their skill at the mental game: their ability to adjust to lane conditions, to the shifting physical environment (temperature, humidity, etc.), and, perhaps most important, to the pressure of a professional tournament. "You bowl for a week, forty-two games," Pezzano says, "and then the tournament is decided in a one-game match. It's almost like having a golf tournament in which you play thirty-six holes and then the final decision is determined by one hole. This makes winning a lot more difficult."

Lane conditions vary from one lane to another to a considerable extent, a fact, says Pezzano, little known to the general public. A bowler may release the ball at the first board, at the last, or anywhere in between. But, while the point of release may vary by more than two feet, bowling remains a game of inches, because an error of one inch side to side at the foul line can result in an error of three to five inches at the finish.

"This," Pezzano continues, "is what the pro has to figure out. The pro who succeeds is the one who has what we call "a working ball," that is, a ball that allows a player to miss the intended target a little bit and still carry the pins."

At the beginning of a tournament, Pezzano reports, the pro player is allowed eight practice shots, during which the "scoring conditions" must be determined. "An easy condition," says Pezzano, "is one in which everything favors the bowler. If he rolls the ball out and it comes in late, it sweeps the pins. If it comes in high on the head pin, it still carries. The opposite situation, known as a 'grind-out condition,' is that in which very little carries, and even when you hit the pocket one of the end pins may stand." A grind-out condition may mean that a 200 game will be enough to win; an easy condition may require a score in the 250s or 260s.

Lane conditions determine, as well, which balls the players select. From the six or seven balls a pro bowler may bring to a tournament, the choice of a ball with which to begin will be made in the practice frames. But, says Pezzano, a bowler may play half a game—another five to ten balls—and decide to change. "The key to equipment these days," Pezzano explains, "is the surface of the ball—its softness or hardness. A softer ball will grip the lane more and will give you more action on the ball as it hits the pins. (Sometimes this can be a disadvantage, because excessive grip will cause the ball to hook too much.) A harder ball, which creates less friction with the lane surface, will have a tendency to skid and so miss the pocket."

Another variable is the manner of drilling. Almost no players use a two-hole ball these days; three is the norm, and some players may use a four-hole ball, with a hole for every finger but the pinky. Some players have been known to use a "slot," in which all four fingers are inserted together in one elongated hole.

Then there is the approach, which can also vary greatly from one player to another. Most players, says Pezzano, use four-step and five-step approaches, while some players—including Mark Roth—may take six or seven steps before releasing the ball. "Normally," Pezzano explains, "the reason for taking more steps is to build up more speed. Obviously, though, if you take long steps, you cannot take too many. Many women bowlers do very well with only three steps. There is no hard and fast rule."

"Normally," Pezzano continues, "a medium speed is best for mixing the pins. You cannot carry the pins unless they mix around on the lane bin. If the ball is thrown too fast, it goes right through and the pins don't have a chance to mix around, so too fast is no good. Then again, if the lanes are hooking too much, a player needs that extra speed to hold the ball in the pocket. But generally a medium speed works best."

Strange as it may seem, professional bowlers will probably not be looking at the pins when they release their shot. "On the lane, there are arrows embedded at five-board intervals. The pros generally use these as their guide. They will shoot at the third arrow, or two boards to the left or right of it. Some will look at the foul line or a few feet beyond it, where there are rows of dots. Some will look even further down the lane, trying to pick out a board that is somewhat darker in color than the ones surrounding it. The choice of a target near to or far from the foul line is a matter of individual preference."

Television, Pezzano points out, has had a marked impact on professional bowling, resulting not just in increased tournament purses but also in an increased understanding of the game. Seeing the ball go down the lane and into the pins, he says, viewers can see the way the ball moves, rotates, hooks, and is deflected by the pins. Those pins, Pezzano adds, are a good deal bigger and farther apart than they look from the foul line. On a perfect hit, the ball makes contact with only four pins. The rest is caused by pins hitting other pins. Slow-motion replays on television make it easy to see the complex way the pins interact.

Another welcome result of televised bowling is the growth in popularity of women's bowling tournaments, and the emergence of such stars as Donna Adamek, who in three successive years was national high school champion, collegiate champion, and the winner of a pro tournament—an unprecedented achievement. So far, though, says Pezzano, few women have developed the "killer instinct" that marks the best bowlers.

Professional bowlers—or those 150 or so who participate in at least half the tournaments on the national tour—require much physical stamina in addition to skill. They may bowl between 30 and 35 weeks a year; during that time they will constantly experiment with different equipment and exchange information. The result is a growing number of players who, in any given tournament, have a real chance for victory.

Though it is every amateur bowler's dream, the 300 game—in which the bowler makes twelve strikes in a row—has, in Pezzano's opinion, been vastly overrated by the general public. "A 300 game is just something that comes," he says. "The pros are happy to get it. They love to have one. But they're not looking for it, and they're not thinking about it. Most pros have had several 300 games, so it isn't such a big deal to them—unless they occur during a televised tournament. Then there may be a large cash prize."

When a player has a string of strikes leading off a game, and 300 begins to loom as a possibility, there is, says Pezzano, "a certain tenseness, a certain nervousness, and regardless of what pro bowlers say, they feel it. But that doesn't deter them from performing well. Every great athlete—and bowlers are athletes in the same sense that golfers are athletes—has the ability to perform well under pressure. If you look closely at the players on TV who have a shot at a 300 game, you will see their knees shaking a bit, or their arms. But this does not prevent them from performing well."

The idea in bowling, Pezzano observes, is to stand up there and make the same shot every time. The shot may be predictable, but people are not, and no bowler can make precisely the same shot twice. But the goal is always the same: "to go up to the line the same way, to release the ball the same way, to have the same angle and the same speed going into the pins every time." If people are not perfect, neither are machines. A laboratory in Milwaukee, Pezzano says, has a machine designed to send bowling balls down alleys under scientifically controlled conditions. "I don't think," says Pezzano with a smile, "that machine has ever bowled 300!"

Main Events

PBA NATIONAL CHAMPIONSHIP

Year	Winner	Year	Winner
1980	Johnny Petraglia	1975	Earl Anthony
1979	Mike Aulby	1974	Earl Anthony
1978	Warren Nelson	1973	Earl Anthony
1977	Tommy Hudson	1972	Johnny Guenther
1976	Paul Colwell	1971	Mike Lemongello

ABC TOURNAMENT CHAMPIONSHIP, CLASSIC DIVISION

Year	Winner	Year	Winner
1980	Mike Eaton	1975	Les Zikes
1979	Ed Biro	1974	Jim Godman
1978	Bill Beach	1973	Jimmy Mack
1977	Mickey Higham	1972	Teata Semiz
1976	Jim Schroeder	1971	Gary Dickinson

ABC MASTERS TOURNAMENT CHAMPIONS

Year	Winner	Year	Winner
1980	Neil Burton	1975	Ed Ressler
1979	Doug Meyers	1974	Paul Colwell
1978	Frank Ellenburg	1973	Dave Soutar
1977	Earl Anthony	1972	Bill Beach
1976	Nelson Burton, Jr.	1971	Jim Godman

WIBC WOMEN'S OPEN CHAMPIONSHIPS

Year	Winner	Year	Winner
1980	Betty Morris	1975	Paula Carter
1979	Diane Silva	1974	Patty Costello
1978	Donna Adamek	1973	Mildred Martorella
1977	Betty Morris	1972	Lorrie Nichols
1976	Patty Costello	1971	Paula Carter

WIBC NATIONAL CHAMPIONSHIPS

Year	Winner	Year	Winner
1980	Betty Morris	1975	Barbara Leicht
1979	Betty Morris	1974	Shirley Garms
1978	Mae Bolt	1973	Bobby Buffaloe
1977	Akiko Yamaga	1972	D. D. Jacobson
1976	Bev Shonk	1971	Ginny Younginer

QUEENS TOURNAMENT CHAMPIONSHIPS

Year	Winner	Year	Winner
1980	Donna Adamek	1975	Cindy Powell
1979	Donna Adamek	1974	Judy Soutar
1978	Loa Boxberger	1973	Dorothy Fothergill
1977	Dana Stewart	1972	Dorothy Fothergill
1976	Pam Buckner	1971	Mildred Martorella

All-Time Greats

Courtesy PBA

Don Carter
(July 29, 1926–)

Known for his unorthodox playing styles (he keeps his arm crooked and stoops while delivering), Carter was named Bowler of the Year in 1953, 1954, 1957, 1958, 1960, and 1962. He was the first (and only) bowler to win the Grand Slam of match-games (1961). Carter, who won a total of 20 titles, retired in the mid-1960s following a knee injury.

Courtesy WIBC

Marion Ladewig
(Oct. 30, 1914–)

Ladewig, who claimed that she bowled every day from 1940 through 1962, took her first championship at the Western Michigan Golden Pin Classic in 1940–41. By 1954 she had been elected Bowler of the Year nine times. She set the record for All-Star two-game scores (279 and 255), and a record eight-game average of 247.6. She retired in 1955.

Enrico ("Hank") Marino
(Nov. 27, 1889–July 12, 1976)

American Bowling Congress

One of the better all-round players in the history of bowling, Marino got a late start in bowling but continued to rack up amazing scores well into middle age. He entered his first PBA title event when he was 45 and entered tournaments regularly for the next 10 years. A small man, at 5 feet 6 inches and 145 pounds, Marino was noted especially for his doubles wins, for his instinctive feel for different balls and conditions—and for spinning the ball while it hung from his thumb.

Floretta McCutcheon
(July 22, 1888– Feb. 2, 1967)

Courtesy WIBC

McCutcheon, who did not begin to bowl until she was 35, shocked champion Jimmy Smith by defeating him during one of the pro's exhibition tours. She stayed in the game for 10 years, maintaining an average of more than 200. An enthusiastic promoter of bowling, she toured the country giving clinics and is said to have taught an estimated half-million women how to bowl.

Jimmy Smith
(Sept. 19, 1882–Apr. 21, 1946)

American Bowling Congress

In 1910, Smith went out on what was to have been a year's exhibition tour—it lasted until 1924. During that time, he played more than 12,000 games, with a 205 average. He was considered the match king during his heyday (1915–24) and was distinguished by his seemingly effortless style.

Dick Weber
(Dec. 23, 1929–)

Courtesy PBA

Three-time Bowler of the Year, Weber is known for his "killer instinct" and the fact that he has won more PBA titles than anyone else (24). Weber has completed at least 17 sanctioned games of 300 and 7 sanctioned games of 299.

HALL OF FAME

National Bowling Hall of Fame
5301 S. 76 St.
Greendale, WI 53129
(414) 421-6400

1941
Joseph Bodis
Adolph Domianus ("Swede") Carlson
Charley Daw
Peter Howley
John Koster
Herbert W. Lange
Mortimer J. Lindsey
Enrico ("Hank") Marino
James Smith
Harry H. Steers
Gilbert Zunker

1951
Joseph ("Buck") Wilman

1952
Edward P. ("Ned") Day

1953
Goldie Greenwald
Grayce Hatch
Emma Jaeger
Louise Stockdale
Marie Warmbier

1954
William Knox
Dorothy Miller
Joseph J. Norris

1955
James Blouin
Philena Bohlen
James ("Junie") McMahon, Jr.

1956
Floretta McCutcheon

1957
Emily Chapman
Andrew Varipara

1958
Frank Benkovic
Catherine Burling

1959
Josephine Mraz
Walter G. Ward

George Young

1960
Albert R. Brandt
Violet E. ("Billy") Simon

1961
Addie Ruschmeyer
William Sixty, Sr.
Phil Wolf

1962
John ("General") Crimmins (Krzyminski)
Anita Rump

1963
Elmer H. Agumgarten
Charles O. Collier
Ebber D. ("Sarge") Easter
Basil ("Buzz") Fazio
Jack Hagerty
Jeanette Knepprath
Abraham L. Langtry
Steve J. Nagy
Louis P. Petersen
Esther Ryan

1964
Nelson Burton, Sr.
Nora Kay
Marion Van Oosten Ladewig
Sally Twyford

1965
Therman Gibson
Emma Phaler
Myrtle Schulte

1966
Harold J. Allen
Herbert B. ("Buddy") Bomar
Deana Fritz
Sylvia W. Martin
Berdie Speck

1967
Fred Bujack
Madalene Hochstadter
Frank C. ("Midge") Kartheiser
Iolia Lasher
Walter ("Skand") Mercurio

1968
William Bunetta
Louis Campi
William Doehrman
Alfred J. ("Lindy") Faragalli
Russell H. Gersonde
Cornelius ("Cone") Hermann
Edwards Kawolics
Joseph F. Kristof
Paul A. Krumske
Bertha McBride
Charles O'Donnell
Conrad A. Schwoegler
Louis A. Sielaff
Grace Smith
Tony ("Ace") Sparando
Barney ("Jumping Jack") Spinella

1969
Robert F. Bensinger
Margaret Higley
Joseph G. Joseph
David Luby
John O. Martino
Leona Robinson

1970
Donald J. ("Bosco") Carter
Helen Duval
Catherine Fellmeth
Richard A. Weber
Sam Weinstein
Ann Wood

1971
Shirley Garms
Sam Levine
Edward A. Lubanski
Howard W. McCullough
Tess Morris Small
Otto Stein, Jr.
Frank ("Sykes") Thoma

1972
Martin Cassio
LeRoy Chase
Stella Hartrick
William T. Lilliard
Beverly Ortner
Milton Raymer
Gertrude Rishling

1973
Raymond A. ("Bloop") Bluth
Walt Ditzen
Edward H. Krems
Connie Powers
Pearl Switzer

1974
Joan Holm

Richard Lee Hoover
Mort Luby, Sr.
Merle Matthews
Claude ("Pat") Patterson, Jr.
Dennis J. Sweeney
Georgia E. Veatch

1975
Frank K. Baker
Joseph L. ("Chesty") Falcaro
Mildred Martorella
William J. Welu
Mildred White
Vern E. Whitney
Cecilia Winandy

1976
Winifred Berger
Edward J. Brosius, Jr.
Grazio Castellano
Doris Coburn
Olga Gloor
Thomas M. Hennessey
Joseph F. Kissoff
Henry ("Hank") Lauman
Judy Soutar
Elvira Toepfer
Fred Wolf

1977
Helen Baetz
Nina Van Camp Burns
LaVerne Carter
Dorothy Taylor Haas
Helen Shablis

1978
Harold Aspound
Vince Lucci, Sr.
Harry Smith
J. Elmer Reed

1979
Glenn Allison
Bill Golembiewski
Lee Jougland
Roland ("Tony") Lindemann
Carmen Salvino

1980
J. B. Coker
Dr. H. A. Hattstrom
Frank Klause
Joe Thumb
Wayne Zahn

1981
Don Ellis
Bob Kennedy

For the Record

PROFESSIONAL BOWLERS ASSOCIATION

Most titles, career
36   Earl Anthony

Most titles, season
8   Mark Roth   1978

Most 300s on national tour, one year
6   Guppy Troup   1979

Greatest margin of victory (1 match)
172 pins   Larry Laub   1975

Highest score, six games
1,613   Tom Baker   1981

Highest score, 42 games
10,383   Tom Baker   1981

WOMEN'S INTERNATIONAL BOWLING CONGRESS

Most consecutive strikes
21   Betsy Corrigan   1978–79
     Sharon Graff   1978–79

Most consecutive spares
27   Joan Taylor   1973–74

Most 300 games, career
5   Betty Morris

Highest average, season
227   Patty Ann   1979–80

Greatest game-to-game margin
212   Lynne Santucci   1971–72

Did you know?

1. The Petersen Classic in Chicago lasts nine months, attracts more than 30,000 bowlers, and offers more than $800,000 in prize money; yet the ABC refuses to sanction it. Why?

2. Many religious figures in the past condemned all types of sports as frivolous, accusing sports of taking people's thoughts away from higher things. One major religious figure, however, thought bowling was not only moral but a noble occupation. Who was that person?

3. Who was the first bowler to earn more than $100,000 in a season?

4. Where was the first recorded bowling tournament held and what was the prize?

5. What military leader's passion for bowling could have cost a nation its navy?

Answers: 1. The tournament is intentionally designed to give bowlers the most miserable conditions possible, including uneven lanes, dropped pins, abrupt changes in temperature, pools of oil lying throughout the alley, animals wandering through the lanes, and sudden blaring announcements. Tournament directors say this keeps scores low and gives mediocre players a chance to win! **2.** Martin Luther (1483–1546), leader of the Reformation, was so enamored of the game that he had a bowling alley built in his home. He felt that bowling could be used as an instrument to teach moral homilies; **3.** Earl Anthony, by capturing seven national titles in 1975; **4.** The competition was held in Breslau (now Wrocław), Poland, in 1518. The winner was awarded an ox; **5.** Sir Francis Drake was given news of the impending attack of the Spanish Armada while he was bowling. He did not react until he finished his game.

Key Words

alley   a bowling lane or bowling center.

all events   the total of games bowled by an individual in one tournament, usually three games in the team event, three in doubles, and three in singles. Sometimes, the total for the three events by the five members of one team.

anchorman   the last player in a team line-up.

approach   the area, a minimum of 15 feet long, on which a player walks to the foul line.

baby split   the 2–7 or 3–10 leaves.

backup   a ball that fades away from the pocket; also, a reverse hook.

backswing   the path of the arm behind the body during the next to last step in the delivery.

bedposts   the 7–10 split.

bellying   a ball rolled in a wide-curving arc.

big four   the 4–6–7–10 split.

blind   the number of pins given a team when a player is absent, the total being based on the absent player's average.

blow   failure to convert a spare. Also called an error or miss.

blow a rack   score a perfect strike hit.

boards   the number of boards, usually 39, in the width of a bowling lane. Also, the aiming target in the delivery; "playing the tenth board," for example, means that the bowler rolls the ball over a predetermined point on the tenth board from the gutter, the board adjacent to the gutter being the first board.

Brooklyn   a ball rolling to the 1–2 pocket for a right-hander, 1–3 for a left-hander, also called a crossover.

channel   drop-off area on both sides of a lane. The gutter.

cherry   chopping off the front pin by driving it straight back past any other standing pins to the right or left; an error, blow.

clean game   a game without a miss or split.

clutch hit   an important strike.

count   the number of pins knocked down on the first ball.

cross lane   a shot in which the ball rolls diagonally at the corner pin spare, crossing a maximum number of lane boards, as opposed to rolling at the pin in the direction of the board.

curve   a ball rolled in a wide-sweeping arc. Different from the hook delivery, which veers more sharply into the pocket.

deuce   a 200 average or a 200 game.

dodo   an illegally balanced or weighted ball.

dog   the player with the lowest score in a team game and/or series.

double   two strikes in succession.

double pinochle   the 4–6–7–10 split.

drives   bowling lanes.

driving ball   a ball that rolls into the pocket with power.

fast lanes   in some areas, lanes that allow the ball to take a wide hook; in others, lanes that hold down the hook. Also known as *running lanes*.

fence posts   the 7–10 split.

field goal   a shot in which the ball rolls between a split without hitting any pins.

fill   the number of pins knocked down on the first delivery following a spare.

fill the wood box   a strike on the final ball of a game; also called *load the boat* and *full count*.

fingers   applies lift to the ball on release.

foul   to touch or go beyond the foul line while delivering the ball.

foul line   the line separating the approach and the lane.

foundation   a strike in the ninth frame.

four bagger   four consecutive strikes. Also two bagger, three bagger, and so on, for any number of strikes in a row.

fudge shot   a poorly delivered ball, usually caused by the player trying to make a last-second adjustment when releasing the ball.

graveyard   a low-scoring lane or bowling establishment.

grinder   a powerful hook or curve ball.

grip   the manner in which a bowling ball is drilled to accommodate the thumb and, usually, the two middle fingers.

gutter   the drop-off area to the immediate left and right of the lane.

gutter ball   a delivery that rolls off the lane into the gutter.

gutter shot   a delivery from the extreme edge of the lane, paralleling the gutter until veering toward the pocket.

handicap   a means of placing bowlers and teams with varying degrees of skill on as equitable a basis as possible for their competition against each other.

hang a pin   leave one pin standing after an apparent strike ball.

heads   the first 16 feet of the lane forward of the foul line.

headpin   no. 1 pin.

high board   an expanded or loose board in a lane that can cause a ball to veer from its intended course.

high hit   a ball rolling almost as full in the pocket as a nose hit.

hook   a ball that breaks sharply toward the pocket.

hooking lane   a lane that allows the ball to break into the pocket.

holding lane   a lane that resists hooking action.

inside angle   the path a ball travels that is aimed away from the pocket and hooks or curves back into the pocket; the starting point on the approach varies but is usually left of center for a right-hander, the opposite for a left-hander.

Jersey side   the strike pocket.

leadoff   the first player in a team line-up.

leave   pins remaining after the first ball delivery.

lift   imparting forward motion with an upward follow-through of the arm as the ball falls off the fingers at the delivery release point.

light hit   a ball that barely hits the pocket.

lily   a delivery that leaves the 5–7–10 split; also called *sour apple*.

line   the path of the ball from the release point to the pocket.

line ball   a ball delivered with a minimum of hook.

load   the low scorer on a team.

lofting   tossing the ball in the air beyond the foul line.

mark   a strike or spare.

mixer   a ball that hits the pocket lightly, causing the pins to spin and ricochet, usually resulting in a strike. Also known as a "sweeper," a "schleifer," or a "swisher."

move in   to start from or near a center position on the approach.

move out   to start from or near a corner position on the approach.

nose hit   a hit full on the headpin.

on a limb   the anchorman's turn after all teammates have rolled strikes.

open   a frame in which the player fails to strike or spare.

out and in   similar to "inside angle"—rolling the ball toward the gutter and having it curve or hook to the pocket. A delivery often used on running lanes.

pinching the ball   gripping the ball hard enough to cause an unnatural delivery.

pitch   the angle at which a hole is bored into the ball.

playing the lane   moving the ball release point and, thereby, the ball angle in relation to a fast or slow lane.

pocket   the area between the 1–2 pins for a left-hander, the 1–3 for a right-hander.

punching out   striking out in the final frame.

pushaway   pushing the ball forward as part of the first step in delivering the ball.

railroad   a split. Also called a "sleeper."

rap   the pin left standing on a pocket hit. Also called a "solid 10" or a "ringing 8."

ringing 8   the 8 pin left standing on a pocket hit.

rocking 4   the 4 pin (or any single pin) that wobbles but does not fall over for a strike.

roll-off   the tenth frame. Also, a match between players or teams to determine a championship or position finish.

running lane   a hooking lane.

rushing the foul line   a common fault, wherein the player reaches the foul line too quickly, ready to release the ball while the arm and ball still are in the backswing.

scratch   the actual score, without a handicap.

short pin   a pin rolling on the lane that fails to knock down a standing pin.

sleeper   a pin hidden behind another; sometimes called a *railroad.*

slots   high-scoring lanes.

solid   a ball that hits the strike pocket resoundingly, yet sometimes leaves standing a solid 10 pin or the like.

spare   the knocking down of all the pins with two deliveries.

split   combinations of pins left standing after the first delivery with a pin down immediately ahead of or between them. The headpin must be down to record a split.

spot   the sighting or target area on the lane where the player aims.

stepladder   a series in which a player improves the score by one pin in each game.

stiff lane   a nonhooking lane.

strike   the knocking down of all ten pins on the first ball.

strike out   make at least three strikes in a row to finish a game.

string   three or more consecutive strikes. Also called a "full game." (In some areas, three strings constitute a series.)

stroke   armswing and follow-through in delivery.

sweep bar   the part of an automatic pin-setting device that removes fallen pins from the deck after the first ball and remaining pins after the second ball.

tap   a pin left standing on an apparent solid pocket hit.

thin   a light hit.

track   a path to the pins created by many balls previously rolled in the same general area.

trip 4   a late-falling 4 pin on a strike, often resulting from the 2 pin rebounding off the kickback.

turkey   three consecutive strikes in a single game.

turn   the motion imparted to the ball on release at the foul line to impart the hook or curve. Often occurring in the phrase "lift and turn" to describe the release action.

up the hill   coaxing the ball into the pocket.

vacancy   the number of pins assigned in league play when the team roster is incomplete.

washout   generally the 1–2–10, 1–2–4–10, 1–3–7, or 1–3–6–7 left after the first ball. Not a split.

working ball   a ball that drives into the pocket carrying all 10 pins.

Courtesy PBA

Marshall Holman watches with obvious satisfaction as his ball finds the pocket.

6 BOXING

There were no rings, no gloves, no fancy footwork in the early boxing matches held thousands of years ago in Mesopotamia. Two boxers merely sat nose to nose on square stones and, on signal, began swinging, continuing until one fell off. The winner then bludgeoned the loser to death. Boxing's approach today is much more scientific, with increased knowledge about training and diet, but the object is essentially the same: to batter one's opponent until he is knocked out or unable to continue fighting, or to simply outclass him as a fighter by throwing better punches and impressing the judges at ringside.

After its appearance in the "cradle of civilization," boxing was to be found in ancient Greece, where it was a popular event in the Olympics. The Romans later adopted the sport, embellishing it with such devices as spikes on the fists. By this time, boxers were standing and facing each other. Boxing was not limited to punching, as it is today; anything was legal, including gouging, wrestling, throwing, and holding.

Boxing remained much the same until, centuries later, some innovative English boxers found a few well-aimed punches on the jaw more simple and effective than taking turns throwing each other to the mat. Of these early pugilists, the eighteenth-century fighter James Figg is most famous. Figg is credited with popularizing punching, and his style of bareknuckle fighting remained the boxing norm well into the next century.

About 1743, the first attempts to "civilize" boxing were made when Jack Broughton, a great fighter, drew up boxing rules later amended and codified as the "London Prize Ring rules." Under these rules, which were widely adopted and observed, boxers fought in a chalked-off area, with a referee, judges, or umpires to enforce the rules and settle disputes. A boxer was not permitted to strike an opponent who had fallen down until the opponent was back on his feet. The London Prize Ring rules became the basis for rules devised about a century later by the Marquis of Queensberry, whose Queensberry rules, designed to make the sport safer, are still observed today; they introduced the use of gloves, the 10-second count, and 3-minute rounds with a minute's rest between rounds. Classification of boxers by weight also began about this time. The earliest weight classes were lightweight, middleweight, and heavyweight.

It wasn't until the late nineteenth century that boxing gained the popularity in the United States that it had long enjoyed in England. The relatively few American fights were bareknuckle affairs that attracted a few fans, and the fans it did attract were, to say the least, not members of the upper class—as they often were in England. In fact, throughout much of the United States, it was illegal to fight with bare fists. Boxing cannot be said to have caught on in this country until an American fighter named John L. Sullivan donned a pair of gloves and toured the country with a theater troupe, giving exhibitions. Sullivan would arrive in a town and announce that he would "take on all comers" by fighting a three-minute round under the Queensberry rules. When he was accused of hiring people to lose to him, Sullivan offered first a $400 and then a $500 prize to anyone who could defeat him in four rounds. This caused a new surge of interest in boxing. Boxing schools developed in response to youngsters who said they wanted to "grow up like Sullivan." Sullivan became the first of many U.S. heavyweight champions, whose ranks also include such boxing greats as Jack Johnson, Jim Corbett, Jack Dempsey, Joe Louis, and Muhammad Ali.

Today, boxing has grown to the point where it is possible to have 3 world champions in each of 11 weight classes—a situation that exists because three organizations recognize world champions: the World Boxing Association, the World Boxing Council, and *Ring Magazine*. Such amateur contests as the Golden Gloves are designed to build the confidence of young men by teaching them the art and science of self-defense. For many of these athletes, boxing is a way—perhaps the only way—to gain fame, to achieve wealth, and to become a hero across one's own country or even, perhaps, around the world.

Great Moments

1719 James Figg, originator of bareknuckle fighting, becomes the first British bareknuckle champion.

1743 The British fighter Jack Broughton draws up London Prize Ring rules, which were used into the next century.

1792 The first welterweight championship is held. The welterweight class attracts little attention until the late 1880s.

1816 Jacob Hyer is declared the United States' first boxing champion.

1850s   English pugilists tour the United States, fighting American boxers.

1865   The Marquis of Queensberry introduces new rules. Intended to make boxing safer, the rules remain in use today.

1868   Abe Hicken defeats Pete McGuire and declares himself the first U.S. lightweight champion.

1872   For the first time, boxers fight for trophies. That same year, they are paired according to weight. The major fights, however, continue to be held between large men.

1882   The American bareknuckle fighter John L. Sullivan tours the United States, giving boxing exhibitions under the Queensberry rules. Boxing takes a leap in popularity.

1884–85   Middleweight and bantamweight classes are established.

1888   Amateur boxing is established when the first Amateur Athletic Union Championships are held. AAU boxing, however, remains loosely organized until 1900.

1892   In a match held in New Orleans, James ("Gentleman Jim") Corbett defeats John L. Sullivan, under the Queensberry rules, becoming the first heavyweight champion in the United States.

1896   New York becomes the first state to legalize boxing, followed, in 1897, by Nevada.

1919   Jack Dempsey knocks out Jess Willard in the third round, to win his first world heavyweight title.

1925   Madison Square Garden is opened and becomes the center for boxing in New York City.

1927   The Golden Gloves championships for amateur fighters are established by the New York *Daily News.*

1930   The controversial Max Schmeling–Jack Sharkey bout ends with Schmeling gaining the decision because of a foul by Sharkey in the fourth round. Schmeling is later stripped of the crown.

1936   Joe Louis suffers his first knockout, by Max Schmeling in the twelfth round of a title bout.

1949   Ezzard Charles and Jersey Joe Walcott meet to determine the heavyweight title vacated by Joe Louis, who had retired. Charles wins by a decision.

1959   Sweden's Ingemar Johansson becomes the first non-U.S. fighter to hold the world heavyweight title since 1933, by knocking out Floyd Patterson in the third round.

1964   Cassius Clay (Muhammad Ali) wins the heavyweight title for the first time, when champion Sonny Liston fails to answer the bell for the seventh round.

1971   Joe Frazier defeats Cassius Clay (Muhammad Ali) in a 15-round unanimous decision and retains the title he had gained during Ali's "retirement."

1976   American boxers Ray Leonard, Michael Spinks, and Leon Spinks come away from the Montreal Olympics with gold medals in the light welterweight, middleweight, and light heavyweight classes, respectively.

1978   World champion and heavy favorite Muhammad Ali loses a 15-round decision to Leon Spinks in a highly publicized bout. The rematch six months later, once again, ends in a 15-round decision, but this time Ali regains the title.

1980 Sugar Ray Leonard, the favorite to beat Roberto Duran to retain the light welterweight title, loses a June twentieth bout by a unanimous decision. A rematch in November goes to Leonard when Duran leaves the ring in the eighth round.

The Setup

Nationally, professional boxing is governed by state and local boxing commissions and associations. These groups sanction matches, provide medical supervision and officials, and enforce rules. Most of the groups belong to the World Boxing Association, which has affiliates in other countries. The relatively new World Boxing Council also sponsors international professional matches; along with the WBA and *Ring Magazine,* the council recognizes champions.

In the United States, amateur boxing is governed by the Amateur Athletic Union. The AAU sponsors national and international competitions and funds the training and transportation of Olympic boxers. The Golden Gloves Association, which sponsors the annual Golden Gloves boxing championships for young amateur boxers, is affiliated with the AAU.

GOLDEN GLOVES ASSOCIATION
8801 Princess Jeanne NE
Albuquerque, NM 87112
(505) 298-9286
Stan Gallup, exec. sec.

U.S. AMATEUR BOXING
  FEDERATION
Amateur Athletic Union
3400 W. 86th St.
Indianapolis, IN 46268
(317) 872-2900
Robert J. Surkein, national boxing chairman

WORLD BOXING ASSOCIATION
Panama 1
Republica de Panama
Rodrigo Sanchez, pres.

WORLD BOXING COUNCIL
Apartado Postal 75-254
Mexico 14, D.F. Mexico
Jose Sulaimain, pres.

The Basics

Object To outbox an opponent by knocking him out or, failing that, to outclass the opponent by landing more punches and earning the highest score from the referee and judges.

The ring The ring must be no less than 12 feet square and no more than 20 feet square. It is marked off by three parallel ropes. The ring, raised three to four feet above the ground, has a floor that is covered, first with a layer of thick felt, then with canvas.

Equipment Padded leather gloves weighing six ounces (for professional championship bouts) to eight ounces; a mouthguard made of plastic, to protect the teeth; tape for the hands; and boots.

Officials A referee, judges, a timekeeper, and seconds. The referee: controls the bout, stopping it when he feels a boxer is unable to continue; counts when a boxer is down; and cautions boxers when necessary. In Great Britain, the referee is the sole judge of the contest's outcome; elsewhere, as many as three judges, one of whom may be the referee, may score the fight. Judges rate boxers according to their performance. Professional boxers are allowed three seconds; amateurs are allowed one.

Duration A fight lasts a specified number of rounds, set before the fight. Amateur bouts usually last three rounds; a professional fight goes for 4 to 15 rounds. The fight ends sooner if there is a knockout. Each round begins and ends with a bell, and boxers have a one-minute break between rounds.

Rule 1   Weigh-in All boxers must weigh in before a bout on the day of an event. This is important because boxers are classified according to their weight. The following classifications are recognized by the World Boxing Council, the World Boxing Association, or both.

heavyweight	more than 190 lb	junior lightweight	up to 130
cruiserweight	up to 190	featherweight	up to 126
light heavyweight	up to 175	junior featherweight	up to 122
middleweight	up to 160	bantamweight	up to 118
junior middleweight	up to 154	junior bantamweight	up to 115
welterweight	up to 147	flyweight	up to 112
junior welterweight	up to 140	junior flyweight	up to 108
lightweight	up to 135		

Rule 2   Punching Only punching is allowed; no wrestling, holding, tripping, butting with the head, kicking, or other forms of fighting are permitted.

Rule 3   Illegal punches Some illegal blows are: punching below the belt; "rabbit" punches (blows to the back of the neck); "pivot" punches (see "Key Words"); and "kidney" punches (to the small of the back).

Rule 4   Knockdowns A boxer is considered knocked down when: any part of his body except for his feet is on the floor (except in case of a slip); when he is outside the ropes, between them, or hanging over them; or until he has gotten up after being knocked down.

Rule 5   The count If a boxer is not back on his feet within 10 seconds of the start of the count after he is knocked down, he is considered "knocked out," and loses the fight. The count on a knocked-down boxer begins after his opponent has moved to a neutral corner.

Rule 6   Technical knockout When a boxer is unable or unwilling to continue but has not been down for a 10-count, the opponent wins by technical knockout (TKO). The referee may stop a fight if he feels a boxer is unable to defend himself or risks serious injury; the fight is then awarded to the opponent, by a TKO. If a boxer is disqualified, his opponent wins by a TKO.

Rule 7   The decision   A bout is won by decision of the judges scoring the fight if a knockout or technical knockout has not occurred and all the rounds have been fought. The point system for most amateur bouts is based on 20 points. The top score of 20 is awarded to the winner of a round; the loser of the round receives fewer points. In professional boxing, the point system, which is somewhat controversial, is based on a maximum of 5 to 20 points, depending on where the fight is held.

How to watch

with Bert Randolph Sugar

In the old days of boxing, it was clear to onlookers who had won and who had lost a fight: the winner could still move at the end of the contest; the loser usually could not.

Modern boxing is not a fight to the bitter end, or even, necessarily, to a knockout. "Boxing is really mental chess," says Bert Randolph Sugar, editor in chief of *Ring Magazine* and *The Ring Record Book*. "The idea is to hit and not get hit—to win without getting hurt."

Indeed, some famous fighters, such as Sugar Ray Robinson, "took great pride in the fact that they never got their hair mussed during a fight." They relied instead on outscoring their opponents. According to Sugar, this was good not only for hair but for boxers as well. "If you don't stand around trying to hit, you don't get hit." It has, however, made the job of watching a bout much more difficult—both for spectators and for judges. Instead of looking for a knockout, the fan must also watch style and strategy, keeping track of punches landed and deflected.

"Boxing is highly subjective," Sugar says. Every judge and referee has his own ideas about what wins a round and what doesn't. According to Sugar, the guidelines that judges, in general, follow are:

Clean hitting—a fighter who lands the cleanest blows usually wins the round. Blows deflected by the arms and gloves do not count. Body punches count just as much as punches to the head. Jabs count but not as much.

Effective aggressiveness—the key word here is "effective." A fighter who is forcing his opponent backward is not effective unless he is landing blows. The fighter moving forward and landing blows is the more effective fighter. He is the one who receives points towards winning the round.

Defense—this is the most difficult area to judge. It takes a sharp eye to see the subtle defensive measures a boxer takes to try and make a puncher miss his mark. Such greats as Willie Pep have won rounds without landing a punch. They got points by making their opponents miss with their punches.

Ring strategy—a subjective interpretation of how a fighter conducts himself in the ring, whether he seems to be in control, moving his opponent to his advantage, effectively keeping him at bay, making him fight your kind of fight.

Main Events

PROFESSIONAL BOXING CHAMPIONSHIPS

Professional boxing has no annual tournaments. Instead, championship bouts are individually organized by fight promoters and managers of individual fighters. Boxing fans generally look to one or all of the major sanctioning organizations to determine the champion in each weight class. The World Boxing Association (WBA) and the World Boxing Council (WBC) sanction fights and recognize champions. *Ring Magazine*, though not involved with organizing matches, does recognize champions in 12 weight classes.

PROFESSIONAL BOXING CHAMPIONS*

World Boxing Council	World Boxing Association	*Ring Magazine*
heavyweight (190+)		
Larry Holmes	Mike Weaver	Larry Holmes
cruiserweight (to 190)		
Carlos DeLeon	(not recognized)	(not recognized)
light heavyweight (to 175)		
Matthew Saad Muhammad	Michael Spinks	Matthew Saad Muhammad
middleweight (to 160)		
Marvin Hagler	Marvin Hagler	Marvin Hagler
junior middleweight (to 154)		
Wilfredo Benitez	Sugar Ray Leonard	Sugar Ray Leonard
welterweight (to 147)		
Sugar Ray Leonard	Thomas Hearns	Sugar Ray Leonard
junior welterweight (to 140)		
Saoul Mamby	Aaron Pryor	Aaron Pryor
lightweight (to 135)		
Alexis Arguello	Sean O'Grady	Alexis Arguello
junior lightweight (to 130)		
Cornelius Boza-Edwards	Samuel Serrano	Samuel Serrano
featherweight (to 126)		
Salvador Sanchez	Eusebio Pedroza	Salvador Sanchez
junior featherweight (to 122)		
Wilfredo Gomez	Sergio Palma	Wilfredo Gomez
bantamweight (to 118)		
Guadalupe Pintor	Jeff Chandler	Jeff Chandler
junior bantamweight (to 115)		
Chul-Ho Kim	(vacant)	(not recognized)

flyweight (to 112)
Antonio Avelar   Luis Ibarra   Antonio Avelar

junior flyweight (to 108)
Hilario Zapata   Hwan-Jin Kin   (not recognized)

*As of July 30, 1981.

OLYMPIC BOXING CHAMPIONS

106-LB LIGHT-FLYWEIGHT

1980 Shamil Sabirov, USSR
1976 Jorge Hernandez, Cuba
1972 Gheorghi Gedo, Hungary
1968 Francisco Rodriguez,
     Venezuela

112-LB FLYWEIGHT

1980 Peter Lessov, Bulgaria
1976 Leo Randolph, USA
1972 Gheorghi Kostadinov, Bulgaria
1968 Ricardo Delgado, Mexico
1964 Fernando Atzori, Italy
1960 Gyula Torok, Hungary
1956 Terence Spinks, Great Britain
1952 Nathan E. Brooks, USA

119-LB BANTAMWEIGHT

1980 Juan Hernandez, Cuba
1976 Yong Jo Gu, North Korea
1972 Orlando Martinez, Cuba
1968 Valeri Sokolov, USSR
1964 Takao Sakurai, Japan
1960 Oleg Grigoryev, USSR
1956 Wolfgang Behrendt, Germany
1952 Pentti Hamakainen, Finland

125-LB FEATHERWEIGHT

1980 Rudy Fink, East Germany
1976 Angel Herrera, Cuba
1972 Boris Kousnetsov, USSR
1968 Antonio Roldan, Mexico
1964 Stanislav Stepashkin, USSR
1960 Francesco Musso, Italy
1956 Vladimir Safronov, USSR
1952 Jan Zachara, Czechoslovakia

132-LB LIGHTWEIGHT

1980 Angel Herrera, Cuba
1976 Howard Davis, USA
1972 Jan Szczepanski, Poland
1968 Ronnie Harris, USA
1964 Jozef Grudzien, Poland
1960 Kazmierz Pazdzior, Poland

1956 Richard McTaggart, Great Britain
1952 Aureliano Bolognesi, Italy

139-LB LIGHT-WELTERWEIGHT

1980 Patrizio Oliva, Italy
1976 Ray Leonard, USA
1972 Ray Seales, USA
1968 Jerzy Kulej, Poland
1964 Jerzy Kulej, Poland
1960 Bohumil Nemecek,
     Czechoslovakia
1956 Vladimir Enguibarian, USSR
1952 Charles Adkins, USA

147-LB WELTERWEIGHT

1980 Andreas Aldama, Cuba
1976 Jochen Bachfeld, GDR*
1972 Emilio Correa, Cuba
1968 Manfred Wolke, GDR
1964 Marian Kasprezyk, Poland
1960 Giovanni Benvenuti, Italy
1956 Necolae Linca, Romania
1952 Zigmunt Chychla, Poland

156-LB LIGHT-MIDDLEWEIGHT

1980 Armando Martinez, Cuba
1976 Jerzy Rybicki, Poland
1972 Dieter Kottysch, FRG*
1968 Boris Lagutin, USSR
1964 Boris Lagutin, USSR
1960 Wilbert McClure, USA
1956 Laszlo Papp, Hungary
1952 Laszlo Papp, Hungary

165-LB MIDDLEWEIGHT

1980 Jose Gomez, Cuba
1976 Michael Spinks, USA
1972 Viatcheslav Lemechev, USSR
1968 Chris Finnegan, Great Britain
1964 Valery Popenchenko, USSR
1960 Eddie Crook, USA
1956 Gennady Chatkov, USSR
1952 Floyd Patterson, USA

*German Democratic Republic (East Germany).
*Federal Republic of Germany (West Germany).

178-LB LIGHT-HEAVYWEIGHT

1980 Slobodan Kacar, Yugoslavia
1976 Leon Spinks, USA
1972 Mate Parlov, Yugoslavia
1968 Dan Pozniak, USSR
1964 Cosimo Pinto, Italy
1960 Cassius Clay, USA
1956 James Boyd, USA
1952 Norvel L. Lee, USA

HEAVYWEIGHT

1980 Teofilo Stevenson, Cuba
1976 Teofilo Stevenson, Cuba
1972 Teofilo Stevenson, Cuba
1968 George Foreman, USA
1964 Joseph Frazier, USA
1960 Francesco de Piccolo, Italy
1956 Peter Rademacher, USA
1952 Hayes Sanders, USA

GOLDEN GLOVES CHAMPIONSHIPS

The New York *Daily News* originated and sponsored the Golden Gloves tournaments in 1927. The program, aimed at young amateur boxers from the inner city, has since become national and international in scope. The climax comes when the winners of the Eastern championships (held in New York) and the winners of the Western championships (held in Chicago) fight for the national Golden Gloves championships. The national championships are held each spring at various locations. National champions from the last 10 years are listed below.

112-LB CLASS

1980 Jerome Coffee
1979 Jerome Coffee
1978 William Johnson
1977 Orlando Maldonado
1976 Julio Rodriguez
1975 Leo Randolph
1974 Greg Richardson
1973 Miguel Ayala
1972 Greg Lewis
1971 James Martinez

132-LB CLASS

1980 Melvin D. Paul
1979 Johnny Bumphus
1978 Dave Armstrong
1977 Samuel Ayala
1976 Aaron Pryor
1975 Aaron Pryor
1974 Curtis Harris
1973 Ray Leonard
1972 James Busceme
1971 James Busceme

156-LB CLASS

1980 James Schuler
1979 James Schuler
1978 Donald Bowers
1977 Curtis Parker
1976 Don Carbin
1975 Ray Phillips
1974 Michael Spinks
1973 Dale Grant
1972 Lamont Lovelady
1971 Samuel Nesmith

119-LB CLASS

1980 Myron Taylor
1979 Kenneth Baysmore
1978 Jackie Beard
1977 Wayne Lynum
1976 Barnard Taylor
1975 Miguel Ayala
1974 Dan Hermosillo
1973 James Martinez
1972 Ray Theragood
1971 Johnny Moreno

139-LB CLASS

1980 Terry Silver
1979 Lemuel Steeples
1978 Ronnie Shields
1977 Thomas Hearns
1976 Ronnie Shields
1975 Paul Sherry
1974 Ray Leonard
1973 Larry Bonds
1972 Ray Seales
1971 Wiley Johnson

165-LB CLASS

1980 Lamont Kirkland
1979 Antonio Ayala
1978 Wilford Scypion
1977 Keith Broom
1976 Michael Spinks
1975 Tom Sullivan
1974 Michael Spinks
1973 Dale Grant
1972 Marvin Johnson
1971 Jerry Dobbs

125-LB CLASS

1980 Bernard Taylor
1979 Roland Cooley
1978 Bernard Taylor
1977 Bernard Taylor
1976 Dave Armstrong
1975 Ronnie Shields
1974 Dan Hermosillo
1973 Morice Watkins
1972 Louis Self
1971 Louis Self

147-LB CLASS

1980 Don Curry
1979 Michael McCullum
1978 Jeffrey Stoudemire
1977 Michael McCallum
1976 Clinton Jackson
1975 Clinton Jackson
1974 Clinton Jackson
1973 Harold Beal
1972 Jesse Valdez
1971 Larry Carlisle

178-LB CLASS

1980 Steve Eden
1979 Leroy Murphy
1978 Greg Singletary
1977 Rick Jester
1976 Rick Jester
1975 Frankie Williams
1974 Robert Stewart
1973 D.C. Barker
1972 Verbie Garland
1971 Marvin Johnson

HEAVYWEIGHT CLASS

1980	Michael Arms	1976	Michael Dokes	1972	Duane Bobick
1979	Marvis Frazier	1975	Emory Chapman	1971	Ronald Draper
1978	Greg Page	1974	Emory Chapman		
1977	James Clark	1973	Johnny Hudson		

AAU CHAMPIONSHIPS

The Amateur Athletic Union (AAU) National Championships are the culmination of a year of amateur tournaments held throughout the United States. Held annually at varying locations, the championships feature boxers from the organizations affiliated with the AAU.

125-LB

1980	Clifford Gray
1979	Bernard Taylor
1978	Euchi Jumawan
1977	Johnny Bumphus
1976	David Armstrong
1975	David Armstrong
1974	Michael Hess
1973	Howard Davies
1972	Jerome Artis
1971	Rickey Boudreaux

132-LB

1980	Melvin Paul
1979	David Armstrong
1978	Melvin Paul
1977	Anthony Fletcher
1976	Howard Davis
1975	Hilmer Kenty
1974	James Kentyn
1973	Aaron Pryor
1972	Norman Goins
1971	James Busceme

139-LB

1980	Johnny Bumphus
1979	Lemuel Steeples
1978	Donald Curry
1977	Thomas Hearns
1976	Milton ("Pete") Seward
1975	Ray Leonard

1974	Ray Leonard
1973	Randy Shield
1972	Carlos Palomino
1971	Ray Seales

147-LB

1980	Gene Hatcher
1979	Donald Curry
1978	Roger Leonard
1977	Michael McCallum
1976	Clinton Jackson
1975	Clinton Jackson
1974	Clinton Jackson
1973	William Tuttle
1972	Fred Washington
1971	Sammy Maul

156-LB

1980	Don Bowers
1979	Jeff Stoudemire
1978	J. B. Williamson
1977	Clinton Jackson
1976	J. B. Williamson
1975	Charles Walker
1974	Jerome Bennett
1973	Dale Grant
1972	Henry Johnson
1971	Billy Daniels

165-LB

1980	Martin Pierce
1979	Alex Ramos

1978	Jeff McCracken
1977	Jerome Bennett
1976	Keith Brown
1975	Tommy Brooks
1974	Vonzell Johnson
1973	Marvin Hagler
1972	Michael Colbert
1971	Joey Hadley

178-LB

1980	Jeff Lampkin
1979	Tony Tucker
1978	Elmer Martin
1977	Larry Strogen
1976	Leon Spinks
1975	Leon Spinks
1974	Leon Spinks
1973	D. C. Barker
1972	Hernando Molyneaux
1971	Marvin Johnson

HEAVYWEIGHT

1980	Marvis Frazier
1979	Tony Tubbs
1978	Greg Page
1977	Greg Page
1976	Marvin Stinson
1975	Mike Dokes
1974	Dwayne Bonds
1973	James Chapman
1972	Nick Wells
1971	Duane Bobick

PAN AMERICAN BOXING CHAMPIONSHIPS

LIGHT-FLYWEIGHT

1979	Hector Ramirez, Cuba
1975	Jorge Hernandez, Cuba
1971	R. Carbonell, Cuba

FLYWEIGHT

1979	Alberto Mercado, Puerto Rico
1975	Ramon Duvalon, Cuba

1971 Francisco Rodriguez,
      Venezuela
1967 Francisco Rodriguez,
      Venezuela
1963 Floreal G. LaRosa, Uruguay
1959 Miguel Botta, Argentina
1955 Hilario Correa, Mexico
1951 Alberto Barenghi, Argentina

BANTAMWEIGHT

1979 Jackie Beard, USA
1975 Orlando Martinez, Cuba
1971 Pedro Flores, Mexico
1967 Juvencio Martinez, Mexico
1963 Abel C. Aimariz, Argentina
1959 Waldo Claudiano, Brazil
1955 Salvador Enriquez, Venezuela
1951 Rica do Gonzales, Argentina

FEATHERWEIGHT

1979 Bernard Taylor, USA
1975 David Armstrong, USA
1971 Juan Garcia, Mexico
1967 Miguel Garcia, Argentina
1963 Rosemiro Santos, Brazil
1959 Carlos Aro, Argentina
1955 Osualdo Insfran, Argentina
1951 Francisco Nunez, Argentina

LIGHTWEIGHT

1979 Adolfo Horta, Cuba
1975 Chris Clarke, Canada
1971 Luis Davila, Puerto Rico
1967 Enrico Bianco, Cuba
1963 Roberto Caminero, Cuba
1959 Abel Laudonio, Argentina
1955 Miguel Pendola, Argentina
1951 Oscar Galareo, Argentina

LIGHT-WELTERWEIGHT

1979 Lemuel Steeples, USA
1975 Ray Leonard, USA
1971 Enrico Reguiferos, Cuba
1967 James Wallington, USA
1963 Adolfo Moreira, Argentina
1959 Vincent Shomo, USA
1955 J.C.R. Fernandez, Argentina

WELTERWEIGHT

1979 Andres Aldama, Cuba
1975 Clinton Jackson, USA
1971 Emilio Correa, Cuba
1967 Andres Modina, Cuba
1963 Misael Vilugeron, Chile
1959 Alfredo Cornejo, Chile
1955 Joseph Dorando, USA
1951 Oscar Pietta, Argentina

LIGHT-MIDDLEWEIGHT

1979 Jose Molina, Puerto Rico
1975 Rolando Garbey, Cuba
1971 Rolando Garbey, Cuba
1967 Rolando Garbey, Cuba
1963 Elecio Neves, Brazil
1959 Wilbert McClure, USA
1955 Paul Wright, USA

MIDDLEWEIGHT

1979 Jose Gomez, Cuba
1975 Alejandro Montoya, Cuba
1971 Faustino Quinalex, Venezuela
1967 Jorge Ahumada, Argentina
1963 Luiz Cezar, Brazil
1959 Abrao de Souza, Brazil
1955 Orville E. Pitts, USA
1951 Ubadio Pereura, Argentina

LIGHT-HEAVYWEIGHT

1979 Tony Tucker, USA
1975 Orestes Pedrozo, Cuba
1971 Raymond Russell, USA
1967 Arthur Redden, USA
1963 Fred Lewis, USA
1959 Amos Johnson, USA
1955 Luis Ignacio, Brazil
1951 Rinaldo Ansaloni, Argentina

HEAVYWEIGHT

1979 Teofilo Stevenson, Cuba
1975 Teofilo Stevenson, Cuba
1971 Duane Bobick, USA
1967 Forrest Ward, USA
1963 Lee Carr, USA
1959 Allen Hudson, USA
1955 Alesci P. Ochoa, Argentina
1951 Jorge Vertone, Argentina

All-Time Greats

Muhammad Ali
(Jan. 17, 1942–)

Probably the most compelling boxing star ever, Ali is perhaps the best-known athlete in the world. He first gained national attention in 1960, when, as a light heavyweight, he won the AAU national Golden Gloves competition and the Olympic light heavyweight gold medal in the same year. Over the next three and a half years, Ali (then known as Cassius Clay) took on 19 opponents before getting the chance, in 1964, to fight Sonny Liston for the world heavyweight boxing championship. The fight ended with Ali knocking out Liston in the seventh round for the title. He held the title until 1971, when he lost it to Joe Frazier. Frazier then held the title for two years after Ali withdrew from prizefighting amid controversy over his refusal to be drafted into the army. In 1974, Ali regained the world title by knocking out George Foreman. He held the title until he lost it, by a decision, to Leon Spinks. Seven months later, Ali fought Spinks again, this time winning by decision. Ali retired as champion, but in 1980 returned to challenge Larry Holmes, who had become champion in the meantime; Ali lost the fight but continues to talk of another comeback. Ali's style—as a public figure and as a boxer—has made him a legend. Many fans both loved and hated his flamboyance and boastful nature (his slogan is "I am the greatest!"); anyone who saw him in his prime could admire his quick, dancing feet in the ring and his fast, powerful punch.

John Arthur ("Jack") Johnson
(Mar. 31, 1878–June 10, 1946)

Jack Johnson, the underweight son of a janitor and part-time preacher, as a youth had to depend on his older sister to fend off bullies—not always successfully. He became the world's first black heavyweight champion and one of the best heavyweight fighters of all time. During the years before Johnson beat Tommy Burns and gained the heavyweight title, he faced prejudice, poverty, and the fists of fighters who used him merely as a sparring partner but who later found him an awesome opponent. Johnson traveled around the country, looking for a chance to take on the current white heavyweight champion. It was a challenge no black man had ever made, and one no white man had ever risked accepting. The Burns fight—fought in Sydney, Australia, on December 26, 1908—was arranged by an Australian promoter who agreed to pay Burns $35,000, win or lose, but Johnson only $5,000. After 14 rounds, Johnson emerged the undisputed champion. Over the next 15 years, he defended his title successfully, eventually losing to Jess Willard, in Havana. The award-winning play and film *The Great White Hope* are based on Johnson's life.

Joe Louis
(May 13, 1914–Apr. 12, 1981)

The Ring Magazine

Joe Louis was a heavyweight champion not content to rest on his laurels. After winning the title in August 1937, he took on challenger after challenger, defending his crown 25 times. A steady, methodical boxer, Louis faced a series of fighters who, collectively, came to be known as the Bum of the Month Club. The Brown Bomber was knocked out only twice in his entire 71-bout career—once by Max Schmeling in 1936 and then by Rocky Marciano in 1951. He first retired in 1949, having successfully defended his crown against every challenge. In 1950, Louis attempted a comeback but lost in a world heavyweight title bout to Ezzard Charles.

Rocky Marciano
(Sept. 1, 1923–Aug. 31, 1969)

The Ring Magazine

A talented athlete who had tried a professional baseball career before turning to boxing, Marciano waged a boxing campaign beginning in 1947 that culminated, five years later, in a shot at the world heavyweight championship held by Jersey Joe Walcott. Marciano knocked Walcott out in the thirteenth round, and in a rematch in 1953 he knocked out Walcott at 2:25 of the first round to retain the title. Known for his powerful punch, Marciano won 43 of his bouts by knockout. He defended the title successfully six times, and retired in 1956, having suffered no defeats in his 49-bout career. He died in an airplane accident the day before his 46th birthday.

Floyd Patterson
(Jan. 4, 1935–)

The Ring Magazine

Floyd Patterson first learned to box at the correctional institution where he was sent as an adolescent. In the 1952 Olympics, he won a gold medal in the light middleweight division, and four years later he won the vacant world heavyweight championship by knocking out Archie Moore in the fifth round. Patterson was knocked out by Ingemar Johansson in 1959 and lost the crown; one year later, he knocked out the Swede in a rematch, becoming the first boxer to regain the heavyweight title. Patterson later lost championship bouts to Sonny Liston (twice), Muhammad Ali, and Jimmy Ellis (WBA title). Out of a total of 64 bouts, Patterson won 40 by knockout in a career that spanned 20 years.

"Sugar Ray" Robinson
(May 3, 1920–)

The Ring Magazine

Born Walker Smith, "Sugar Ray" Robinson, at his peak, was regarded as the best boxer, pound for pound, of his day. He was dubbed "Sugar Ray" because of his "sweet" style—he protected his no-muss look with swift and hard punching. Robinson won his first world title, the welterweight, by defeating Tommy Bell in 1946. He successfully defended the title until 1951, when he won the *middleweight* title by knocking out Jake LaMotta. When he retired in 1952, he had lost only 3 of 137 bouts he had fought. Robinson came out of retirement in 1954 and by 1955 had won the world middleweight title again. Twice he lost attempts to retain the title, but he came back in 1958 to defeat Carmen Basilio and win a world title for a record fifth time. By the time he retired in 1965, Sugar Ray had fought 201 bouts, winning more than half of them by knockout.

John L. Sullivan
(Oct. 15, 1858–Feb. 2, 1918)

The Ring Magazine

The career of John L. Sullivan marks the beginning of professional boxing in the United States. He was the nation's last bareknuckle champion, retaining the title in a bout in 1889 against Jake Kilrain. In 1892, however, Sullivan lost the Queensberry world title to James Corbett. Known early in his career as the "Boston Strong Boy," Sullivan is credited with popularizing boxing by staging fights throughout the country. He went along with theatrical troupes for exhibition matches, with gloves, taking on all comers for $100—and later, for $500—if they could knock him out in less than four rounds.

BOXING HALL OF FAME

Membership in the Boxing Hall of Fame is divided into three categories: Pioneer Group, Old-Timers, and Modern Group. Pioneers, elected by the board of directors of *Ring Magazine*, may or may not have boxed professionally, but must have made a significant contribution to the sport. Old-timers, elected by a panel of experts, were active more than 30 years ago. Moderns, chosen by sportswriters, broadcasters, and other boxing experts, are outstanding boxers who have been active in the past 35 years, but who have been retired for at least two years. Following is a table listing the members of the Hall of Fame.

Pioneer Group

Barney ("Young") Aaron	Pete Herman
Jack Broughton	Leo Houck
James Burke	Joe Jeannette
Arthur Chambers	James J. Jeffries
Tom Chandler	Jack Johnson
Nobby Clark	Stanley Ketchel
Sam Collyer	The Dixie Kid (Aaron L. Brown)

Tom Cribb
Dick Curtis
Dan Donnelly
Mike ("Prof") Donovan
Tommy Burns
Georges Carpentier
George ("K.O.") Chaney
Joe Choynski
James J. Corbett
Young Corbett, II
Johnny Coulon
Jack Delaney
Jack Dempsey
Jack Dillon
George Dixon
Jem Driscoll
Jackie Fields
Bob Fitzsimmons
Tiger Flowers
Joe Gans
Frankie Gerano
Mike Gibbons
Tom Gibbons
Young Griffo

James Figg
Joe Goss
John Gully
John C. Heenan
Jacob Hyer
"Gentleman John" Jackson
Peter Jackson
Jake Kilrain
Tom King
Jem Mace
Daniel Mendoza
Tom Molineaux
John Morrissey
Ned Price
Bill Richmond
Paddy Ryan
Young Dutch Sam
Tom Sayers
Tom Spring
William ("Bendigo") Thompson
Jem Ward

Old-Timers

Abe Attell
Paul Berlenbach
Jimmy Britt
Johnny Kilbane
Frank Klaus
Fidel LaBarba
Sam Langford
George ("Kid") Lavigne
Battling Levinsky
Ted ("Kid") Lewis
Jack McAuliffe
Charles ("Kid") McCoy
Packey McFarland
Terry McGovern
Peter Maher
Charley Mitchell
Owen Moran

Battling Nelson
"Philadelphia" Jack O'Brien
Billy Papke
Willie Ritchie
Jack Root
Tommy Ryan
Tom Sharkey
Jeff Smith
John L. Sullivan
Pancho Villa
Joe ("Barbados") Walcott
Freddie Welsh
Jimmy Wilde
Jess Willard
"Kid" Williams
Harry Wills
Ad Wolgast

Modern Group

Lou Ambers
Sammy Angott
Fred Apostoli
Henry Armstrong
Max Baer
Carmen Basilio
Jackie ("Kid") Berg
Jack Britton

Gus Lesnevich
Joe Louis
Jimmy McLarnin
Rocky Marciano
Joey Maxim
Archie Moore
Floyd Patterson
Willie Pep

Tony Canzoneri
Marcel Cerdan
Ezzard Charles
"Kid Chocolate" (Eligio Sardinias)
Billy Conn
Jack Dempsey
Johnny Dundee
Sixto Escobar
Gene Fullmer
Ceferino Garcia
"Kid" Gavilan
Rocky Graziano
Harry Greb
Beau Jack
Lew Jenkins
Benny Leonard

Pascual Perez
Billy Petrolle
"Sugar Ray" Robinson
Maxie Rosenbloom
Barney Ross
Max Schmeling
Yoshio Shiral
Lew Tendler
Dick Tiger
Gene Tunney
"Jersey Joe" Walcott
Mickey Walker
Ike Williams
Chalky Wright
Tony Zale
Fritzie Zivic

For the Record

Longest consecutive winning streak, total bouts
180   Hal Bagwell   1938–48

Most knockouts scored in major competition
141   Archie Moore   1936–63

Most consecutive knockouts (20 or more)
44   Lamar Clark   1958–60

Undeated throughout career (25 or more bouts)
Jimmy Barry   1891–99
Cruz Marcano   1966–70
Rocky Marciano   1947–55
Jack McAuliffe   1884–97
Laszlo Papp   1957–64

Fastest one-round knockout in a title bout, heavyweight class
55 sec.   James J. Jeffries over Jack Finnegan   1900

Fastest one-round knockout in a title bout, middleweight class
45 sec.   Al McCoy over George Chip   1914

Fastest one-round knockout in a title bout, lightweight class
1 min. 6 sec.   Tony Canzoneri over Al Singer   1930

Most world championships
6   Sugar Ray Robinson

Oldest to hold a world title (gloves)
age 48   Archie Moore   1961

Most rounds in a heavyweight championship fight
110 rounds   Bowen vs Burke   April 1893

Greatest weight in a fight, two-fighter total
601 lb   Ewart Potgieter (335) and Bruce Olsen (266)   1957

Greatest weight difference between fighters
140 lb   Bob Fitzsimmons (167 lb) over Ed Dunkhurst (327 lb)   1900

First million-dollar gate
Jack Dempsey over Georges Carpentier   1921

Did you know ?

1. What world heavyweight champion had to pay a fine for winning his title?

2. One of Jack Dempsey's sparring partners later became one of the richest men in the world. Who was he?

3. So far, four heavyweight champions have retired undefeated. Three of them are James Jeffries, Gene Tunney, and Rocky Marciano. Who was the fourth?

4. Who is the only heavyweight champion to win his title three times?

5. Who was the youngest fighter to become the heavyweight champion of the world?

6. Henry Armstrong was the first fighter to hold titles in three weight classes simultaneously. What was his nickname?

7. Who was considered the best boxer in ancient Greece?

8. Have boxing matches ever been held on horseback?

9. Who took the heavyweight title from Jack Johnson?

10. Who was nicknamed the "Manassa Mauler"? Why?

11. What is Jersey Joe Walcott's real name?

12. Who did George Foreman beat to win the heavyweight title in 1973?

13. Who refereed the famous Sullivan–Corbett fight in 1892?

14. What famous U.S. marshal refereed a match between Bob Fitzsimmons and Tom Sharkey?

Answers: 1. John L. Sullivan. After Sullivan defeated Jake Kilrain in 75 rounds in 1899, he and Kilrain were arrested and charged with assault and battery—boxing was then illegal. Kilrain was sentenced to a short jail term, Sullivan to one year, which was eventually converted to a fine of $1,000. **2.** J. Paul Getty; **3.** Joe Louis; **4.** Muhammad Ali; **5.** Floyd Patterson. In 1956, at the age of 21, Patterson took the title from Archie Moore; **6.** "Homicide Hank." Armstrong held the featherweight, lightweight, and welterweight titles in 1938; **7.** Theagenes, who fought and defeated 1,425 opponents, often to the death; **8.** Yes. Germany held such matches in 1912, in the belief that they were good preparation for warfare; **9.** Jess Willard, in 1915; **10.** Jack Dempsey was nicknamed the "Manassa Mauler"; he was born in Manassa, Colorado; **11.** Arnold Raymond Cream; **12.** Joe Frazier, by a technical knockout; **13.** Professor John Duffy; **14.** Wyatt Earp.

Key Words

belt   an imaginary line across a boxer's middle below which it is illegal to strike.

blocking   using the arms to deflect an opponent's blows.

bob and weave   to move from side to side or up and down quickly and continuously to make oneself a moving, and therefore difficult, target.

bout   a boxing match. An amateur bout lasts three rounds; professional bouts last up to fifteen rounds, but most often, ten.

clinch   to tie up an opponent with one or both arms, thus making it difficult to exchange punches. Tired or hurt fighters use it as a stall.

cross   a hook shot thrown above an opponent's lead.

(down for the) count   when a boxer is knocked down, the referee begins to count to 10. If the boxer is still down when the count is completed, his opponent wins the match.

ducking   dodging a blow from an opponent by quickly stooping or by lowering the head and shoulders.

glass jaw   susceptibility to being knocked out.

gloves   thickly padded leather mitts worn by boxers.

headlock   holding firmly the head of an opponent.

hook   a short, circular-motion blow delivered with the arm bent at the elbow and held rigid.

jab   a quick, straight punch made without the full force of the body behind it.

kidney punch   an illegal blow to the small of the back.

knockout   the act of hitting a boxer until he loses consciousness and falls to the mat; a knockout also occurs when the fighter knocked down cannot get to his feet before the referee counts to 10. The abbreviation "KO" is often used.

lead   the first punch in a series; usually the hand or punch favored by the fighter.

low blow   an illegal punch landing below the belt.

mouthguard   a plastic mold worn in the mouth during a fight, to protect the teeth.

pivot blow   an illegal blow in which a boxer keeps his arm rigid and pivots, striking his opponent full force with an outstretched arm.

ring   the marked-off fight area. The typical ring is a square with three parallel ropes 20 feet long on each side. Usually, the ring (including the floor, which is covered with felt and canvas) is raised from the surrounding area.

ringside   the area just outside the boxing ring.

ropes   markers, of soft material, used to delineate the fight area.

round the period during a bout in which boxers actually fight. In professional boxing, a round is three minutes long; in amateur competition, a round is two to three minutes long.

second someone who aids a boxer. Seconds are permitted in the ring between rounds.

shadow box sparring with an imaginary opponent.

slip (a punch) to avoid a punch by moving the head to one side.

spar practice boxing. A sparring partner helps a boxer train by standing in for the boxer's opponent.

speed bag an inflated leather punching bag suspended at eye level; it is used in practice to improve speed and reflexes.

technical knockout a fight stopped because a boxer is either unwilling or unable to continue, but who is not "down for the count." Such a knockout, often abbreviated "TKO," is determined by the referee.

uppercut a short punch thrown from the waist upward, with the arm bent.

weighing in a standard procedure followed before bouts, in which the contestants are weighed to ensure that they meet the weight requirements for their fight class.

ABC Sports

ABC Sports

7 FOOTBALL

In the 60 years since formal professional football began, the sport has gained in prominence to become the most popular sport in the United States. Its annual grand finale—the Super Bowl, which draws an audience of 30 million homes or more—generally rates as one of the most watched television programs of the year.

The game of football began in the nineteenth century among American college students, some of whom favored soccer as a model and some of whom preferred to play rugby. It also was popular among local athletic clubs, and intense rivalries developed. As a result of the fierce competition, the first major football tournament was organized. In 1902, four teams competed in a "world series" of football at Madison Square Garden: the Philadelphia Athletics, the New York Knickerbockers, the Watertown (New York) Red and Blacks, and the Syracuse Athletic Club. Syracuse won the first game, which was also the first indoor football game ever played, and went on to win the tournament.

Pockets of football formed in Ohio and Indiana as the game slowly caught on. Its popularity was boosted when Olympic star Jim Thorpe signed with a professional team and, in 1916, led the Canton Bulldogs to the championship. By 1920, it was clear that more rules and better organization were needed. A number of teams met in August of that year and, on September 17, the American Professional Football Association (APFA) was formed, with teams from five states: the Akron Pros, Canton Bulldogs, Cleveland Indians, Dayton Triangles, and Massillon Tigers, from Ohio; the Hammond Pros and Muncie Flyers, from Indiana; the Racine Cardinals, Rock Island Independents, and Decatur Staleys, from Illinois; the Rochester Jeffersons, from New York; and a team called simply "Wisconsin."

In 1922, the APFA became the National Football League. Teams came and went. Four years later, a nine-team American Football League was formed, but it folded in 1927. By the end of the 1920s, football had stabilized somewhat, and in 1929 the Green Pay Packers, led by Johnny ("Blood") McNally, Cal Hubbard, and Mike Michalske, were declared the first NFL champions.

Some important rule changes were made in pro football in 1933, calling for standard inbound lines, or hash marks, 10 yards from the sidelines, and goal posts on the goal lines. Divisions were designated, with division winners to meet in a championship game at the end of the season. The Chicago Bears beat the New York Giants, 23–21, to win the first NFL championship game.

Pro football met college football for the first time in 1934, in the first all-star game. The match between the Chicago Bears and the college stars was a stand-off. With the introduction of the college draft in 1936, college ball became inextricably tied to pro ball; colleges and universities are now the training ground for almost all professional players. With the legalization, in the 1930s, of the forward pass from anywhere behind the line of scrimmage, passing became an effective offensive weapon. From that point on, the game would never be quite the same. (Previously, the passer had to be at least five yards behind the line of scrimmage.)

The close relationship of football and television began in 1939, when the Brooklyn Dodgers–Philadelphia Eagles game was broadcast in New York City to the lucky few who had television sets. Television has since contributed heavily to the success of professional football.

World War II depleted the ranks of pro football, and a number of teams merged for the duration of the war. A postwar count showed that 638 men who had played in league games had served in the armed forces, and 21 of them had been killed. Despite a scandal surrounding the 1946 championship game, football maintained its standing, even strengthening its position as an emerging major sport. The end of the war brought a new league, the All-American Football Conference (AAFC), but by 1950 the league had been forced to merge some of its teams with the stronger NFL. That year, the American and National conferences replaced the Eastern and Western divisions, although in 1954 they became the Eastern and Western conferences.

Rules were added and changed during the 1950s. Baltimore reentered the NFL, and the Giants moved from the Polo Grounds to Yankee Stadium. At the end of the decade, the NFL had its first strong challenge in some time. Lamar Hunt, representing Dallas, met with representatives from five other cities. On August 14, 1959, they formed the American Football League (AFL). Three more cities joined, and in 1960 the AFL began its first season.

New franchises were granted and transfers were made in the NFL, and a battle for players developed between the two leagues. The AFL took the NFL to court in the early 1960s, charging monopoly. Because the AFL could neither win nor survive, it agreed to a merger with the NFL in 1966. Two years later, the new league, now consisting of 24 teams, was expanded by two. The AFL and NFL would maintain separate schedules until 1970, although, beginning in 1967, they met annually in a world championship game (the Super Bowl).

The newly merged leagues even received the blessing of Congress. Still more shifting of franchises and realignment of teams made organization of the sport difficult to follow. The first Super Bowl pitted the Green Bay Packers, of the NFL, against the Kansas City Chiefs, of the AFL, with the winning Packer players picking up $15,000 each. Although the NFL was clearly the superior league during the transition years, the underdog New York Jets of the AFL, with Joe Namath at quarterback, won the Super Bowl in 1969, defeating Baltimore, 16–7, at Miami.

With the exception of the expansion to 28 teams in the midseventies, the NFL, outwardly, has changed little since 1970. There was some competition from the World Football League, but that association soon folded under the pressure of stiff competition. Beneath the apparent stability in the postmerger era, however, professional football has changed. Players are coming out of college primed for the pro game. Salaries have increased. More and more players are becoming household names. Clearly, television is responsible for the tremendous increase in the game's popularity with spectators. Football is made for television. The game is easier to follow on television than in person, and nothing compares with a slow-motion, instant replay of a beautiful touchdown run. Practically no one doubts that viewers will ever tire of the sound of cracking shoulder pads or the sight of a deep pass reception by a player in full stride.

COLLEGE

Football began as an amateur sport played on college campuses in the eastern United States. It wasn't until this century that it was played professionally to any extent. Football's heritage is a blend of the English games of soccer and rugby and the numerous games involving a kicked ball that preceded it.

The contest between Princeton and Rutgers on November 6, 1869, is widely recognized as the first intercollegiate football game, although the game resembled soccer more closely than it does today's football. Nevertheless, 1869 is a date often used to mark the beginning of what became intercollegiate football competition. That momentous game spurred the organization and codification of football, and in 1873 Yale led a movement to combine Harvard, Princeton, Columbia, and Rutgers in a league. Harvard refused to attend, wishing instead to continue playing football according to the "Boston Game," a set of rules that differed considerably from those used by the other schools. The American Intercollegiate Football Association (AIFA) was formed without Harvard, and the teams competed according to the association's rules, which were based on English soccer.

In the early 1880s, football began taking a shape distinctive from that of its predecessors. The number of players on a side was reduced gradually from 25 to 11, and the number of downs, or chances to advance the ball, was allotted—three downs in which to move the ball forward five yards.

The AIFA was disbanded in 1895, Pennsylvania having withdrawn the year before. The resulting disorder and lack of rules led to a high incidence of serious injuries and even deaths from playing the "friendly" game of college football. President Theodore Roosevelt, outraged at the rowdiness of the game, ordered schools to make play safer. Representatives of the major school teams met and devised rules designed to accomplish this. College football had begun its ascent to preeminence in collegiate sports competition.

The introduction of the forward pass in 1906, in a game between Wesleyan and Yale, marked a major change for football. It became more of a throwing than a kicking game, and it represented a sharp departure from English soccer and rugby. Football had become a distinctly American game. At about the same time, another great football tradition emerged: the bowl game. Major bowl games were scheduled to end the collegiate season and start the new year. Currently, 15 major bowl games are played annually, and another 22 major bowls have been discontinued.

College football has evolved over the years to become a game quite distinct from its professional partner. The halftime show, the atmosphere, the school spirit—all are as much a part of the college game as the contest itself. College football has become a means of drawing continued alumni financial support in an inexpensive and excellent training ground from which professional teams can replenish their ranks. In spite of some recent setbacks from scandals involving recruitment and other practices, college programs are getting stronger, players are getting better, and attendance is increasing. Collegiate football continues to score.

Great Moments

PROFESSIONAL

1915 Jim Thorpe signs with the Canton (Ohio) Bulldogs for $250 a game.

1925 On November 22, when the University of Illinois' season ends, Red Grange signs with the Chicago Bears.

1929 The Green Bay Packers win the first of what would become a string of NFL championships.

1932 December 18: the first playoff in NFL history takes place, in Chicago Stadium, with the Chicago Bears defeating the Portsmouth (Ohio) Spartans, 9–0.

1934 The NFL legalizes forward passes made from anywhere behind the line of scrimmage.

1946 The NFL grants Cleveland permission to transfer their franchise to Los Angeles, making them the first NFL team on the West Coast.

1947 Los Angeles halfback Fred Gehrke paints horns on the Rams' helmets, and the helmet emblem is introduced in pro football.

1951 The Pro Bowl game is revived under a new format, pitting all-stars of each conference against each other.

1958 December 28: Weeb Ewbank's Baltimore Colts defeat the New York Giants, 23–17, in the first sudden-death NFL championship game.

1964 On September 12, the New York Jets trounce Denver, 30–6, in the first football game played at Shea Stadium.

1967 August 5: an AFL team defeats an NFL team for the first time—Denver over Detroit, 13–7.

1971 An AFC divisional playoff game lasts 82 minutes and 40 seconds, making it the longest football game in history; Miami defeats Kansas City, 27–24, in sudden-death overtime on a field goal by Garo Yepremian.

1974 Seattle and Tampa Bay are granted an NFL franchise, expanding the league to 28 teams.

1977 December 4: Cincinnati wins the NFL's five-thousandth game, defeating Kansas City, 27–7.

COLLEGE

1869 Princeton and Rutgers play the earliest recognized intercollegiate football games, with Rutgers winning the first game, 6–4, and Princeton the second, 8–0.

1873 Yale and Princeton play the first game of what becomes the longest series in college football history.

1876 Yale claims the first championship of the newly formed American Intercollegiate Football Association by virtue of defeating three of its four member teams.

1882 A major change in the rules of the game is marked by the advent of "downs," or chances to advance the ball; a team that does not gain 5 yards, or that loses 10 yards in three downs, must relinquish possession.

1889 The first All-America selections are made by Yale's Walter Camp; the players selected are from Harvard, Yale, and Princeton.

1902 The first Rose Bowl game is played, with Michigan trouncing Stanford, 49–0; the rivalry is discontinued until 1916.

1906 A player from Wesleyan throws the first forward pass.

1912 A rule change stipulates four downs, instead of three, and a gain of 10 yards to receive a first down.

1914 The Yale Bowl opens and is recognized as the most outstanding stadium of its type in the world.

1935 The first Heisman Memorial Trophy, honoring the outstanding college football player of the year, is awarded to Jay Berwanger, a halfback from the University of Chicago.

1943 Notre Dame wins its first national championship.

1952 The first game played under the NCAA television plan is televised on September 20; Kansas defeats Texas Christian University, 13–10.

1958 The first scoring rule-change in almost half a century calls for a choice in conversions after touchdowns; a successful kick is worth one point, and a successful pass or run is worth two points.

1975 Running back Archie Griffin, of Ohio State, becomes the first college player to win the Heisman Trophy twice.

1980 Portland State quarterback Neil Lomax finishes the season having captured four major all-time, NCAA all-division records, including career total offensive yards and season total offensive yards.

The Setup

The National Football League (NFL) organizes professional football in the United States. The league is divided into two conferences: American Football Conference (AFC) and National Football Conference (NFC). Each conference has an Eastern, Central, and Western division. After the regular season, a series of playoff games is played in each conference until a conference winner is decided. The AFC winner and the NFC winner meet in the Super Bowl to determine the NFL championship.

AMERICAN FOOTBALL CONFERENCE

Eastern Division	Central Division	Western Division
Baltimore Colts	Cincinnati Bengals	Denver Broncos
Buffalo Bills	Cleveland Browns	Kansas City Chiefs
Miami Dolphins	Houston Oilers	Oakland Raiders
New England Patriots	Pittsburgh Steelers	San Diego Chargers
New York Jets		Seattle Seahawks

NATIONAL FOOTBALL CONFERENCE

Eastern Division	Central Division	Western Division
Dallas Cowboys	Chicago Bears	Atlanta Falcons
New York Giants	Detroit Lions	Los Angeles Rams
Philadelphia Eagles	Green Bay Packers	New Orleans Saints
St. Louis Cardinals	Minnesota Vikings	San Francisco 49ers
Washington Redskins	Tampa Bay Buccaneers	

NATIONAL FOOTBALL LEAGUE
410 Park Ave.
New York, NY 10022
(212) 758-1500
Pete Rozelle, commissioner
Lamar Hunt, pres., American Football Conf.
George Halas, pres., National Football Conf.

AMERICAN FOOTBALL CONFERENCE

BALTIMORE COLTS
P.O. Box 2000
Owings Mills, MD 21117
(301) 356-9600
Robert Irsay, pres.
(games played at Memorial Stadium)

BUFFALO BILLS
One Bills Dr.
Orchard Park, NY 14127
(716) 648-1800
Ralph C. Wilson, Jr., pres.
(games played at Rich Stadium)

CINCINNATI BENGALS
200 Riverfront Stadium
Cincinnati, OH 45202
(513) 621-3550
John Sawyer, pres.
(games played at Riverfront Stadium)

CLEVELAND BROWNS
Tower B
Cleveland Stadium
Cleveland, OH 44114
(216) 696-5555
Arthur B. Modell, pres.
(games played at Cleveland Stadium)

DENVER BRONCOS
5700 Logan St.
Denver, CO 80216
(303) 623-8778
Allan R. Phipps, pres.
(games played at Denver Mile High
 Stadium)

HOUSTON OILERS
Box 1516
Houston, TX 77001
(713) 797-9111
K. S. ("Bud") Adams, Jr., pres.
(games played at the Astrodome)

KANSAS CITY CHIEFS
One Arrowhead Dr.
Kansas City, MO 64129
(816) 924-9300
Lamar Hunt, owner
(games played at Arrowhead Stadium)

MIAMI DOLPHINS
330 Biscayne Blvd.
Miami, FL 33132
(305) 379-1851
Joseph Robbie, managing gen. partner
(games played at the Orange Bowl)

NEW ENGLAND PATRIOTS
Schaefer Stadium
Route 1
Foxboro, MA 02035
(617) 543-7911
William H. Sullivan, Jr., pres.
(games played at Schaefer Stadium)

NEW YORK JETS
598 Madison Ave.
New York, NY 10022
(212) 421-6600
Jim Kensil, pres.
(games played at Shea Stadium)

OAKLAND RAIDERS
7850 Edgewater Dr.
Oakland, CA 94621
(415) 562-5900
Al Davis, managing gen. partner
(games played at Oakland–Alameda
 County Coliseum)

PITTSBURGH STEELERS
300 Stadium Circle
Pittsburgh, PA 15212
(412) 323-1200
Arthur S. Rooney, Sr., chairman of board
(games played at Three Rivers Stadium)

SAN DIEGO CHARGERS
P.O. Box 20666
San Diego, CA 92120
(714) 280-2111
Eugene V. Klein, pres.
(games played at San Diego Stadium)

SEATTLE SEAHAWKS
5305 Lake Washington Blvd.
Kirkland, WA 98033
(206) 827-9777
Herman Sarkowsky, managing gen. partner
(games played at the Kingdome)

NATIONAL FOOTBALL CONFERENCE

ATLANTA FALCONS
Suwanee Rd. at I-85
Suwanee, GA 30174
(404) 588-1111
Rankin M. Smith, Sr., chairman of board
(games played at Atlanta–Fulton County
 Stadium)

CHICAGO BEARS
55 E. Jackson Blvd.
Chicago, IL 60604
(312) 663-5100
George S Halas, Sr., pres.
(games played at Soldier Field)

DALLAS COWBOYS
6116 N. Central Expwy.
Dallas, TX 75206
(214) 369-8000
Clint W. Murchison, Jr., pres.
(games played at Texas Stadium)

DETROIT LIONS
1200 Featherstone Rd.
Pontiac, MI 48057
(313) 335-4131
William Clay Ford, pres.
(games played at Pontiac Silverdome)

GREEN BAY PACKERS
1265 Lombardi Ave.
Green Bay, WI 54303
(414) 494-2351
Dominic Olejniczak, pres.
(games played at Lambeau Field or
  Milwaukee County Stadium)

LOS ANGELES RAMS
2327 W. Lincoln Ave.
Anaheim, CA 92801
(714) 535-7267
Georgia Rosenbloom, pres.
(games played at Anaheim Stadium)

MINNESOTA VIKINGS
7110 France Ave. S
Edina, MN 55435
(612) 920-4805
Max Winter, pres.
(games played at Metropolitan Stadium)

NEW ORLEANS SAINTS
1500 Poydras St.
New Orleans, LA 70112
(504) 587-3034
John W. Mecom, Jr., pres.
(games played at Louisiana Superdome)

NEW YORK GIANTS
Giants Stadium
East Rutherford, NJ 07073
(201) 935-8111
Wellington T. Mara, pres.
(games played at Giants Stadium)

PHILADELPHIA EAGLES
Philadelphia Veterans Stadium
Broad and Pattison Sts.
Philadelphia, PA 19148
(215) 463-2500
Leonard H. Tose, pres.
(games played at Philadelphia Veterans
  Stadium)

ST. LOUIS CARDINALS
200 Stadium Pl.
St. Louis, MO 63102
(314) 421-0777
William V. Bidwell, pres.
(games played at Busch Memorial Stadium)

SAN FRANCISCO 49ers
711 Nevada St.
Redwood City, CA 94061
(415) 365-3420
Edward J. DeBartolo, Jr., pres.
(games played at Candlestick Park)

TAMPA BAY BUCCANEERS
One Buccaneer Pl.
Tampa, FL 33607
(813) 870-2700
Hugh F. Culverhouse, pres.
(games played at Tampa Stadium)

WASHINGTON REDSKINS
P.O. Box 17247
Dulles International Airport
Washington, DC 20041
(703) 471-9100
Jack Kent Cooke, chairman of board
(games played at Robert F. Kennedy
  Stadium)

COLLEGE

The National Collegiate Athletic Conference (NCAA) began classifying college football into divisions I, II, and III in 1973. Five years later, Division I was further divided into Division I-A and Division I-AA, with major college teams constituting Division I-A. Most colleges also are members of athletic conferences, and some remain independent. Interconference games are played, however; often, seasons pass before two teams in the same conference meet. In spite of that fact, conference champions are declared at the end of every season. Those champions, along with successful independents, usually are invited to compete in bowl games at the end of the regular season. The following selected Division I schools are members of major athletic conferences or are leading independent schools:

ATLANTIC COAST

Clemson Tigers
Duke Blue Devils
Maryland Terps
North Carolina Tar Heels
North Carolina State Wolfpack
Virginia Cavaliers
Wake Forest Demon Deacons

SOUTHWEST

Arkansas Razorbacks
Baylor Bears
Houston Cougars
Rice Owls
Southern Methodist Mustangs
Texas Longhorns
Texas A&M Aggies
Texas Christian Horned Frogs
Texas Tech Red Raiders

ABC Sports

BIG EIGHT

Colorado Buffaloes
Iowa State Cyclones
Kansas Jayhawks
Kansas State Wildcats
Missouri Tigers
Nebraska Cornhuskers
Oklahoma Sooners
Oklahoma State Cowboys

IVY LEAGUE

Brown Bruins, Bears
Columbia Lions
Cornell Big Red
Dartmouth Big Green
Harvard Crimson
Pennsylvania Quakers
Princeton Tigers
Yale Bulldogs, Elis

BIG TEN

Illinois Fighting Illini
Indiana Fightin' Hoosiers
Iowa Hawkeyes
Michigan Wolverines
Michigan State Spartans
Minnesota Gophers
Northwestern Wildcats
Ohio State Buckeyes
Purdue Boilermakers
Wisconsin Badgers

SOUTHEASTERN

Alabama Crimson Tide
Auburn Tigers
Florida Gators
Georgia Bulldogs
Kentucky Wildcats
Louisiana State Fighting Tigers
Mississippi Rebels
Mississippi State Bulldogs
Tennessee Volunteers
Vanderbilt Commodores

PACIFIC TEN	*MAJOR INDEPENDENTS*
Arizona Wildcats	Army Cadets
Arizona State Sun Devils	Florida State Seminoles
California Golden Bears	Georgia Tech Yellow Jackets
Oregon Ducks	Navy Midshipmen
Oregon State Beavers	Notre Dame Fighting Irish
Southern Cal. Trojans	Penn State Nittany Lions
Stanford Cardinals	Pittsburgh Panthers
UCLA Bruins	Rutgers Scarlet Knights
Washington Huskies	South Carolina Fighting Gamecocks
Washington State Cougars	Syracuse Orangemen
	Temple Owls
	Tulane Green Wave

The Basics

Object of the game   To score the most points by carrying or successfully passing the ball over the opponent's goal line or kicking the ball through the opponent's goal posts.

The playing field   The field (shown in the diagram) is 120 yards long and 53⅓ yards wide, including two end zones, each 10 yards deep. Goal posts—18½ feet wide, with a crossbar at least 10 feet off the ground and vertical posts extending at least 30 feet above the crossbar—stand at either end of the field.

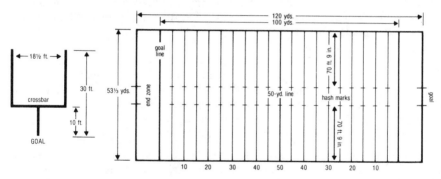

Equipment   An inflated oval-shaped leather football is used. Players wear helmets, shoulder pads, and other protective gear, along with the team uniform.

Players   Each team is permitted 11 men on the field at the snap, with unlimited substitution permitted when the ball is dead. (In college football, a player may enter the game only twice per quarter.) A team comprises a center, two tackles, two guards, a quarterback, two ends, two halfbacks, and a fullback.

Officials   The game has seven officials: a referee, umpire, head linesman, line judge, back judge, side judge, and field judge. (College football is overseen by a referee, umpire, field judge, linesman, and an electric-clock operator.)

Scoring   A touchdown, worth six points, is scored when the ball passes over the opponent's goal line in the hands of an offensive player or when it is caught by a receiver behind the goal line. A field goal, kicked from the line of scrimmage, is

worth three points to the kicking team. A conversion—either a run, a kick, or a pass—after a touchdown is worth one point (in college football, two points for a run or pass), and a safety is worth two points.

Timing   A game is divided into four 15-minute periods, with 2-minute intermissions between periods and 15 minutes at halftime. If the score is tied at the end of four periods of regulation play, sudden-death overtime begins, and the first team to score wins the game.

Rule 1   The kickoff   The kickoff is made from the kicking team's 35-yard line (the 40-yard line in college football) at the start of each half, after a field goal, or after a point-after-touchdown. To be legal a kickoff must travel at least 10 yards or be touched by a member of the receiving team.

Rule 2   The snap   At the snap, the offensive team must have at least seven players on the line, with those offensive players not on the line at least one yard back. No interior lineman may move after taking or simulating a three-point stance.

Rule 3   Possession   A team retains possession of the ball until it fails to advance 10 yards, until it scores, or until it fumbles a ball that is recovered by the opposing team.

Rule 4   Advancing on the field   A team in possession of the ball has four chances, or downs, to advance 10 yards. Failure to do so forces the offensive team to relinquish possession.

Rule 5   Passing   The passer must be behind his own line of scrimmage. A forward pass may be touched or caught by eligible receivers on the offensive team or by any members of the defensive team.

Rule 6   Pass blocking   A player's hands must be inside the blocker's elbows and may be thrust against an opponent below the neck, in a legal block.

Rule 7   ***Pass completion***   A pass touched by one offensive player but caught by another eligible offensive player is legal. A forward pass is complete when a receiver touches the ground with both feet in bounds while in possession of the ball (in college football, only one foot must be in bounds).

Rule 8   ***Pass interference***   Interference with a forward pass thrown from behind the line is illegal. The penalty for defensive pass interference is an automatic first down at the spot where the foul occurred.

Rule 9   ***Contact***   No offensive player may assist a runner except by blocking for him. Interlocking interference is illegal. Only a ball carrier may ward off opponents with his hands or arms.

Rule 10   ***Fumble***   A fumble may be advanced by any player on either team regardless of whether recovered before or after the ball hits the ground.

Rule 11   ***Measuring***   Measurements are made from the forward point of the ball.

Rule 12   ***Penalties***   An automatic first down is awarded to the offensive team for all defensive fouls except offside, delay of game, encroachment, illegal substitution, and excessive time-outs. Some other penalties are: 15 yards for clipping or for pulling an opponent by the face mask; 10 yards for holding; and 5 yards for being offside.

How to watch

Pittsburgh Steelers

with Lynn Swann

Lynn Swann, gifted wide receiver for the Pittsburgh Steelers, manages to gain a particularly broad perspective on the game both as a receiver downfield and as a commentator for ABC Sports. Football is a complex game, and therefore difficult for the uninitiated to follow. Swann suggests that the viewer try to take in as much of the action as possible; but beginners might first focus on the ball, and later try to analyze the offensive and defensive formations. Although different teams will try different plays, depending on their own strengths and weaknesses, those of their opponents, as well as other factors, fans can usually expect certain plays in certain situations. Swann outlines what the viewer can expect to see in the following general situations:

First down-and-10: Early in the game, the first series of plays will attempt to exploit the weaknesses of the opponent as determined by studying films and reviewing statistics. The most popular offensive strategy is to establish the running game early; first down is usually a running down in spite of recent rule changes that encourage more passing. Fewer mistakes are made running, the offense has better control of the ball, and running plays keep the clock moving. A running play also tests the opponent's defensive line. A gain of four yards or more is considered a successful play.

Second down: The play for second down depends, of course, on how many yards were gained on the first play. Given that the first play was successful, and that at least four yards were gained, there are a number of possibilities for second-and-6. The offense could run a sweep to test the outside speed of its opponent. The quarterback might try a swing pass (a short pass to a back running to the outside) or a play-action pass (faking a hand-off to a back and then throwing the ball). San Diego, effective in giving the ball to the running back through the air, often uses a short pass to a back instead of a hand-off. Faking the run could give the offensive back on a swing pass anywhere from 5 to 10 yards before making contact with a defender.

Third down and short yardage: A team without a big, strong defensive line will go for position and use their speed to try to cut off the outside quickly. A team with strong blockers will get the ball off quickly and power its way up the middle for the few yards needed for the first down. Houston and Oakland are two straight blocking teams that generally are successful with this ploy.

Third-and-long: An obvious passing situation. The defense is expecting the pass, and will gear its strategy accordingly. With the element of surprise removed, in this situation, skill, technique, and execution are necessary to carry it off.

Fourth-and-short: This situation is often critical. If a team is down, time is running out, and they don't expect to get the ball again soon, they will usually go for it. If they are deep in the opponent's territory and have to score to win, they will also go for it, figuring that if they don't make it, they aren't giving their opponent good field position even if they have to give up the ball. If there is so little time left in the ball game that a field goal would get them close but wouldn't help much, then a team will probably go for it. They might try a field goal, and then an onsides kick, to maintain possession; but the chances of success aren't very good. If it is early in the game, most teams will go for the field goal—provided they are in range.

Swann also discussed some outstanding quarterbacks, their different styles, and why they are successful with their respective teams. "Bob Griese was perfect for a team like the Miami Dolphins," says Swann, "because he was so smart, because he had the talent for passing—short or deep—and because he had an excellent touch. Even his short pass was easy to catch." Swann describes Griese, who retired from football after the 1980–81 season, as a leader and a tactician. "He would give the ball to [Larry] Csonka at the right time and pound away at the middle. Then he would use [Nat] Moore and [Paul] Warfield for the big passing plays, using their ability and experience to outmaneuver the defensive secondary."

Roger Staubach is another example of a quarterback who worked well with his coach and his team. Cool under pressure, Staubach would "scramble, and yet still look downfield for an open receiver." Although coach Tom Landry calls the plays for Dallas, Staubach was talented enough to call an audible when necessary and call the right play. He always managed to come up with the big play when the pressure was on, the deep passes that made for the comeback ball game so often identified with Dallas and Staubach." The "shotgun" formation was used often by Landry and his quarterback in obvious passing situations. Since the defense sensed that he was going to pass, Staubach eliminated any possible surprise by going into shotgun, using the extra few seconds to read the secondary and, often, to outmaneuver it.

San Diego's Dan Fouts is a quarterback whose style is ideal for the revised rules, which encourage greater use of the play that is probably the fans' favorite—the pass. "Dan's style works well because he's got the quick release and a good touch," Swann observes. He points out that the Chargers do not use the deep pass all that often; they simply pass steadily and "pick away at you." Although San Diego's opponents expect the pass, Fouts's quick release and ability to pop the ball off immediately take some of the pressure off his offensive line. Fouts is also a quick reader: "He makes the decision very quickly whether to go to a wide receiver downfield or dump it off to a running back."

Like offensive strategies and quarterback styles, a team's defense is based on the particular talents of its personnel. Swann analyzed the defense of the team he knows best—Pittsburgh. "We have excellent personnel across the board, with solid people in every position." One of the reasons the Steelers' defense is so successful is, as Swann put it, "You can't put a guy one-on-one against Joe Greene. Defensive ends L. C. Greenwood and Dwight White would certainly force the issue." Many teams approach the "problem" of Joe Greene by double-teaming him and his talented cohorts. "Even if our guys don't make the tackle, they are occupying two men, and that can give Jack Lambert room to run around and make all the tackles."

Teams that don't have this kind of defensive personnel will adapt a strategy to fit their abilities. Swann used the example of the Atlanta Falcons in the years before they made it into the playoffs. "They had a few All-Pros, but their linebacking corps wasn't solid, and their secondary was only fair." The strategy that worked for them was the blitz. They used it as often, and in as many different ways as possible, to confuse the blockers." This strategy forced their opponents to go to the deep pass; and since the quarterback often did not have enough time, the Falcons were able to make the sack.

Some of the factors that affect the game are outside the control of the coach and the players. Weather, for one. It's a factor in many regular season games, although the Super Bowl is always played in a warm climate or indoors. On a cold, clear day, Swann says, the viewer can expect to see some passing, but more play will be on the ground. Quarterbacks try to avoid putting the ball in the air when it's raining or snowing; receivers can't see it well, and fumbles are more likely when the ball is wet. AstroTurf, or any other synthetic surface, makes for a faster game because players can get better traction; more injuries are likely with artificial surfaces, though.

Because football is possibly the "consummate team sport," it is important for the viewer to watch as much of the action as he or she can take in. By focusing too much on, say, the offense, or the defense, or the ball, the viewer will be fooled by the fake, won't notice the penalty, or will miss the open receiver downfield. And sometimes these tactics—or just one of them—can mean the ball game.

Main Events

NATIONAL FOOTBALL LEAGUE

Super Bowl XV
Jan. 25, 1981   Oakland (AFC) 27, Philadelphia (NFC) 10   at New Orleans

Super Bowl XIV
Jan. 20, 1980   Pittsburgh (AFC) 31, Los Angeles (NFC) 19   at Pasadena

Super Bowl XIII
Jan. 21, 1979   Pittsburgh (AFC) 35, Dallas (NFC) 31   at Miami

Super Bowl XII
Jan. 15, 1978   Dallas (NFC) 27, Denver (AFC) 10   at New Orleans

Super Bowl XI
Jan. 9, 1977   Oakland (AFC) 32, Minnesota (NFC) 14   at Pasadena

Super Bowl X
Jan. 18, 1976   Pittsburgh (AFC) 21, Dallas (NFC) 17   at Miami

Super Bowl IX
Jan. 12, 1975   Pittsburgh (AFC) 16, Minnesota (NFC) 6   at New Orleans

Super Bowl VIII
Jan. 13, 1974   Miami (AFC) 24, Minnesota (NFC) 7   at Houston

Super Bowl VII
Jan. 14, 1973   Miami (AFC) 14, Washington (NFC) 7   at Los Angeles

Super Bowl VI
Jan. 16, 1972   Dallas (NFC) 24, Miami (AFC) 3   at New Orleans

Super Bowl V
Jan. 17, 1971   Baltimore (AFC) 16, Dallas (NFC) 13   at Miami

Super Bowl IV
Jan. 11, 1970   Kansas City (AFL) 23, Minnesota (NFL) 7   at New Orleans

Super Bowl III
Jan. 12, 1969   New York (AFL) 16, Baltimore (NFL) 7   at Miami

Super Bowl II
Jan. 14, 1968   Green Bay (NFL) 33, Oakland (AFL) 14   at Miami

Super Bowl I
Jan. 15, 1967   Green Bay (NFL) 35, Kansas City (AFL) 10   at Los Angeles

MAJOR COLLEGE BOWL GAMES

ROSE BOWL (PASADENA)

Jan. 1, 1981	Michigan 23, Washington 6
Jan. 1, 1980	Southern Cal 17, Ohio State 16
Jan. 1, 1979	Southern Cal 17, Michigan 10
Jan. 2, 1978	Washington 27, Michigan 20
Jan. 1, 1977	Southern Cal 14, Michigan 6
Jan. 1, 1976	UCLA 23, Ohio State 10
Jan. 1, 1975	Southern Cal 18, Ohio State 17
Jan. 1, 1974	Ohio State 42, Southern Cal 21
Jan. 1, 1973	Southern Cal 42, Ohio State 17
Jan. 1, 1972	Stanford 13, Michigan 12
Jan. 1, 1971	Stanford 27, Ohio State 17

ORANGE BOWL (MIAMI)

Jan. 1, 1981	Oklahoma 18, Florida State 17
Jan. 1, 1980	Oklahoma 24, Florida State 7
Jan. 1, 1979	Oklahoma 31, Nebraska 24
Jan. 2, 1978	Arkansas 31, Oklahoma 6
Jan. 1, 1977	Ohio State 27, Colorado 10

Jan. 1, 1976	Oklahoma 14, Michigan 6
Jan. 1, 1975	Notre Dame 13, Alabama 11
Jan. 1, 1974	Penn State 16, LSU 9
Jan. 1, 1973	Nebraska 40, Notre Dame 6
Jan. 1, 1972	Nebraska 38, Alabama 6
Jan. 1, 1971	Nebraska 17, LSU 12

COTTON BOWL (DALLAS)

Jan. 1, 1981	Alabama 30, Baylor 2
Jan. 1, 1980	Houston 17, Nebraska 14
Jan. 1, 1979	Notre Dame 35, Houston 34
Jan. 2, 1978	Notre Dame 38, Texas 10
Jan. 1, 1977	Houston 30, Maryland 21
Jan. 1, 1976	Arkansas 31, Georgia 10
Jan. 1, 1975	Penn State 41, Baylor 20
Jan. 1, 1974	Nebraska 19, Texas 3
Jan. 1, 1973	Texas 17, Alabama 13
Jan. 1, 1972	Penn State 30, Texas 6
Jan. 1, 1971	Notre Dame 24, Texas 11

SUGAR BOWL (NEW ORLEANS)

Jan. 1, 1981	Georgia 17, Notre Dame 10
Jan. 1, 1980	Alabama 24, Arkansas 9
Jan. 1, 1979	Alabama 14, Penn State 7
Jan. 2, 1978	Alabama 35, Ohio State 6
Jan. 1, 1977	Pittsburgh 27, Georgia 3
Dec.31,1975	Alabama 13, Penn State 6
Dec.31,1974	Nebraska 13, Florida 10
Dec.31,1973	Notre Dame 24, Alabama 23
Dec.31,1972	Oklahoma 14, Penn State 0
Jan. 1, 1972	Oklahoma 40, Auburn 22
Jan. 1, 1971	Tennessee 34, Air Force 13

NATIONAL CHAMPIONS

(Based on an Associated Press poll of sportwriters and United Press International's poll of coaches.)

Year	AP	UPI
1980	Georgia	Georgia
1979	Alabama	Alabama
1978	Alabama	Southern Cal
1977	Notre Dame	Notre Dame
1976	Pittsburgh	Pittsburgh
1975	Oklahoma	Oklahoma
1974	Oklahoma	Southern Cal
1973	Notre Dame	Alabama
1972	Southern Cal	Southern Cal
1971	Nebraska	Nebraska
1970	Nebraska	Texas

HEISMAN MEMORIAL TROPHY

(Honoring the outstanding college football player in the United States; chosen by members of the sports media and presented by the Downtown Athletic Club of New York.)

Year	Name	School	Position
1980	George Rogers	South Carolina	HB
1979	Charles White	Southern Cal	HB
1978	Billy Sims*	Oklahoma	HB
1977	Earl Campbell	Texas	HB
1976	Tony Dorsett	Pittsburgh	HB
1975	Archie Griffin	Ohio State	HB
1974	Archie Griffin*	Ohio State	HB
1973	John Cappelletti	Penn State	HB
1972	Johnny Rodgers	Nebraska	FL
1971	Pat Sullivan	Auburn	QB
1970	Jim Plunkett	Stanford	QB

*Junior.

All-Time Greats

Sammy Baugh
(Mar. 17, 1914–)

Sammy Baugh, the best passer of his era, was a quarterback for the Washington Redskins from 1937 to 1952. He holds the record for most seasons leading the league in passing (six); he has the highest career average for punting, with 45.1 yards; and he shares the record for most interceptions in a game (four). At Texas Christian University, Baugh perfected the fast release and practiced long and hard the forward pass, developing it into an offensive weapon of great accuracy. He used the pass as a standard tactic rather than for surprise or in desperation.

Jim Brown
(Feb. 17, 1936–)

Brown, who began his career with the Cleveland Browns as Rookie of the Year in 1957, lived up to that achievement in the rest of his career. He holds numerous NFL records, including career records for most touchdowns scored (126), most combined net yards gained (15,459), and most yards gained rushing (12,312). He also led the league in rushing for eight seasons—another record. Upon retiring from football, Brown became an actor.

George ("Papa Bear") Halas
(Feb. 2, 1895–)

Halas epitomizes the all-round sports hero. A pioneer of professional football, "Papa Bear" stuck with the sport even when its future seemed doubtful; he was involved as player, manager, coach, and owner of the Chicago franchise known successively as the Decatur Staleys, Chicago Staleys, and Chicago Bears. Halas took up baseball and played for the New York Yankees. After an injury in 1919, he returned to football. He holds the record for most seasons as a coach (40) and is second with the longest fumble run for a touchdown—98 yards against the Oorang Indians in 1923. Today, Halas serves as president of the National Football Conference.

Elroy ("Crazylegs") Hirsch
(June 17, 1923–)

From 1946 to 1948, Hirsch played halfback and end for the Chicago Rockets, of the All-American Football Conference, and for the Los Angeles Rams from 1949 to 1957. Along with two other players, he shares the record for most touchdown passes caught in a season, 17, as well as sharing the record for catching touchdown passes in nine consecutive games, spanning the 1950 and 1951 seasons.

Don Hutson
(Jan. 31, 1913–)

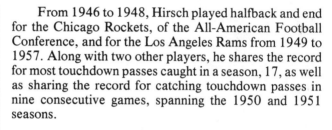

Hutson, an end whose career with the Green Bay Packers spanned the years 1935 to 1945, holds career records for most touchdown passes caught (99), most seasons leading the league in touchdown receptions (9), and most seasons leading the league in pass receiving (8). He also led the league in scoring for five years, a record he shares with several other players.

Dick ("Night Train") Lane
(Apr. 16, 1928–)

A defensive halfback for the Los Angeles Rams, Chicago Cardinals, and Detroit Lions, from 1952 to 1965, "Night Train" Lane was an aggressive player who, while possessing the abilities needed to be a good offensive player, preferred the freedom of defensive play, with its extensive body contact and use of the hands and arms. Lane set a season record for most interceptions caught (14), and he shares the record for most seasons leading the league in interceptions (2).

Gale Sayers
(May 30, 1943–)

Pro Football Hall of Fame

A running back for the Chicago Bears from 1965 to 1971, Sayers was a versatile runner and receiver, as well as a record-holding specialist in kick returns. Known as a modest man (his motto: "God is first, friends are second, I am third"), Sayers holds the record for most points scored by a rookie (132) and most touchdowns by a rookie (22); he shares the record for most touchdowns in a game (6, against San Francisco, on December 12, 1965).

O. J. Simpson
(July 9, 1947–)

Robert L. Smith

O. J. Simpson, a star running back out of USC, brought a certain style and grace to the game of football. Despite playing his entire professional career with losing teams (Buffalo and San Francisco), he led the AFC in rushing four times, accumulating numerous records along the way. During his 1973 season with Buffalo, Simpson set a record for most yards gained (2,003) and, in the 1975 season, most touchdowns (23). Upon retiring, he began a career in acting.

Fran Tarkenton
(Feb. 3, 1940–)

ABC Sports

Fran Tarkenton set numerous passing records in his 11 seasons with the NFL. A minister's son, Tarkenton played college ball at the University of Georgia. He joined the Minnesota Vikings as quarterback in 1961, but left the team in 1967 to play for the New York Giants. Tarkenton returned to Minnesota in 1972, and remained there until his retirement, in 1978. A versatile quarterback who could scramble when yardage was needed, Tarkenton holds the record for most touchdown passes in a career, with 342, as well as career records for most pass attempts (6,467) and most pass completions (3,686). Although he led Minnesota to three Super Bowls, Tarkenton was never able to beat his AFC opponents. He is now a commentator for ABC's *Monday Night Football.*

Jim Thorpe
(May 28, 1888–Mar. 28, 1953)

Pro Football Hall of Fame

Jim Thorpe, football's first legend even though he never played with one team for two full seasons, possessed great speed and strength, two characteristics that were amply demonstrated in his running and tackling. Part Indian, Thorpe first played football for Pop Warner at the Carlisle Indian School. At the 1912 Olympics, he earned gold medals in the decathlon and the pentathlon—an unprecedented feat that remains unmatched today. Thorpe was later stripped of the medals when he admitted to having played semipro baseball one summer before the Olympic games. In 1920, the man called "the world's greatest athlete" was elected the first president of the National Football League.

Emlen Tunnell
(Mar. 29, 1925–July 23, 1975)

According to the legend, Tunnell hitchhiked to his professional tryout. He played safety for 12 years, first with the New York Giants (1948–58) and then with the Green Bay Packers (1959–61). He holds the career record for most yards gained through interceptions (1,282). A player who could have succeeded equally as well as a ball carrier or a receiver, Tunnell had 79 pass interceptions, a record that is second only to Paul Krause's 81 interceptions.

Johnny Unitas
(May 7, 1933–)

In a brilliant career spanning the years 1956 to 1972, Johnny Unitas set numerous records, including most consecutive games with touchdown passes (47). He played semiprofessional ball with the Bloomfield Rams, was cut by Pittsburgh, then was picked up by Baltimore almost by accident. Unitas spent most of his career as a quarterback for the Baltimore Colts, playing only his last season, 1973, with the San Diego Chargers. He stands just behind Fran Tarkenton in career records for most touchdown passes, most yards gained passing, and most passes attempted. Named Player of the Year three times, Unitas led the Colts to two titles, in 1958 and 1959.

Photos courtesy Pro Football Hall of Fame

Pro Football Hall of Fame
2121 Harrison Ave. NW
Canton, OH 44708
(216) 456-8207
Joe Horrigan, curator-historian

The members of the Pro Football Hall of Fame are:

1963
Sammy Baugh
Bert Bell*
Joe Carr*
Earl ("Dutch") Clark
Red Grange
George Halas
Mel Hein
Wilbur ("Pete") Henry
Cal Hubbard
Don Hutson
Earl ("Curly") Lambeau
Tim Mara*
George Preston Marshall*
Johnny ("Blood") McNally
Bronko Nagurski

Ernie Nevers
Jim Thorpe

1964
Jimmy Conzelman
Ed Healey
Clarke Hinkle
Roy ("Link") Lyman
Mike Michalske
Art Rooney*
George Trafton

1965
Guy Chamberlain
John ("Paddy") Driscoll
Dan Fortmann

Otto Graham
Sid Luckman
Steve Van Buren
Bob Waterfield

1966
Bill Dudley
Joe Guyon
Arnie Herber
Walt Kiesling
George McAfee
Steve Owen
Hugh ("Shorty") Ray
Clyde ("Bulldog") Turner

1967
Chuck Bednarik

Paul Brown*
Bobby Layne
Dan Reeves*
Ken Strong
Joe Stydahar
Emlen Tunnell

1968
Cliff Battles
Art Donovan
Elroy ("Crazylegs") Hirsch
Wayne Millner
Marion Motley
Charley Trippi
Alex Wojciechowicz

1969
Glen ("Turk") Edwards
Earle ("Greasy") Neale
Leo Nomellini
Joe Perry
Ernie Stautner

1970
Jack Christiansen
Tom Fears
Hugh McElhenny
Pete Pihos

1971
Jim Brown
Bill Hewitt
Frank ("Bruiser") Kinard

Vince Lombardi*
Andy Robustelli
Y. A. Tittle
Norm Van Brocklin

1972
Lamar Hunt*
Gino Marchetti
Ollie Matson
Clarence ("Ace") Parker

1973
Raymond Berry
Jim Parker
Joe Schmidt

1974
Tony Canadeo
Bill George
Lou Groza
Dick ("Night Train") Lane

1975
Roosevelt Brown
George Connor
Dante Lavelli
Lenny Moore

1976
Ray Flaherty*
Len Ford
Jim Taylor

1977
Frank Gifford
Forrest Gregg
Gale Sayers
Bart Starr
Bill Wills

1978
Lance Alworth
Weeb Ewbank*
Alphonse ("Tuffy") Leemans
Ray Nitschke
Larry Wilson

1979
Dick Butkus
Yale Lary
Ron Mix
Johnny Unitas

1980
Herb Adderley
David ("Deacon") Jones
Bob Lilly
Jim Otto

1981
Red Badgro
George Blanda
Willie Davis
Jim Ringo

*Nonplayer.

For the Record

PROFESSIONAL

Most points, game
40   Ernie Nevers   Chicago Cardinals vs Chicago Bears   Nov. 28, 1929

Most consecutive games scoring
151   Fred Cox   Minnesota   1963–73

Most touchdowns, career
126   Jim Brown   Cleveland   1957–65

Most touchdowns, season
23   O. J. Simpson   Buffalo   1975

Most touchdowns, game
6   Ernie Nevers   Chicago Cardinals vs Chicago Bears   Nov. 28, 1929
    Dub Jones   Cleveland vs Chicago Bears   Nov. 25, 1951
    Gale Sayers   Chicago vs San Francisco   Dec. 12, 1965

Most consecutive games scoring touchdowns
18   Lenny Moore   Baltimore   1963–65

Most field goals, game
7   Jim Bakken   St. Louis vs Pittsburgh   Sept. 24, 1967

Most yards gained, season
2,003   O. J. Simpson   Buffalo   1973

Most yards gained, game
275   Walter Payton   Chicago vs Minnesota   Nov. 20, 1977

Longest run from scrimmage (TD)
97 yds   Andy Uram   Green Bay vs Chicago Cardinals   Oct. 8, 1939
         Bob Gage   Pittsburgh vs Chicago Bears   Dec. 4, 1949

Most passes completed, career
3,686   Fran Tarkenton   Minnesota and N.Y. Giants   1961–78

Most passes completed, game
37   George Blanda   Houston vs Buffalo   Nov. 1, 1964

Most consecutive passes completed
17   Bert Jones   Baltimore vs N.Y. Jets   Dec. 15, 1974

Longest pass completion (TD)
99 yds   Frank Filchock
         (to Andrew Farkas)   Washington vs Pittsburgh   Oct. 15, 1939

         George Izo
         (to Robert Mitchell)   Washington vs Cleveland   Sept. 15, 1963

         Karl Sweetan
         (to Patrick Studstill)   Detroit vs Baltimore   Oct. 16, 1966

         Sonny Jurgenson
         (to Gerald Allen)   Washington vs Chicago   Sept. 15, 1968

Most pass receptions, game
18   Tom Fears   Los Angeles vs Green Bay   Dec. 3, 1950

Longest field goal
63 yds   Tom Dempsey   New Orleans vs Detroit   Nov. 8, 1970

Longest punt
98 yds   Steve O'Neal   N.Y. Jets vs Denver   Sept. 21, 1969

Most fumbles, game
7   Len Dawson   Kansas City vs San Diego   Nov. 15, 1964

COLLEGE, NCAA DIVISION 1-A

Most yards gained (total offense), game
599   Virgil Carter   Brigham Young vs Texas–El Paso   Nov. 5, 1966

Most yards gained (total offense), season
3,580   Marc Wilson   Brigham Young   1979

Most touchdowns (TDs scored and passed for), game
9   Dennis Shaw   San Diego State vs New Mexico State   Nov. 15, 1969

Most touchdowns (TDs scored and passed for), career
79   Rick Leach   Michigan   1975–78 (4 yrs)
73   Danny White   Arizona State   1971–73 (3 yrs)

Most points (scored and passed for), game
56   Jerry Rhome   Tulsa vs Louisville   Oct. 17, 1964

Most points (scored and passed for), career
474   Rick Leach   Michigan   1975–78

Most yards gained rushing, game
356   Eddie Lee Ivery   Georgia Tech vs Air Force   Nov. 11, 1978

Most yards gained rushing, career
6,082   Tony Dorsett   Pittsburgh   1973–76

Most touchdown passes, game
9   Dennis Shaw   San Diego State vs New Mexico State   Nov. 15, 1969

Most touchdown passes, career
69   Steve Ramsey   North Texas State   1967–69

Most pass receptions, game
22   Jay Miller   Brigham Young vs New Mexico   Nov. 3, 1973

Most pass receptions, career
261   Howard Twilley   Tulsa   1963–65

Most consecutive games catching a pass
42   John Filliez   Marshall   1973–76
     John Jefferson   Arizona State   1974–77

Most points scored, game
43   Jim Brown   Syracuse vs Colgate   Nov. 17, 1956

Most points scored, season
174   Lydell Mitchell   Penn State   1971

Most points scored, career
356   Tony Dorsett   Pittsburgh   1973–76

Most touchdowns scored, game
7   Arnold Boykin   Mississippi vs Mississippi State   Dec. 1, 1951

Most touchdowns scored, career
59   Tony Dorsett   Pittsburgh   1973–76
     Glenn Davis   Army   1943–46

Most field goals made, career
56   Tony Franklin   Texas A&M   1975–78

Longest field goal made
67 yds   Joe Williams   Wichita State vs Southern Illinois   Oct. 21, 1978
             Steve Little   Arkansas vs Texas   Oct. 15, 1977
             Russell Erxleben   Texas vs Rice   Oct. 1, 1977

Did you know ?

1. Who was the first person openly paid to play football?

2. Who bought the New York City NFL franchise in 1925, and how much did it cost?

3. Name the first city to have its baseball team win the World Series and its football team win the NFL Championship in the same year.

4. Who is the only athlete enshrined in both the Baseball Hall of Fame and the Pro Football Hall of Fame?

5. Who is the first known individual club owner? What was the name of his team?

6. What was the first pro team to use an out-of-town training camp? When? Where was the camp?

7. Name the two teams that played in the first AFL championship. Who was the winner, and what was the score?

8. What is the oldest continuing team in professional football?

9. For three months, ending March 3, 1950, the National Football League went by another name. What was it?

10. In 1946, Commissioner Bell moved the league headquarters from Chicago to a Philadelphia suburb, now the headquarters of the Major Indoor Soccer League. What is the name of the suburb?

11. How did the Green Bay Packers get their name?

12. Name the only team sponsored by a dog kennel; the only team to give its profits to charity. *Hint:* both teams were from Ohio.

13. What coach, and what team, were the only ones to beat Vince Lombardi and the Green Bay Packers in a playoff game?

14. What Heisman Trophy winners are also enshrined in the Pro Football Hall of Fame?

15. Only one player on a losing Super Bowl team has been named Most Valuable Player. Who was he, and what was his team?

16. What sportswriter made Notre Dame's 1924 backfield legendary by dubbing them the "Four Horsemen"?

17. What two football players were the only ones to win the annual Sullivan Award for the best amateur athlete in the United States?

18. Only two Big Ten teams have played in the Rose Bowl and not won. Who were they?

19. Who won the first Outland Trophy, awarded to the best interior lineman of the season?

20. Who was the leading rusher and scorer in the NCAA's first year of gathering statistics, and what is his current occupation?

Answers: 1. Former Yale star William ("Pudge") Heffelfinger was paid $500 by the Allegheny Athletic Association, on November 12, 1892, making him the first known professional football player; **2.** Tim Mara and Billy Gibson, $500; **3.** Detroit, 1935; **4.** Cal Hubbard; **5.** William Temple bought the Duquesne Country and Athletic Club's Pittsburgh Duquesnes in 1898; **6.** In August 1929, the Chicago Cardinals set up their training camp in Coldwater, Michigan; **7.** The Houston Oilers defeated the Los Angeles Chargers, 24–16, at Houston in 1961; **8.** The Morgan Athletic Club, founded in 1898 on Chicago's South Side, became, successively, the Chicago Normals, Racine Cardinals, Chicago Cardinals, and St. Louis Cardinals; **9.** National-American Football League; **10.** Bala Cynwyd; **11.** When they were organized in 1919, the Indian Packing Company provided the equipment and the nickname (in 1921, T. E. Clair, of the Acme Packing Company, was granted the franchise); **12.** The Oorang Indians, of Marion, Ohio, were sponsored by the Oorang Dog Kennels, and the Frankford Yellow Jackets, of Philadelphia, Ohio, gave their profits to charity; **13.** Coach Buck Shaw and the Philadelphia Eagles beat the Packers, 17–13, in 1960, leading the Eagles to the NFL title; **14.** None; **15.** Chuck Howley of the Dallas Cowboys (Super Bowl V, Baltimore 16, Dallas 14); **16.** Grantland Rice; **17.** Doc Blanchard, Army, in 1945, and Arnold Tucker, Army, in 1946; **18.** Indiana and Wisconsin; **19.** George Connor, a tackle from Notre Dame, won the first Outland Trophy, in 1946; **20.** Byron ("Whizzer") White, of Colorado, is a justice on the U.S. Supreme Court.

Key Words

blitz   when one or more defensive backs assist the linemen in rushing the passer, either tackling him or forcing him to throw hastily.

chucking   warding off an opponent who is in front of a defender by making contact with him by quickly extending the arms, followed by return of the arms to a flexed position. Chucking is illegal when it occurs more than five yards beyond the line of scrimmage.

clipping   an illegal block by a player who throws his body across the back of an opponent's leg or hits him from behind—unless the opponent is the ball carrier or the action takes place three yards on side of the line of scrimmage.

conversion   one point scored by kicking or passing the ball after a touchdown (in college ball, two points for a successful pass).

crackback   an illegal block by an eligible receiver who moves outside the tackle, then cuts back toward the middle of the line.

dead ball   a ball not in play.

down   period of action when the ball is put in play, ending when the referee signals that the ball is dead. A team gaining possession of the ball is allowed 4 downs in which to advance the ball 10 yards.

eligible receivers   offensive players on either end of the line (except for the center, guard, or tackle) or players at least one yard behind the line at the snap.

encroachment   a player in the neutral zone at the snap, or a player who makes contact with an opponent before the snap.

end zone   the area (10 feet deep) beyond the goal line but within the field of play.

extra point   a point scored after a touchdown by kicking two or more yards from the goal line; also called "point after touchdown" (PAT).

fair catch   an unhindered catch of a kick by a receiver who has signaled with an arm raised full length above his head while the ball is in flight.

field goal   a ball drop- or place-kicked between the goal posts from the line of scrimmage; it is worth three points to the kicking team.

flea flicker   a play that starts out as a double reverse intended to fool the defense, but in which the ball is given back to the quarterback, who throws a long pass. The term also indicates a long pass caught by a receiver who then laterals the ball to a teammate behind him.

fumble   loss of possession of the ball.

gridiron   the playing field; also, a synonym for "football."

hash marks   the inbound lines.

holding   illegal use of the hands or arms by an offensive player except the ball carrier, to ward off an opponent; it results in a 10-yard penalty (under college rules, a 15-yard penalty). The term is also used to indicate illegal holding or tackling of anyone but the ball carrier by a defensive player, resulting in a 5-yard penalty (15 yards in college play).

I formation   a pattern, usually for a run, in which both setbacks line up directly behind the quarterback.

intentional grounding   an illegal forward pass that strikes the ground after the passer throws, tosses, or lobs the ball in an attempt to prevent loss of yardage. The penalty may be loss of yards or loss of down.

interception   a forward pass caught by a defensive player.

late hit   a defensive player intentionally running into the passer after the ball has left his hand. The referee must determine whether the opponent had a reasonable chance to stop his momentum during an attempt to block the pass or tackle the passer while he still had the ball.

lateral   a pass thrown parallel to the line of scrimmage.

line of scrimmage   an imaginary line on which the ball is placed and where play begins; also the two imaginary lines on either side of the line of scrimmage on which players must line up before the ball is snapped.

offside   a player is offside when any part of his body is over his line of scrimmage at the snap.

pass rush   a move by the defensive linemen to tackle the passer before he releases the ball, or at least to rush his passing attack.

pocket   a horseshoe-shaped space defined by blockers, in which the quarterback stands for protection before passing.

pro set   an offensive formation with the two running backs behind the quarterback, the other back wide, and the end on the opposite side playing wide. Also called a "pro T."

punt   a kick by a player (who drops the ball and kicks it while it is falling) toward the opposing team's territory. The punt is used when it seems better to give up the ball than to retain possession and risk having to relinquish possession of the ball deep in one's own territory.

quarterback   the back who calls the signals to start a play (except on a punt). This player usually passes the ball, hands it off to a runner, or runs with it himself.

recover a fumble   to gain possession of a loose ball, whether it was lost by a teammate or by an opponent.

reverse   a play intended to deceive the defense by making it appear that a running play is going in a certain direction, whereas the ball carrier hands off to another player headed in a different direction.

roughing the kicker   an illegal move by a defensive player, who runs into or knocks down the kicker before touching the ball; the penalty for this personal foul is a loss of 15 yards and automatic first down.

rushing   yards accumulated by a ball carrier.

sack   defensive players bringing down a passer (usually a quarterback) behind the line of scrimmage before he can release or run with the ball.

safety   the situation obtaining when the ball is dead on or behind the goal of the team in possession of the ball, if the action that led to the ball's being there originated with a player on that team. In this case, the opposing team scores two points.

shotgun   a pass formation consisting of a quarterback taking the snap while standing a few yards behind the center. The play is intended to give the passer a few seconds' extra time in which to throw.

snap   passing the ball from the center to the quarterback, which begins play.

sudden death   the extension of a tied game into overtime; the team that scores first—by a safety, a field goal, or a touchdown—wins the game.

T formation   an offensive formation, in which the quarterback lines up just behind the center and the fullback lines up behind the quarterback, with the halfbacks on either side of the fullback.

touchback   a situation occurring when the ball is dead on or behind a team's own goal line, provided the movement of the ball came from an opponent, and provided the action is not a touchdown or a missed field goal.

touchdown   a score of six points; a touchdown is made whenever any part of the ball legally in possession of a player inbounds is on, above, or over the opponent's goal line, provided the action is not a touchback.

wild card   the team with the best conference record, but which has not clinched a division championship. A wild-card team qualifies for the playoffs.

wishbone   an offensive formation used primarily in college football, that resembles the T formation. In the wishbone, the quarterback stands behind the center, with the fullback slightly farther back. The two halfbacks stand on either side of the fullback, and slightly behind him.

8 GOLF

Woodrow Wilson called it "an attempt to move a ball into a hole with instruments entirely unsuited to the task." Mark Twain thought it ruined a good walk. James Reston insists it's "a plague invented by Calvinist Scots as a punishment for man's sins." And Britain's Max Beerbohm says it perfectly expresses "our national stupidity." Even Babe Didrikson, who became one of the most outstanding American female golfers, at first thought golf "a little silly."

Despite its sometimes tongue-in-cheek detractors, however, golf has become a major sport in the United States, played by some 12 million Americans on approximately 12,000 golf courses.

Although golf may seem today to be the perfect recreational sport for the more staid members of our society, its reputation was not always so pristine. Several fifteenth-century English kings banned the game, and people who played when they should have been in church were fined. In 1657, in Albany, New York, a complaint was filed against three men whose golf-playing, it was charged, endangered public morals. Despite the outcries of good citizens, the sport remained popular, especially in Scotland and among members of the Scottish-American community.

The early game was played with wooden balls and clubs that bore a marked resemblance to sledge hammers, lending a certain excitement to most matches. By the early nineteenth century, balls were made of rubber and clubs of metal, tees replaced mounds of dirt, and golf began to take on other refinements as it continued to spread across the United States and Canada. Much of its popularity in the United States was a result of the efforts of John ("Jock") Reid, a Scotsman who founded the St. Andrews Golf Club of Yonkers, New York, and led the "Apple Tree Gang," a group of enthusiasts who, in addition to recommending an apple tree be built on each course, did much to spread the word about their favorite pastime.

When Francis Ouimet, a 20-year-old American caddie, defeated major European players at the 1913 U.S. Open, the game became firmly entrenched in American culture.

In golf's early days, the most frequent version of the game was called "match golf," in which whoever scored the lowest for a single hole won that hole, and the winner was the person who won the most holes in a game. While match play had the advantage of not letting one bad hole ruin a game, it also diminished enthusiasm and excitement, because the entire 18 holes usually were not played out. As professional golf, and eventually televised golf, grew more prominent, match play was replaced by stroke play, in which the lowest score for the entire 18 holes wins the game. This is the version of golf now played most often in the United States.

Although golf was long considered the exclusive property of the upper classes— who lived near the large green areas needed to play, and who had the time to practice frequently a game requiring three or four hours per round—various innovations have made golf more accessible and exciting to the general public. The advent of auto transportation and public golf courses has meant that working people can still have the opportunity to hit the fairway on weekends.

Also, the innovation of the handicap system has made it possible for "duffers"—occasional players who have not yet mastered the game—to be able to play with more expert golfers without necessarily losing by consistently wide margins.

According to the handicap system, a player is rated on his or her average score for an 18-hole course, and then receives a handicap. At the end of the game, the player may deduct the amount of the handicap from the number of strokes used to derive the final score. Use of the handicap system makes golf one of the few sports in which mismatched players can meet each other with the outcome of the game in doubt—making golf, in a sense, a more democratic game than most, despite its elite image.

That—along with the chance golf offers to play a sport outdoors in beautiful surroundings—may be the reason that golf remains one of the nation's favorite sports.

Great Moments

ca. 1552 St. Andrews, one of the earliest and most famous of golf courses, is established.

1873 The Royal Montreal Golf Club, the first in North America, is formed.

1888 John ("Jock") Reid, the "father of modern golf," founds the St. Andrews Golfing Club in Yonkers, New York. The club, the oldest continuing golf club in the United States, first plays on a six-hole course in the cow pasture that was Reid's backyard.

1900   British golfer Harry Vardon's exhibition tour through the United States, beginning February 3, stimulates great interest in golf. Vardon, ranked the top golfer in the world, is sponsored by A. G. Spalding and Brothers to promote the new "Vardon Flyer" guttie golf ball.

1902   "Sandy" Herd wins the British Open, using the new rubber ball. International recognition of the rubber ball follows, marking the first major change in golf-ball design in 50 years.

1904   American Walter Travis, at 35, a latecomer to golf, is the first outsider to win the British Amateur championship.

1905   Willie Anderson becomes the first and only golfer to capture three consecutive U.S. Open championships.

1911   John McDermott of the Atlantic City Country Club becomes the first home-grown golfer to win the U.S. Open, a feat he repeats in 1912. (Americans have dominated their own title ever since.)

1913   Twenty-year-old amateur Francis Ouimet, aided by his ten-year-old caddie, plays the last six holes of the U.S. Open at two under par to tie veterans Harry Vardon and Ted Ray. Ouimet easily defeats the two in the playoff on the rain-soaked Brookline Country Club course.

1914   Ouimet proves his Open victory was not just lucky by taking the U.S. Amateur, defeating Jerome Travers in the final round. This year marks a changing of the guard with the last major victory of the "Great Triumvirate" (Vardon–British Open), and American Walter Hagen's first victory.

1915   Amateur Charles ("Chick") Evans becomes the first to win the U.S. Open and the U.S. Amateur championships in the same year.

1916   The Professional Golfers Association of America (PGA) is formed, on January 17, and stages its first National Championship at Siwanoy Country Club, in New York. James Barnes defeats Jock Hutchison in the final of the all-match-play event.

1922   The first international golf match is held at Southampton, New York, on August 28–29. The United States defeats Great Britain to win the first Walker Cup.

1930   Bobby Jones sets a record by winning the U.S. Open, the U.S. Amateur, the British Open, and the British Amateur.

1950   Babe Didrikson Zaharias sets a money-winning record for women golfers by winning $14,800.

1955   Journeyman golfer Jack Fleck wins the U.S. Open, defeating favorite Ben Hogan, who had won in the past four years.

1962   Jack Nicklaus joins the PGA Tour and wins his first tournament—the prestigious U.S. Open.

1977   Nancy Lopez wins $161,000, the most money won officially by a rookie in men's or women's professional golf.

1980   Tom Watson becomes the first golfer to win more than $500,000 in purses in a single year.

The Setup

Although men and women golfers often enjoy playing together, professional golf is strictly segregated by gender. Under the aegis of their respective professional associations, the Professional Golfers Association (PGA) and the Ladies Professional Golf Association (LPGA), individual men and women players compete in tours (series of tournaments) for prize money donated by corporations or other sponsors.

A player may not enter a PGA tournament unless he has a card (and actual cards are given to each player) that certifies his eligibility. To earn a card, a player must: (1) have won a Tournament Players Championship (TPC), World Series, American PGA, U.S. Open, or Masters tournament in the past five years; (2) have been a leader in PGA Tour Official Standings for each of the past five years; (3) have won the British Open in the past calendar year; (4) have been a member of the most recent U.S. Ryder Cup Team; (5) have won any PGA-designated tournaments in the past calendar year; or (6) have been one of the top 30 leaders in PGA Tour Official Money in the past calendar year. Certain wins, such as major opens or being at the top of the money list, entitle a player to exempt status—he may enter any PGA tournament regardless of his current record.

Goals and policies for PGA tournaments are established by the Tournament Policy Board, which includes four directors elected by players, three directors representing the public interest, and three directors who are national officers of the PGA. A Players Advisory Council consults with the Policy Board. The board appoints the commissioner, who is chief administrator of PGA tours, and supervises the tournament staff, which conducts tournament play.

In addition to supervising and coordinating sponsored tournaments, the PGA also administers the TPC games and the World Series of Golf.

The LPGA operates similarly to the PGA, with its board of directors establishing standards for tournament play and organization. The board has responsibility for long-range planning and final authority on general policy matters. It maintains a liaison with the Tournament Sponsors Board, which looks after the interests of tournament sponsors, and with the LPGA Player Council, through which players themselves have a voice in tour operations. The LPGA also ranks players, and determines eligibility to compete in tournaments through a series of preliminary competitions for new players. In addition to coordinating and supervising sponsored tournaments, the LPGA conducts its own championship and selects the winners of several professional awards.

ABC Sports

PROFESSIONAL GOLFERS'
  ASSOCIATION
Sawgrass
Ponte Vedra Beach, FL 32082
(904) 285-3700
Deane R. Beman, commissioner

LADIES PROFESSIONAL GOLF
  ASSOCIATION
919 Third Ave.
New York, NY 10022
(212) 751-8181
Ray Volpe, commissioner

The Basics

Object of the game To use clubs to hit a ball into a series of holes on a specially designed course, using fewer strokes than one's opponents.

The ball The dimpled ball must not weigh more than 1.62 ounces or be less than 1.68 inches in diameter; its maximum velocity may not exceed 250 feet per second.

The course There are no standard specifications for a golf course, but each has 18 holes, and each hole has a teeing area from which the ball is "launched," a fairway, a putting green on which the actual hole is located, natural hazards (water, trees, sand traps, etc.), and rough (untrimmed areas on the boundaries of the hole). The distance from the tee to the green is usually 300 to 500 yards, and an entire course may cover as much as 200 acres.

Number of players Two or more people per grouping, who participate either singly or as partners. A common grouping, of four players, is called a *foursome.*

Equipment A supply of balls, no more than fourteen clubs, tees, and a golf bag that is usually carried by a caddie.

Rule 1   Order of play The order of play is established by drawing for the first tee shot at the first hole. On subsequent holes, the player with the lowest score for the preceding hole has the privilege of deciding who will tee off first at the next hole. After the tee shot, the ball farthest from the hole is played first. If a player accidentally plays out of turn, the ball is nevertheless deemed to be in play without penalty.

Rule 2   Practice swing A player may not take a practice swing during play of a hole or while the ball is in play.

Rule 3   Striking the ball The ball must be struck with the head of the club, not pushed or scraped. If a player strikes the ball twice while making a stroke, a penalty stroke is added to his score. The ball must not be deliberately moved or touched except when the player is addressing it.

Rule 4   Assisting a player One caddie may accompany a player, and advise him or mark the position of a ball. If a player assists or advises another player, both players are penalized.

Rule 5   Lie of ball A player may not interfere with growing things, loose soil, and the like on the course in order to improve the line of play. He must play the ball as it lies.

Rule 6   Flagstick Before and during the stroke, a player may have the flagstick attended, removed, or held up to indicate the position of the hole.

Rule 7   Interference If a player thinks an opponent's ball will interfere with his shot, the player may ask to have it removed; if the player believes that his ball may help an oppponent's shot, the ball may be removed. In either case, a marker is used to indicate the position of the ball.

Rule 8   Ball lost or unplayable If a ball is lost, anywhere except in a water hazard, or shot out of bounds, the player takes the next stroke as close as possible from the original spot and adds a penalty stroke to the score for the hole. A player may stand out of bounds to play a ball lying within bounds. If a ball lies in a water hazard, the player may drop the ball and take a penalty of one stroke.

Rule 9   Dropping or placing ball   A player must drop the ball himself, facing the hole and dropping the ball behind his shoulder. A ball to be placed or replaced after it has been purposely or accidentally moved should be placed as near as possible to the place where it lay but not nearer the hole, and in as similar a lie as that which it originally occupied.

Rule 10   Scoring   Scoring is the responsibility of each player. Men's rules stipulate that a player mark the card for his partner, recording the number of strokes for each hole. In women's play, the player marks her own card. At the end of the game, the player with the fewest strokes wins.

How to watch

with Dale Antram

Dale Antram, of the Professional Golfers Association, says television viewers of golf must realize that only the very finest players make it to the last part of the tournament, which is the part that is televised. Golf tournaments cover seventy-two holes over four days, and only those players who have not yet been eliminated make it to the final round. Most television coverage of golf tournaments concentrates on the last holes of the final round.

Very often, the winner of a tournament is the person who makes one or two key shots, either an approach that puts the ball close to the pin or a key putt, in the final two or three holes. According to Antram, it can be this key shot that determines the outcome, and often the real challenge of the game is for someone to make a birdie or two in the last holes.

Both the approach shots and the putts are extremely important to the outcome of a golf game, but they are completely different skills. "Tour players are so skillful in their approaches that they can hit a shot from a distance of 180 yards (almost twice the length of a football field) and have it come within fifteen feet of the pin," says Antram. They are so accurate with their irons that if they hit the ball more than twenty feet from the pin, they consider it unacceptable. One of the most important things to look for in a golfer is thus the ability to shoot long distances with reasonable accuracy, he says.

The putt, which actually sinks the ball, is, obviously, also crucial to the outcome of the tournament. The key to tournament championships is therefore the combination of the approach shot with a successful putt, making a birdie that influences the outcome of the tournament.

When observing golfers in action , it is usually easy to tell whether or not their swing is good—there are prescribed ways of holding oneself and the club that have proved to hold up under pressure. For television viewers, the person who is doing the commentary will usually explain the intricacies of the swing and evaluate the golfer's performance.

Putting, however, is an entirely different skill. Each player has his or her own approach, and the only thing that matters is whether or not it works. Stances vary—golfers stand straight, bend over, keep their arms stiff, bend their elbows, etc. "Putting is so personal an activity that style and technique don't matter," says Antram. "All that matters is that it works."

Antram believes one of the most exciting aspects of golf to be the lure of a perfect game, which has never been played, but which is a goal that makes players always want to do better. Golf is exciting because players compete against themselves as well as other players. One week, a golfer may be up against someone with great putting; next week, he or she may have to match the skill of a long-distance driver.

Antram points out that another variable in golf is the course—no two are exactly alike, and conditions on the same course change with the weather—and with shifting pin placement. Therefore, no two shots in a golfer's career are ever exactly the same.

Key weather factors are wind and rain. Play during a light rain has no adverse effect on players, except perhaps to annoy golfers who wear glasses. Because a soft rain makes the greens soft, the players can fly their approach shots directly to the pin and not worry about bouncing or rolling the ball off the green. Games played in a misty rain usually result in lower scores.

Conversely, one of the toughest conditions under which a golfer can play is high winds on a course that is very firm and fast (in which the turf is cut short and the surfaces are hard). In that situation, it is quite difficult to get the ball close to the pin with the approach shots. Some players—especially those from Texas and Oklahoma—have learned to shoot low, where the ball is less affected by the wind, and so have a better chance of winning under gusty conditions.

The differences in terrain on each course, says Antram, also influence the outcome of a tournament. "On a short, tight golf course, the player who is a very straight driver, who can hit the irons well, and who is also a decent putter, can be expected to win," he says. "Other courses, such as the Firestone Country Club in Akron, Ohio, are long, broad, and fairly easy to putt on." The greens also are not much of a problem. The important skill on these courses is the ability to hit the ball a long way with a good deal of accuracy. The test becomes how far a player can hit the ball and still keep it on the fairway. The character of each course causes a slight shift in emphasis. The more a player has been exposed to a particular course, the greater advantage he or she has.

Golf is a game in which personalities and emotions play an important role, says Antram. Each player has a different way of dealing with the pressure. "Lee Trevino chats, quips and never lets himself get tense," according to Antram. "Nicklaus is composed and organized—very meticulous in his play." Antram says Fuzzy Zoeller is easy-going and Jerry Pate doesn't mind wearing a live microphone while he is playing; they are, he adds, two players who rarely let the pressure get to them.

Antram also mentions Curtis Strange, who has won a few times and given the winners a run for their money in other tourneys, as a player to watch. "Everybody thinks this guy is going to be a real superstar. He just needs to get over his trouble making the key shot that means a victory," according to Antram. As for Tom Watson, the dominant player of the last four years, Antram says he has been having trouble off the tee, but fans can expect golf's leading money winner to be out on the practice tee until he gets it right.

In the end, Antram says, it is the skill of the golfer—his or her ability to remain composed under quite tense conditions and shoot approaches and putts that combine to form winning birdies—that distinguishes the champion from the rest of the crowd.

Main Events

PGA

MASTERS

Year	Winner	Year	Winner
1981	Tom Watson	1976	Ray Floyd
1980	Severiano Ballesteros	1975	Jack Nicklaus
1979	Fuzzy Zoeller	1974	Gary Player
1978	Gary Player	1973	Tommy Aaron
1977	Tom Watson	1972	Jack Nicklaus

U.S. OPEN

Year	Winner	Year	Winner
1981	David Graham	1976	Jerry Pate
1980	Jack Nicklaus	1975	Lou Graham
1979	Hale Irwin	1974	Hale Irwin
1978	Andy North	1973	Johnny Miller
1977	Hubert Green	1972	Jack Nicklaus

BRITISH OPEN

Year	Winner	Year	Winner
1980	Tom Watson	1975	Tom Watson
1979	Severiano Ballesteros	1974	Gary Player
1978	Jack Nicklaus	1973	Tom Weiskopf
1977	Tom Watson	1972	Lee Trevino
1976	Johnny Miller	1971	Lee Trevino

PGA CHAMPIONSHIP

Year	Winner	Year	Winner
1980	Jack Nicklaus	1975	Jack Nicklaus
1979	David Graham	1974	Lee Trevino
1978	John Mahaffey	1973	Jack Nicklaus
1977	Lanny Wadkins	1972	Gary Player
1976	David Stockton	1971	Jack Nicklaus

VARDON TROPHY
(Awarded to the PGA member with the best playing average in PGA-sanctioned events)

Year	Winner	Year	Winner
1980	Lee Trevino	1975	Bruce Crampton
1979	Tom Watson	1974	Lee Trevino
1978	Tom Watson	1973	Bruce Crampton
1977	Tom Watson	1972	Lee Trevino
1976	Don January	1971	Lee Trevino

PGA PLAYER-OF-THE-YEAR AWARD
(Based on a point system developed by the PGA)

Year	Winner	Year	Winner
1980	Tom Watson	1975	Jack Nicklaus
1979	Tom Watson	1974	Johnny Miller
1978	Tom Watson	1973	Jack Nicklaus
1977	Tom Watson	1972	Jack Nicklaus
1976	Jack Nicklaus	1971	Lee Trevino

LPGA

COLGATE–DINAH SHORE

Year	Winner	Year	Winner
1980	Donna C. Young	1975	Sandra Palmer
1979	Sandra Post	1974	JoAnn Prentice
1978	Sandra Post	1973	Mickey Wright
1977	Kathy Whitworth	1972	Jane Blalock
1976	Judy Rankin		

LPGA CHAMPIONSHIP

Year	Winner	Year	Winner
1980	Sally Little	1975	Kathy Whitworth
1979	Donna C. Young	1974	Sandra Haynie
1978	Nancy Lopez	1973	Mary Mills
1977	Chako Higuchi	1972	Kathy Ahern
1976	Betty Burfeindt	1971	Kathy Whitworth

U.S. WOMEN'S OPEN

Year	Winner	Year	Winner
1980	Amy Alcott	1975	Sandra Palmer
1979	Jerilyn Britz	1974	Sandra Haynie
1978	Hollis Stacy	1973	Susie Berning
1977	Hollis Stacy	1972	Susie Berning
1976	JoAnne Carner	1971	JoAnne Carner

VARE TROPHY
(Awarded for the lowest average of the year)

Year	Winner	Year	Winner
1980	Amy Alcott	1975	JoAnne Carner
1979	Nancy Lopez	1974	JoAnne Carner
1978	Nancy Lopez	1973	Judy Rankin
1977	Judy Rankin	1972	Kathy Whitworth
1976	Judy Rankin	1971	Kathy Whitworth

LPGA PLAYER-OF-THE-YEAR AWARD
(Based on a point system developed by the LPGA)

Year	Winner	Year	Winner
1980	Beth Daniel	1975	Sandra Palmer
1979	Nancy Lopez	1974	JoAnne Carner
1978	Nancy Lopez	1973	Kathy Whitworth
1977	Judy Rankin	1972	Kathy Whitworth
1976	Judy Rankin	1971	Kathy Whitworth

All-Time Greats

Patty Berg
(Feb. 13, 1918–)

LPGA Photo

Patty Berg turned professional in 1935 and enjoyed a 38-year career marked by such milestones as a victory in the first U.S. Women's Open in 1946 and twice being named Associated Press Woman Athlete of the Year. Berg was the first president of the LPGA, and she continues to promote golf by teaching, writing, and giving golf exhibitions around the world. In 1976 she became the first woman to receive the Humanitarian Sports Award, on behalf of her work against cerebral palsy, and in 1978 the LPGA announced the establishment of the Patty Berg Award, given annually for outstanding contributions to women's golf.

Walter C. Hagen
(Dec. 21, 1892–Oct. 6, 1969)

World Golf Hall of Fame

Walter Hagen was the first full-time professional tournament golfer. Known for his expert putting ability, he advanced the standing of professional golfers both by fighting to improve their conditions and, through his relaxed and friendly personality, attracting new fans to the sport. Beginning with his victory in the U.S. Open in 1914, Hagen pursued a career that lasted well into the late 1930s.

Robert Tyre Jones, Jr.
(Mar. 17, 1902–Dec. 17, 1971)

World Golf Hall of Fame

Bobby Jones won his first championship at the Atlanta Athletic Club when he was nine years old. Also known as the "Boy Wonder" and "Grand Slammer," Jones had won both the Georgia State Championship and the Southern Amateur Championship by the time he was 15. He went on to win the U.S. Open four times, the U.S. Men's Amateur five, and the British Open three. He was the first man to complete the Grand Slam of golf. After retiring at the age of 28, he continued to participate in golf by founding the Masters tournament and the World Amateur Team championship, despite a crippling muscle disease that eventually killed him.

John Byron Nelson
(Feb. 4, 1912–)

World Golf Hall of Fame

Byron Nelson might have been America's greatest golfer had not the height of his playing career coincided with World War II, during which most major tournaments were cancelled. Nelson holds the record for the most tournament wins in a calendar year; he took 18 tournaments in 1945.

Jack Nicklaus
(Jan. 21, 1940–)

ABC Sports

Known as the "Golden Bear" because of his once-portly build and his Nordic coloring, Nicklaus has won a major tournament every year but one since joining the PGA Tour in 1962. He has won the Masters five times, the U.S. Open four, and the British Open three. The five-time PGA Player of the Year hit a dry spell in 1979, winning no tournaments, and sports fans thought his career was on the decline. But the "Golden Bear" surprised everyone with a strong comeback in 1980, winning both the U.S. Open (by four strokes) and the PGA Championship (by seven strokes).

Arnold Palmer
(Sept. 10, 1929–)

PGA Photo

The son of a country-club golf pro, Palmer was given his first clubs when he was three years old. Taught by his father, Palmer developed the versatility to play any shot. His personality is so engaging that "Arnie's Army," a legion of enthusiastic fans, follows and cheers him on whenever he plays. Palmer has earned several Vardon Trophies and has won the Masters four times, the U.S. Open once, and the British Open twice.

Glenna Collett Vare
(June 20, 1903–)

World Golf Hall of Fame

Vare was the best woman golfer of her time, winning the U.S. Amateur a record six times, and earning multiple wins in the Canadian, French, British, and North and South championships. She set the U.S. Golf Association record for the most consecutive wins (19) and won 49 amateur championships in her 18-year career. The prized Vare Trophy, awarded by the LPGA, is named for her.

Kathy Whitworth
(Sept. 27, 1939–)

Kathy Whitworth is the leading all-time money winner in the LPGA. Her 80 official Tour victories come in second only to Mickey Wright's 82, and she has won both the Player-of-the Year designation and the Vare Trophy seven times. One of the greatest putters in the history of women's golf, Kathy is known for her ability to adapt to all conditions, her versatility in maneuvering shots, and her grace under pressure.

Mary Kathryn ("Mickey") Wright
(Feb. 14, 1935–)

Mickey Wright may be the greatest player in LPGA history. Starting in 1956, she won from 1 to 13 tournaments each year for 14 consecutive years, and she leads in number of career victories (82) and number of wins in a calendar year (13). The only golfer who has twice won the LPGA championship and U.S. Open in one season, she was also twice named Associated Press Woman Athlete of the Year.

HALL OF FAME

Professional Golfers Association of American Hall of Fame
P.O. Box 12458
Lake Park, FL 33403
(305) 626-3600

Members of the Professional Golfers Association of America Hall of Fame are:

1940	1955	1961
Willie Anderson	Leo Diegel	Johnny Farrell
Thomas D. Armour		Lawson Little
James M. Barnes	**1956**	Henry C. Picard
Charles ("Chick") Evans, Jr.	Craig R. Wood	
Walter Hagen		**1962**
Bobby Jones	**1957**	Olin Dutra
John J. McDermott	Herman D. ("Denny") Shute	E. J. ("Dutch") Harrison
Francis Ouimet		
Gene Sarazen	**1958**	**1963**
Alex Smith	Horton Smith	Ralph Guldahl
Jerry Travers		John Revolta
Walter Travis	**1959**	
	Harry Cooper	**1964**
1953	Jock Hutchison, Sr.	Edward B. Dudley
Ben Hogan	Paul Runyan	Lloyd E. Mangrum
Byron Nelson		
Sam Snead	**1960**	**1965**
	Michael J. Brady	Vic Ghezzi
1954	Jimmy Demaret	
Macdonald Smith	Frederick R. McLeod	**1966**
		William ("Billy") Burke

1967
Bobby Cruickshank

1968
Melvin R. ("Chick") Harbert

1969
Chandler Harper

1974
Julius N. Boros
Cary ("Doc") Middlecoff

1975
Jack Burke, Jr.
Doug Ford

1976
Mildred ("Babe") Didrikson Zaharias

1978
Patty Berg

1980
Arnold Palmer

ABC Sports

World Golf Hall of Fame
Pinehurst, NC 28374
(919) 295-6651

Members of the World Golf Hall of Fame are:

1974
Patty Berg
Walter Hagen
Ben Hogan
Bobby Jones
Byron Nelson
Jack Nicklaus
Francis Ouimet
Arnold Palmer
Gary Player
Gene Sarazen
Sam Snead
Harry Vardon
Babe Didrikson Zaharias

1975
Willie Anderson
Fred Corcoran

Joseph C. Dey
Chick Evans
Tom Morris, Jr.
John H. Taylor
Glenna C. Vare
Joyce Wethered Amory

1976
Tommy Armour
James Braid
Tom Morris, Sr.
Jerry Travers
Mickey Wright

1977
John Ball
Bobby Locke
Herb Graffis

Donald Ross

1978
Dorothy Campbell
Billy Casper
Bing Crosby
Harold Hilton
Hurd Howe
Cliff Roberts

1979
Louise Suggs
Walter Travis

1980
Henry Cotton
Lawson Little

For the Record

PGA

Best 18-hole score
59   Al Geiberger   1977 Memphis Classic (second round)

Best 72-hole score
257   Mike Souchak   1955 Texas Open

Longest sudden-death playoff
11 holes   Cary Middlecoff and Lloyd Mangrum (tie)   1949 Motor City Open

Most consecutive birdies
8   Bob Goalby   1961 St. Petersburg Open (fourth round)
    Fuzzy Zoeller   1976 Quad Cities Open (first round)

Most consecutive events without missing the cut
113   Byron Nelson   1940s

Most consecutive victories
11   Byron Nelson   Mar. 11, 1945–Aug. 4, 1945

Most PGA victories, career
84   Sam Snead

Oldest tour winner
52 yrs 10 mos   Sam Snead   1965 Greater Greensboro Open

Widest winning margin
16   Bobby Locke   1948 Chicago Victory National Championship

Youngest tour winner
20 yrs 4 mos   Gene Sarazen   1922 U.S. Open

LPGA

Best 18-hole score
62   Mickey Wright   1964 Tall City Open (fourth round)

Best 72-hole score
271   Hollis Stacy   1977 Rail Muscular Dystrophy Classic

Fewest putts, one round
19   Beverly Klass   1978 Women's International (second round)

Most birdies, one round
10   Nancy Lopez   1979 Mary Kay Classic

Most consecutive birdies
7   Carol Mann   1975 Borden Classic (first round)

Most consecutive tournament wins
5   Nancy Lopez   1978

Most tournament wins, career
82   Mickey Wright

Most tournament wins, year
13   Mickey Wright   1963

Most eagles, one round
3   Alice Ritzman   1979 Colgate European Open (second round)

Widest winning margin
14   Louise Suggs   1949 USGA Women's Open

Did you know?

1. Many athletes feel that golf is an excellent way to keep in shape for other sports, but one famous sports expert violently disagreed. Who was it?

2. Although balls are sometimes lost and golf clubs sometimes broken, golf courses themselves rarely suffer major physical damage at the hands of men. Name a notable exception.

3. How many dimples are on a golf ball?

4. Movies about football, baseball, and track heroes abound; but only one movie was ever made about a championship golfer. What are the names of the movie and its star, and what golfer's story does the movie tell?

5. What are the odds against a golfer making a hole in one?

Answers: 1. Ty Cobb, as manager of the Detroit Tigers, had such a violent distaste for golf that in 1925 he banned it for his players and confiscated their clubs; **2.** In 1929, the entire fifth green—300 square feet—of the North Hills Golf Course, in Douglaston, New York, was dug up by thieves and removed during the night; **3.** 336; **4.** Glenn Ford played Ben Hogan in the 1951 film *Follow the Sun*; **5.** Experts say the odds are 300,000 to 1 against making an "ace."

Key Words

ace   a hole in one (player drives the ball into the hole from the tee).

address the ball   take one's position over the ball and prepare to swing.

birdie   one stroke under par for a hole.

bogey   one stroke over par for a hole.

brassie   number 2 wood.

bunker   a sand trap.

chip shot   a short shot that allows the ball to roll on the green; also called a pitch-and-run shot.

draw   for a right-handed golfer, a shot that intentionally veers sharply to the left; also called a "pull."

driver   number 1 wood, often used to tee off.

dub   miss the ball completely.

duffer   a player of mediocre skill, usually as a result of playing only on weekends.

eagle   two strokes under par for a hole.

fade   for a right-handed golfer, a shot that intentionally veers sharply to the right.

fairway   a mowed strip of ground between the putting green and the tee area.

green   a closely manicured, irregularly shaped area immediately surrounding the hole.

hook   a shot that accidentally veers sharply to the left.*

honor   designation of the player who will shoot first at the next hole, awarded to the player with the lowest score at the preceding hole.

iron   a club with a metal head.

lie   position of ball in relation to green, sand traps, fairway, etc.

match play   a form of golf in which each hole is considered separately, and the winner of the most holes is the winner of the game.

par   an arbitrary standard of play governing golf, or the number of strokes from the tee to the hole necessary to sink the ball on a given hole. Par varies from one hole to another, and from one golf course to another.

pin   the pole that supports a flag marking the hole; the flag usually carries the number of the hole being played.

putt   a stroke taken when the ball is on the green.

putter   club with a vertical face that can top the ball with maximum control, used on the green.

rough   the area, usually not landscaped, on either side of the fairway.

sand trap   an artificial hazard filled with loose sand.

shanking   hitting the ball with the heel of the clubhead or the shaft.

skying   hitting the ball almost straight up, like a pop fly in baseball.

slice   a shot that accidentally curves sharply to the right.*

stroke   movement of the club head forward (even if it does not touch the ball).

tee   a wooden spike with a concave tip used to elevate the ball for tee shots.

tee shot   the first shot of a hole, and the only shot for which the player uses a tee.

water hazard   a stream or pond incorporated in a course, and intended to present a challenge to players.

wedge   a number 10 iron, used either for lifting the ball out of a sand trap (sand wedge) or making a high, short approach shot from the fairway (pitching wedge).

wood   a club with a wooden head, used for long drives.

*For a righthander; to opposite side for a lefthander.

9 GYMNASTICS

Although the ancient Greeks used a form of gymnastics for physical conditioning, modern gymnastics originated in early nineteenth-century Germany. There, the sport was part of an overall educational program. When German immigrants brought gymnastics to the United States during the nineteenth century, they left its rigorous "educational" aspects behind and enjoyed it as recreation and physical conditioning. For decades thereafter, however, Americans were indifferent to gymnastics and the activity remained almost exclusively German.

With the revival of the Olympic Games in 1896 and the formation of collegiate gymnastics societies, gymnastics became more acceptable. Although the Russians and Japanese have dominated international competitions during most of this century, American gymnasts have recently been performing very respectably.

Part of the reason for this improvement is that Americans, particularly the women, are beginning to take an interest in gymnastics while they are still young enough to be trained for high-quality competition. The immense popularity of Olga Korbut and Nadia Comaneci has sent thousands of young American girls to their local YWCAs or to gymnastics schools to learn how to swing on the uneven bars and do cartwheels on the balance beam.

The impact of Korbut and Comaneci on gymnastics is not only a result of personal appeal, but of stylistic changes they have wrought which make gymnastics more exciting. Korbut, with her bouncy style, lively music, and successful execution of extremely difficult, unprecedented maneuvers, led the way for a new generation of bold, imaginative gymnasts.

Although some criticize the new style, claiming that gymnasts are risking severe injury by incorporating dangerous stunts into their routines, and also that the "new wave" of younger competitors makes it impossible for women with more mature bodies to compete successfully, the new gymnastics seems here to stay. In the future, Americans are likely to be watching more younger gymnasts performing exercises of greater technical difficulty than ever before.

Great Moments

1817　The U.S. Military Academy establishes a gymnasium for its students.

1866　The Normal College of the American Gymnastics Institute is founded. It is the first American facility for training gymnastics teachers.

1885　For the first time, parallel and horizontal bars are used in American gymnastics.

1887　The YMCA sets up a physical training program. The "Y" becomes a major force in gymnastics.

1897　The Amateur Athletic Union becomes the governing body for amateur gymnastics in the United States.

1928　Women's gymnastics becomes part of Olympic competition.

1931　The AAU holds its first national gymnastics tournament for women.

1936　The National Collegiate Athletic Association holds its first annual gymnastics competition.

1959　The National Association of College Gymnastics Coaches founds the Gymnastics Hall of Fame.

1970　Cathy Rigby becomes the first American woman to win a medal in international competition.

1972　Olga Korbut's performance at the Munich Olympics thrills the world and leads to a surge of interest in gymnastics.

1976　Fourteen-year-old Nadia Comaneci's seven perfect scores at the Montreal Olympics dazzle fans and judges alike.

The Setup

Almost all gymnastics competition takes place at the amateur level. International amateur gymnastics is governed by the International Gymnastics Federation

(IGF), which is closely allied with the International Olympic Committee. In the United States, the U.S. Gymnastics Federation (USGF) governs the sport, setting standards and selecting American participants for the World Cup and other international competitions. The USGF works closely with the AAU, which sponsors national championships each year and, along with the U.S. Olympic Committee, serves as the American governing body for Olympic competition.

At the college level, gymnastics for men is governed by the NCAA; women's competition comes under the jurisdiction of the Association for Intercollegiate Athletics for Women.

AMATEUR ATHLETIC UNION
3400 W. 86th St.
Indianapolis, IN 46268
(317) 297-2900
Ollan C. Cassell, exec. dir.

ASSOCIATION FOR
  INTERCOLLEGIATE ATHLETICS
  FOR WOMEN
1201 16th St. NW
Washington, DC 20036
(202) 833-5485
Ann Uhlir, dir.

INTERNATIONAL GYMNASTICS
  FEDERATION
Juraweg 12, 3250 Lyss
Switzerland
290 24 71
Max Bangerter, sec.-gen.

NATIONAL COLLEGIATE ATHLETIC
  ASSOCIATION
Nall Ave. at 63rd St.
P.O. Box 1906
Shawnee Mission, KS
(913) 384-3220
Walter Byers, exec. dir.

U.S. GYMNASTICS FEDERATION
P.O. Box 7686
Fort Worth, TX 76111
(817) 485-7630
Roger Counsil, exec. dir.

The Basics

Object   To perform compulsory and voluntary stunts and exercises with grace, strength, and precision.

The arena   Gymnastics competition takes place in a gymnasium. For floor exercises, a mat 12 meters square is used.

Equipment   Equipment for men's gymnastics consists of: rings (two circles 7⅛ inches in diameter suspended from a bar 17 feet 11 inches above the floor; even parallel bars 5 feet 3 inches high; a vaulting horse 4 feet 5 inches high and 5 feet 4⅛ inches long, placed near a small springboard; a horizontal bar 8 feet 5 inches high; and a pommel horse (a leather-covered, horizontal cylinder with metal handles placed in the center) 3 feet 7 inches high. Women's equipment consists of: a balance beam 3 feet 11 inches high, 16 feet 3 inches long, and 4 inches wide; a vaulting horse 3 feet 7 inches high and 5 feet 4⅛ inches long, placed near a small springboard; and two uneven parallel bars each 11 feet 5 inches long and 4 feet 11 inches and 7 feet 6 inches high, respectively.

Scoring   In Olympic competition, four judges rate (independently) each entrant in each event. The highest and lowest of these scores are discarded, and the two remaining are averaged to arrive at the final score. The highest number of points possible is 10; gymnasts begin with 10 and are then subjected to reduction of points for both general weaknesses (lack of grace or strength, failure to attempt difficult maneuvers) and specific flaws (falling, stumbling, going off the mat) in the performance.

In the scoring for the best "all-around" performance, each of the top competitors performs one compulsory and one optional routine for each event, and added to the total points for these is half the points he or she earned in the team event. The gymnast with the highest total points is the winner in all-around competition.

Order of competition   In Olympic events, team competitions take place first; the highest scorers in the team events are then allowed to compete for individual titles.

Officials   The officials usually present are four judges, timekeepers, scorekeepers, and supervisors.

OLYMPIC COMPETITION

Men's Events

In men's Olympic competition, the events are:

Rings: a series of mandatory and optional movements while the competitor is suspended from the rings; the rings must remain stationary throughout the event.

Pommel horse (or side horse): a series of movements consisting of mounting, swinging on, and dismounting from the side horse, with clean swings and no stopping. The body may not touch the horse.

Horizontal bar: a series of movements undertaken while mounting, holding onto, and dismounting from the horizontal bar, alternating both hands and one hand.

Parallel bars: swinging and holding exercises, including the mount and the dismount, from the even parallel bars; this event must include pivots on one hand.

Long horse vault: a jump from a small springboard to the vaulting horse, landing on the hands, with a subsequent thrust over the horse and high into the air.

Floor exercise: a series of compulsory and optional movements designed to display the overall skill of the competitor. All elementary movements should be technically correct and all available floor space should be used.

Team competition: the members of each nation's team perform one mandatory and one voluntary routine on each piece of equipment and on the floor. The five highest scores achieved by members of the teams are totaled, and the team with the highest score wins.

Women's Events

The women's events are:

Long horse vault: same as for men, but both hands must be on the horse.

Uneven parallel bars: continuous swinging from and around the bars, paying special attention to suspension and movement of the hands from bar to bar.

Balance beam: a series of acrobatic movements performed while on an elevated beam four inches wide; attention is paid to the mount and dismount.

Floor exercise: a series of exercises put together by the gymnast, including certain compulsory moves, that displays her overall ability and grace. Musical accompaniment contributes to the performance. The feet may never cross the edge of the mat.

Team competition: the same as for men.

How to watch

Nissen Corp.

with Dick Mulvihill

Dick Mulvihill, gymnastics coach at the National Academy of Gymnastics, has watched many gymnasts—former champions and hopefuls. Although the following pointers refer specifically to women's events, viewers of gymnastics generally can use most of the same criteria for evaluating and enjoying the performance of men gymnasts. The major distinctions between men's and women's gymnastics are that men's events usually call more for a display of sheer strength, such as holding a difficult position on the rings, while women are encouraged to project a dancerlike image. Mulvihill believes that as women in gymnastics continue to explore more daring and spectacular stunts, some of the differences between men's and women's gymnastics will lessen. The championship coach analyzes each women's event:

Vault: In vaulting events, the purpose is for the gymnast to make contact with the horse in such a way that she is repelled from it, much the way that a thrown rock bounces across the surface of a body of water. This "repulsion" then propels the gymnast high in the opposite direction.

Therefore, a gymnast's sprint to the Reuther board, and her jump onto the vault, should be quick and powerful, since a slow approach will not provide the momentum necessary for a good vault. Upon contact and repulsion, the gymnast should go high in the opposite direction, with her arms outstretched. The vault itself should be high and should include such difficult movements as half-twists, full twists, and somersaults. The landing should be firm, with no faltering or steps taken. The gymnast's head should be back behind her ankles; leaning the head forward will cause the body to follow it, resulting in extra steps. As in most gymnastics events, it is the dismount that leaves a lasting impression on the judge and the audience; it should be as nearly perfect as possible.

Uneven bars: The trend is for women gymnasts to use the higher bar of the uneven bars as men use the horizontal bar—as a foundation for daring and spectacular maneuvers. While on the high bar, a good gymnast will perform a variety of bold, potentially dangerous moves that look spectacular, and are. Good gymnasts continuously try to come up with stunts that have not been performed before; to do so is a decided plus.

Definitions of what exactly a movement is are often different in the minds of judges and gymnasts. This is sometimes important in scoring since there is a rule specifying no more than five movements in succession on one bar without changing to the other. So spectators may sometimes see a "great" performance on the uneven bars receive a low score. The gymnast might consider each triple twist, for example, as one movement, while the judges say it is three. The difference in definition thus might result in a violation of the rule, from the judges' point of view.

A good gymnast usually works with the uneven bars as widely separated as possible. She will change direction frequently, especially when going from one bar to another. Transitions should be smooth and the routine should be varied, including many different elements arranged in an interesting way. Difficult moves that fit in with the individual gymnast's style should be part of the exercise.

Americans tend to perform routines that are lengthy and contain many difficult movements; Russian gymnasts lean toward short, simple exercises interspersed with some movements that are extremely difficult. In general, routines that are daring and contain some risk (the risk either of a bad fall or of imperfectly executing a complicated maneuver) are what the fans and judges are looking for.

The dismount should be executed cleanly, with no faltering. The gymnast must land securely on both feet with her hands high over her head. An original or especially daring dismount can make a good performance great.

Balance beam: It is in the balance beam, the most difficult of all gymnastic events, that the true precision and art of the sport is shown, according to Mulvihill.

A top gymnast will work the balance beam high up on her toes, which is much more difficult than working flat-footed. Her routine will have a varied pace, using music that changes rhythm frequently—from waltz to march to jazz. She will use all of the beam, moving back and forth along its length and also working from side to side, frequently changing direction.

Stunts on the balance beam should demonstrate the gymnast's willingness to take risks, and her dramatic flair. As in other events, the development of any new movement is encouraged. The difficulty of the dismount should be in keeping with that of the routine; although a gymnast will be given credit for doing an intricate dismount after a simple routine, a performer who opts for an easy dismount after a hard routine will not score as well as possible.

The best performers also will relate to the audience while on the balance beam. Although they must be centered on the beam at all times, they should not appear to be looking down or overly concerned with the placement of their feet.

The gymnast should always present a "feminine" appearance, without calling attention to any displays of strength, always maintaining the desired smooth, dancelike quality of the routine.

Floor exercise: Even more than in any other event, the routine for the floor exercise should be tailored to the individual gymnast. This is her chance to display her own personality, and her performance should be unique, not an imitation of a Comaneci or a [Tracee] Talavera. In all cases, the music should be varied and the pace should change, but the overall tone of the exercise should be in keeping with the physique and style of the gymnast. Tiny, wiry women tend toward a jazzy performance and taller, willowy gymnasts favor routines with a more balletic quality.

Although tumbling and acrobatics are theoretically not of great importance in the floor exercise, in actuality they make up a major proportion of most routines. Such acrobatics should consist of aerial stunts (such as flips and no-handed somersaults) and complex floorwork, in various combinations—the more difficult the stunts and the more interesting the combinations, the higher the score.

The gymnast should make use of the entire mat, working now diagonally, then in a circle, and sometimes from side to side, so that she will retain the audience's interest.

One of the most exciting things about the floor exercise is its suitability for individual expression. Elements of acrobatics, ballet, modern dance, tumbling, and almost any other physical activity can be incorporated into the routine, providing an endless variety of possible styles.

In general, when watching gymnastics, a viewer should keep in mind that, as a rule, each country has its own style. The Chinese teams, for example, are very disciplined and almost seem to be doing calisthenics when on such apparatus as the balance beam. Russian gymnastics teams are now beginning to put some movements from modern dance, such as those devised by Isadora Duncan, into their floor exercises—a move that Americans, who have the best modern dancers in the world, could well emulate.

Although teams have their own styles, each member should perform in an individual way. The best gymnastics teams are those in which each individual member can develop her own style of movement. Teammates should not appear to have been cloned from one another. Individuality, originality, and the courage to be different are just as important to the performance of a top gymnast as is technical expertise.

The 1970s saw the beginning of certain trends in gymnastics that are likely to persist for some time. As noted, there has been a move toward high-risk, spectacular maneuvers; more fluid, and jazzier exercises are also on the increase.

Mulvihill thinks, however, that one recent trend will probably soon reverse itself. If the 1970s were marked by the very young gymnast, with children as young as eleven competing in the Olympics, the 1980s will see a return to appreciation of the mature woman, Mulvihill predicts.

Although the child gymnast may be a bit more fearless than the older person who has received some injuries, and although the child's more limber body may more easily be able to perform some spectacular stunt, the "older" gymnast (in her 20s) definitely has a place in today's arena, he says. The maturity of the older performer, her extra experience and the fact that she is comfortable with her body, can make her more appealing than the talented, but unseasoned adolescent. As the older gymnasts come to realize this, Mulvihill believes, they will be less intimidated by the child prodigies coming up behind them, and more inclined to stay with gymnastics past age 20. And today's younger gymnasts, who are being trained in extremely difficult stunts at an early age, will have a much better foundation for making gymnastics part of their lives and not merely part of their childhoods.

Main Events

OLYMPIC COMPETITION

Men
ALL-AROUND

Year	Name	Country
1980	Alexander Dityatin	USSR
1976	Nikolai Andrianov	USSR
1972	Sawao Kato	Japan
1968	Sawao Kato	Japan
1964	Yukio Endo	Japan
1960	Boris Shakhlin	USSR
1956	Victor Tchoukarine	USSR
1952	Victor Tchoukarine	USSR
1948	V. Huhtanen	Finland

FLOOR EXERCISE

Year	Winner	Country
1980	Roland Bruckner	GDR*
1976	Nikolai Andrianov	USSR
1972	Nikolai Andrianov	USSR
1968	Sawao Kato	Japan
1964	Franco Menichelli	Italy
1960	Albert Azarian	USSR
1956	Albert Azarian	USSR
1952	Grant Chaguinian	USSR
1948	K. Frei	Switzerland

LONG HORSE

Year	Winner	Country
1980	Nikolai Andrianov	USSR
1976	Nikolai Andrianov	USSR
1972	Klaus Koeste	GDR
1968	Mikhail Voronin	USSR
1964	Haruhiro Yamashita	Japan
1960	Boris Shakhlin	USSR
	Takashi Ono	Japan
1956	Helmuth Bantz	FRG*
	Valentine Mouratov	USSR
1952	Victor Tchoukarine	USSR
1948	P. J. Aaltonen	Finland

*GDR: German Democratic Republic (East Germany); FRG: Federal Republic of Germany (West Germany).

POMMEL HORSE

Year	Winner	Country
1980	Zoltan Magyar	Hungary
1976	Zoltan Magyar	Hungary
1972	Viktor Klimenko	USSR
1968	Miroslav Cerar	Yugoslavia
1964	Miroslav Cerar	Yugoslavia
1960	Eugen Ekman	Finland
	Boris Shakhlin	USSR
1956	Boris Shakhlin	USSR
1952	Victor Tchoukarine	USSR
1948	P. J. Aaltonen	Finland

HORIZONTAL BAR

Year	Winner	Country
1980	Stoyan Deltchev	Bulgaria
1976	Mitsuo Tsukahara	Japan
1972	Mitsuo Tsukahara	Japan
1968	Mikhail Voronin	USSR
1964	Boris Shakhlin	USSR
1960	Takashi Ono	Japan
1956	Takashi Ono	Japan
1952	Jack Gunthard	Switzerland
1948	Josef Stalder	Switzerland

PARALLEL BARS

Year	Winner	Country
1980	Alexander Tkachyov	USSR
1976	Sawao Kato	Japan
1972	Sawao Kato	Japan
1968	Akinori Nakayama	Japan
1964	Yukio Endo	Japan
1960	Boris Shakhlin	USSR
1956	Victor Tchoukarine	USSR
1952	Hans Engstar	Switzerland
1948	M. Reusch	Switzerland

RINGS

Year	Winner	Country
1980	Alexander Dityatin	USSR
1976	Nikolai Andrianov	USSR
1972	Akinori Nakayama	Japan
1968	Akinori Nakayama	Japan
1964	Takuji Hayata	Japan
1960	Albert Azarian	USSR
1956	Albert Azarian	USSR
1952	Grant Chaguinian	USSR
1948	K. Frei	Switzerland

TEAM COMPETITION

Year	Winner	Year	Winner
1980	USSR	1960	Japan
1976	Japan	1956	USSR
1972	Japan	1952	USSR
1968	Japan	1948	Finland
1964	Japan		

Women

ALL-AROUND

Year	Winner	Country
1980	Yelena Davydova	USSR
1976	Nadia Comaneci	Romania
1972	Ludmilla Turischeva	USSR
1968	Vera Caslavska	Czechoslovakia
1964	Vera Caslavska	Czechoslovakia
1960	Larisa Latynina	USSR
1956	Larisa Latynina	USSR
1952	Maria Gorokhovakaja	USSR

BALANCE BEAM

Year	Winner	Country
1980	Nadia Comaneci	Romania
1976	Nadia Comaneci	Romania
1972	Olga Korbut	USSR
1968	Natalia Kuchinskaya	USSR
1964	Vera Caslavska	Czechoslovakia
1960	Eva Bosakova	Czechoslovakia
1956	Agnes Keleti	Hungary
1952	Nina Botcharova	USSR

FLOOR EXERCISE

Year	Winner	Country
1980	Nadia Comaneci	Romania
	Nelli Kim	USSR
1976	Nelli Kim	USSR
1972	Olga Korbut	USSR
1968	Vera Caslavska	Czechoslovakia
1964	Larisa Latynina	USSR
1960	Larisa Latynina	USSR
1956	Agnes Keleti	Hungary
	Larisa Latynina	USSR
1952	Agnes Keleti	Hungary

HORSE VAULT

Year	Winner	Country
1980	Natalya Shaposhnikova	USSR
1976	Nelli Kim	USSR
1972	Karin Janz	GDR
1968	Vera Caslavska	Czechoslovakia
1964	Vera Caslavska	Czechoslovakia
1960	Margarita Nikolaeva	USSR
1956	Larisa Latynina	USSR
1952	Ekaterina Kalinthouk	USSR

UNEVEN PARALLEL BARS

Year	Winner	Country
1980	Maxi Gnauck	GDR
1976	Nadia Comaneci	Romania
1972	Karin Janz	GDR
1968	Vera Caslavska	Czechoslovakia
1964	Polina Astakhova	USSR
1960	Polina Astakhova	USSR
1956	Agnes Keleti	Hungary
1952	Margit Korondi	Hungary

TEAM COMPETITION

Year	Winner	Year	Winner
1980	USSR	1964	USSR
1976	USSR	1960	USSR
1972	USSR	1956	USSR
1968	USSR	1952	USSR

1980 NCAA GYMNASTICS CHAMPIONS

DIVISION I

Event	Winner	School
All-Around	Jim Hartung	Nebraska
Floor exercise	Steve Elliot	Nebraska
Pommel horse	David Stoldt	Illinois
Rings	Jim Hartung	Nebraska
Long horse vault	Ron Galimore	Iowa State
Parallel bars	Philip Cahoy	Nebraska
Horizontal bar	Philip Cahoy	Nebraska
Team championship	university team	Nebraska

DIVISION II

Event	Winner	School
All-Around	Casey Edwards	Wisconsin–Oshkosh
Floor exercise	Casey Edwards	Wisconsin–Oshkosh
Pommel horse	Paul Gretzinger	Wisconsin–Oshkosh
Rings	Casey Edwards	Wisconsin–Oshkosh
Long horse vault	Casey Edwards	Wisconsin–Oshkosh
Parallel bars	Dave Russell	Wisconsin–Oshkosh
Horizontal bar	Casey Edwards	Wisconsin–Oshkosh
Team competition	university team	Wisconsin–Oshkosh

1980 AIAW CHAMPIONS

DIVISION I

Event	Winner	School
All-Around	Sharon Shapiro	UCLA
Balance beam	Sharon Shapiro	UCLA
Floor exercise	Sharon Shapiro	UCLA
Vault	Sharon Shapiro	UCLA
Uneven parallel bars	Sharon Shapiro	UCLA
Team competition	university team	Penn State

DIVISION II

Event	Winner	School
All-Around	Beth Johnson	Centenary
Balance beam	Jill Brown	Centenary
Floor exercise	Margo Todd	Centenary
Vault	Beth Johnson	Centenary
Uneven parallel bars	Beth Johnson	Centenary
Team competition	university team	Centenary

All-Time Greats

Nikolai Andrianov
(1952–)

ABC Sports

Nikolai Andrianov, of the Soviet Union, began training in gymnastics when he was 11 years old. In his first international competition, the European Championships in 1969, he gave a mediocre performance. For the next four or five years, he competed with varied results, winning some events and performing poorly in others. With determination and practice, Andrianov was able to transform himself from a talented but inconsistent performer into the world's leading all-around gymnast. In 1975 he won a gold medal in the all-around at the World Cup, surpassing the Japanese champions to become the world's top-ranked men's gymnast. Andrianov's best performance came at the 1976 Olympics in Montreal, where he scored 9.65 or better in every event he entered, achieving an unprecedented all-around score of 116.65. He took gold medals in the floor exercise, stationary rings, vault, and all-around events.

Nadia Comaneci
(Nov. 12, 1961–)

ABC Sports

One of the things that makes the sport of gymnastics unique is that so young a performer as Comaneci is already part of the story of gymnastics. By the end of the first day of the 1976 Olympics, the Romanian gymnast was already established as the most exciting performer in a galaxy of exciting performers. At 14, Nadia amazed Olympic judges and spectators with her virtually flawless routines, which incorporated the extremely difficult stunts pioneered by Olga Korbut, yet were executed with such impeccable skill that she earned the first perfect score in the history of Olympic gymnastics, and then went on to earn six more. Nadia, who had won the European championship the previous year, had already racked up 19 perfect scores in international competition. She won three Olympic gold medals that year and returned to win two more in Moscow in 1980.

Olga Korbut
(May 15, 1955–)

ABC Sports

Although she was to be overshadowed by Nadia Comaneci, Soviet Olympic star Olga Korbut, now married and retired from international competition, will be remembered as one of the most important contributors to gymnastics, in terms of both technical expertise and promotional efforts. Korbut, who stole the show at the 1972 Olympic Games, won the admiration of judges for her unconventional routines, which featured difficult stunts, some never tried before. She also exhibited a presence that delighted the fans, and practically the whole world sympathized when she burst into tears following a fall that probably cost her the All-Around gold medal. Korbut did, however, pick up gold medals that year for the balance beam, her best event, and for her floor exercise. She was only 17 years old. Despite her fall, Korbut did not lose her confidence, and she continued to perform routines that were highly risky, setting the standard for an entirely new type of gymnastics.

Cathy Rigby Mason
(Dec. 12, 1952–)

ABC Sports

When Cathy Rigby won a silver medal at the World Games in 1970, she became the first American gymnast to take a prize in international competition. Rigby, who overcame a childhood lung ailment to become perhaps the best known U.S. gymnast, began learning gymnastics at age ten. At 15, she was a member of the 1968 U.S. Olympic Team, placing 15th in overall competition. This was the highest standing ever achieved by an American up to that point. Two years later she took a medal at the World Games in Yugoslavia, defeating world all-around champion Ludmilla Turischeva of the Soviet Union and showing that Americans were, at last, able to compete with the best. Before the 1972 Olympics in Munich, Rigby suffered an injury that kept her from competing in the trials. The U.S. Olympic Committee made an exception to its rules and allowed her to be on the team without taking part in the trials. Rigby went on to place tenth at Munich, again setting a record for Americans. Rather than retaining her amateur status to provide for a chance at a 1976 gold medal, Rigby settled on a professional career. Now married, she currently performs as an actress on television, does commercials for various products, serves as a sports commentator for ABC Sports, and runs the Cathy Rigby Gymnastics Camp in Mission Viejo, California.

Kurt Thomas
(Mar. 29, 1956–)

ABC Sports

Thomas is considered not only the best gymnast America has produced, but also the one who has managed to give the United States real credibility in international competition. Many observers think he would have been the first U.S. Olympic gold medalist in gymnastics had the United States participated in the 1980 Olympics in Moscow. Thomas, who began learning gymnastics when he was 14 years old—what many now would consider a very late start—got his first taste of competition at the University of Indiana, where he was an NCAA All-American. He quickly progressed to the international arena where, in 1976, he was part of the U.S. team in both the Pan-American games and the Olympics. In the Pan-Am games he was the highest placed American, finishing third in the all-around competition. An innovative gymnast, Thomas is known for developing the "Thomas Flair," a stunt involving a whirling leg motion used on the pommel horse and in the floor exercise. In 1978 Thomas won a gold medal at the World Championships, and in 1979 improved to two gold medals (in the floor exercise and the horizontal) and three silver medals (for the parallels, the pommel horse, and the all-around). He retired from competition in 1980 and now coaches and serves as a commentator for ABC Sports.

HALL OF FAME

Gymnastics Hall of Fame
Citizens Savings Hall of Fame Athletic Museum
9800 S. Sepulveda Blvd.
Los Angeles, CA 90045
(213) 670-7556
W. R. ("Bill") Schroeder, dir.

Induction Year

Unrecorded
Dallas Bixler
Marshall Brown
Vincent D'Autorio
Gus Kern
Rene J. Kern
Paul Kremple
John Mais
William Matthei
Adolph Picker
Curtis Rottman
James Rozanas
Henry Smidl
Erwin Volze
Herman Witzig

1959
Raymond Bass
Frank Cumiskey
George Gulack
Frank Haubold
Gustav Heineman

Daniel L. Hoffer
Alfred Jochim
Leslie J. Judd
Frank Kriz
Louis H. Mang
Frederick Mayer
Roy E. Moore
Ralph A. Piper
Arthur Pitt
Ben Price
Hartley Price
George Wheeler
Roland Wolfe
Maxmillian W. Younger
Leopold Zwarg

1963
Alfred Bergmann
William Denton
E. A. Eklund
Lester Griffin
Abe Lober
Chester W. Phillips

Henry Schroeder
Charles Vavra
Gene Wettstone

1964
Harry G. Nelson
Emil Preiss
Lyle Welser
Fred Zitta

1965
George P. Nissen

1966
Joseph Giallombardo
Charles Pond
Ted Steeves

1967
Charles W. Graves

1970
Harold Frey

Bruno A. Johnke
Carl A. Patterson
George Szypula
John Van Aalten

1971
Newt Loken
Tom Maloney

1973
Hubert Dunn
Eric Hughes
Paul E. Pina

1974
Meta Neumann Elste
Walter J. Lienert
Clara Schroth Lomady
William Meade
Tony Rossi
Henry Schiget
Helen Schifano Sjursen
Paul Uram
Herbert Vogel
Erna Wachtel

ABC Sports

1975
Marian Twining Barone
Chuck Keeney
George Lewis
Mildred Prchal
William H. Roetzheim
Courtney Shanken

Robert Stout
Frank A. Wolcott

1977
Clayton ("Bud") Marquette
Bernhard Unser
Walter Zwickel

Bill Sorenson
Jerry Todd

1979
Jacquelyn Fie
Abie Grossfeld
Armando Vega

1976
Jack Beckner
Margaret C. Brown
Consetta Caruccio Lenz

1978
Bill Coco
Joe Kotys

1980
Ted Muzyczko
Ed Scrobe
Don Tonry

For the Record

Youngest Olympic team
Romania   1976

Most perfect scores, Olympics
7   Nadia Comaneci, Romania   1976

Most Olympic individual gold medals
7   Victor Tchoukarine, USSR
    Boris Shakhlin, USSR
    Vera Caslavska, Czechoslovakia

Most individual world championships
10   Boris Shakhlin, USSR
     Larisa Latynina, USSR

Youngest international competitor
11   Anita Jokiel, Poland   1977

Most World Cup wins in a single year
5   Ludmilla Turischeva, USSR

Most NCAA titles, single year
5 John Crosby,
Southern Connecticut State 1973

Most NCAA titles, career
12 John Crosby,
Southern Connecticut State

Most NCAA team championships
9 Penn State

Most NCAA individual championships
39 University of Illinois

Did you know ?

1. Who was the only gymnast ever to win the AAU Sullivan Award for amateur athlete of the year?

2. True or False: Nadia Comaneci of Romania is the only gymnast ever to win a perfect score in the Olympics.

3. How many gold medals did Olga Korbut win at the 1976 Olympics in Montreal?

4. What gymnast holds the world's record for the most Olympic medals won during a career?

5. How many people are on an Olympic gymnastics team?

6. How long do women's floor routines last? How many musical instruments may be used to accompany women's floor exercises?

7. What is the highest number of points that can be awarded during team competition?

8. Which of the following did not win an Olympic medal in 1972: Ludmilla Turischeva, Cathy Rigby, Mitsuo Tsukahara, Nelli Kim, Olga Korbut, or Sawao Kato?

9. Name three events that were once part of gymnastics competition but are no longer.

10. The first gymnastics organizations in the United States were social and educational associations imported from Germany. What were they called?

Answers: 1. Kurt Thomas was voted the award in 1979. **2.** False. In 1976, the first year any gymnast ever received a perfect score, Comaneci earned seven and Nelli Kim earned two; **3.** None; **4.** Larisa Latynina of the Soviet Union holds nine gold medals, five silver, and four bronze, for a grand total of 18 Olympic medals; **5.** Six; **6.** From 60 to 90 seconds; one; **7.** 600 for men; 400 for women; **8.** Cathy Rigby and Nelli Kim; **9.** Trampolining, tumbling, and rebound tumbling, which were dropped in 1969; **10.** Turnverein.

Key Words

aerial cartwheel   a type of flip that looks like a cartwheel but is performed without the hands touching anything.

Arabian handspring   a handspring that is begun out of a jump rather than from a standing position.

croup   the end of a vaulting horse nearest the gymnast as he approaches it, or the right side of a pommel horse.

dismount   process of coming off a piece of equipment, such as the horse or parallel bars.

dive   any stunt that begins with a jump onto hands or arms and ends with the gymnast falling into a roll.

false grip   a method of grasping equipment in which the wrist is bent and the heel of the hand is leaning on the equipment.

flic-flac   a backward handspring.

grip   the position of the hands on any piece of equipment.

handspring   a type of somersault in which the gymnast performs a momentary handstand; only the hands and feet may touch the floor.

Hecht vault   a leap over a vaulting horse with the legs and the body held straight.

kip   a rapid straightening from a pike position, also called a kip-up.

lever   in men's gymnastics, a position in which a gymnast on the rings holds the body parallel to the floor.

low bar   a bar used to practice exercises normally performed on the horizontal bar. The low bar is adjustable and usually at hip level.

neck   the part of a vaulting horse farthest away from the gymnast, or the left side of a pommel horse.

needle scale   posture in which one leg is extended straight or nearly straight and the body is parallel to that or the other leg.

overgrip   a manner of grasping equipment in which the palms face outward from the near side of the apparatus; also called front grip or regular grip.

pike   a position in which the body is bent at the waist, legs are straight, and back is bowed—the body resembles a "V."

pivot   a turn on one leg with the other leg extended.

Reuther board   a small springboard used to aid a vault.

saddle   the middle area of a pommel horse, located between the pommels.

salto   a somersault in the air, either forward or backward, usually performed during the floor exercise.

scale a position in which the gymnast is standing on one leg with the other leg extended up to the side or straight back.

stoop through a backward swing on the horizontal bar in men's gymnastics. The gymnast tucks the straightened legs inside the arms, between the chest and the bar, before piking upward; also called a jam.

straddle mount method of mounting a piece of equipment by leaping up and landing on it, legs spread apart.

straddle seat a position in which the gymnast is supported on the parallel bars by the hands, with the legs in a straddling position.

straddle stand a position in which the gymnast has feet wide apart and pointing in the same direction.

straddle vault a leap over an object using the hands for impetus, with the legs extended out to both sides.

undergrip a way of holding on to equipment with the palms facing inward from the far side; also called reverse grip.

underswing a swing on a piece of equipment, with the body hanging below the hands.

uprises movements from a hanging position on rings or bars to a position where the body is straight and supported by the arms; also called a stem.

V seat a position in which a seated gymnast holds legs and body in the air in the shape of a "V."

vault the use of the hands to propel oneself over an object.

walkover an exercise in which the gymnast bends forward or backward from a standing position, puts both hands on the floor, goes into a handstand by lifting one leg at a time, and descends one leg at a time.

ABC Sports

10   HOCKEY

o the uninitiated observer, an ice hockey match may look like a bizarrely choreographed free-for-all played and watched by people who enjoy nothing so much as a Sunday afternoon of gratuitous violence. In fact, though, ice hockey is a game that demands intense grace, agility, and concentration, not to mention intricate footwork and incredibly precise timing. Compared to its earliest counterparts, moreover, modern ice hockey is a paragon of gentility.

The site of the first hockey match is a matter of heated dispute among several Canadian cities. Most sources agree that the game began as a makeshift attempt to play cricket and other European lawn games during the frigid North American winter. These early players, logically enough, played their game on ice—often one hundred strong. Out of these early free-for-alls, in the 1880s, modern ice hockey gradually emerged, first in Canada, and later in the United States.

The game that eventually developed—played by six-man teams consisting of one goalie, three forwards, and two wings each—is now one of the major draws in professional sports.

Unlike most sports, hockey's rules of conduct are not centered around the idea that sportsmanlike behavior precludes violence. In hockey, violence is acceptable, but must be kept within specific bounds. Penalties are awarded for violence that is deemed "excessive"—a term only vaguely defined—and many rules, such as that only a team captain may speak to a referee, or that a third player may not enter a fight between two others, were written to try to contain some of the more extreme violence in a sport where ramming a person with one's body or slamming him against the side boards are perfectly legitimate moves.

Despite its reputation as a violent sport, a hockey game is usually won by the players who show the most control. The legendary Montreal Canadiens, who hold the record for Stanley Cup wins, are noted less for their brute strength than for their skating skill, precision timing, and coordinated team effort. Such great players as Bobby Orr, "Rocket" Richard, and Phil Esposito are better known for their special skills and keen sense of timing than for their ability to inflict injuries on their opponents.

Although for almost a hundred years North America, and Canada in particular, was considered the exclusive domain of ice hockey, in recent decades the sport has gained popularity internationally. In the Soviet Union, for example, the game is taken so seriously that, unlike many teams in North America, Soviet hockey teams train all year round and practice between matches. The Soviets' military-style approach to ice hockey earned them the Olympic championship in 1972, but that approach has never caught on with North American fans, who prefer the fluidity, excitement, and seeming confusion of a sport that began (and many believe still belongs) in the wild terrain of their own backyards.

Great Moments

1875   In the first known newspaper reference to ice hockey, the *Montreal Gazette* announces an evening game to be played on March 3 in the Victoria Skating Rink.

1888   James Creighton forms the Rideau Hall Rebels hockey club, among whose early members are two sons of Lord Stanley, the governor general.

1890   The Ontario Hockey Association, the first provincial league, is formed.

1892   Lord Stanley donates a cup for the Canadian championship, won by the Montreal Amateur Athletic Club. (The Stanley Cup remains the most prized award in hockey.)

1893   Yale and Johns Hopkins play the first recorded college hockey game.

1896   The U.S. Amateur Hockey League is formed.

1917   The first game of the newly formed National Hockey League is played, on December 19.

1918   The NHL institutes the center red line to permit forward passing in the center ice area, thus speeding up the game.

1920   The Allan Cup champions (from Canada) compete in and win the first Olympic international hockey competition. The Canadians dominate the sport for the next 50 years.

1924   The Boston Bruins become the first U.S. team to join the NHL. The Montreal Maroons also join that year.

1936 The International League and the Canadian–American League merge to become the American Hockey League.

1947 The first NHL All-Star game is held, in Toronto.

1961 The Hockey Hall of Fame opens, in Toronto.

1967 The NHL doubles its size from 6 to 12 teams in response to pressure from television stations that want West Coast teams and from threats by some cities to form a new league.

1970 The NHL expands to 14 teams with the addition of the Buffalo Sabres, the Vancouver Canucks, and the Chicago Black Hawks.

1972 The Atlanta Flames and New York Islanders join the NHL. The World Hockey Association is formed, with teams from Vancouver, Calgary, Edmonton, Winnipeg, Quebec City, Cleveland, Phoenix, Cincinnati, and Indianapolis.

1974 The NHL expands to 18 teams with the addition of the Kansas City Scouts and the Washington Capitals. Two conferences (Prince of Wales and Campbell) of two divisions each are formed.

1979 The NHL expands to 21 teams, with the Edmonton Oilers, the Hartford Whalers, the Quebec Nordiques, and the Winnipeg Jets joining.

1980 The underdog U.S. hockey team wins a gold medal at the Winter Olympics at Lake Placid, New York.

The Setup

Of the three professional ice hockey leagues, the largest is the National Hockey League (NHL) with 21 teams from the United States and Canada. The American Hockey League (AHL) also includes both U.S. and Canadian teams; the Central Hockey League includes nine teams, all from American cities.

AMERICAN HOCKEY LEAGUE
Suite 533
31 Elm St.
Springfield, MA 01103
(413) 781-2030
Jack A. Butterfield, pres. and treas.

CENTRAL HOCKEY LEAGUE
Suite 718
6060 N. Central Expwy.
Dallas, TX 75206
(214) 692-6261
Norman Poile, pres.

NATIONAL HOCKEY LEAGUE
(CANADIAN OFFICE)
960 Sun Life Bldg.
Montreal, Quebec
Canada H3B 2W2
(514) 871-9220
Brian F. O'Neill, vice-pres.

NATIONAL HOCKEY LEAGUE
(U.S. OFFICE)
14th Floor
1221 Avenue of the Americas
New York, NY 10020
(212) 398-1100
John A. Ziegler, Jr., pres.

NATIONAL HOCKEY LEAGUE

PRINCE OF WALES CONFERENCE

Norris Division	Adams Division
Detroit Red Wings	Boston Bruins
Hartford Whalers	Buffalo Sabres
Los Angeles Kings	Minnesota North Stars
Montreal Canadiens	Quebec Nordiques
Pittsburgh Penguins	Toronto Maple Leafs

CLARENCE CAMPBELL CONFERENCE

Patrick Division	Smythe Division
Calgary Flames	Chicago Black Hawks
New York Islanders	Colorado Rockies
New York Rangers	Edmonton Oilers
Philadelphia Flyers	St. Louis Blues
Washington Capitals	Vancouver Canucks
	Winnipeg Jets

NHL CLUBS

BOSTON BRUINS
150 Causeway St.
Boston, MA 02114
(617) 227-3223
Paul A. Mooney, pres.
(games played at Boston Garden)

BUFFALO SABRES
Memorial Auditorium
Buffalo, NY 14202
(716) 856-7300
Seymour H. Knox III, chairman of board
and pres.
(games played at Memorial Auditorium)

CALGARY FLAMES
P.O. Box 1540, Station M
Calgary, Alberta T2P 3B9
(403) 233-8383
Nelson Skalbania, pres. and gov.
(games played at the Stampede Corral)

CHICAGO BLACK HAWKS
Chicago Stadium
1800 W. Madison St.
Chicago, IL 60612
(312) 733-5300
Arthur M. Wirtz, chairman
(games played at Chicago Stadium)

COLORADO ROCKIES
McNichols Sports Arena
One McNichols Plaza
Denver, CO 80204
(303) 573-1800
Arthur E. Imperatore, chairman of board
(games played at McNichols Sports Arena)

DETROIT RED WINGS
Joe Louis Sports Arena
600 Civic Center Dr.
Detroit, MI 48226
(313) 963-8400
Bruce A. Norris, chairman and pres.
(games played at Joe Louis Sports Arena
and Olympia Stadium)

EDMONTON OILERS
Northlands Coliseum
Edmonton, Alberta
Canada T5B 4M9
(403) 474-8561
Glen Slather, pres.
(games played at Northlands Coliseum)

HARTFORD WHALERS
1 Civic Center Pl.
Hartford, CT 06103
(203) 728-3366
Howard L. Baldwin, gov. and mng. gen.
partner
(games played at Hartford Civic Center)

LOS ANGELES KINGS
3900 W. Manchester Blvd.
Box 10–The Forum
Inglewood, CA 90306
(213) 674-6000
Dr. Jerry Buss, chairman of board
(games played at The Forum)

MINNESOTA NORTH STARS
Met Center
7901 Cedar Ave., S
Bloomington, MN 55420
(612) 853-9333
George Gund III, chairman of board
(games played at Met Center)

MONTREAL CANADIENS
2313 St. Catherine St., W
Montreal, Quebec H3H 1N2
(514) 932-6181
Morgan McCammon, pres.
(games played at Montreal Forum)

NEW YORK ISLANDERS
Nassau Veterans Memorial Coliseum
Uniondale, NY 11553
(516) 794-4100
John O. Pickett, Jr., chairman of board and
    gov.
(games played at Nassau Coliseum)

NEW YORK RANGERS
Madison Square Garden
4 Pennsylvania Pl.
New York, NY 10001
(212) 563-8000
Michael Burke, chairman
(games played at Madison Square Garden)

PHILADELPHIA FLYERS
The Spectrum–Pattison Pl.
Philadelphia, PA 19148
(215) 465-4500
Joseph C. Scott, chairman of board
(games played at the Spectrum)

PITTSBURGH PENGUINS
Civic Arena
Gate #7
Pittsburgh, PA 15219
(412) 434-8911
Vincent J. Bartimo, chairman of board and
    pres.
(games played at Civic Arena)

QUEBEC NORDIQUES
5555 3rd Ave. W
Charlesbourg, Quebec G1H 6R1
(418) 627-3801
Jean Lesage, chairman of board
(games played at the Quebec Coliseum)

ABC Sports

ST. LOUIS BLUES
The Checkerdome
5700 Oakland Ave.
St. Louis, MO 63110
(314) 781-5300
R. Hal Dean, chairman of board
(games played at the Checkerdome)

TORONTO MAPLE LEAFS
Maple Leaf Gardens
60 Carlton St.
Toronto, Ontario M5B 1L1
(416) 977-1641
Harold E. Ballard, pres. and mng. dir.
(games played at Maple Leaf Gardens)

VANCOUVER CANUCKS
Pacific Coliseum
100 N. Renfrew St.

Vancouver, British Columbia V5K 3N7
(604) 254-5141
Frank A. Griffiths, chairman
(games played at Pacific Coliseum)

WASHINGTON CAPITALS
Capital Centre
Landover, MD 20786
(301) 350-3400
Abe Pollin, pres. and gov.
(games played at Capital Centre)

WINNIPEG JETS
15-1430 Maroons Rd.
Winnipeg, Manitoba R3G 015
(204) 772-9491
R. G. Graham, chairman of board
(games played at Winnipeg Arena)

The Basics

Object of the game   To score the most goals by the end of three 20-minute playing periods. The team in control of the puck attempts to score by shooting the puck past the opposing goalie. The defending team attempts to block the attackers from scoring and to gain control of the puck themselves.

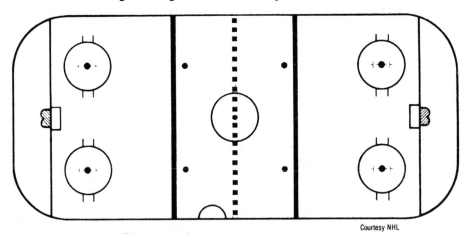

Courtesy NHL

Indoor ice rink   (Diagram above)

Equipment   Players wear special ice skates and use long sticks with a blade at the bottom to push a small, flat, circular hard-rubber puck across the ice into a goal. Goaltenders may wear heavily padded protective clothing and face masks. All players wear gloves.

Players   Six players make up a team: a center, two wingers, a left and right defense, and a goalie. A team may have 15 players and a regular and spare goalkeeper in uniform at the beginning of the game. Players may be substituted at any time during the game.

Length of game   A game lasts for three 20-minute playing periods, with 10-minute breaks between them. If at the end of three periods the score is even, the game ends in a tie (except in playoff competition).

Officials   A referee, two linesmen, two goal judges, an official scorer, a game time-keeper, a penalty timekeeper, and a statistician are present at every NHL game.

Rule 1   ***Face-off***   The game begins in the center circle of the rink with two opposing players attempting to gain control of the puck.

Rule 2   ***The puck***   The puck must be kept in motion at all times. Only the goalie may use his hands to direct the puck (except when a player must deflect a flying puck). No one may direct the puck by kicking it.

Rule 3   ***Stopping play***   The referee may whistle for all play to stop if: he has lost sight of the puck; the puck is out of the rink; a goal has been scored; or a violation has been committed.

Rule 4   ***Violations***   Violations include excessive boarding, fighting, kicking the puck, intentionally shooting the puck outside the rink, delaying the game, overly violent body checking, interference, icing, and harassing the goalie.

Rule 5   ***Blue line***   No member of the attacking team may cross the defensive blue line (into an opponent's end zone) ahead of the puck.

Rule 6   ***Red line***   Players on their own side of the red line may not shoot the puck across the goal line of the opposing team (unless the team is short-handed because a player is serving a penalty off the ice).

Rule 7   ***Offside***   A player may not be in the attacking zone ahead of the puck at the time a teammate has propelled the puck over the blue line; a player cannot receive a pass when he is in the neutral zone, over the red line, if the pass is from a teammate in the defending zone and the puck has crossed the blue line and the red line.

Rule 8   ***Penalties***   For a minor penalty, any player, other than a goalkeeper, must leave the ice for two minutes, during which time no substitute is permitted. For the first major penalty of a game, the offender, except for the goalkeeper, must leave the ice for five minutes, during which time no substitute is permitted. For the third major penalty in one game, the same player is ejected from the game, but a substitute may replace him after five minutes. Misconduct penalties require removal of the player from the game for 10 minutes, but a substitute player may replace him.

Rule 9   ***Delayed penalties***   If a third player of any team is penalized while two players of the same team are serving penalties, the penalty time of the third player begins after the penalty time of one of the first two has elapsed.

Rule 10   ***Penalty shot***   Certain rule violations require that the opposing team have an opportunity for a shot on goal, in which a designated player attempts to score from the center face-off spot, without interference except by the opposing goalkeeper.

Rule 11   Scoring   A goal is scored when the puck completely crosses an opponent's goal line. Each goal is worth one point.

Rule 12   Points system   Points determine the ranking of a player and of a team. A point is awarded for each goal and for each assist a player accomplishes. A goaltender is rated on the number of goals that were scored against him.

How to watch

New York Rangers

with Phil Esposito

Phil Esposito, who retired last year after an outstanding career with the Chicago Black Hawks, the Boston Bruins, and the New York Rangers, says that a good hockey player is, first and foremost, a good athlete. Hockey differs from such sports as football and soccer, he says, in the obvious way that the sport involves skating "with razor blades on your feet and a club in your hand." But it resembles these and many other sports in several respects. "Coordination is important, naturally, and the ability to manipulate on skates. But a guy has to be a thinker. He has to have a 'hockey sense,' the ability to anticipate, to act on the spur of the moment, to make up his mind quickly." The reason, Esposito explains, is that hockey has relatively few set plays. Such plays as there are generally apply in power-play situations, where a team is playing with a one-man advantage, or in a penalty-killing situation, where a team playing shorthanded is trying to run down the penalty clock.

Because hockey plays are not planned in advance, communication between team members on the ice is common, and often constant. "The team that talks most on the ice," says Esposito, "is usually the team that wins." Because the game is so fast, players often have to depend on recognizing a teammate's voice to know where to send the puck. Sometimes, Esposito observes, a player will pass the puck behind him directly into the possession of an opposing player. That, he explains, is often because that other player is "yelling like crazy at him, yelling his name," and convincing his opponent that he is on the same team.

Though hockey has few set plays, it is still very much a team sport. "Very seldom," Esposito says, "does one player dominate the team—or even a game. Bobby Orr did it, and I believe Wayne Gretzky does it now. But I don't remember any other guys doing it." He continues: "I think that the Islanders, for example, would win without Denis Potvin, or without Mike Bossy, the Rangers without Ron Duguay, the Montreal Canadiens without Lafleur—not as much, perhaps, but they would win."

How much a team wins depends on the coach as well as the players. "I never thought a coach was important till I reached the end of my career," Esposito admits.

"Then I realized how important the coach is to a hockey team. He has to be a leader, a babysitter, and a psychiatrist all in one." These requirements are made more acute, he notes, because a hockey team has only one or two coaches. "If I'm ever lucky enough to become the manager or head of an NHL team, I plan to use three, or even four coaches. The defensemen would practice first, for 15 minutes or a half-hour, then the forwards, and then everyone together—under my tutelage. I have a lot of ideas that differ from the traditional ones."

One area besides coaching technique where Esposito sees room for improvement is in the televised coverage of hockey games. Hockey presents a special challenge for TV crews, as the speed of the game makes it very difficult for a TV camera to follow. "The Canadian TV crews," Esposito says, "do a better job than the American ones because they're more familiar with the game. It's the national game up there so they spend more money, not on production but on more cameras." The best way he knows of to improve hockey coverage, he says, is to put two cameras in each of three zones. "With a super director—one who knows hockey—anticipating where the puck is going to be, using split-screen, and so forth, I think watching the game on television would be more enjoyable. It's good, but it could be better." (One notable exception, Esposito adds, is Al Michaels, who covered hockey in the most recent Olympics. "He was terrific because he created excitement. The announcers have to create excitement, they have to keep the people's interest. When you're at a game live, you're there. You hear the noises, you hear the crowd roaring, you see the body checks, you're watching the action in front of the net instead of the puck at the blue line.")

Ice is ice, or is it? "Madison Square Garden, up until two years ago, was considered the worst ice in hockey," Esposito remarks. "It was chippy, and controlling the bouncing puck was very difficult. Since that time, they've come on really well and their ice is now good. Some other rinks, though, still have soft ice, and some have ice that is harder and chippier." Like ice, the characteristics of the boards of one rink in rebounding the puck may differ from those of another.

What makes a young hockey player gravitate toward one or another hockey position: goaltender, forward, defenseman? That, says Esposito, is not an easy question. "As far as a goaltender is concerned, I can only speak of my brother. He just had a knack for the position, he wanted to be a goalie, and he could skate better than I could." Despite a common notion, a goaltender, says Esposito, has to skate as well as anyone else on the team. "He has to have excellent balance." A forward must have good mobility on the ice, and a good sense of where the goal is and of how to get the puck into it. A good defenseman is one who lacks fear, who is willing to block shots without goal pads on, to take the heavy hits in front of the net, and to be a little bit more physical than the other players. Not incidentally, Esposito adds, he must be a player willing to forego some of the fame attendant on a star forward.

Young players to watch? Ron Duguay, Barry Beck, Ron Greschner, Darryl Sutter, Steve Christoff, Wayne Babych, and Glen Anderson, Esposito offers. But, he adds, "there are many who have ability. Whether they have the determination and the dedication is another story. If they do, they can become very successful. If they don't, they will be just average, run-of-the-mill players."

Esposito was once asked, by someone close to him, what he had had to give up to be successful in hockey. "Youth," he had answered, meaning that the dedication it had taken to excel at the game had not left much time, when he had been a youngster, for anything else. "I had to do that," "Espo" says, "because I really had to work at it. Other people don't have to do that. But it does demand discipline from the time you're 17, and if you can discipline yourself, you've got it made. If you can't discipline yourself, then you're wasting everybody's time."

Main Events

THE STANLEY CUP (NHL)

Year	Winner	Loser
1980	N.Y. Islanders 4	Philadelphia 2
1979	Montreal 4	N.Y. Rangers 1
1978	Montreal 4	Boston 2
1977	Montreal 4	Boston 0
1976	Montreal 4	Philadelphia 0
1975	Philadelphia 4	Buffalo 0
1974	Philadelphia 4	Boston 2
1973	Montreal 4	Chicago 2
1972	Boston 4	N.Y. Rangers 2
1971	Montreal 4	Chicago 3
1970	Boston 4	St. Louis 0

PRINCE OF WALES TROPHY

Presented each year to the team finishing with the most points in the Prince of Wales Conference at the end of the regular season.

Year	Winner	Year	Winner
1979–80	Buffalo Sabres	1974–75	Buffalo Sabres
1978–79	Montreal Canadiens	1973–74	Boston Bruins
1977–78	Montreal Canadiens	1972–73	Montreal Canadiens
1976–77	Montreal Canadiens	1971–72	Boston Bruins
1975–76	Montreal Canadiens	1970–71	Boston Bruins

CLARENCE S. CAMPBELL BOWL (NHL)

Year	Winner	Year	Winner
1979–80	Philadelphia	1974–75	Philadelphia
1978–79	N.Y. Islanders	1973–74	Philadelphia
1977–78	N.Y. Islanders	1972–73	Chicago
1976–77	Philadelphia	1971–72	Chicago
1975–76	Philadelphia	1970–71	Chicago

HART MEMORIAL TROPHY (NHL)

Awarded annually by the Professional Hockey Writers Association to a team's most valuable player.

Year	Winner	Year	Winner
1980	Wayne Gretzky (Edmonton)	1975	Bobby Clarke (Philadelphia)
1979	Bryan Trottier (N.Y. Islanders)	1974	Phil Esposito (Boston)
1978	Guy Lafleur (Montreal)	1973	Bobby Clarke (Philadelphia)
1977	Guy Lafleur (Montreal)	1972	Bobby Orr (Boston)
1976	Bobby Clarke (Philadelphia)	1971	Bobby Orr (Boston)

CALDER MEMORIAL TROPHY (NHL)

Awarded annually to the player selected by Professional Hockey Writers Association as the most proficient in his first year in the NHL.

Year	Winner	Year	Winner
1980	Ray Bourque (Boston)	1975	Eric Vail (Atlanta)
1979	Bobby Smith (Minnesota)	1974	Denis Potvin (N.Y. Islanders)
1978	Mike Bossy (N.Y. Islanders)	1973	Steve Vickers (N.Y. Rangers)
1977	Willi Plett (Atlanta)	1972	Ken Dryden (Montreal)
1976	Bryan Trottier (N.Y. Rangers)	1971	Gilbert Perreault (Buffalo)

All-Time Greats

Jean A. Beliveau
(Aug. 31, 1931–)

Montreal Canadiens

"Le Gros Bill," who was six feet three and weighed 210 pounds, so impressed the Montreal Canadiens in 1953 that they bought the entire Quebec Senior League to protect their rights to him. He became the highest paid player and the highest scoring center in the history of the NHL, scoring 507 goals in 18 seasons. In 1955–56, Beliveau scored 47 goals and 41 assists, setting another NHL record. In 1971, Beliveau retired, after leading the Montreal Canadiens to their tenth Stanley Cup victory since he joined them.

Phil Esposito
(Feb. 29, 1941–)

Boston Bruins

Esposito joined the Chicago Black Hawks in 1963, directly from a minor league team in Sault Ste. Marie. Traded by Chicago to the Boston Bruins, he went on to become a hockey superstar, second only to Gordie Howe in most NHL careers goals, most NHL career points, most goals including playoffs, most points including play-offs, most 20-or-more-goal seasons, and most consecutive 20-or-more-goal seasons; he shares with Bobby Hull the record for most 40-or-more-goal seasons. In addition, Esposito holds the NHL records for most games scoring three or more goals, most consecutive 40-or-more-goal seasons, most 100-or-more point seasons, most goals and most points in one season (including and excluding playoffs), most power-play goals in one season, and most shots on goal in one season. Traded from Boston to the New York Rangers in 1975, Esposito retired from play in 1981.

Gordie Howe
(Mar. 31, 1928–)

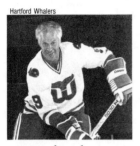
Hartford Whalers

Gordie Howe is one of the most durable, as well as remarkable, players in hockey history. Howe, who retired in 1971 from the Detroit Red Wings at the age of 43 (he began his career with the same team when he was 18) surprised the hockey world by joining his two sons on the AHL Houston Aeros two years later. Howe then joined the Hartford Whalers for the 1979–80 season. Among the many accomplishments in Howe's remarkable career are setting NHL records for the most seasons played, most games played, most goals (including and excluding playoffs), most assists, most points (including and excluding playoffs), and most 30-or-more-goal seasons. Howe is the NHL's all-time top scoring leader, all-time career-point leader, and all-time career assists leader, and he is considered by most fans, and by players themselves, to be the greatest all-round hockey player in the history of the sport.

Bobby Hull
(Jan. 3, 1939–)

Hartford Whalers

The fastest skater in hockey, Hull is the third highest scorer in the history of the NHL. He turned pro in 1957 when he joined the Chicago Black Hawks, and was the first player to earn $100,000 a year (1968–69). He has had six 100-or-more-point seasons. Known for his wicked slap shot and controlled style of playing, Hull has also completed a record 13 consecutive seasons scoring 30 or more goals.

Bobby Orr
(Mar. 20, 1938–)

Boston Bruins

Bobby Orr, inducted into the Hockey Hall of Fame in 1979, was largely responsible for turning the Boston Bruins into a top hockey club. Orr, who played for Chicago, Winnipeg, and Hartford as well, holds the career record for most-assists-per-game average, and shares the record for most 100-or-more-point seasons (1969–74 seasons). Orr also comes in second only to Esposito for most points in one season and three times set the record for most assists in one season. He scored more goals in a season than any other defenseman (setting five records) and more points in a season than any other defense player (setting three records).

Maurice Richard
(Aug. 14, 1924–)

Montreal Canadiens

Maurice Richard played with the Montreal Canadiens from 1942 until his retirement in 1960. Despite a series of injuries, "The Rocket" was the first player to score 50 goals in a 50-game season, many of them earned through the exercise of sheer brute strength. He was also known for a temper that got him suspended from the 1955 Stanley Cup games for assaulting two Boston players, but he was nevertheless inducted into the Hockey Hall of Fame in 1961, after scoring 544 goals and 421 assists in his 978-league-game career.

Hockey Hall of Fame
Canadian National Exhibition Park
Toronto, Ontario M6K 3C3
(416) 366-7551

Members of the Hockey Hall of Fame are:

1945
Donald H. ("Dan") Bain
Hobart ("Hobey") Baker
Russell Bowie
Aubrey ("Dit") Clapper
Charles Robert ("Chuck") Gardiner
Eddie Gerard
Aurel Joliat
Frank McGee
Howie Morenz
Frank Nighbor
Lester Patrick
Tommy Phillips
Harvey Pulford
Arthur Howie Ross
Edward W. ("Eddie") Shore
Hod Stuart
Frederic ("Cyclone") Taylor
Georges Vezina

1950
Allan M. ("Scotty") Davidson
Charles Graham Drinkwater
Michael ("Mike") Grant
Silas Seth ("Si") Griffis
Edouard Charles ("Newsy") Lalonde
Joseph ("Joe") Malone
George Taylor Richardson
Harry J. Trihey

1952
Richard R. ("Dickie") Boon
William Osser Cook
Frank Xavier ("Moose") Goheen

Ernest ("Moose") Johnson
Duncan ("Mickey") MacKay

1958
Frank Boucher
Francis Michael ("King") Clancy
Sprague Cleghorn
Alex Connell
Mervyn A. ("Red") Dutton
Frank Foyston
Frank Frederickson
Herbert Martin ("Herb") Gardiner
George Hay
James Dickenson ("Dick") Irvin
Ivan ("Ching") Johnson
Gordon ("Duke") Keats
Hugh Lehman
George McNamara
Patrick Joseph ("Paddy") Moran

1959
John James ("Jack") Adams
Cyril ("Cy") Denneny
Cecil R. ("Tiny") Thompson

1960
George ("Buck") Boucher
Sylvio Mantha
John Phillip ("Jack") Walker

1961
Charles Joseph Sylvanus ("Syl") Apps
Charles W. Conacher
Clarence Henry ("Hap") Day

George Hainsworth
Joseph Henry Hall
Percy LeSueur
Frank Rankin
R. J. Maurice ("Rocket") Richard
Milton Conrad ("Milt") Schmidt
Oliver Levi Seibert
Bruce Stuart

1962
Harry L. ("Punch") Broadbent
Harold Hugh ("Harry") Cameron
Samuel Russell ("Rusty") Crawford
John Proctor ("Jack") Darragh
James Henry ("Jimmy") Gardner
Hamilton Livingstone ("Billy") Gilmour
Wilfred ("Shorty") Green
William Milton ("Riley") Hern
Charles Thomas ("Tom") Hooper
John Bower ("Bouse") Hutton
Harry M. Hyland
Jean Baptiste ("Jack") Laviolette
Fred G. ("Steamer") Maxwell
William George ("Billy") McGimsie
Edward Reginald ("Reg") Noble
Didier ("Pit") Pitre
J. D. ("Jack") Ruttan
David ("Sweeney") Schriner
Harold Edward ("Bullet Joe") Simpson
Alfred E. Smith
Russell ("Barney") Stanley
Nelson ("Nels") Stewart
Martin ("Marty") Walsh
Harry E. Watson
Harry Westwick
Fred Whitcroft
Gordon Allan ("Phat") Wilson

1963
Ebenezer R. ("Ebbie") Goodfellow
A. Joseph Primeau
Earl Walter Seibert

1964
Douglas Wagner Bentley
William Ronald Durnan
Albert C. ("Babe") Siebert
John Sherratt ("Black Jack") Stewart

1965
Martin J. ("Marty") Barry
Clinton S. Benedict
Arthur F. Farrell
George Reginald ("Red") Homer
Sydney Harris Howe
John ("Jack") Marshall
William ("Billy") Mosienko

Blair Russel
Ernest Russell
Fred Scanlan

1966
Maxwell H. L. Bentley
Hector ("Toe") Blake
Emile Joseph ("Butch") Bouchard
Francis Charles Brimsek
Theodore Samuel ("Teeder") Kennedy
Elmer James Lach
Robert Blake Theodore ("Ted") Lindsay
Walter ("Babe") Pratt
Kenneth Joseph Reardon

1967
Walter Edward ("Turk") Broda
Neil MacNeil Colville
Harry Oliver

1968
William Mailes Cowley

1969
Sidney Gerald Abel
Bryan Aldwyn Hextall
Leonard Patrick ("Red") Kelly
Roy Worters

1970
Cecil Henry ("Babe") Dye
William Alexander Gadsby
Thomas Christian Johnson

1971
Harvey ("Busher") Jackson
Gordon Roberts
Terrance Gordon ("Terry") Sawchuk
Ralph ("Cooney") Weiland

1972
Jean Arthur Beliveau
Joseph ("Boom Boom") Geoffrion
Harry ("Hap") Holmes
Gordon Howe
Reginald ("Hooley") Smith

1973
Douglas Norman Harvey
Claude Earl ("Chuck") Rayner
Thomas James Smith

1974
Billy Burch
Arthur Edmund Coulter
Thomas Dunderdale
Richard Winston Moore

1975
George Edward Armstrong
Irvine Wallace ("Ace") Bailey
Gordon Arthur Drillon
Glenn Henry Hall
Joseph Albert Pierre Paul Pilote

1976
John William Bower
Hubert George ("Bill") Quackenbush

1977
Alex Delvecchio
Miles Gilbert ("Tim") Horton

1978
Andrew James ("Andy") Bathgate
Joseph Jacques Omer Plante
Joseph Rene Marcel Pronovost

1979
Henry Vernon ("Harry") Howell
Robert Gordon Orr
Joseph Henri Richard

1980
Harry Lumley
Joseph Lynn Patrick
Lorne John ("Gump") Worsley

For the Record

INDIVIDUAL RECORDS

Most goals, career
801   Gordie Howe   26 seasons

Most assists, career
1,049   Gordie Howe   26 seasons

Most points, career
1,850   Gordie Howe   26 seasons

Most games scoring 3 or more goals
32   Phil Esposito   17 seasons

Most 50-or-more goal seasons
6   Guy Lafleur   9 seasons

Most goals, season
76   Phil Esposito   1970–71

Most points, season
164   Wayne Gretzky   1980–81

Most goals by a rookie, season
53   Mike Bossy   1977–78

Most shorthanded goals, season
10   Marcel Dionne   1974–75

Longest undefeated streak by a goaltender
32 games   Gerry Cheevers   1971–72

Most goals, game
7   Joe Malone   1920

Most points, game
10   Darryl Sittler   1976

Most penalties, game
9   Jim Dorey   1968

Fastest goal from start of a period
4 sec.   Claude Provost   1957

TEAM RECORDS

Most points, season
132   Montreal Canadiens   1976–77

Most wins, season
60   Montreal Canadiens   1976–77

Most ties, season
24   Philadelphia Flyers   1969–70

Most goals, season
399   Boston Bruins   1970–71

Most shorthanded goals, season
25 Boston Bruins 1970–71

Most assists, season
697 Boston Bruins 1970–71

Most scoring points, season
1,096 Boston Bruins 1970–71

Most 100-or-more-point scorers in one season
4 Boston Bruins 1970–71

Most shutouts, season
22 Montreal Canadiens 1928–29

Fewest goals against, season (min. 70 games)
131 Toronto Maple Leafs 1953–54
     Montreal Canadiens 1955–56

Most goals by one team, game
16 Montreal Canadiens 1920

Most points by one team, game
40 Buffalo Sabres 1975

Most penalties by one team, game
42 Boston Bruins 1981
    Minnesota North Stars 1981

Longest winning record
14 games Boston Bruins Dec. 1929–Jan. 1930

Longest undefeated record in one season
35 games Philadelphia Flyers Oct. 1979–Jan. 1980

Did you know?

1. What was the "Curse of Muldoon?"

2. To what did the New York Rangers attribute their amazing rise from a .500 record in December 1951 to winning 9 of 11 games by early January?

3. Many sets of three brothers have played in the NHL, but what *four* brothers had successful professional hockey careers?

4. When was the NHL's only no-score, no-penalty game?

5. Only one player not on the Montreal Canadiens has ever scored two Stanley Cup winning goals. Who was this player and what years did he score the winning goals?

6. Hockey is unique among sports in that it has a special official solely to keep track of penalty time served. What player has served the most penalty time in the history of the NHL?

7. Hockey is known for its violence, and many players have suffered bruises or more serious injuries from being hit by puck, sticks, or other players. Only one player, however, was ever set on fire during a game. Who was he and how did it happen?

8. What team won the 1938 Stanley Cup despite a dismal season record of 14 wins, 29 losses, and 9 ties?

Answers: 1. In 1927, former Chicago Black Hawks coach Pete Muldoon, bitter over being fired, declared: ''This team will never finish first.'' The Black Hawks did not finish first for more than 40 years; **2.** Restaurateur Gene Leone had concocted a ''Magic Elixir'' which, when the Rangers drank it, seemed to cause them to win. Belief in the mixture was so complete that the Toronto Maple Leafs tried to have the Rangers' supply confiscated at the airport before a game. Eventually, the effects of the elixir wore off, and the Rangers finished the season in fifth place; **3.** The Bouchers of Ottawa. George (''Buck'') Boucher played for the Ottawa Senators, the Montreal Maroons, and the Chicago Black Hawks; Frank played for Ottawa and the New York Rangers; Billy played for the Montreal Canadiens and the New York Americans; and Bob played 12 games for the Montreal Canadiens; **4.** The only such game occurred at Chicago Stadium on February 20, 1944, between the Toronto Maple Leafs and the Chicago Black Hawks; **5.** Bobby Orr of the Boston Bruins had the winning goal in 1970 (against St. Louis) and in 1972 (against the New York Rangers); **6.** Dick Schultz, ''enforcer'' for the Philadelphia Flyers, served 2,294 penalty minutes in nine seasons; **7.** In a 1930 Quebec Junior Amateur Game, goalie Abie Goldberry was hit by a flying puck that ignited his pocket, setting his uniform on fire. He was badly burned before his teammates could put the fire out; **8.** Despite their miserable season, the Chicago Black Hawks qualified for the playoffs because other teams had done even worse. During the playoffs, they got their game together and defeated the Toronto Maple Leafs to take the championship, 4–1.

Key Words

assist   passage of the puck to the player who scores; points are awarded (for individual and team statistics purposes) for up to two assists per goal.

attacking zone   the zone farthest from the goal the team is defending.

back checking   covering one's opponent so that he can't be entirely free to play the puck.

backhand   a shot delivered from the left side of a right-handed player or the right side of a left-handed player, with the player's arms crossed in front of him.

bench minor   a penalty that requires removal of a player for a specified time period, with no substitute allowed.

boarding   causing an opponent to be violently thrown against the boards.

body checking   blocking an opponent with one's hip or shoulder.

breakaway   also called a rushing game, a style of play aimed at getting more attackers than defenders out front with the puck heading toward the opponent's goalie.

butt-ending   jabbing an opponent with the top of the stick.

center   forward player who skates in the center of the ice.

center line   a red line across the rink midway between the goal lines.

center zone   the middle portion of the playing area.

ABC Sports

ABC Sports

The U.S. Hockey Team exults in their un-expected victory at the 1980 Winter Olympics, defeating the Soviet Union and then Finland for the gold medal.

centering pass   a pass used when shots are being taken at the goal.

change on the fly   substitution of one player for another while the game is in progress.

charging   delivering a body check after taking more than two steps toward the opponent.

clearing pass   a pass made when a defender wants to clear the puck from his own goal area.

crease   a 4-foot-by-8-foot rectangle directly in front of the goal.

cross-checking   stopping an opponent with a stick held off the ice in both hands.

defensive zone   the zone nearest to the goal the team is defending.

deking   faking out one's opponents by, for example, pretending to pass in one direction and then passing in another.

drop pass   pass made by skating with the puck and then leaving it on the ice to be picked up by another player.

dumping   shooting a puck across the defensive blue line into an empty part of the ice.

flip pass   pass in which the puck is scooped up and sent flying above the ice surface.

forechecking   making a direct attempt to rob the puck from a player while facing him.

forehand   shot delivered from the right side of a right-handed player or left side of a left-handed player.

freezing the puck   stopping the motion of the puck during the game.

hat trick   three goals scored by a single player in a single game.

headmanning   repeatedly passing the puck to the player who is farthest ahead on the attack.

high stick   a stick carried above shoulder height.

hook checking   attempting to hook the puck away from the person carrying it.

icing   shooting the puck across an opponent's goal line while standing behind one's own red line.

lie of the stick   the angle between the blade and shaft of the stick; can be varied and is numbered from 1 to 10, depending on the degree of the angle.

line   three forward players (center and wingers) on a team.

major penalty   a penalty that consists of (1) the first time in a game, removing the player from the ice for five minutes with no substitute allowed; and (2) the second time in a game, barring the player responsible from the rest of the game and allowing a substitute after five minutes.

match penalty   a penalty that sends a player to the dressing room for the duration of the game and makes him unable to play again until his case is disposed of by disciplinary authorities.

misconduct penalty   a penalty that, when given for the first time in a game, keeps the player off the ice for ten minutes but allows a substitute; the second time in a game, the player goes to the dressing room for the rest of the game, but a substitute is allowed.

pattern game   a style of play that involves much intricate skating and passing.

penalty shot   a free shot from the center spot taken by any member of the non-offending team.

poke checking   poking the blade of the stick at the puck.

power play   portion of the game played with five men against four (because one team has a player in the penalty box).

slap shot   a shot in which the player raises his stick to shoulder height and brings it forward to hit the ice and the puck at the same time.

spearing   illegally poking an opponent with the blade of the stick.

stick handling   carrying the puck with the stick while skating, controlling it by short taps from side to side.

sweep pass   a pass in which the stick is directed at the puck in a sweeping motion.

tight game   a style of play emphasizing defensive strategy and heavy checking.

wrist shot   a shot delivered with a snapping motion of the wrist.

ABC Sports

11 HORSE RACING

No one knows when, or under what circumstances, the first horse race was held, but it obviously occurred after people learned to ride and control the fleet-footed animal, and it probably involved wagering. The earliest known form of horse racing was, in effect, the harness race: the Greeks included chariot-racing in their Olympics. Centuries later, the Spanish raised, on breeding farms, horses much larger and stronger than those the Greeks had used. The "Arabian" horses the Spanish developed through selective breeding were faster than any animal bred by man, though they could sustain their maximum speed for only a limited time; they could, however, do with ease what no earlier horses could do: carry a full-grown, fully armed and armored man for long distances and, when necessary, at high speed.

When England's King Henry I learned of the existence of Spain's equine treasure, he obtained an Arabian stallion as breeding stock for his own stable. The year was A.D. 1110, and the English horses subsequently developed—crosses of Henry's Arabian and his sturdy but slow English mares—were the progenitors of every Thoroughbred horse since.

To qualify as a Thoroughbred, a horse must be descended from one of three "foundation sires": Godolphin Arabian, Byerly Turk, and Darley Arabian. Few horse owners can trace their horses' lineage so far back, but ancestry that can be traced back to the eighteenth-century horses "Matchem," "Herod," or "Eclipse"is considered adequate proof of breeding.

The first English horse races were held on stretches of English public road temporarily and informally appropriated by competing horse owners. Racing soon became a standard feature of county fairs and festivals, and in 1714, Queen Anne took horse racing a step further when she sanctioned the first sweepstakes: a race in which each competitor must put up a sum of money to enter, the aggregate amount becoming the winner's prize. Within 50 years, horse breeders had set up a series of annual races, including the St. Leger's race and the Epsom Derby. In 1752, the Jockey Club was formed in London; it continues to be the international horse-racing authority.

The first known American horse race—in which horses were used that were descended from those brought to the New World by early Spanish explorers—was held in Hempstead, New York, about 1665. The first Thoroughbred horse racing took hold in the years that followed, many more Thoroughbreds were shipped from England to America.

One of these Thoroughbreds, "Messenger," shipped to America in 1788, was the progenitor of the Standardbred, or harness-racing, horse. The difference between the Standardbred and the Thoroughbred is that the Thoroughbred is allowed to use its fastest natural gait, the gallop, whereas the Standardbred must trot or pace, a gait it must be trained to sustain. "Hambletonian," a descendant of "Messenger," is considered the sire of today's American Standardbred horse. Harness racing was born on back roads and at country fairs, just as Thoroughbred racing had been. By the 1850s, it was established and today rivals Thoroughbred racing in popularity.

As racing became better established, so did wagering. Bookmaking was a standard feature of horse racing in America by 1873. Pari-mutuel betting, which involves betting machines, originated in France in 1865 and was introduced in the United States about 1875; its popularization was impeded, however, by reforms in the early part of this century that shut such betting down in all but two states, Kentucky and Maryland. Today pari-mutuel betting is legal in some 30 states and is featured in both Thoroughbred and harness-racing tracks.

Horse racing was once known as the "sport of kings," because of the great wealth it took then to engage in it. Today, anyone with two dollars to bet can participate.

Great Moments

ca. 800 B.C.	Horseback riding contests become part of the Greek Olympics.
A.D. 1110	King Henry I of England purchases the first Arabian stallion to breed with the slower, stronger English mares.
A.D. 1174	The first public race track, the Smithfield Track, is built, in London, an event that marks the beginning of organized racing under a saddle.
1609	A silversmith's error results in prizes for second- and third-place winners in a race. Until now, only first prizes have been awarded.
1668	The first recorded race in the United States is held—at "Newmarket Course," near Hempstead, New York.

1674 The first turf race is held, in Virginia.

1704 Darley purchases an Arabian horse in Syria and has it shipped to England; descendants of Darley's Arabian are among horse racing's most famous horses.

1748 "Matchem"—one of the three foundation sires of Thoroughbred horses, and descended from Godolphin's Arabian stallion—is foaled.

1751 The Jockey Club is organized, in England. The world's oldest horse-racing club, it becomes the most prestigious as well.

1758 "Herod" is foaled. One of three foundation sires of Thoroughbred horses, he is descended from Byerly's Turkish stallion.

1762 Jockey Club members register their colors for the first time.

1764 "Eclipse," one of the three foundation sires of Thoroughbred horses, is foaled. The horse is descended from Darley's Arabian stallion.

1776 Colonel St. Leger arranges the first race for three-year-olds, in Doncaster. It becomes the world's oldest stakes race.

1797 Williams Race Track, Kentucky's first, is built near Lexington.

1780 The Earl of Derby establishes another race for three-year-olds of both genders. The race becomes known as the Epsinison English Derby. That same year, The Jockey Club sanctions a race for two-year-olds.

1788 "Messenger," a gray Thoroughbred stallion, is imported into the United States from England. He goes on to sire some of harness racing's best trotters.

1791 The English Stud Book is created.

1806 A trotter is clocked at less than three minutes for the first mile, in Harlem, New York.

1867 The Belmont Stakes are inaugurated, at Elmont, New York.

1873 The Preakness, the second of the Triple Crown Series, is inaugurated at Pimlico Race Track, in Baltimore. That year, bookmakers appear at race tracks for the first time.

1875 Churchill Downs opens in Lexington, Kentucky.

1892 The bicycle-wheel sulky is introduced into harness racing.

1919 "Sir Barton" becomes the first horse to win the Triple Crown.

1930 The daily double is introduced for pari-mutuel wagers.

1950 The Triple Crown trophy is officially established, and is granted retroactively to the eight horses that have won the Kentucky Derby, Preakness, and Belmont Stakes in the past.

1966 Johnny Longden retires after the longest career by a modern jockey— 40 years.

1973 "Secretariat" becomes the first horse to win the Triple Crown in 25 years.

1978 At age 18, Steve Cauthen becomes the youngest jockey to win the Triple Crown, riding "Affirmed" to victory.

The Setup

THOROUGHBRED RACING

Thoroughbred racing is conducted at individually operated tracks throughout the United States. Most tracks are members of the Thoroughbred Racing Associations of America, an umbrella group that coordinates efforts by all parts of the horse-racing world, from jockeys to those interested in the welfare of the horses. Horses are entered in races according to class (breeding and speed). These races are held around the country (horses are not necessarily raced regionally, as they sometimes are in harness racing).

THE JOCKEY CLUB
300 Park Ave.
New York, NY 10022
(212) 355-6146
Nick Jemas, ntl. mng. dir.

THOROUGHBRED RACING
  ASSOCIATIONS
3000 Marcus Ave., Suite 2W4
Lake Success, NY 11040
(506) 328-2660
Robert S. Gunderson, pres.

THOROUGHBRED RACING
  PROTECTIVE BUREAU
P.O. Box 3557
New Hyde Park, NY 11042
(516) 328-2010
Clifford Wickman, pres.

UNITED THOROUGHBRED
  TRAINER'S ASSOCIATION OF
  AMERICA
19363 James Couzens Hwy.
Detroit, MI 48235
(313) 342-6144
Ruth LeGrove, sec.

HARNESS RACING

All harness racing in the United States and the Maritime Provinces (Canada) is supervised by the United States Trotting Association. Its formation, in 1938, centralized all harness-racing interests, eliminating three other organizations that had sponsored harness racing.

Harness racing is operated on three levels: the Grand Circuit, the Fair Circuit, and pari-mutuel. The Grand Circuit is a national program of races designed to attract the top trotters and pacers, primarily colts. The Fair Circuit comprises races run at local fairs throughout the country; these allow local horse owners to race often against comparable competition without having to travel far. Pari-mutuel racing, or racing at tracks where pari-mutuel betting is conducted, is responsible for the growth of harness racing as a spectator sport in recent years.

STANDARDBRED OWNERS
  ASSOCIATION
539 Old Country Rd.
Westbury, NY 11590
(516) 333-5663
Carl C. Benevento, exec. dir.

UNITED STATES TROTTING
  ASSOCIATION
750 Michigan Ave.
Columbus, OH 43215
(614) 224-2291
William R. Hilliard, exec. vice-pres.

The Basics

Object   For the horse and jockey to complete a circuit of the track ahead of all other horses.

Track   (see diagram)   Track surfaces in the United States are most commonly dirt, although some are grass. Major American tracks are flat, oval, and between one mile and one-and-one-half miles long.

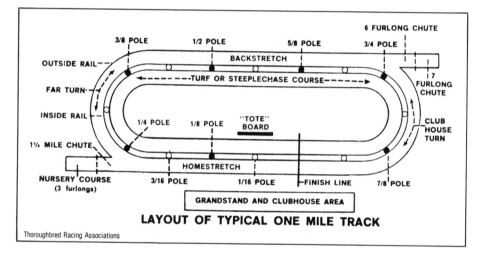

LAYOUT OF TYPICAL ONE MILE TRACK

Thoroughbred Racing Associations

Equipment   A jockey wears racing silks in the registered racing colors of the horse owner, in addition to a helmet, boots, and gloves. A jockey may use a riding crop or similar instrument. The horse's equipment consists of a lightweight racing saddle, bridle, bit, and reins. A saddle blanket or pad is placed between the saddle and the horse's back.

Officials   The tasks of the officials (who are numerous) are, for example, verification of identity, inspection, and weigh-in. Some other officials are patrol judges and stewards, who watch the race for violations, and stewards, who make rulings in case of protests.

Rule 1   Eligibility   Eligibility requirements vary, and each type of race has specific rules governing weight carried by the horse, age of the animal, class, registration dates, and so on.

Rule 2   Weigh-in   The horse and jockey must be weighed in before and after the race. The assigned weight that a horse carries is the combined weight of the jockey and the saddle. Metal weights are sometimes placed in the jockey's pockets to meet a weight requirement. In Triple Crown events, all horses must carry 126 pounds.

Rule 3   The start   Horses and jockeys are assigned to one of the 12 to 14 stalls and are positioned there. An electric starting gate is used to ensure a fair start.

Rule 4 **Interference**   A horse may be disqualified for crossing in front of another horse and thereby impeding it; a horse or a jockey may be disqualified for jostling another horse or jockey; a jockey may be disqualified for striking another horse or jockey during a race. A jockey may claim a foul against a horse or another jockey, in which case the film of the race is studied by the stewards, who then rule on the alleged offense.

Rule 5 **Leaving the course**   If a horse leaves the course for any reason during a race, it must return to the starting point and begin again to qualify as a finisher.

Rule 6 **Mishandling a horse**   A jockey who is judged to have mishandled a horse, or prevented it from running the best possible race, faces disqualification and possible suspension.

Rule 7 **Rerunning a race**   If a race is run by the field at wrong weights, or for an incorrect distance, or if a judge is not in the stands when the horses pass the winning post, the race may be run again after the last race of the day, or no later than 30 minutes after the wrong race was run.

Rule 8 **Illegal substances**   Samples of urine and/or saliva from the winning horse are tested to determine whether the horse won while under the influence of an illegal substance. If a prohibited substance is found, the horse is disqualified and the jockey, owner, and trainer are subject to fines and/or suspension.

Rule 9 **The finish**   A special camera is positioned to photograph the finish. In a close race, it may be used to determine the winner.

Rule 10 **Official results**   The results of a race are not official until the winning jockeys have weighed in and are certified as having carried the designated weight.

HARNESS RACING

Object   For a horse to trot or pace (not gallop) around a designated track and cross the finish ahead of all other competitors while pulling a sulky (a lightweight, two-wheeled cart).

Equipment   Equipment is similar for trotters and pacers, although each requires some special equipment.

Equipment for Trotters

Elbow boots   These are sheepskin-lined pads worn on the front legs to protect the leg from cuts caused when the front hoof is folded back in top-stride.

Hind shin boots   These leather guards protect the lower hind legs from cuts caused when the front legs graze them during the race.

Toe weights   Brass or lead weights used to extend a horse's stride. These weigh two to four ounces and are clipped to the horse's front hoofs.

Quarter boots   These are close-fitting boots on the front heel to protect the heel of the foot from being cut by the hind shoes.

Martingale   This is a strap running from between the horse's front legs to the reins that are threaded through the strap to prevent the horse from raising its head too much.

Equipment for Pacers

Hobbles   Hobbles are leather straps connecting the front and hind legs on the same side of the horse. This helps keep the horse on stride.

Shadow roll   A large sheepskin roll worn just above the horse's nose to cut off its view of the track so the horse will not be distracted by shadows or objects.

Knee boots   These leather boots are fitted around the horse's knees to protect blows to the area from the opposite foot.

Head pole   This is usually a pool cue fastened alongside the horse's head to keep its head straight.

Gaiting strap   This strap is strung inside the shafts of the sulky to keep the horse from swinging its rear end to the right and left and traveling sideways on its gait.

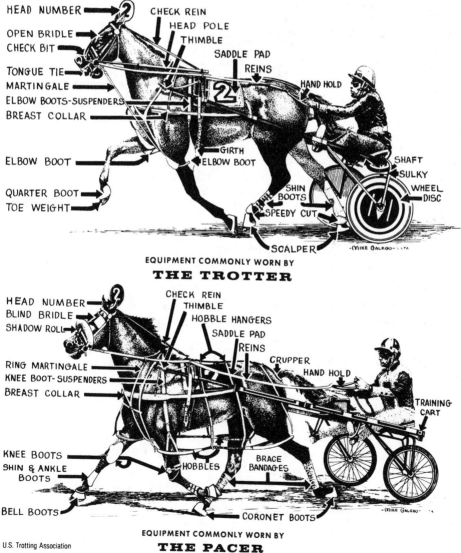

HEAD NUMBER
OPEN BRIDLE
CHECK BIT
TONGUE TIE
MARTINGALE
ELBOW BOOTS-SUSPENDERS
BREAST COLLAR
ELBOW BOOT
QUARTER BOOT
TOE WEIGHT
CHECK REIN
HEAD POLE
THIMBLE
SADDLE PAD
REINS
HAND HOLD
GIRTH
ELBOW BOOT
SHIN BOOTS
SPEEDY CUT
SHAFT
SULKY
WHEEL
DISC
SCALPER
—MIKE GALEGO—

EQUIPMENT COMMONLY WORN BY
THE TROTTER

HEAD NUMBER
BLIND BRIDLE
SHADOW ROLL
RING MARTINGALE
KNEE BOOT-SUSPENDERS
BREAST COLLAR
KNEE BOOTS
SHIN & ANKLE BOOTS
BELL BOOTS
CHECK REIN
THIMBLE
HOBBLE HANGERS
SADDLE PAD
REINS
CRUPPER
HAND HOLD
TRAINING CART
HOBBLES
BRACE BANDAGES
CORONET BOOTS
—MIKE GALEGO—

EQUIPMENT COMMONLY WORN BY
THE PACER

U.S. Trotting Association

Rule 1 The start A mobile starting gate is used to line up the field for the start. A horse can be penalized for delaying the start, failure to obey the starter's instructions, rushing ahead of the inside or outside wing of the gate, starting out of position, crossing over before reaching the starting point, interference with another driver, or failure to come into position.

Rule 2 Interference Under the driving rules, the driver is held responsible and can be penalized for crowding or jostling other drivers, crossing sharply in front of another horse, or otherwise interfering unfairly with other horses and drivers.

Rule 3 The pace If a horse breaks its stride, or begins to gallop, the driver must pull the horse over to the side and correct it. The driver is not permitted to gain any ground during a break.

How to watch

THOROUGHBRED

with Joe Hirsch

According to Joe Hirsch, executive writer for *The Daily Racing Form,* in Thoroughbred racing, the start is all-important. No race, however, is decided until the last stride.

"The start is more important in sprint races, because they are shorter," Hirsch adds. Some horses, however, such as Pleasant Colony in 1981, have made a specialty of starting a bit behind the pack and pouring on the juice for the end.

How can the spectator tell a good start from a bad one?

"A good start is when everyone gets away together. It sounds simple, but it's harder than that. The starter has to be sharp. He must see that all of the horses are flat-footed. Assistant starters must have a hold on the horses that are acting up. They must also remember to let go at the right time."

The start, or the first one-sixth of a mile, also affects a horse's position during a race. "If you have speed," Hirsch adds, "you can get position. If you have no speed, you can't. And, if you aren't in a good position at the start, you probably wouldn't get one."

Position is very important during a race, Hirsch says. "This doesn't mean staying close to the rail. Position means being where it is most suitable for your horse in relation to the other horses. For instance, a horse with some speed could be positioned just off the leader's shoulder, so the rider could keep an eye on him and make his move at the right time."

All through the race, jockeys are looking for the best place to "make a move." According to Hirsch, those behind are looking for a way to move up or to "box" those on the rail, preventing them from moving ahead. Others are staying on the outside, trying to avoid being trapped. There are certain landmark posts, such as the half-mile post along the track, where a jockey usually makes a move. "Most horses accelerate at the half-mile pole," Hirsch says.

Important aids to watching a horse race are knowing who the favorite is and what his records are on the type of track being run that day. Just as horses vary between sprinters and long-distance runners, tracks vary between smooth, firm surfaces and soft, sandy ones which are generally slower.

HARNESS RACING

with Stan Bergstein

Any horse can run, but not all can trot or pace. That is one of the beauties of harness racing, according to Stan Bergstein, president of Harness Tracks of America. "There is inherent beauty in the gaited horse," he says. "I've always been captivated by the athletic ability of a trotter at high speed."

Harness horses also are more durable than other horses—and more predictable, which is a good reason for bettors to flock to the harness pari-mutuel track. "A harness horse that can run a mile-track in two-oh-three one time will, more than likely, run it again at two-oh-three. The consistency of the harness horse attracts a lot of people."

From a bettor's point of view, Bergstein says, a pacer is a safer bet than a trotter as far as consistency is concerned. A trotter is more likely to break his stride than a pacer, because the pacer's legs are synchronized by the set of hobbles—leather straps—he wears.

Harness racing differs from Thoroughbred racing in several other respects. For instance, the harness horse is a "rated" horse, whereas the Thoroughbred, basically, runs downhill from the start.

"A typical strategy for a harness horse is to set a fast pace for the first quarter, then pull back a bit for the second and third, and speed up again for the final quarter." "Usually," Bergstein says, "a Thoroughbred starts fast and loses speed as he goes."

The start also differs, in that it is a moving start. A mobile starting gate attached to a car circles the track until all the horses are resting their noses on the gate. The gate is then lifted, and the horses take off together. Many people are convinced that the starting position has an effect on the outcome of the race. It is usually considered preferable to be on the rail, according to Bergstein.

"In case of rain or a sloppy track—when water would drain toward the rail and make the area muddy and sloppy—an outside post position, or at least one not on the inside, might be preferable."

Drivers must adapt their technique to their horses. If a horse is "useable"—that is, if the horse is easy to handle and is responsive to the lines, the driver has more time to pay attention to his strategy.

This means using the first quarter of the race to get position by going as fast as possible, rating the horse for the middle quarters, and then going for a very fast final quarter. A driver very rarely holds his horse back; the rating process is more a means of "holding the horse together" so he doesn't tire or break his gait.

"A driver's hands are critically important," says Bergstein. "The driver can use his hands to transfer a special strength and confidence to the horse, so the horse will race bolder and be more tenacious in staying up front. The expression a 'great pair of hands' refers to the driver's ability to transfer commands to the horse through the lines, and have the horse respond to those commands. "The good drivers have these hands," says Bergstein.

Main Events

TRIPLE CROWN

The Triple Crown is a series of three races for three-year-olds that begins with the Kentucky Derby held every spring at Churchill Downs, outside Louisville, Kentucky. The Derby is followed by the Preakness, at Pimlico Park in Maryland, and the Belmont Stakes, in Belmont, New York, The Derby is a one-and-one-quarter-mile track; the Preakness is one and three-sixteenth miles; and the Belmont Stakes is one and one-half miles. Since the late nineteenth century, only 11 horses have won all three races in the same season.

TRIPLE CROWN WINNERS

The following horses are Triple Crown Winners; that is, they are three-year-olds who have won the Kentucky Derby, Preakness, and Belmont Stakes in a single season.

Year	Winner	Year	Winner
1978	Affirmed	1941	Whirlaway
1977	Seattle Slew	1937	War Admiral
1973	Secretariat	1935	Omaha
1948	Citation	1930	Gallant Fox
1946	Assault	1919	Sir Barton
1943	Count Fleet		

KENTUCKY DERBY

Three-year-olds compete in this one-and-one-quarter-mile race at Churchill Downs, in Kentucky. It is the first race in the Triple Crown series, which also includes the Belmont Stakes and the Preakness. Winners of the Kentucky Derby for the past 10 years are:

Year	Winner	Year	Winner
1981	Pleasant Colony	1976	Bold Forbes
1980	Genuine Risk	1975	Foolish Pleasure
1979	Spectacular Bid	1974	Cannonade
1978	Affirmed	1973	Secretariat
1977	Seattle Slew	1972	Riva Ridge

PREAKNESS

The second race in the Triple Crown series. Three-year-olds run a one-and-three-sixteenths-mile race at Pimlico, near Baltimore, Maryland. Winners from the past 10 years include:

Year	Winner	Year	Winner
1981	Pleasant Colony	1976	Elocutionist
1980	Codex	1975	Master Derby
1979	Spectacular Bid	1974	Little Current
1978	Affirmed	1973	Secretariat
1977	Seattle Slew	1972	Bee Bee Bee

BELMONT STAKES

The third race in the Triple Crown series. Three-year-olds run one-and-one-half-mile, held at Belmont Park, in Elmont, New York. Winners from the past 10 years include:

Year	Winner	Year	Winner
1981	Summing	1976	Bold Forbes
1980	Temperence Hill	1975	Avatar
1979	Coastal	1974	Little Current
1978	Affirmed	1973	Secretariat
1977	Seattle Slew	1972	Riva Ridge

ECLIPSE AWARDS

HORSE OF THE YEAR

1980	Spectacular Bid
1979	Affirmed
1978	Affirmed
1977	Seattle Slew
1976	Forego
1975	Forego

OUTSTANDING JOCKEY

1980	Chris McCarron
1979	Laffit Pincay, Jr.
1978	Darrel McHargue
1977	Steve Cauthen
1976	Sandy Hawley
1975	Braulio Baeza

OUTSTANDING TRAINER

1980	Bud Delp
1979	Lazaro Barrera
1978	Lazaro Barrera
1977	Lazaro Barrera
1976	Lazaro Barrera
1975	Steve DiMauro

HARNESS-RACING TRIPLE CROWN

There are no official Triple Crown ceremonies in either trotting or pacing, but both forms of harness racing have three races each year that are equivalent in prestige and importance to the Kentucky Derby, Preakness, and Belmont Stakes in

Thoroughbred racing. For trotters, these races are the Hambletonian, the Kentucky Futurity, and the Yonkers Trot. For pacers, the races (for three-year-old horses) are Little Brown Jug, William Cane Futurity, and Messenger Stakes.

Trotting "Triple Crown" winners are "Scott Frost" (1955), "Speedy Scott" (1963), "Ayres" (1964), "Nevele Pride" (1968), and "Lindy's Pride" (1969). "Super Bowl" is the only horse to have won all three trots in the past ten years; "Niatross" won the three paces in 1980.

HAMBLETONIAN

The Kentucky Derby of harness racing, the Hambletonian, held every summer, is a one-mile race for three-year-old trotters. The winners are:

Year	Winner	Year	Winner
1980	Burgomeister	1975	Bonefish
1979	Legend Hanover	1974	Christopher T.
1978	Speedy Somolli	1973	Flirth
1977	Green Speed	1972	Super Bowl
1976	Steve Lobell	1971	Speedy Crown

KENTUCKY FUTURITY

The Kentucky Futurity is one of the most prestigious and lucrative races for three-year-old trotters (the others are the Hambletonian and the Yonkers Trot). All three together make up the trotter's Triple Crown. The race is held in Lexington, Kentucky. Winners from the past 10 years are:

Year	Winner	Year	Winner
1980	Final Score	1975	Noble Rogue
1979	Classical Day	1974	Waymaker
1978	Doublemint	1973	Arnie Almahurst
1977	Texas	1972	Super Bowl
1976	Quick Pay	1971	Savoir

George Smallsreed/USTA

YONKERS TROT

The Yonkers Trot, the third race in harness racing's Triple Crown, is a half-mile race held in Yonkers, New York. Winners for the past 10 years are:

Year	Winner	Year	Winner
1980	Nevele Impulse	1975	Surefire Hanover
1979	Chiola Hanover	1974	Spitfire Hanover
1978	Speedy Somolli	1973	Tamerlane
1977	Green Speed	1972	Super Bowl
1976	Steve Lobell	1971	Quick Pride

WILLIAM CANE FUTURITY

The William Cane Futurity, held every summer in Yonkers, New York, is a mile-long race for three-year-old pacers. Recent winners are:

Year	Winner	Year	Winner
1980	Niatross	1975	Nero
1979	Happy Motoring	1974	Boyden Hanover
1978	Armbro Tiger	1973	Smog
1977	Jade Prince	1972	Hilarious Way
1976	Keystone One	1971	Albatross

LITTLE BROWN JUG

The Little Brown Jug is a mile-long race run in Delaware, Ohio, every summer for three-year-old pacers. Past winners are:

Year	Winner	Year	Winner
1980	Niatross	1975	Seatrain
1979	Hot Hitter	1974	Armbro Omaha
1978	Happy Escort	1973	Melvin's Woe
1977	Skipper	1972	Strike Out
1976	Keystone Ore	1971	Nansemond

MESSENGER STAKES

The Messenger Stakes, named for the foundation sire of today's Standardbred horses, is held every summer at Roosevelt Raceway, in Westbury, New York. Three-year-olds pace a mile-long course. Recent winners are:

Year	Winner	Year	Winner
1980	Niatross	1975	Bret's Champ
1979	Hot Hitter	1974	Armbro Omaha
1978	Abercrombie	1973	Valiant Bret
1977	Governor Skipper	1972	Silent Majority
1976	Windshield Wiper	1971	Albatross

HARNESS HORSE OF THE YEAR

The Harness Horse of the Year is chosen by a USTA poll of harness-racing writers and racing secretaries.

Year	Winner	Year	Winner
1980	Niatross	1975	Savoir
1979	Niatross	1974	Delmonica Hanover
1978	Abercrombie	1973	Sir Dalrae
1977	Green Speed	1972	Albatross
1976	Keystone Ore	1971	Albatross

All-Time Greats

JOCKEYS

Eddie Arcaro
(Feb. 19, 1916–)

TRA Photo

Eddie Arcaro, along with Johnny Longden and Willie Shoemaker, are considered the best jockeys of the past half-century. Arcaro rode all the best horses of his day—"Citation," "Whirlaway," "Kelso," "Bold Ruler," and "Assault"—repeatedly winning the Kentucky Derby (five times), the Preakness and Belmont Stakes (six times each), and Triple Crowns. Of 24,092 races he entered, Arcaro won 4,779 times, finished second 3,807 times, and took third 3,302 times. His career winnings upon his retirement in 1961 were $30,039,543.

Johnny Longden
(Feb. 14, 1907–)

TRA Photo

Longden began his racing career in 1927 atop a nine-year-old Thoroughbred named "Hugo K. Asher." He rode the horse to victory only once, however, taking seconds and thirds after that. It would be nine more years before Longden's winnings reached the hundred-thousand-dollar mark ($102,255, in 1935); but for the rest of his 40-year career, he never earned less than $100,000 in a single year. Longden rode 6,032 winners—among them the Triple Crown winner "Count Fleet"—a record that stood from 1956 to 1970. Longden finished his career with a victory at the San Juan Capistrano Handicap.

William Lee ("The Shoe") Shoemaker
(Aug. 19, 1931–)

Pimlico Photo

Willie Shoemaker is horse-racing's all-time top money-winner. In a career spanning 32 years, he amassed more than 7,000 wins. In 1956, Shoemaker became the first jockey to win more than $2 million in purses in one year, a record he broke several times after that. "The Shoe," once called "The Silent Shoe" because of his reserve, is as well known off the track as he is on it, and he has become a kind of ambassador of racing. The four-foot-eleven-inch jockey was named to the National Museum of Racing Hall of Fame in 1958, just 10 years after his career began.

HORSES

Hambletonian
(1849–76)

Hall of Fame of the Trotter

The horse known as the "foundation sire" of harness racing never raced. He just produced the pacers and trotters that went on to win race after race, and whose descendants are the top pacers and trotters of harness racing today. "Hambletonian" had an unlikely beginning. He was the product of a union between the Thoroughbred "Abdallah" and a crippled mare owned by a New York farmer named Jonas Seely. Seely, unimpressed by the foal, sold the mare and colt to his hired man for $125, not a bad price for a horse that earned more than $300,000 in stud fees over the next 26 years. Named for a famous trotter, the colt became a perfectly developed show horse. After two appearances at the prestigious Orange County Fair, where "Hambletonian" won championships two years in a row for appearance alone, his owner could command stud fees of $10 and later $25. A total of 1,900 mares were sent to Hambletonian, and 1,300 produced foals. Because so many of the foals "Hambletonian" sired became good racers, exhibiting his strength and other traits, the horse is said to have founded the Standardbred horse line. Practically all Standardbreds registered today can trace their lineage to "Hambletonian."

"Man o' War"
(1917–47)

TRA Photo

The greatest of the greats, "Man o' War" lost only one race during his two-year career on the track. Sired by August Belmont's "Fair Play," a horse with a fiery disposition, "Man o' War" was bought by Samuel D. Riddle in 1918. The yearling distinguished himself from the 10 other horses Riddle bought in that year's Saratoga Springs yearling sale with his long stride (four feet longer than the average), his muscular build, and his voracious appetite. "Man o' War" loved to run. His first race was in 1919, at the Belmont race track in New York City. The inexperienced horse broke slowly from the gate, trailing the field. He proceeded to astonish the crowd by pulling even with the field and cantering to the finish six lengths ahead of the nearest horse. That race set the tone for all "Man o' War's" subsequent starts. Only one race went sour. A rookie starter handled the big two-year-old roughly, leading him away from the starting gate as the gate broke. In a valiant effort, the horse took off in pursuit of the field and barely missed overtaking the winner. "Man o' War" set numerous records: the American record for the one-and-three-eighths miles, at Belmont; the one-and-one-half miles, in the Jockey Club Stakes; and the one-and-one-sixteenth miles (carrying an unprecedented 138 pounds). He was retired to stud with earnings of $249,465—a record at the time. He then broke the record for the highest stud fee up to that time, of $5,000. He proved to be worth the price. "Man o' War" sired 379 foals that won a total of 1,300 races.

"Secretariat"
(1970–)

TRA Photo

Many consider "Secretariat" the only other horse in the same class as "Man o' War." A Triple Crown winner and the winner of all but 2 of his 21 starts, "Secretariat" had the same strength and speed as the other horse. He first attracted publicity by winning seven of his nine races as a two-year-old (a record that has since been broken) and, in 1973, bringing the highest price of any horse in history: $6,080,000. As a three-year-old, "Secretariat" won the Triple Crown and set track records in the Belmont and the Kentucky Derby. He ran the Preakness in record time as well; but a malfunctioning course clock did not reflect this, and the record remains unofficial. "Secretariat," like "Man o' War," ended his career in Canada, where he won the Canadian International Championship and brought his total career earnings to $1,306,818—or about $62,000 per race.

HALL OF FAME

National Museum of Racing Hall of Fame
Union Ave.
Saratoga Springs, NY 12866
(518) 584-0400

Jockeys who are members of the National Museum of Racing Hall of Fame are:

F. ("Dooley") Adams	William Hartack	Winnie O'Connor
John Adams	Albert Johnson	George Odom
Edward Arcaro	William ("Willie") Knapp	Frank O'Neill
Theodore ("Ted") Atkinson	Clarence Kummer	Gil Patrick
Carroll K. Bassett	Charles Kurtsinger	Samuel Purdy
George H. ("Pete") Bostwick	John Loftus	John Reiff
Samuel Boulmetis	John Longden	Earl Sande
Steve Brooks	Linus ("Pony") McAtee	Carroll Schilling
Frank Coltiletti	Conn McCreary	William Shoemaker
Robert ("Specs") Crawford	Rigan McKinney	Todhunter ("Tod") Sloan
Levelle ("Buddy") Ensor	James McLaughlin	Jimmy Stout
Laverne Fator	Danny Maher	Fred Taral
Andrew ("Mack") Garner	Walter Miller	Bayard Tuckerman
Edward ("Snapper") Garrison	Isaac Murphy	Nash Turner
Henry F. Griffin	Ralph Neves	Raymond ("Sonny") Workman
Eric Guerin	Joseph Notter	George Woolf

Horses that have been enshrined in the Hall of Fame are:

American Eclipse	Domino	Neji
Armed	Elkridge	Old Rosebud
Artful	Equipoise	Omaha
Assault	Exterminator	Pan Zareta
Battleship	Fair Play	Peter Pan
Beldame	Gallant Fox	Regret
Ben Brush	Gallorette	Roseben
Blue Larkspur	Good and Plenty	Round Table
Bold Ruler	Grey Lag	Salvator
Boston	Hanover	Sarazen
Broomstick	Hindoo	Seabiscuit
Buckpasser	Imp	Secretariat
Busher	Jay Trump	Sir Archy
Bushranger	Jolly Roger	Sir Barton
Cicada	Kelso	Swaps
Citation	Kingston	Sysonby
Colin	Lexington	Tom Fool
Commando	Longfellow	Top Flight
Count Fleet	Luke Blackburn	Twenty Grand
Damascus	Man o' War	Twilight Tear
Dark Mirage	Miss Woodford	War Admiral
Discovery	Nashua	Whirlaway
Dr. Fager	Native Dancer	

For the Record

THOROUGHBRED

Most races won, one year
19   "Citation"   1948

Most consecutive races won, one year (since 1900)
15   "Citation"   1948

Most consecutive races won
16   "Citation"   1948–49

Most stakes races won, lifetime
33   "Exterminator"   1917–24

Most consecutive stakes races won
14   "Colin"   1907–08
      "Man o' War"   1919–20

Most races won, lifetime
89   "Kingston   1886–94

Most races won, lifetime (since 1900)
78   "Tippity Witchet"   1917–29

Jockeys

Most years, annual leader, purses earned
10   Willie Shoemaker

Most consecutive years, annual leader, purses earned
7   Willie Shoemaker   1958–64

ABC Sports

Most races won, lifetime
7,923   Willie Shoemaker

Most races won, one year
546   Chris McCarron   1974

Most races won, apprentice, one year
546   Chris McCarron   1974

Most stakes races won, one year
46   Willie Shoemaker   1971

Most years, annual leader, races won
5   Willie Shoemaker

Most consecutive years, annual leader, races won
3   Bill Hartack   1955–57

Most races won, one day
8   Hubert S. Jones   June 11, 1944   Caliente Race Track (13 mounts)
   Jorge Tejeira   June 16, 1976   Keystone and Atlantic City (two programs;
      12 mounts)
   David Gall   Oct. 18, 1978   Cahokla Downs (10 mounts)

Most consecutive races won, world record
12   Gordon Richards   Oct. 3–5, 1933   Nottingham, Chepston, Eng.
   Pieter Phillipus Stroebel   June 7–July 7, 1958   Bulawayo Turf Club,
      Rhod.

Most consecutive races won, North American record
9   Albert Adams   Sept. 10–12, 1930   Marlboro, MD

Most years as rider, since 1900
40   Johnny Longden   1927–66

Triple Crown

Only undefeated winner of Triple Crown
"Seattle Slew"   1977   (9 wins)

Worst record before Triple Crown
none   6 starts   "Sir Barton"   1919

Best record of Triple Crown winner as 3-year-old
undefeated in 8 starts   "War Admiral"   1937

Most Triple Crown championships, jockey
2   Eddie Arcaro   ("Whirlaway," "Citation")

Youngest jockey to win Triple Crown
Steve Cauthen   18   "Affirmed"   born May 1, 1960

Ten That Just Missed

The ten horses that won the first two legs of the Triple Crown—the Kentucky Derby and the Preakness Stakes—and then were defeated in the Belmont Stakes:

1944	"Pensive," finished second; winner, "Bounding Home"
1958	"Tim Tam," finished second; winner, "Cavan"
1961	"Carry Back," finished seventh; winner, "Sherluck"
1964	"Northern Dancer," finished third; winner, "Quadrangle"
1966	"Kauai King," finished fourth; winner, "Amberoid"
1968	"Forward Pass," finished second; winner, "Stage Door Johnny"
1969	"Majestic Prince," finished second; winner, "Arts and Letters"
1971	"Canonero II," finished fourth; winner, "Pass Catcher"
1979	"Spectacular Bid," finished third; winner, "Coastal"
1981	"Pleasant Colony," finished third; winner, "Summing"

ABC Sports

HARNESS RACING

Drivers

Most consecutive wins, one raceway program, single dashes
7   Augustine Ratchford   Sackville Downs   Halifax, N. S.   Feb. 21, 1976

Most 2-minute drives, one raceway program
6   John Campbell   Meadowlands   East Rutherford, NJ   June 5, 1981

Most wins by driver, one meeting
269   William O'Donnell   Saratoga Harness   1979

Most wins, one day, one track
11 Clint Hodgins   Dufferin Park   Toronto, Ont.   Nov. 25, 1939
     Joe O'Brien   Truro Raceway   Truro, N. S.   Sept. 16, 1942

Most wins, one raceway program, single dashes
8   Herve Filion   Hinsdale Raceway   Hinsdale, NH   Sept. 10, 1978

Record U.D.R.S. driver, single year
100–199 starts   .696   Fred Johnson   1951
200–299 starts   .629   William Miller   1949
300–up starts   .566   C. J. Osborn   1979

Youngest driver, 2-minute mile
Alma Sheppard (12 years)   Dean Hanover   1:58.2   Sept. 24, 1937

Horses

Most heats or dashes won, lifetime
350   "Goldsmit Maid"   1864–77

Most $100,000 races won, one year
9   "Niatross"   1980

Most 2-minute miles, lifetime
71   "Rambling Willie"   1972–80

Most consecutive 2-minute miles
18   "Niatross"   1980

Most 2-minute miles, one year
24   "Niatross"   1980

Longest winning streak
41   "Carty Nagle"   1937–38

Did you know ?

1. What horse was the only one to run unbeaten in 54 races?

2. What Triple Crown winner sired another Triple Crown winner?

3. What three races make up Great Britain's Triple Crown?

4. Where is the oldest race track in the United States?

5. Who was the first jockey to win both Jockey of the Year and Apprentice Jockey of the Year?

6. What horse was the first with career winnings of more than a $1 million?

7. What race did "Canonero II," the surprise colt from Venezuela, lose when he missed the Triple Crown by one race, in 1971?

8. Who is the oldest jockey to ride in a race?

9. What jockey tied Eddie Arcaro's record of riding five Kentucky Derby winners?

10. "Man o' War" won the Belmont Stakes, the Preakness, the Kenilworth Park Gold Cup, and the Kentucky Derby during his career. Is this true?

11. What race was the only one "Man o' War" lost?

12. Who was the first woman jockey to ride 100 winners?

13. Who was the first woman to ride in the Kentucky Derby?

14. "Hambletonian," the foundation sire of today's Standardbred horses, was also a champion at the race track. True?

15. What Standardbred pacer broke Dan Patch's record of 30 two-minute-or-faster miles?

16. What American jockey is credited with developing the crouching position used by jockeys today?

17. What horses raced in the first $100,000 race in the United States?

Answers: 1. "Kincsem," in races in Austria, Great Britain, France, and Germany; **2.** "Gallant Fox," the 1930 Triple Crown winner, sired "Omaha," the winner in 1935; **3.** The English, or Epsom's Derby; the St. Leger's; and the 2,000 Guineas; **4.** Hempstead, NY; **5.** Steve Cauthen; **6.** "Citation"; **7.** The Belmont Stakes; "Canonero II" lost to "Pass Catcher"; **8.** Levi Barlingame; **9.** Bill Hartack; **10.** False, "Man o' War" never rode in the Kentucky Derby (it wasn't considered a prestigious race at the time by his owner, Samuel Riddle); **11.** The Sanford Memorial Stakes, at Saratoga, NY; **12.** Mary Bacon; **13.** Diane Crump; **14.** False, "Hambletonian" never raced; **15.** "Bret Hanover"; **16.** Tod Sloan; **17.** "Zev," a Kentucky Derby winner, and "Papyrus," an English Derby winner, in 1923, at Belmont Park; "Zev" won.

acey deucey a style of riding in which the jockey uses a much longer stirrup on the left, or inside, leg.

action a horse's movement; an even, smooth stride is said to be "good action."

also ran a horse that does not finish among the first three.

backstretch the straightaway on the far side of the race track; also used as a reference to the stable area.

barrier a synonym for "starting gate."

Bill Daly a horse that breaks in front and sets the pace is said to be "on the Bill Daly." This manner of running is thought to be the principal tactic developed and drilled into jockeys by "Father Bill" Daly, a colorful trainer prior to the turn of the century.

blanket finish a finish in which several horses finish with their noses and heads apart, or so closely grouped that figuratively speaking, they could be covered by a blanket.

blinkers eye cups used to block a horse's side and rear vision.

blowout a brief, final workout given a day or two before a race, intended to sharpen and maintain a horse's condition.

boxed in a situation in which a horse is surrounded by horses—in front, behind, and on the side—pinning the horse to the hub rail.

break when a trotter or pacer goes off its gait and starts galloping.

breezing a horse working a short distance under restraint.

brush the brief peak or peaks of speed reached by a harness horse in a race or a training mile; drivers like to preserve a horse's "brush" for the stretch drive.

chalk the favorite or most heavily played horse in a race; also called a "chalk horse."

choked down a trainer or driver attempting to restrain or rate a harness horse, which inadvertently cuts off the animal's breathing; in this case, the horse blacks out and often falls.

climbing a fault in a horse's stride which, instead of letting the horse reach out, causes its "action" to be abnormally high.

clubhouse turn the last turn before the homestretch.

colors the distinctively colored silk or nylon jacket and cap provided by the owner and worn by the jockey; the colors are registered with the Jockey Club and the state racing authority.

cushion the loose surface of a race track.

dead heat   a race so close that even the photo-finish camera shows no difference in the finish of two horses; in such cases, the race is declared a dead heat, or tie.

driving   a horse running under extreme pressure.

dwelt   a horse slow to break from the starting gate.

eighth pole   on a race track, the pole one-eighth of a mile before the finish line.

extended   a horse running at or near its top speed and being pressured by its rider to achieve even more speed.

far turn   the turn coming off the backstretch.

furlong   a distance of one-eighth of a mile; it was originally a furrow long, or the length of a plowed field.

garden spot   the position occupied by a horse racing in second position on the rail; the lead horse is close enough to cut the wind for the second-place horse, yet the latter is still in position to make a bid for the lead in the stretch.

TRA Photo

garrison finish   a late rush resulting in a narrow margin of victory, so called because Edward ("Snapper") Garrison, a prominent rider around 1900, specialized in such finishes.

gelding   a castrated male horse.

hand   four inches; a unit of measure used to express a horse's height; one hand is placed above the other, from the ground to the withers or the point where the saddle sits. A horse that measures 16 hands is 5 feet 4 inches tall at the withers.

handle   the total money wagered on a race, day, meeting, or season.

homestretch   the straightaway leading to the finish line.

in the money   a horse finishing first, second, or third.

irons   stirrups.

lapped on   juxtaposition at the wire, where a horse's nose is at least opposite the hindquarters of the horse ahead.

morning line   the approximate odds, usually printed in the program and posted on the totalizator board before the betting begins. It is a forecast of how the betting is expected to go in a particular race.

near side   the left side of a horse (facing in the same direction as the horse), the side on which a horse is led, mounted, or dismounted.

odds-on   betting odds of less than even money (one dollar to one dollar); a winner at a payoff of less than four dollars is "odds-on."

off side   the right-hand side of a horse, facing in the same direction as the horse.

paddock   the area of the race track where horses are saddled and viewed before a race.

parked out   the position of a trotter or a pacer when its rivals are positioned so as to prevent it from reaching the rail; a horse forced to race on the outside must travel a longer distance, and thus rarely wins.

post   the starting point for a race.

post position   horses' positions in the starting gate, counting from the inner rail out; positions are decided by a drawing at the close of entries the day before a race.

post time   the starting time for a race; at post time, all horses are required to be at the post, ready to start.

purse   technically, a race prize to which owners do not contribute.

quarter horse   a breed of horse recently established; it is extremely fast over short distances.

quarter pole   on a one-mile track, the pole at the turn into the stretch one quarter of a mile before the finish line.

scratch   to withdraw a horse from a race.

short   in a race, a horse that drops out of contention in the stretch or near the finish line.

silks   the jacket and cap worn by a jockey.

stallion   a male horse, usually one retired from racing and which stands at stud on a breeding farm.

stayer   a horse that runs well at longer distances.

stick   slang for a jockey's whip.

stretch   the last eighth of a mile before the finish line.

stud   a stallion used for breeding.

tack   the saddle and other equipment worn by a horse during racing or exercise.

totalizator board   a display of data in the infield, posted electronically, which is useful to racegoers; the board gives such information as approximate odds; total amount bet in each pool (on some boards); track condition; post time; time of day; race results; official sign, or inquiry or objection sign, if a foul is claimed; running time; and payoff prices after a race declared official.

walkover   a race in which only one starting horse goes to the post; in this rare event, the horse is required only to gallop the distance of the race to be declared the winner and collect the purse.

weanling or yearling   all horses are considered weanlings from the time they are taken from their mothers until they reach their first birthday (always January 1, regardless of the day they were born); a horse is called a "yearling" from the time it reaches age one until it reaches age two.

ABC Sports   ABC Sports

12 ICE SKATING

he exact origin of ice skating is not known. Although early Scandinavians surely developed some methods of traveling on frozen surfaces, it is impossible to tell whether early references to "ice skates" may not actually be to crude versions of skis or snowshoes, developed to ease overland foot travel in Arctic climates.

The oldest recognizable pair of ice skates, made from bones attached to a shoe, was found in Switzerland. They are thought to be at least 4,000 years old. The now indispensable metal blade did not make its appearance until the late Middle Ages, when enterprising Dutchmen attached sharpened strips of iron to the bottoms of their wooden clogs. These strips, or blades, enabled skaters to move by shifting their weight from one skate to the other in a gliding motion. This movement, known as the "Dutch roll," is still considered the fundamental ice-skating step.

Given the ease of movement made possible by metal skates, ice skaters soon became a common sight, both in the Low Countries, where people skated on frozen canals, and in Britain (especially Scotland) on iced-over lakes in the Lake District. By the late eighteenth century, skating was so popular in Scotland that the world's first skating club was formed there, in Edinburgh. In both England and the Low Countries, skating was taken seriously; it was a participatory athletic event—something to do, not watch.

In the Netherlands, skating was a means of transportation. When contests were held, they were races from one town to another designed to test speed, not grace. The English approached skating almost scientifically, considering the best skaters those who performed staid, somewhat stilted movements with dignity and precision. It wasn't until the early nineteenth century that skating came to be viewed as something more than functional. A group of French intellectuals who had taken to ice skating incorporated twists, pirouettes, jumps, and other dancelike movements in their skating routines.

By 1868, Jackson Haines, an American ballet teacher, was treating ice skating as though it were a form of dance, choreographing routines solely for skaters. He went to England, where his ideas were not well received. Finally, he settled in Vienna, where, partly because of the city's tradition of, and interest in, dancing, ice skating to music took hold. Pair skating, and eventually ice dancing, developed directly from Viennese ice skating.

In England, skaters were attempting to make ice skating more precise. "Figure skating"—tracing intricate figures on ice—became more complex and increasingly difficult. At the same time, speed skating was developing into a full-fledged sport. Meanwhile, other games on ice, such as curling, ice hockey, and bandy were growing in popularity.

By the late nineteenth century, ice skating in its various forms was sufficiently popular throughout the world to justify formation of the International Skating Union, which remains the governing body of sport skating to this day.

Whereas speed skating has changed little since its introduction (the basic object is still simply to skate faster than anyone else), figure skating, at least at competitive levels, has undergone significant changes, all related to changes in the relative influences of the English and Viennese schools of skating.

The so-called English school, which stresses precision execution of figures on the ice, has, since about 1970, been overshadowed by "freestyle" skating, both figure and ice dancing. In Olympic competition, for example, the "school figures" portion of a skater's performance has been reduced to only 30 percent of the total score, while free skating accounts for 50 percent of the score. In recent years a segment requiring seven compulsory freestyle elements, 20 percent of the total score—has been added, further diminishing the importance of school figures. In pair skating, as in singles skating, freestyle elements count for much more than do figure techniques. Also in 1976 ice dancing, which consists solely of free movements performed to standard dance rhythms, became an Olympic event.

The success of such skaters as John Curry, Dorothy Hamill, Tai Babilonia, and Randy Gardner, all of whom have extensive training in dance, is another indication that modern competitive skating, though still demanding enormous precision and discipline, has been enhanced by the growing acceptance of artistic self-expression.

Great Moments

1879   The National Skating Association of Great Britain, the first of its kind in the world, is founded to unite speed skaters in the British Isles.

1881   Figure skating is recognized by the National Skating Association of Great Britain.

1887 The Skating Club of the United States is formed, in Philadelphia.

1888 Pair skating is performed for the first time, in Vienna, Austria.

1892 The International Skating Union (ISU) is formed.

1896 The ISU holds its first international championships, in St. Petersburg.

1908 The ISU holds its first pairs championships. That same year, pair skating becomes an Olympic event.

1914 The first American national figure-skating championship competition is held, in New Haven, Ct.

1921 The first U.S. speed-skating competition for women is held.

1924 Winter sports events are made part of the Olympic Games. That year, 12-year-old Sonja Henie wins her first title, the Norwegian national figure-skating championship.

1936 Following her final Olympic victory at the Berlin Olympics, Henie tours the United States with history's first professional ice show.

1952 Ice dancing is accepted as an event in world-championship competition.

1960 Women's speed skating is introduced at the Olympic Games.

1962 Donald Jackson of Canada executes the first competition triple jumps and triple loops, at the world championships in Prague.

1969 Olympic rules for figure skating are revised to give equal weight in scoring to school figure- and free-skating routines.

1970 The 1,000-meter race is added to ISU men's speed skating competition.

1972 In an effort to reduce the disadvantage of freestyle skaters, rules for the Olympics are changed to give the compulsory figures only 40 points and to reduce the number of compulsory figures from six to three; a short program of compulsory freestyle movements is introduced.

1976 Ice dancing and the 1000-meter race are accepted as Olympic events.

1979 Beth Heiden wins the women's World Championship, taking gold medals in all four events.

1980 Eric Heiden, of the United States, wins all five Olympic speed-skating gold medals, becoming the first athlete to win five gold medals in one Winter Olympics.

The Setup

Both figure and speed skating are Olympic sports and as such are governed by the International Olympic Committee. Aside from various ice shows, which are sponsored by individual promoters, skating is a predominantly amateur sport.

Amateur figure skating—which includes singles skating, pair skating, and ice dancing—is governed in the United States by the United States Figure Skating Association (USFSA). USFSA sets the standards for competition, defines amateur status, and sanctions and classifies competitions while maintaining a liaison with the U.S. and International Olympic Committees.

The national governing body for metric, or Olympic-style, speed skating is the U.S. International Speedskating Association (USISA). It selects the U.S. Olympic team and sets the rules for metric-style speed skating. The Amateur Skating Union of the United States (ASU) governs races in pack-style speed skating and is affiliated with the USISA.

AMATEUR SKATING UNION OF
  THE UNITED STATES
4423 Deming Place
Chicago, IL 60639
(312) 235-9581
Lawrence R. Ralston, exec. sec.

U.S. INTERNATIONAL
  SPEEDSKATING ASSOCIATION
Beggs Isle
Oconomowoc, WI 53066
(414) 567-6051
George Howie, pres.

UNITED STATES FIGURE SKATING
  ASSOCIATION
20 First St.
Colorado Springs, CO 80906
(303) 635-5200
Roy Winder, exec. dir.

The Basics

Object To perform any of several types of routines on ice with precision and grace, using figure skates.

The rink Most competitive figure skating takes place on an indoor rink large enough to provide each competitor with an adequate area of relatively unblemished ice on which to perform.

Equipment The major piece of equipment necessary is figure skates, which consist of a metal blade attached beneath heavy leather boots. Figure skating blades are concave, so that the inside and outside edges of the blades meet the ice separately (top quality skaters do not skate with both edges of a blade on the ice at the same time). At the front of the blade is a "toe" with serrated teeth that can add impetus to jumps and also aid stopping.

The only other equipment required by a figure skater is a costume that allows freedom of movement. Skaters choose their own costumes; selecting a costume that adds to the performance and enhances the musical interpretation is important.

Officials Officials present at skating competitions include a referee, several judges, a timekeeper, and a scorekeeper.

SINGLES SKATING

The program Singles skating competitions are divided into three parts. The first is a series of three compulsory figures that must be traced on the ice. These are called "school figures," and performance in them counts for 30 percent of the total score.

The second required element is the "short program," a sequence of seven compulsory freestyle movements that is worth 20 percent of the total. The third element, which makes up half of the aggregate score, is a free skating composition of the skater's choice.

Compulsory Figures

The routine Three compulsory, or school, figures all based on variations of a circle, must be traced. The skater must trace the figures using the prescribed edge of the prescribed skate; their diameters should be about three times the skater's height.

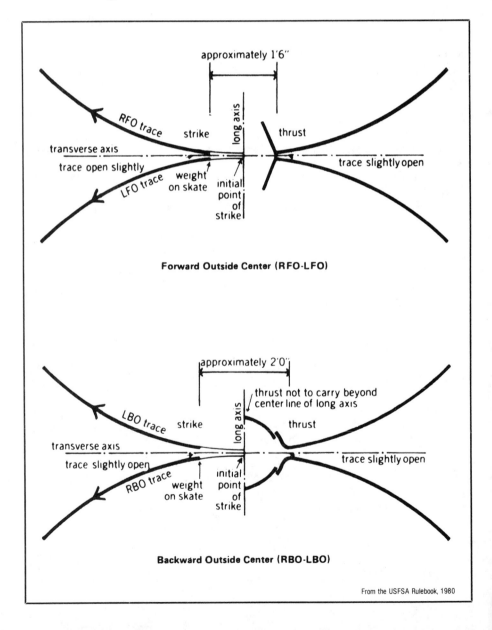

Forward Outside Center (RFO-LFO)

Backward Outside Center (RBO-LBO)

From the USFSA Rulebook, 1980

Rule 1   Starting   Before starting, the skater should indicate the long axis of the figure to be skated. The skater starts, when signaled by the referee, from the intersection of the long and short axes of the figure. The skater must make a clean start with no preliminary movement.

Rule 2   Tracings   The skater should select as smooth a piece of ice as possible so that his or her tracings are clear. Skaters may not follow the tracings of a previous skater. If they make a faulty tracing on the first tracing, it should be corrected in subsequent repetitions.

Rule 3   Repetitions   Skaters must skate each figure three times on each foot.

Rule 4   False starts   One false start is permitted without penalty. Starting on the wrong foot, skating the wrong figure, beginning before the referee indicates, and taking a preliminary step are all considered false starts.

Rule 5   Scoring   Each figure is judged on a scale of zero (not skated) to six (flawless). Points are deducted if, among other things, a figure is too large or too small, the skater selects unclear ice or follows someone else's tracings, the figure is not finished in a reasonable length of time, or the skater is awkward, unsure, or lacking in grace.

Short Program

The routine   The short program, which may last no longer than two minutes, consists of seven compulsory free-skating movements chosen from four groups of such movements by the ISU. The free-skating elements consist of jump combinations, spin combinations, straight and circular step sequences, and connecting steps.

Rule 1   Music   The skater chooses the music to be used, and judges consider how well it suits the movements chosen.

Rule 2   Connecting steps   The skater may use connecting steps of his or her choice. The steps are marked, and a skater is penalized for using any more steps than are absolutely necessary.

Rule 3   Extra elements   Extra elements, including repetitions of required movements that were not executed properly the first time, are not allowed.

Rule 4   Scoring   Skaters are scored on a scale of one to six, with six being a perfect score. In scoring, judges consider time (the routine should take as little time as possible), technical merit, and composition and style. In considering technical merit, judges note execution of jumps (height, length, technique, clean start, and landing) and spins (strength and control of rotation, number of revolutions, speed of rotation, and centering of the spin).

In considering style and composition, judges note: the harmony of the composition, including the connecting steps, as a whole and as an expression of the character of the chosen music; the difficulty of the connecting steps; ease of movement; rhythm; originality; and utilization of all the available ice.

Free Skating

The routine   A series of movements chosen entirely by the skater. There should be a great deal of variety, and difficult elements of free skating—for example, jumps, spins, dance steps, and linking movements—should be included. The maximum length for men's singles is five minutes; the maximum for women's singles is three.

Rule 1   Jumps   Jumps must be clean, starting and ending on one skate. No jumps may begin or end on both feet. Somersault-type jumps are prohibited.

Rule 2   Two feet   No unnecessary or prolonged movements on two feet are permitted.

Rule 3   Repetitions   Repetitions of movements are permitted, but the full score for a particular maneuver may be given only once.

Rule 4   Ice area   Skaters should utilize the entire ice area available to them.

Rule 5   Music   The skater selects the music for the routine.

Rule 6   Scoring   Scoring for both technical merit and composition and style is based on the same criteria used in judging the short program. *Note:* Although free skating accounts for 70 percent of the total score, as opposed to 30 percent in school figures, it is still possible for a performer who is strong in compulsory figures to defeat a strong free skater. This happens because judges tend to score the figures on a wide scale, using the entire spectrum from zero to ten; but they score free skating within a narrow range. Thus a good figure skater who gets a four point lead over a good freestylist early in the program may be able to maintain that lead and win the event despite coming in with somewhat lower marks in free skating and the short program.

PAIR SKATING

Object   For two people to skate in unison with such harmony that they give the impression of being a single unit.

The program   Pair skating programs consist of a five-minute freestyle program chosen by the pair and a short program of compulsory movements. Pairs competition is held between man-woman pairs, woman-woman pairs, or man-man pairs.

The skaters   The skaters should be of approximately the same height and physique. A skater should pay particular attention to the choice of a partner, because points are deducted for skating with an inappropriate partner.

Free Skating

The routine   The routine should be varied and contain an adequate number of difficult movements. It should display such traditional pair-skating movements as spirals, spins, and lifts and have many singles skating movements, performed simultaneously, either in parallel (shadow skating) or symmetrically (mirror skating).

Rule 1   Movement   Partners do not have to perform the same movements at all times; separate movements, however, should be coordinated to give the impression of unity.

Rule 2   Assisted jumps   Assisted jumps must consist of one continuous ascending and descending movement interrupted by no more than three complete revolutions of the partner doing the lifting. A skater may not touch the legs of the partner. No lifts which result in one partner being held in a horizontal position are permitted and a skater may not merely carry the other partner.

Rule 3 Lifts A lift must be completed with the lifting arm fully extended; lifts only to shoulder height are not counted.

Rule 4 Spins A skater is not allowed to spin the partner around in the air while holding the partner's hand or foot. No partner is allowed to rotate while the other skater is gripping his or her leg, arm, or neck. Twistlike movements, in which the woman is turned while her skating foot leaves the ice, are not allowed. The "death spiral spin," in which one skater is spun around the other, is permitted as long as one of the spun partner's skates remains on the ice.

Rule 5 Scoring Performance is judged on technical merit and on style and composition. When forbidden movements are performed, judges must deduct in both categories. Judging is according to the same criteria as in singles free skating, except that close attention is paid to accurate performance in unison.

Short Program

The routine The short program consists of a series of seven compulsory movements chosen the day before the competition from one of four ISU-recognized groups of short program movements. These movements include multiple flips, spins, spirals, lifts, jumps, and step sequences. The short program may not last longer than two minutes and fifteen seconds.

Rule 1 Spins Spins must contain at least six revolutions on the prescribed foot or, if performed on both feet, five revolutions on each foot. Solo spins may not begin with a jump.

Rule 2 Step sequences All step sequences should be executed as closely together as possible, in keeping with the music.

Rule 3 Connecting steps Skaters may chose their connecting steps. Although the steps are marked, their number should be kept to the minimum necessary to link the movements in a unified routine.

Rule 4 Scoring Judging is according to the same criteria as for the short program in singles skating, except that attention is also paid to the harmony of the pair. Deductions are made for failing at or omitting the prescribed double jump or the prescribed double lift. Less severe deductions are made for other flaws.

ICE DANCING

Object To perform formal dance movements on ice with musical accompaniment.

The skaters A dance couple consists of a man and a woman.

The program An ice-dancing program consists of compulsory dances, an original set pattern dance, and a free dance of the skaters' choice.

Compulsory Dances

The dances The ISU recognizes 18 compulsory dances, most of them variations on the waltz, tango, or foxtrot.

Performance Each couple performs three compulsory dances, drawn by lot the day before the competition.

Rule 1 Starts Starts may not exceed seven introductory steps for either partner.

Rule 2 Poses Theatrical poses at the beginning or end of the dance are forbidden.

Rule 3 Music The dance couple must choose their own music for the dances drawn. It must conform with the type and tempo of the dances.

Rule 4 Scoring The compulsory dance makes up 30 percent of the couple's total score. The highest possible score for each event is six. Scores for each dance are added together and divided by 2.5 for the final mark in the compulsory dances.

Original Set Pattern Dance

The dance The original set pattern dance is performed to a dance rhythm selected by the ISU each year and is the same for all competing couples. Couples must make the choices of instrumental music, steps, connecting steps, and movements, as long as they conform to the chosen rhythm.

Rule 1 Starts As in the compulsories, starts are restricted to seven introductory steps.

Rule 2 Poses Theatrical poses are forbidden.

Rule 3 Separations Partners may not separate except to change their hold. Changes of a hold cannot last longer than one musical measure.

Rule 4 Movement restrictions Hand-in-hand skating with outstretched arms is not permitted; otherwise, there are no restrictions on holds, arm movements, or handclasps.

Rule 5 Scoring The original set-pattern dance is judged on composition and presentation. This segment accounts for 20 percent of the couple's total score. As in other skating events, marks are awarded on a scale of zero to six. Typical composition criteria are originality, difficulty, and variety of movements; utilization of the ice surface, and conformity to the chosen pattern. Presentation is judged on correct timing of movement to music, expression of the music, cleanness, harmony in unison, and style.

Free Dancing

The dance The free dance consists of any series of dancelike steps and movements selected by the skaters and performed to music.

Duration The dance must last no longer than four minutes.

Music Couples choose their own music. Music must be instrumental dance music; no more than three changes of tune are allowed.

The routine The routine should consist of a nonrepetitive sequence of dance movements, new or standard, choreographed in a unified, expressive whole. The movements should be of a significant degree of difficulty.

Rule 1   ***Steps***   All steps are permitted, although solely ballet dancing on ice is considered pair skating, not ice dancing, and is not allowed. Difficult, original, and intricate footwork is expected of performers. Standing and sitting are not considered appropriate to ice dancing and are penalized.

Rule 2   ***Separations***   Partners may separate to change hold or position as often as they wish. Separations to execute arabesques or other movements may last no longer than five seconds, and the partners may never be over two arm lengths away from each other. Only five such separations are permitted.

Rule 3   ***Stops***   The couple may not remain stationary on the ice for more than two measures of music while twisting or posing.

Rule 4   ***Movements***   Although a certain amount of lifting, jumping, and other pair-skating movements is permitted if they are in character with the music and augment the dance, the use of too many such movements is considered inappropriate to ice dancing and is penalized.

Rule 5   ***Scoring***   The free dance receives two marks on a scale of zero to six, one for technical merit and one for composition and style. Technical merit includes the originality, difficulty, and variety of the dance, utilization of the ice area, and appropriate selection of music; composition and style involve correct timing, cleanness, and the style and harmony of the couple. The free dance represents 50 percent of the total score.

SPEED SKATING (OLYMPIC-STYLE)

Object   To cover a specified distance on ice in the shortest possible time, wearing skates.

The track   Speed skating may take place indoors or outdoors. The standard Olympic track is a closed oval course with two straightaways and two curved ends. All lanes are at least four meters wide, with a ridge of snow separating them. The backstretch is designated as a lane-changing zone. Skaters skate counterclockwise.

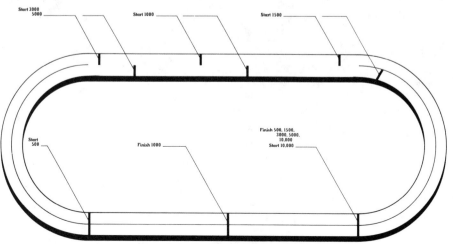

Courtesy Champion International Corporation

Equipment Skates with long, sharp blades and uppers of thin leather. Skaters wear skintight uniforms to permit free movement and reduce air resistance.

Officials Officials present at major speed-skating races are a referee and four assistant referees, a starter and an assistant, three track scorers, lap scorers, timekeepers, flagman, and a chief judge and at least three other judges.

Distances In Olympic competition, men compete in five races: the 500-meter, 1,000-meter, 1,500-meter, 5,000-meter, and 10,000-meter. Women compete in 500-meter, 1,000-meter, 1,500-meter, and 3,000-meter events.

Rule 1 ***Order of competition*** Speed skaters compete one against another. The order of competition is determined by a skater's time in previous races; in the Olympics, racers draw for starting order and race in heats, two skaters at a time.

Rule 2 ***The start*** Skaters must stand still in an upright position until the starter calls ready; then they may take their starting position. They must not move until the starting pistol is fired, again, however. The 5,000-meter and 10,000-meter races have staggered starts. Skaters are recalled if there is a false start. A skater is disqualified for two false starts in the same race.

Rule 3 ***Changing lanes*** Skaters must change lanes each time they come to the crossover, so the skater in the inner lane will have skated as far as the opponent in the outer lane. The skater crossing from the outer lane to the inner lane has the right of way. An official with a flag directs the skaters.

Rule 4 ***Illegal moves*** A skater may be disqualified for interfering with an opponent by either charging, pushing, or tripping.

Rule 5 ***The winner*** The winner of the race is the skater who, after all heats have been completed, has the shortest elapsed time for covering the specified distance.

ABC Sports

How to watch

Courtesy ProServ, Inc.

with Tai Babilonia

Ice skating demands the grace of a ballerina, the endurance of a long-distance runner, and the precision of a diamond cutter. But the hardest part of all, says world-champion pair skater Tai Babilonia, now a star of the Ice Capades, is to make the entire exercise look easy.

The best ice skaters, she says, excel in both athleticism and artistry, combining the two in a way that seems effortless. In the school figures, where the skater must etch intricate designs on the ice, concentration is all-important. Singles skaters must compete in both figures and freeskating, skills that seldom go together. Thus a truly great figure skater will have the athletic ability to excel technically, but he or she will also exemplify the grace and style characteristic of the beat freeskaters.

According to Tai Babilonia, judges look for both originality and flawlessness in skaters. The ultimate goal is a flawless performance, one in which every move is performed smoothly, with no mistakes. Skaters should also have a good edge. This means they should enter and leave different jumps and spins with a speed that does not vary from move to move, so that the entire routine flows.

A skater's performance must exhibit technical mastery as well as artistic interpretation. The music should vary as much as possible in rhythm and tone so the judges' and fans' interest in the performance does not wane. Music and costumes contribute greatly to the effect of a skater's overall performance, and the best skaters make these decisions carefully.

Good skaters will also have a variety of movements in their routines. Some of the most spectacular, such as spreadeagles and spirals, are actually relatively easy for the top skaters to do, Tai Babilonia explains; these moves should be mixed in with truly difficult movements such as the triple rotation jump. Skaters try to use all of the ice, and their programs should contain "a little of everything," including ballet and other forms of dance as well as athletic maneuvers.

The presentation of a skater's movements are as important as the technical skill. Although skaters must have immense concentration, it should appear as though the movements are inevitable, that they grow out of the routine naturally. A good skater will never seem to be looking at his or her feet; and will resist the temptation to lean forward on the skates. A skater who is playing to the audience excessively, however, is in danger of losing that crucial concentration and thus making a mistake.

Skaters should not look timid or betray fear of falling; judges rate confidence highly. In such difficult moves as the lift, the female partner should hold her head erect and her back up, making the maneuver appear as easy and natural as the simpler moves.

In pair skating, the couple's ability to skate in unison is of the utmost importance. They must be intimately familiar with each other's style, timing and technique. Most pair skaters have been training with each other for a long time, usually years, which accounts for their ability to perform in synchronization. The movements of pair skaters should be identical when they are not spinning, lifting or otherwise touching each other. In ice dancing, the partners should also be well matched; the couple should be able to skate through an entire performance on the specified edge of the specified skate, in perfect harmony.

In fact, harmony—both between partners and among the many elements of a routine—is the hallmark of good ice skating. A good skater, or a good pair of skaters, will very likely produce a varied performance, interpreting music well and demonstrating technical virtuosity, while creating the illusion of doing nothing more strenuous than lifting a feather.

How to watch

SPEED SKATING

Speed skating is the fastest way a human being can move on ice under his or her own power. For example, world-champion skaters are capable of sustaining speeds of more than 30 miles an hour in 1,000-meter sprints. The sport is exciting because of the speed and grace of its competitors, and because the rules are fairly simple it is, as sports go, easy to follow. The sport demands from its competitors strength, speed, endurance, and a certain grace, all of which are carefully developed during the speed skater's intensive training.

The stroke is the skater's basic racing movement. Body rhythm and weight distribution are essential to achieving a good stroke. Inevitably, leg movement is the most important part of the stroke. To achieve maximum acceleration and speed, the skater first leans forward and pushes off, using the free leg and the overall body weight. During the stroke, the other leg swings free until it is time for the leg to come down on the ice for another push-off; this leg should land near the skate already on the ice. A skater who uses only the tip of the blade in a push-off will not have a strong, even stroke.

Although a skater's leg movements are essentially the same for races of all distances, arm movements do vary. In the 500-meter sprint, for instance, the arms swing high behind the skater, alternately left-arm-forward-and-right-leg-back, then right-arm-forward-and-left-leg-back. In middle-distance races, of say, 1,000, and 1,500 meters, the skater swings only one arm on the straightaway; the other arm rests behind on the lower back. In longer races, the skater's arms are behind the back, with one hand grabbing the other wrist.

Speed-skating races are begun with competitors at a standstill. The start is somewhat awkward until racers gain momentum and attain the rhythm necessary for top speed. The skater will start with short quick steps. There is almost no gliding until some momentum has been gained.

Whereas the start is important, turns are probably the chief determinant of who wins a race. The laws of physics dictate the skater's technique in a turn. A skater going into a turn too fast has to waste time and energy battling inertial forces, the tendency to move in a straight line. Skaters usually try to maintain their entry speed going into a turn, accelerating as they come out of it, and using centrifugal force to push into the straightaway. As is true on the straightaway, positioning of the arms in a turn varies according to the distance being raced. In a short race, a skater will not lean far forward in the turn, but will instead distribute body weight evenly so the force does not pull too strongly on one part of the body. The arms move quickly back and forth in rhythm, with fast leg movements. Distance skaters rely on longer, gliding strokes to get through a turn efficiently. Although a distance skater will lean forward to glide in the turn, this skater will lean inward rather than rotating the body.

In spite of the importance of technique in speed skating, the sport much more closely resembles track than it does its sister sport, figure skating; speed, and not style, is what wins. Skaters are racing against the clock rather than each other; thus, they prefer tough rather than easy opponents. Viewers can expect the fastest races and the most records in heats pitting two evenly-matched competitors against each other.

Main Events

FIGURE SKATING

Olympics

MEN'S

1980	Robin Cousins	UK
1976	John Curry	UK
1972	Ondrej Nepela	Czechoslovakia
1968	Wolfgang Schwartz	Austria
1964	Manfred Schnelldorfer	FRG *
1960	David Jenkins	USA
1956	Hayes Jenkins	USA
1952	Dick Button	USA
1948	Dick Button	USA

WOMEN'S

1980	Anett Poetzsch	GDR*
1976	Dorothy Hamill	USA
1972	Beatrix Schuba	Austria
1968	Peggy Fleming	USA
1964	Sjoukje Dijkstra	The Netherlands
1960	Carol Heiss	USA
1956	Tenley Albright	USA
1952	Jeannette Altwegg	UK
1948	Barbara Ann Scott	Canada

* German Democratic Republic (East Germany).
* Federal Republic of Germany (West Germany).

PAIRS

1980	Irina Rodnina & Alexander Zaitsev	USSR
1976	Irina Rodnina & Alexander Zaitsev	USSR
1972	Irina Rodnina & Alexei Ulanov	USSR
1968	Ludmilla Belousova & Oleg Protopopov	USSR
1964	Ludmilla Belousova & Oleg Protopopov	USSR
1960	Barbara Wagner & Robert Paul	Canada
1956	Elisabeth Schwartz & Kurt Oppelt	Austria
1952	Ria Falk & Paul Falk	FRG
1948	Micheline Lannoy & Pierre Brunet	Belgium

World Championships
MEN'S

1980	Jan Hoffmann	GDR
1979	Vladimir Kovalev	USSR
1978	Charles Tickner	USA
1977	Vladimir Kovalev	USSR
1976	John Curry	UK
1975	Sergei Yolkov	USSR
1974	Jan Hoffman	GDR
1973	Ondrej Nepela	Czechoslovakia
1972	Ondrej Nepela	Czechoslovakia
1971	Ondrej Nepela	Czechoslovakia

WOMEN'S

1980	Anett Poetzsch	GDR
1979	Linda Fratianne	USA
1978	Anett Poetzsch	GDR
1977	Linda Fratianne	USA
1976	Dorothy Hamill	USA
1975	Dianne de Leeuw	Netherlands
1974	Christine Errath	GDR
1973	Karen Magnusson	Canada
1972	Beatrix Schuba	Austria
1971	Beatrix Schuba	Austria

PAIRS

1980	Chersekova & Shakrai	USSR
1979	Tai Babilonia & Randy Gardner	USA
1978	Irina Rodnina & Alexander Zaitsev	USSR
1977	Irina Rodnina & Alexander Zaitsev	USSR
1976	Irina Rodnina & Alexander Zaitsev	USSR
1975	Irina Rodnina & Alexander Zaitsev	USSR
1974	Irina Rodnina & Alexander Zaitsev	USSR
1973	Irina Rodnina & Alexander Zaitsev	USSR
1972	Irina Rodnina & Alexei Ulanov	USSR
1971	Irina Rodnina & Alexei Ulanov	USSR

SPEED SKATING

Olympics

MEN'S 500-METER

1980	Eric Heiden	USA
1976	Yevgeny Kulikov	USSR
1972	Erhard Keller	FRG
1968	Erhard Keller	FRG
1964	Terry McDermott	USA
1960	Eugeni Grishin	USSR
1956	Eugeni Grishin	USSR
1952	Ken Henry	USA
1948	Finn Helgesen	Norway

MEN'S 1000-METER

1980	Eric Heiden	USA
1976	Peter Mueller	USA

MEN'S 1,500-METER

1980	Eric Heiden	USA
1976	Jan Storholt	Norway
1972	Ard Schenk	Netherlands
1968	Anton Maier	Norway
1964	Ants Anston	USSR
1960	Viktor Kosichkin	USSR
1956	Boris Shilkov	USSR

MEN'S 5,000-METER

1980	Eric Heiden	USA
1976	Sten Stensen	Norway
1972	Ard Schenk	Netherlands
1968	Anton Maier	Norway
1964	Knut Johannesen	Norway
1960	Viktor Kosichkin	USSR
1956	Boris Shilkov	USSR
1952	Hjalmar Andersen	Norway

MEN'S 10,000-METER

1980	Eric Heiden	USA
1976	Piet Kline	Netherlands
1972	Ard Schenk	Netherlands
1968	Johnny Hoeglin	Sweden
1964	Jon Nilsson	Sweden
1960	Knut Johanneson	Norway
1956	Sigge Ericsson	Sweden
1952	Hjalmar Andersen	Norway
1948	Ake Seyffarth	Sweden

WOMEN'S 500-METER

1980	Karin Enke	GDR
1976	Sheila Young	USA
1972	Anne Henning	USA
1968	Ludmilla Titova	USSR
1964	Lydia Skoblikova	USSR
1960	Helga Haase	FRG

WOMEN'S 1,000-METER

1980	Natalya Petruseva	USSR
1976	Tatyana Averina	USSR
1972	Monika Pflug	FRG
1968	Carolina Geijssen	Netherlands
1964	Lydia Skoblikova	USSR
1960	Klara Guseva	USSR

WOMEN'S 1,500-METER

1980	Annia Borckink	Netherlands
1976	Galina Stepanskaya	USSR
1972	Dianne Holum	USA
1968	Kaija Mustonen	Finland
1964	Lydia Skoblikova	USSR
1960	Lydia Skoblikova	USSR

WOMEN'S 3,000-METER

1980	Bjoerg Jensen	Norway
1976	Tatyana Averina	USSR
1972	Stien Baas-Kaiser	Netherlands
1968	Johanna Schut	Netherlands
1964	Lydia Skoblikova	USSR
1960	Lydia Skoblikova	USSR

World Championships

MEN'S 500-METER

1980	Eric Heiden	USA
1979	Eric Heiden	USA
1978	Eric Heiden	USA
1977	Eric Heiden	USA
1976	Eric Heiden	USA
1975	Jan Storholt	Norway
1974	Masaki Suzuki	Japan
1973	Bill Lanigan	USA
1972	Ard Schenk	Netherlands
	Roar Gronvold	Norway
1971	Dag Fornaess	Norway

MEN'S 1,000-METER

1980	Herbert van der Duim	Netherlands
1979	Eric Heiden	USA
1978	Eric Heiden	USA
1977	Amund Sjobrend	Norway
1976	Piet Kline	Netherlands
1975	Amund Sjobrend	Norway
1974	Hans van Helden	Netherlands
1973	Sten Stensen	Norway
1972	Ard Schenk	Netherlands
1971	Ard Schenk	Netherlands

MEN'S 5,000-METER

1980	Mike Woods	USA
1979	Eric Heiden	USA
1978	Sten Stensen	Norway
1977	Sten Stensen	Norway
1976	Piet Kline	Netherlands
1975	Vladimir Ivanov	USSR
1974	Sten Stensen	Norway
1973	Goran Claeson	Sweden
1972	Ard Schenk	Netherlands
1971	Ard Schenk	Netherlands

MEN'S 10,000-METER

1980	Mike Woods	USA
1979	Eric Heiden	USA
1978	Sten Stensen	Norway
1977	Sten Stensen	Norway
1976	Piet Kline	Netherlands
1975	Vladimir Ivanov	USSR
1974	Sten Stensen	Norway
1973	Goran Clauson	Sweden
1972	Ard Schenk	Netherlands
1971	Ard Schenk	Netherlands

WOMEN'S 500-METER

1980	Natalya Petruseva	USSR
1979	Beth Heiden	USA
1978	Tatyana Averina	USSR
1977	V. Bryndzey	USSR
1976	Sheila Young	USA
1975	Sheila Young	USA
1974	Sheila Young	USA
1973	Sheila Young	USA
1972	Dianne Holum	USA
1971	Anne Henning	USA

WOMEN'S 1,000-METER

1980	Natalya Petruseva	USSR
1979	Beth Heiden	USA
1978	Tatyana Averino	USSR
1977	V. Bryndzey	USSR
1976	Sheila Young	USA
1975	Sheila Young	USA
1974	Atje Keulen-Deelstra	Netherlands
1973	Atje Keulen-Deelstra	Netherlands
1972	Atje Keulen-Deelstra	Netherlands
1971	Dianne Holum	USA

WOMEN'S 1,500-METER

1980	Natalya Petruseva	USSR
1979	Beth Heiden	USA
1978	Tatyana Averina	USSR
1977	Galina Stepanskaya	USSR
1976	Sylvia Burka	Canada
1975	Karin Kessow	GDR
1974	Atje Keulen-Deelstra	Netherlands
1973	Galina Stepanskaya	USSR
1972	Atje Keulen-Deelstra	Netherlands
1971	Nina Statkevich	USSR

WOMEN'S 3,000-METER

1980	Bjoerg Jensen	Norway
1979	Beth Heiden	USA
1978	M. Dittman	GDR
1977	Galina Stepanskaya	USSR
1976	Karin Kessow	GDR
1975	S. Tigchelaar	Netherlands
1974	Atje Keulen-Deelstra	Netherlands
1973	S. Tigchelaar	Netherlands
1972	Stien Baas-Kaiser	Netherlands
1971	Stien Baas-Kaiser	Netherlands

All-Around World Champions

MEN'S

1980	Herbert van der Duim, Netherlands	1975	Harm Kuipers, Netherlands
1979	Eric Heiden, USA	1974	Sten Stensen, Norway
1978	Eric Heiden, USA	1973	Goran Claeson, Sweden
1977	Eric Heiden, USA	1972	Ard Schenk, Netherlands
1976	Piet Kleine, Netherlands	1971	Ard Schenk, Netherlands

WOMEN'S

1980	Natalya Petruseva, USSR	1975	Karin Kessow, GDR
1979	Beth Heiden, USA	1974	Atje Keulen, Netherlands
1978	Beth Heiden, USA	1973	Atje Keulen, Netherlands
1977	Vera Bryndzey, USSR	1972	Atje Keulen, Netherlands
1976	Sylvia Burka, Canada	1971	Nina Statkevich, USSR

All-Time Greats

Dick Button
(July 18, 1929–)

USFSA Hall of Fame

Button, the founder of modern freestyle skating, in 1948 became the first American to win an Olympic gold medal in figure skating, an achievement he repeated in 1952. He was also the first to perform a double axel, three consecutive double-loop jumps, and a triple-loop jump. The flying camel spin that he originated is, appropriately enough, called the "Button." Entering his first competition in 1943, he placed second. Over the next three years he won gold medals in every sectional and national contest he entered. In 1947, Button entered the World Championships and placed second. The next year he achieved his first Olympic victory. He was U.S. champion from 1946 to 1952 and World Champion from 1949 to 1952. In addition, he won the North American Championship in 1947, 1949, and 1951, and in 1948 the "Quadruple Crown"—the World, U.S., European, and Olympic championships. Upon retirement from skating, Button entered Harvard Law School. Today he is a lawyer, a businessman, and a commentator for ABC Sports.

John Curry
(Sept. 9, 1949–)

Perhaps more than any skater in recent years, Curry is responsible for blending the beauty of ballet with the athleticism of figure skating. A native of Birmingham, England, Curry won the Junior British Skating Championship in 1967 when he was 17 years old. The next year, he won the Jennings Trophy for free skating and by 1970 was the British National Champion, an honor he earned again in 1975. Curry became a triple champion in 1976, winning the European and World titles as well as taking a gold medal in the Winter Olympics. He turned professional later that year, founding and directing his Theatre of Skating. In 1978 he founded another company, Ice Dancing, exclusively for dancers who skate ballets choreographed by Curry.

Peggy Fleming
(July 27, 1948–)

Peggy Fleming's grace and strength not only earned her an Olympic gold medal in 1968, but also inspired a new generation of youngsters to take up figure skating. Fleming won her first competition, the Central Pacific Girls' Championship, in 1959, then, over the next four years, seven sectional and regional titles. During that time she also won a silver medal in the U.S. Novice Championships (1962) and a bronze in the U.S. Junior Ladies (1963). In 1964, Fleming entered the 1964 Winter Olympics at Innsbruck, placing sixth. She ranked seventh in the World Championships. That year, she also won the first of five consecutive U.S. Championships. In 1966, she became world champion, a title she successfully defended for the next two years. She took a gold medal at the 1968 Winter Olympics. Fleming is known for a combination of skills unusual in a figure skater—successfully incorporating ballet and other dance skills into skating while maintaining strong compulsory figures. A professional skater today, Fleming has also created and starred in several television specials.

Eric Heiden
(June 14, 1958–)

Heiden is the only person to win gold medals in all five speed-skating events during a single Olympic competition, a feat he accomplished in 1980. During the Olympics he also set a record for the fastest 1,000-meter race (1 minute 13.6 seconds). He is now viewed as perhaps the greatest speed skater ever. Heiden won every U.S. speed-skating championship in 1979, as well as the 1,500 and 5,000-meter titles. Between 1979 and 1980, Heiden was world champion in the 500-meter. He also set the world's record for the fastest 3,000-meter race (1978, 4 minutes 56.9 seconds). Heiden first competed in the Olympics in 1976 at the age of 18, taking seventh place in the 1,500-meter and fifteenth in the 5,000-meter. In 1977, he became the first U.S. skater to win the Men's All-Around World Speed-Skating Championship. Heiden retired from competition after his stunning victories at Lake Placid.

Sonja Henie
(1912–Oct. 12, 1969)

ABC Sports

More than anyone else, Sonja Henie was responsible for the growth in popularity of figure skating and for its development as both a sport and an art. Henie won the national championship of Norway at the age of twelve and continued with an amateur career in which she amassed an unprecedented ten consecutive world championships (1927–36), six consecutive European championships (1931–36), and three consecutive Olympic gold medals (1928, 1932, and 1936). In addition to being technically an expert skater, Henie was an innovator who changed profoundly women's figure skating. With her short bright costumes, athletic movements, and thoroughly choreographed routines, she created a new look in skating. Henie was also responsible for another skating first: the professional ice show. Turning professional after her last Olympic victory, in 1936, Henie prepared to tour the United States as a "showgirl on ice." The show was a huge success, and paved the way for such other professional groups as the Ice Follies and Ice Capades. Sonja Henie skated her way through 12 movies, helping focus the attention of Americans on the beauty and grace of figure skating.

HALLS OF FAME

Figure Skating Hall of Fame
U.S. Figure Skating Association
20 First St.
Colorado Springs, CO 80906
(303) 635-5200

Members of the Figure Skating Hall of Fame are:

1976
Tenley Albright (US)
Sherwin C. Badger (US)
Theresa Weld Blanchard (US)
Irving Brokaw (US)
Pierre Brunet (France)
Dick Button (US)
Peggy Fleming (US)
Jacques Gerschwiler (Switzerland)
Gillis Grafstrom (Sweden)
Jackson Haines (US)
Carol Heiss (US)
Sonja Henie (Norway)
David Jenkins (US)
Hayes Alan Jenkins (US)
Oscar Johnson (US)
Andree Joly (France)
Gustave Lussi (Switzerland)
Howard Nicholson (US)
Maribel Vinson Owen (US)
Axel Paulsen (Norway)
T. D. Richardson (UK)

Heaton R. Robertson (US)
Ulrich Salchow (Sweden)
Karl Schafer (Austria)
Edi Scholdan (Austria)
Eddie Shipstad (US)
A. Windsor Weld (US)
Reginald J. Wilkie (UK)
Montgomery Wilson (Canada)

1977
Henry M. Beatty (US)
Willi Bockl (Austria)
Lawrence Demmy (UK)
Beatrix Loughlan (US)
Donald Jackson (Canada)
Jean Westwood (UK)

1978
Ludmilla Belousova (USSR)
Nathaniel Niles (US)
Oleg Protopopov (USSR)

National Speedskaters Hall of Fame
(Amateur Skating Union of the U.S. Hall of Fame)
375 Washington St.
Newburgh, NY 12550
(914) 561-3232
Ed Gordon, dir.

Members of the National Speedskaters Hall of Fame are:

1960
Joseph Donoghue
John S. Johnson

1961
Edmund Lamy
Roy McWhirter
Arthur Staff

1962
Everett McGowan
John A. ("Jack") Shea
Morris Wood

1963
Valentine Bialas
Charles Jewtraw
Ben O'Sickey

1964
Bobby McClean
Joseph Moore
Kit Klein Outland

1965
Norval Baptie
Harley Davidson
John Nilssen

1966
Al Flath
Madeline Horn
Harry Kaad
Henry Kemper
Dorothy Franey Langkop

1967
Charles T. Fisher
Kenneth Hall
Irving Jaffee
Harry Noah
Allan Potts

1968
Kenneth Bartholomew
Leo Freisinger
Elsie Muller McLave
Loretta Neitzel
Edward Schroeder

1969
Carmelita Landry Bernard
Ray Blum
Delbert Lamb
Patricia Gibson Marshall
John Werket

1970
Harry Berz
Kenneth Henry
Arthur Mathew Longso
Lamar Ottsen
Gene Sandvig
William D. Disney
J. O'Neil Farrel
James Sheffield

1972
Edgar J. Dame, Jr.
Mary Novak Sand
Herbert F. Schwartz
Philip O. Krumm

1974
Robert Fitzgerald

1975
Jeanne Ashworth Walker

1976
Barbara Marchetti de Schepper
Don McDermott

1977
Terry McDermott

1978
Benjamin Bagdade
Elaine Bogda Gordon

For the Record

Figure Skating

Most Olympic singles gold medals, men
3   Gillis Grafstrom (Sweden)   1920, 1924, 1928

Most Olympic singles gold medals, women
3   Sonja Henie (Norway)   1928, 1932, 1936

Most Olympic gold medals, pair skating
3   Irina Rodnina (USSR)
     with Alexander Ulanov   1972
     with Alexander Zaitsev   1976, 1980

Most world championships, men's singles
10   Ulrich Salchow (Sweden)   1901–05, 1907–11

Most world championships, women's singles
10   Sonja Henie (Norway)   1927–36

Most perfect marks in one performance, pair skating
11   Irina Rodnina and Alexander Zaitsev (USSR)
     European Championship   1974

Most perfect marks in one performance, singles
7   Donald Jackson (Canada), World Championship   1962

First quadruple twist lift in competition
1977   Sergei Shakrai and Marina Tcherkasova (USSR) Helsinki

Most world championships, pair skating
10   Irina Rodnina (USSR)
     with Alexander Ulanov   1969–72
     with Alexander Zaitsev   1973–78

Most U.S. championships, men's singles
7   Dick Button   1946–52

Most U.S. championships, women's singles
5   Peggy Fleming   1964–68
    Janet Lynn   1969–73

Most U.S. championships, pair skating
5   Tai Babilonia and Randy Gardner   1976–80

Speed Skating

Fastest 500-meter, men
37 sec   Yevgeny Kulikov (USSR)
         1975

Fastest 500-meter, women
40.68 sec   Sheila Young (USA)
            1976

Fastest 1,000-meter, men
1 min 13.6 sec   Eric Heiden (USA)
                 1980

Fastest 1,000-meter, women
1 min 23.46 sec   Tatyana Averina
                  (USSR)   1975

Fastest 1,500-meter, men
1 min 55.18 sec   Jan Storholt
                  (Norway)   1977

Fastest 1,500-meter, women
2 min 7.18 sec   Halida Vorobieva
                 (USSR)   1978

Fastest 3,000-meter, men
4 min 4.01 sec   Eric Heiden (USA)
                 1978

Fastest 3,000-meter, women
4 min 31 sec   Galina Stepanskaya
               (USSR)   1976

Fastest 5,000-meter
6 min 56.9 sec   Kay Arne
                 Stenshjemmet
                 (Norway)   1977

Most Olympic gold medals, women
6   Lydia Skoblikova (USSR)
    1060, 1964

Most Olympic gold medals, men
5   Eric Heiden (USA)   1980
5   Clas Thunbert (Finland)
    1960, 1964

Fastest 10,000-meter, men
14 min 25.71 sec   Dmitri Ogloblin
                   (USSR)   1980

Did you know ?

1. Who won the men's and women's singles titles at the first championships for American figure skaters?

2. Name the only two brothers who both held the World, U.S., North American, and Olympic figure-skating titles.

3. Which of the following did not win both World and U.S. figure-skating titles: Peggy Fleming, Janet Lynn, Carol Heiss?

4. Where was the first artificial skating rink built? When?

5. The first known illustration of skating in a book is a picture of the heroine in *The Life of Liedwi,* a book published in 1498. Who was Liedwi?

6. Where is the world's largest artificial skating rink?

7. What was the title of the first skating film, and when was it made?

8. How many different types of figure eights does the ISU recognize as official school figures?

Answers: 1. Norman Scott and Theresa Weld, at New Haven, Ct., in 1914; **2.** Hayes Alan and Dick Jenkins; **3.** Janet Lynn. Although she was U.S. champion from 1969 to 1973, she never won a world championship; **4.** The Glaciarium, the world's first artificial ice rink, was built in London in 1876; **5.** According to legend, Liedwi was a 16-year old Dutch girl who retired to a convent to live a life of piety after suffering a broken rib while skating. She became the patron saint of ice skaters; **6.** In Japan. The Fujikyu Highland Promenade Rink, built in 1967, has 165,750 square feet of ice; **7.** *The Frozen Warning,* the first film to prominently feature ice skating, made its debut in 1917; **8.** 48.

Key Words

axel   a forward jump from the outside edge of one skate to the back outside edge of the other, making a 540-degree turn.

bracket turn   in figure skating, a school figure in which the skater goes out of the circle, switches to the other edge of the skate called for, and finishes tracing the circle.

camel spin   a turn in which the skater raises one leg up to the rear, parallel to the ice, and rotates the body swiftly; also known as a "parallel spin."

death spiral   in pair skating, a move in which one skater swings the partner in a circle while holding the partner's hand. The partner being swung is parallel to the ice, leaning back with one leg extended and the head as close to the ice as possible without touching it.

double   the immediate repetition of a movement in figure and dance skating.

double jump   a jump in which the skater turns 720 degrees.

Dutch roll   a step in which the skater uses the inside edge of one skate to push backward diagonally while at the same time moving forward on the outside edge of the other skate. It is the main step used in speed skating.

eights a set of figures in which circles are traced, with the skater alternating feet and forming figures in the shape of an 8.

flat a double line on the ice made when both edges of the concave blade of a skate are on the ice at the same time.

freestyle a skating program in which the skater choreographs (to music) his or her moves; the program must include certain compulsory moves.

Grafstrom spin in figure skating, a five-turn spin in which the skater leans the upper body forward, bends the knee on his tracing leg, and keeps the other leg raised.

ice dancing pair skating done to formal dance music; it is a competitive event.

jump a move in which the skater has both feet off the ice at the same time.

loop in figure skating, a tracing made when a loop is formed inside a circle.

loop jump a loop jump is an imaginary loop performed in the air; the skater proceeds on the back outside edge of the skate, makes one revolution in the air, and touches down on the back outside edge of the skate.

Lutz in figure skating, a toe loop performed counterclockwise.

master toe the largest serration, located lowest, on the front of the blade of a figure skate.

pack-style a type of speed skating in which skaters group together at the starting line, then jockey for the best position; the skater who crosses the finish line first wins the race.

Salchow a jump from the back inside edge of one foot to the back outside edge of the other foot.

spin a move in which the skater revolves at least six times (five times in the Grafstrom spin), using one foot as a pivot, while remaining in the same spot on the ice.

spiral in figure skating, a position that is essentially the same as an arabesque in ballet.

spreadeagle in figure skating, a movement in which the feet are both on the ice, pointed 180 degrees from each other, while the skater glides either way on the ice.

three turn in figure skating, a school figure made by the skater changing direction while continuing to trace the figure with the same foot.

toes the "teeth" on the front of the blades of figure skates; used to catch the ice and increase friction, thus providing extra impetus.

toe assist in figure skating, use of the toes of one skate to add power to a jump.

toe loop a jump in which the skater, with the help of a toe assist, jumps from the back outside edge of one foot, executes a full turn, and lands on the back inside edge of the same foot; also known as a "cherry flip."

walley a counterclockwise jump from the back inside edge of a skate, with the skater landing on the same edge of the same skate.

windmill spin a camel spin in which the skater's arms are moved first up and then down.

13   RODEO

For almost 50 weeks each year, in more than 600 rodeos throughout the United States, men and women ride untamed, bucking, spinning broncs and bulls or wrestle 700-pound steers to the ground, using the skills of working ranch hands to win money and trophies and gain glory.

Unlike the cowboys who made their living by breaking horses and rounding up cattle on an open range, today's cowboys are real-estate investors, stock contractors, teachers, or even presidential advisors. They are not drawn to the ring for the money but for the raw thrill of pitting themselves against other men, ornery beasts, and the clock.

Most events in the rodeo ring today have evolved from the day-to-day activities of cowboys who once rode the range for months at a time. Bronc busting—breaking in a wild, bucking horse until it is used to a rider—and steer roping were part of a cowboy's daily routine. He took pride in the strength and skill required. The forerunner of today's rodeo was a contest between cowboys from different ranches, who gathered twice a year for roundups. After all the cattle had been branded and separated into herds, and the day's work was done, the cowboys would put their earnings in a hat, and the best bronc busters and steer ropers from each ranch would compete for the money.

Beginning in the late nineteenth century, these contests gradually moved from the plains to the towns, where people would gather, often with picnic baskets, to cheer their favorites and bet on them. The first true rodeo, one that was advertised in advance and for which prizes were given, was held July 4, 1883, in Pecos, Texas. The prize money totaled $40, not bad for a cowboy who worked for only $12 to $25 a month but a far cry from today's purses of more than $800,000.

With the development of the first Wild West shows in the 1890s, the West became a marketable item. Those who had never set foot on a ranch could enjoy the West vicariously by watching sharpshooters, fancy riders, and—later—bronc riders and steer ropers. The Wild West shows ended in the 1920s. Before long, however, they had been replaced by professional rodeos. Those who had traveled with the shows advertised their talents in newspapers and were organized by such promoters as C. B. Irwin and Tex Austin. Irwin and Austin would set up a rodeo, invite riders to participate (for an entry fee), and award prize money to the winners of each event. By this time, bull riding, calf roping, and team roping were standard events.

The modern rodeo is a professionally run business. Cowboys still pay their own way to competitions, but they often get there in their own trailers, or even in private planes. Although entry fees still go into the general purse, this money, known as "added money," beefs up the already substantial purses. Cowboys even have their own organization, the Professional Rodeo Cowboys Association (PRCA), formed in reaction to unfair promoter practices in the first decade of this century. The PRCA sponsors most of the 600-plus rodeos across the country, including the National Finals Rodeo, where the best riders compete for top national honors.

Rodeo remains essentially unchanged, though. A rider inside the arena leaves the modern world behind and stands proudly. This rider is the last vestige of the American frontier. For a short while, he is back on the open range, where the only things that matter are the animal and the rider's skill and strength.

PRCA Photo

Great Moments

1883 On the Fourth of July, the first authentic rodeo is held, in Pecos, Texas. Similar informal events held throughout the Southwest have until this time been called tournaments—as much social get-togethers as they are contests.

1897 Cheyenne Frontier Days, now one of the largest rodeos, is established, in Cheyenne, Wyoming.

1910 Pendleton Round-Up, another major rodeo, is established, in Pendleton, Oregon.

1912 Calgary Stampede, Canada's most famous rodeo, which now attracts both U.S. and Canadian cowboys, makes its debut in the province of Alberta.

1920s Bull riding, now the most popular (and most dangerous) event, is introduced.

1924 The promoter Tex Austin organizes the first rodeo outside the United States; it is held in London.

1929 The Rodeo Association of America is formed, comprising rodeo-organizing committees from all over the country. The association keeps track of records set and money earned, as well as naming champions.

1937 The Cowboy Turtles Association is formed to prevent rodeo promoters from taking advantage of cowboys participating in their shows.

1945 For the first time, the contestants' organization (the Cowboy Turtles Association) and not rodeo organizers, names the year's champions.

1948 The Girls' Rodeo Association is formed, later becoming the Women's Professional Rodeo Association.

1950 Bareback riding becomes one of rodeo's three standard riding events.

1959 The first National Finals Rodeo is held, in Oklahoma City.

1974 The Rodeo Cowboys Association changes its name to the Professional Rodeo Cowboys Association.

The Setup

Professional rodeo is organized in a circuit system, with 12 regional circuits. At the heart of the system is the Professional Rodeo Cowboys Association (PRCA), which sets the rules for professional rodeo competition and sanctions all but a few of the professional rodeos held in the United States each year.

To compete in a PRCA-sanctioned rodeo, cowboys must be members, permit-holders, or apprentices. The PRCA has more than 5,000 members and another 5,000 or 6,000 permit-holders.

The circuit system, organized about 1977, works in one of two ways. It allows cowboys who are restricted to their home areas, or who compete only part-time, to participate regularly without having to travel far. Circuit champions are named each year by the PRCA. Designated circuit rodeos may also be used to accumulate enough money to qualify for the National Finals Rodeo held in Oklahoma City each December. The 12 circuits are: Badlands, Columbia River, Great Lakes, Lone Star, Montana Summer, Mountain States, Northeastern Seaboard, Prairie, Sierra, Southeastern, Turquoise, and Wilderness.

The PRCA is the central organization for coordinating rodeo activities, presenting awards, circulating news, and maintaining records on rodeo champions. The association does not, however, pay salaries, entry fees, or medical and transportation costs for cowboys; these must be paid by the cowboys themselves.

All earnings by members of the PRCA are computed by the organization, which provides up-to-date standings for members at any time. The PRCA also maintains and enforces a code of behavior for its members. A cowboy may be fined for improper behavior at a PRCA rodeo.

The PRCA has affiliates that promote rodeo at the junior high school, high school, and college levels (see below).

INTERNATIONAL RODEO
  ASSOCIATION
American Fidelity Bldg., Suite 412
P.O. Box 615
Pauls Valley, OK 73075
(405) 238-6488
Tom Abshire, pres.

INTERNATIONAL RODEO WRITERS
  ASSOCIATION
3045 W. 28th Ave.
Denver, CO 80211
(303) 433-7074
Cliff Edwards, treas.

ABC Sports

NATIONAL COWBOY HALL OF FAME
1700 N.E. 63rd
Oklahoma City, OK 73111
(405) 478-2251
Willard Porter, dir. of rodeo div.

NATIONAL FINALS RODEO
  COMMITTEE
(affiliated with the PRCA)
101 Prorodeo Dr.
Colorado Springs, CO 80901
Hugh Chambliss, sec.

NATIONAL HIGH SCHOOL RODEO
  ASSOCIATION
(affiliated with the PRCA)
P.O. Box 35
Edgar, MT 59026
Gene E. Litton, sec.-treas.

NATIONAL INTERCOLLEGIATE
  RODEO ASSOCIATION
Walla Walla Community College
500 Tausick
Walla Walla, WA 99362
(509) 527-4342
Timothy L. Cornfield, exec. sec.

NATIONAL LITTLE BRITCHES
  RODEO ASSOCIATION
1050 Yuma, No. 306
Denver, CO 80204
(303) 893-0602
Tom Mikesell, pres.

PROFESSIONAL RODEO COWBOYS
  ASSOCIATION
101 Prorodeo Dr.
Colorado Springs, CO 80901
(303) 593-8840
Bob Eidson, gen. mgr.

PROFESSIONAL WOMEN'S RODEO
  ASSOCIATION
8909 N.E. 25th St.
Spencer, OK 73084
(405) 769-5322
Lydia Moore, sec.-treas.

RODEO HALL OF FAME
Prorodeo Hall of Champions &
  Museum of the American Cowboy
101 Prorodeo Dr.
Colorado Springs, CO 80901
(303) 593-8840
Ken Stemler, exec. dir.

RODEO NEWS BUREAU
101 Prorodeo Dr.
Colorado Springs, CO 80901
(303) 593-8840
David Allen, exec. dir.

The Basics

Each rodeo sanctioned by the PRCA consists of competition in five standard events: bareback riding, saddle bronc riding, bull riding, calf roping, and steer wrestling. Two other events, team roping and barrel racing, are featured at many rodeos. An eighth event, single-steer roping, is becoming popular but is still not considered a standard event at most rodeos.

Rodeo contestants pay entry fees of $30 to $200 for each event they enter. This money, called "added money," becomes part of the purse distributed among the winners of the events.

Before competing in a PRCA-approved rodeo, the contestants must be members or permit-holders in the PRCA or, in case of the all-women barrel-racing event, members of the Women's Professional Rodeo Association.

Contestants in each event must observe the following rules:

SADDLE BRONC RIDING

Object   To ride a saddled, bucking horse for a minimum of eight seconds and to earn a score of 100.

Equipment   A saddle that complies with measurements set forth by the Professional Rodeo Cowboys Association; braided manila rein, about six feet long and 1.5 inches thick; short-shanked spurs with dull rowels; chaps of light leather, snugged tight around the thighs of the rider.

Rule 1   Disqualification   A rider may be disqualified for:
  a. failing to keep the spurs over the horse's shoulder points until the first jump out of the chute is completed;
  b. touching the horse or equipment with the free hand during the ride;
  c. losing a stirrup;
  d. being bucked off before the official eight seconds is up.

BAREBACK RIDING

Object   To stay on an untamed, unsaddled horse for a minimum of eight seconds and to earn 100 points.

Equipment   Thick leather pad ("rigging") which is cinched onto the horse's back. (A small grip on the rigging is the only handhold for the rider.) The rider wears a glove and spurs and, often, chaps.

Rule 1   Disqualification   A rider may be disqualified for:
   a. failing to keep the spurs over the horse's shoulder points until the first jump out of the chute is completed;
   b. touching the horse or equipment with the free hand during the ride;
   c. being bucked off before the official eight seconds is up.

BULL RIDING

Object   To ride a bull for a minimum of eight seconds and to earn a score of 100 points.

Equipment   a flat, braided length of manila rope looped around the bull's neck. (A weighted bell attached to the rope causes it to fall from the bull's neck at the end of the ride.) The rider wears a riding glove and spurs.

Rule 1   Disqualification   A rider may be disqualified for:
   a. hitting the ground before an official eight-second ride is completed;
   b. failing to have a bell attached to the rope;
   c. touching the bull with the free hand at any time during the ride.

CALF ROPING

Object   To rope and tie a 200- to 350-pound calf in as short a time as possible.

Equipment   a lariat, one end tied to the saddle horn, the other forming the catch loop. A smaller, shorter rope, called "pigging string," for tying the calf's feet.

Rule 1   The start   The roper must remain behind a barrier until the calf crosses a scoreline designated by the judges. The head start given the calf depends on the size of the ring. Breaking through the barrier before the calf crosses the scoreline adds 10 seconds to the rider's time.

Rule 2   Weigh-in   Crossbred Brahma calves must weigh at least 200 and not more than 300 pounds. Native calves, such as Hereford or Angus, must not weigh more than 350 pounds.

Rule 3   After the catch, the roper must throw the calf by hand, cross any three of its legs for the tie, then signal completion by raising both hands.

Rule 4   Throws   A rider is allowed two throws. If he misses both, he gets "no time."

STEER WRESTLING

Object   To leap from a running horse to a running steer's horns, bring the steer to a halt, and wrestle it to the ground in as short a time as possible.

Rule 1 ***The start*** The contestant must wait, with a hazer (see Key Words) posted on the opposite side of the release gate, until the steer crosses the designated scoreline. Breaking the barrier earlier adds ten seconds to the rider's total time.

Rule 2 ***The fall*** The steer must be on its feet before being wrestled down. Falls by the steer itself do not count.

Rule 3 ***Official time*** The steer must be flat on its side, with all four legs extended, before the official time is given.

STEER ROPING

Object To rope a steer's horns, spin the steer to the ground, and tie three of its legs in as short a time as possible.

Equipment A lariat of twisted nylon and a tie string longer and heavier than the pigging string used in calf roping.

Rule 1 ***The throw and catch*** Only one throw of the lariat is permitted. The catch must be "clean" around the steer's horns.

Rule 2 ***The start*** The steer is given a designated head start while the roper waits behind the barrier. Breaking the barrier brings a 10-second penalty.

Rule 3 ***The tie*** The steer must remain tied until the catch is approved by a field judge.

TEAM ROPING

Object For two men on horseback to rope a steer in as short a time as possible. One rider (the "header") ropes the horns of the steer; the other ("the heeler") ropes the hind legs of the steer.

Equipment A 28-foot rope for each rider. Saddles with higher horns are often used by contestants in this event.

Rule 1 ***The start*** The steer gets a designated head start while both riders wait behind the barrier. Breaking the barrier means a 10-second penalty.

Rule 2 ***The throw*** A five-second penalty is assessed if the heeler ropes only one foot, or if the header ropes a front foot along with the head. A total of three throws is permitted.

Rule 3 ***Official time*** Ropers must face their horses toward their steers, with ropes taut, before official time can be called.

BARREL RACING

Object To run a course marked by three numbered barrels in the least time.

Competitors Only women are eligible to enter the event.

Officials The barrel race must have two judges. One is stationed at the starting (same as finish) line. The other judge stands in the arena to check performance on the course.

Rule 1   The circuit   The rider must make a complete circuit of each barrel before returning to the finish line. She is allowed a running start.

Rule 2   Touching a barrel   A five-second penalty is assessed if a barrel is knocked over; touching a barrel is permitted.

Rule 3   The pattern   A rider is disqualified if she fails to follow the pattern for a circuit that is set by the officials.

Rule 4   Rerun   A contestant is allowed to make a rerun after her initial run. The decision to run the course again must be made immediately upon completion of the first run.

How to watch

with Dave Baldridge

People and animals are of equal importance in rodeo. A rider, no matter how good, can look good and score highly only if the rider's horse or bull is in top shape and is either bucking to the best of its ability or, in roping contests, responding quickly to the demands of the rider. Dave Baldridge, director of the PRCA's news bureau, outlines points to watch during a rodeo:

The chute: The chute can be more dangerous than the arena for the rider. "The rider will not waste much time once he or she is on the animal's back. The rider has people helping him get on the horse or the bull; once on, though, the rider wants to get out of the chute as quickly as possible. The big danger is getting a leg pinned between the animal and the chute walls."

Saddle bronc riding: "Judges will be looking for whether the rider's boots are over the horse's withers, or shoulders, as the rider comes out of the chute. The rider then must maintain balance with the upper part of the body, moving the feet in an arc, from the horse's neck to the back of the saddle. The harder the horse bucks, and the higher the rider's boots are over the horse's shoulders, the better the ride."

Bareback riding: "Again, judges look for turned-out toes and lots of spurring action, as well as lots of hard bucking from the horse. In all riding events, the rider must appear in control. Also, in all riding events, the rider's free hand must not touch any part of the horse or the rider's body. If it does, the rider is disqualified."

Bull riding: "Many consider this the most dangerous rodeo event. Bulls don't buck the same way horses do. Some are called spinners because they spin as they buck. They sort of twist around when they buck; so, when a rider falls, he wants to fall on the outside of the circle the bull makes when it's spinning. That way, the rider has a better chance of getting away. Judges are looking for control in the bull-riding event. Toes must be well turned out; a rider who is spurring gets extra points. Most bull riders worth their salt spur the bull."

ABC Sports

Calf roping: A rider who ropes a calf in less than nine seconds has done extremely well. In calf roping, as in team and steer roping, the horse the rider uses is very important. The rider must be able to count on the horse to stop at exactly the right time, once the calf has been roped. "Most riders try to get horses known to be good. They usually get them from stock contractors who travel from rodeo to rodeo. Only a few cowboys ride their own horses because of the constant traveling from rodeo to rodeo."

Steer wrestling: In this event, the rider doing the actual wrestling must have a partner who can be trusted. This partner, called a "hazer," is the one who keeps the steer running in a straight line. Steer wrestling is the only event in which another person shares the arena with the cowboy but does not compete. Once the steer is running straight, it's up to the rider to bring the 400- to 700-pound steer to the ground, using strength and leverage.

Team roping: In this event, any time under ten seconds is considered a good run. Judges make sure the steer is legally roped. The rope must be around both horns, around half the head, or around the neck. Both hind legs must be roped. Good understanding and communication between the riders on the team is crucial.

Planning and strategy play only a small role in rodeo events, according to Baldridge. "There is usually only one right way to ride a bull or bronc, or to rope a calf." A successful rider, though, can adapt to the animal being ridden, no matter what the circumstances. "You can tell when the rider's done that," Baldridge says. "The rider will be moving back and forth on the animal's back in a rhythmic, rocking motion, moving with the horse."

Main Events

THE NATIONAL FINALS RODEO

The National Finals Rodeo (NFR) is the World Series of rodeo—when the top 15 cowboys in each of six standard events get together for 10 days to prove who is number one. Held in early December, in Oklahoma City, this rodeo marks the official end of the rodeo season; the new season begins just a few weeks later.

The top 15 money earners for the year in their specialties are the 15 competitors in the National Finals. Once they make it to the finals, they have the chance to win larger purses than at any other time during the year.

When the NFR is over, every cowboy's earnings for the year, including NFR winnings, are totaled, and the PRCA names the world champion in each event. A big win at the NFR helps, but does not guarantee, the winning of a world championship, which goes to the cowboy who has earned the most money for the entire year, including the finals, in his specialty.

The All-Around Cowboy world championship goes to the cowboy who has won the most money in two or more different events for the year.

SADDLE BRONC RIDING

Year	Winner
1980	Bobby Berger, Lexington, OK
1979	Tom Miller, Faith, SD
1978	Joe Marvel, Battle Mountain, NV
1977	J. C. Bonine, Hysham, MT
1976	Monty Henson, Mesquite, TX
1975	Tom Miller, Faith, SD
1974	Joe Marvel, Battle Mountain, NV
1973	Dennis Reiners, Scottsdale, AZ
1972	Marvin Joyce, East Helena, MT
1971	Ken McLean, Okanagan Falls, Brit. Col., Can.
1970	Ivan Daines, Innisfail, Alberta, Can.

BAREBACK BRONC RIDING

Year	Winner
1980	Bruce Ford, Kersey, CO
1979	Bruce Ford, Kersey, CO
1978	Mickey Young, Ferron, UT
1977	Jack Ward, Springdale, AR
1976	Jack Ward, Springdale, AR
1975	Jack Ward, Odessa, TX
1974	Jack Ward, Odessa, TX
1973	Sandy Kirby, Greenville, TX
1972	Ace Berry, Modesto, CA
1971	Ace Berry, Modesto, CA
1970	John Edwards, Red Lodge, MT

PRCA Photo

BULL RIDING

Year	Winner
1980	Ken Wilcox, Greenbriar, AR
1979	John Davis, Homedale, ID
1978	Lyle Sankey, Augusta, KS
1977	(no average)
1976	Don Gay, Mesquite, TX
1975	Denny Flynn, Springdale, AR
1974	Sandy Kirby, Greenville, TX
1973	Marvin Paul Shoulders, Henryetta, OK
1972	Phil Lyne, George West, TX
1971	Bob Berger, Norman, OK
1970	Gary Leffew, Santa Maria, CA

CALF ROPING

Year	Winner
1980	Chris Lybbert, Coyote, CA
1979	Roy Cooper, Durant, OK
1978	Gary Ledford, Comanche, OK
1977	Jim Gladstone, Cardston, Alberta, Can.
1976	Roy Cooper, Durant, OK
1975	Bobby Goodspeed, High Ridge, MO
1974	Ronnye Sewalt, Chico, TX
1973	Barry Burk, Duncan, OK
1972	Phil Lyne, George West, TX
1971	Olin Young, Peralta, NM
1970	Richard Stowers, Duncan, OK

STEER WRESTLING

Year	Winner
1980	Paul Hughes, Kim, CO
1979	Jack Hannum, Ogden, UT
1978	Tom Ferguson, Miami, OK
1977	Tom Ferguson, Miami, OK
1976	Tommy Puryear, Leander, TX
1975	Bob Christopherson, Glendive, MO
1974	Bob Marshall, San Martin, CA
1973	Bob Marshall, San Martin, CA
1972	Jerry Peveto, Hugo, OK
1971	Bob Christopherson, Sioux City, IA
1970	John W. Jones, Morro Bay, CA

TEAM ROPING

Year	Winner
1980	Tee Woolman, Llano, TX
	Leo Camarillo, Lockwood, CA
1979	Allen Bach, Queen Creek, AZ
	Jesse James, Porterville, CA
1978	Brad Smith, Prescott, AZ
	George Richards, Humboldt, AZ
1977	David Motes, Fresno, CA
	Dennis Motes, Fresno, CA
1976	Doyle Gellerman, Oakdale, CA
	Frank Ferreira, Sr., Fresno, CA
1975	Reg and Jerold Camarillo, Oakdale, CA
1974	Jim Wheatley, Hughson, CA
	John Rodrigues, Castroville, CA
1973	Ken Luman, Visalia, CA
	Jim Rodrigues, Jr., Paso Robles, CA
1972	John Miller, Pawhuska, OK
	Ace Berry, Modesto, CA
1971	Leo Camarillo, Donald, OR
	Reg Camarillo, Mesa, AZ
1970	Leo Camarillo, Donald, OR
	Reg Camarillo, Mesa, AZ

SINGLE STEER ROPING

Year	Winner
1980	Guy Allen, Santa Anna, TX
1979	Gary Good, Elida, NM
1978	Walt Arnold, Silverton, TX
1977	Olin Young, Peralta, NM
1976	Charles Good, Elida, NM
1975	Dewey Lee David, Riverton, WY
1974	Olin Young, Peralta, NM
1973	Eddie Becker, Ashby, NB
1972	Joe Snively, Sedan, KS
1971	James Allen, Santa Anna, TX
1970	Dewey Lee David, Riverton, WY

ALL-AROUND COWBOY WORLD CHAMPIONS

Year	Winner	Year	Winner
1980	Paul Tierney	1974	Tom Ferguson
1979	Tom Ferguson	1973	Larry Mahan
1978	Tom Ferguson	1972	Phil Lyne
1977	Tom Ferguson	1971	Phil Lyne
1976	Tom Ferguson	1970	Larry Mahan
1975	Tom Ferguson		

All-Time Greats

Bob Askin
(May 9, 1900–Oct. 8, 1973)

National Cowboy Hall of Fame

Pete Knight called him the best rodeo cowboy of all time. Although Bob Askin rode before world championships were recorded, he is believed to have been the top money-winner of his time. Askin rode the toughest broncs on the circuit, horses with such names as "No Name" and "Midnight." As a youth he traveled great distances to take on a "reputation" horse (a horse notorious for throwing riders). This competitiveness never left him, even after he returned from a stint in the army in the early 1920s. Askin followed rodeos wherever they were held, winning the prestigious Madison Square Garden championship three times.

Everett Bowman
(1899–1971)

Everett Bowman, sometimes called the "George Washington of organized rodeo cowboys," founded and was the first president of the Cowboy Turtles Association, which ensured fair distribution of entry fees and adequate purses for rodeo winners. Bowman specialized and excelled in timed events. He won 10 world championships during his career, a record that stood until Jim Shoulders set a new mark of 16. Bowman was killed in an airplane crash in 1971.

Tom Ferguson
(Dec. 20, 1950–)

Quiet and consistent—these two qualities have earned Tom Ferguson six consecutive All-Around Cowboy World Champion titles and a record $610,000 in his career. He also holds world championships in his two specialties, calf roping and steer wrestling, a total of nine world championships altogether. A native Oklahoman, Ferguson has been called a "professional rodeo phenomenon" by those who have watched him compete under all conditions, always with the same, calculated consistency. Not large as steer wrestlers and calf ropers go, the 5-foot-11-inch, 175-pound Ferguson relies on skill and a cool approach to prevail over the competition. That's what he did in the 1979 National Finals Rodeo when he vied with Paul Tierney and won—becoming the first to win six consecutive All-Around Cowboy titles. Tierney had entered the NFR only $71 behind Ferguson. The race was close for three rounds, then Ferguson pulled ahead to stay. Ferguson has said his next goal is to win the All-Around Cowboy title a seventh time and win the world championship in steer wrestling—both in the same year.

Don Gay
(Sept. 18, 1953–)

Don Gay's ability to ride bulls longer and better than his competitors has earned him five world-champion bull-riding buckles and has qualified him for the National Finals eight times. A native of Mesquite, Texas, Gay has set money records throughout his career; for instance, he was the first to win $55,000 in a single season of bull riding. In 1977, he set a record-high score in bull riding, with 97 points for his ride on "Oscar," a bull whose tough reputation earned it a role in the Academy Award-winning documentary *The Great American Cowboy*. That record was not broken until 1979, when Denny Flynn scored 98 points aboard "Red One." Gay comes from a rodeo family. His father Neal, a well-known stock contractor, runs a weekly rodeo in Mesquite. It was Neal Gay and the legendary Jim Shoulders who tutored the young bull rider. Now their pupil is only two world championships away from Shoulders' all-time record of seven world bull-riding championships.

Pete Knight
(May 5, 1903–1937)

Pete Knight was the world champion saddle bronc rider for four of the five years he competed in the event. He also held the top Canadian titles. At the fortieth anniversary of the Calgary Stampede, Knight was ranked number one among the four greatest cowboys to compete there. Knight was born in Philadelphia. At the age of two, he moved with his family to Crossfield, Alberta, Canada. There, he learned to break horses for use on his father's ranch; it wasn't long before he began entering rodeos to test his skills against those of others. At the age of 21, Knight lost the Prince of Wales trophy by a mere three percentage points, but went on to win it three times in subsequent years. Knight was thrown and killed by a horse he had ridden successfully five times earlier.

Larry Mahan
(Nov. 21, 1943–)

It has been said that Larry Mahan is to rodeo what the Beatles were to rock music. When the Oregon native hit the professional rodeo circuit in 1963, he didn't look like any other cowboy—his black curly hair was a bit too long, his clothes were a bit too flashy, and his furry beaver hat was not exactly in keeping with the Stetsons worn by others. In his 16 years as a professional cowboy, Mahan has emerged not only as a star in the rodeo world but also the representative of his world to outsiders. He is credited with helping create a resurgence of interest in rodeo. His fierce, competitive style in the arena has earned him six PRCA All-Around Cowboy titles, five of them consecutive, and two world bull riding championships. He has qualified 26 times for the National Finals Rodeo, in bull riding, saddle bronc riding, and bareback riding. Mahan no longer works the two or three rodeos a day he did at the peak of his career. Now, much of his time is devoted to television announcing for major networks covering the big rodeos, touring with his band, the Ramblin' Rodeo Revue, costarring in films, and being interviewed. Known as "Bull" inside the arena, Mahan, outside the ring, has earned the nickname "Mr. Rodeo Cowboy," ambassador of rodeo to the world, for his many other efforts.

Casey Tibbs
(Mar. 5, 1929–)

Casey Tibbs was the Larry Mahan of the 1940s. He was as well known for his colorful personality as he was for his superior saddle bronc riding, which earned him six world champion saddle bronc titles and two All-Around Cowboy titles before he was 29. His first efforts to break into film in 1964 were thwarted by a producer who told him he was not the "type" for the role of a bronc rider in a television commercial. In response, Tibbs emerged from retirement to win nine of ten more rodeos and become a movie producer. In 1974, he became the first living cowboy to be named to the National Cowboy Hall of Fame.

HALL OF FAME

Rodeo Hall of Fame
1700 N.E. 63rd St.
Oklahoma City, OK 73111
(405) 478-2250

The members of the Rodeo Hall of Fame are:

Doff Aber	Eddie Curtis	Burel Mulkey	John Schneider
Bob Askin	Verne Elliott	Johnnie Mullens	Dick Shelton
Tex Austin	Tom Ferguson	Lucille Mullhall	Jim Shoulders
Hugh Bennett	Kid Fletcher	Don Nesbitt	Smokey Snyder
Bertha Blancett	Joe Gardner	Tom Nesmith	Thad Sowder
Ed Bowman	Mike Hastings	Dean Oliver	Jesse Stahl
Everett Bowman	C. B. Irwin	Vincente Oropeza	Fannie S. Steele
John Bowman	Andy Jauregui	Homer Pettigrew	Hugh Strickland
Harry Brennan	Ben Johnson	Bill Pickett	Leonard Stroud
Louis Brooks	Tommy Kirnan	Booger Red Privett	Jackson Sundown
Clyde Burk	Pete Knight	Gene Rambo	Earl Thode
Chester Byers	Bill Linderman	Florence Randolph	Casey Tibbs
Lee Caldwell	Tad Lucas	Benny Reynolds	Harry Tompkins
Leo Camarillo	Phil Lyne	Coke Roberds	Fritz Truan
Yakima Canutt	Eddie McCarty	Gerald Roberts	Leonard Ward
Paul Carney	Jake McClure	Lee Robinson	Guy Weadick
Clay Carr	Clay McGonagill	Ike Rude	Todd Whatley
J. Ellison Carroll	Larry Mahan	Buck Rutherford	Oral Zumwalt
Bob Crosby	King Merritt	Paddy Ryan	

For the Record

PRCA

Highest score in bareback riding
93   Joe Alexander   1974

Highest score in bull riding
98   Denny Flynn   1979

Highest score in saddle bronc riding
95   Doug Vold   1979

Fastest calf roping
5.7 sec   Bill Reeder   1978

**Fastest steer-wrestling,
without barrier**
2.2 sec   Oral Zumwalt   1930s

**Fastest steer-wrestling,
with barrier**
3.5 sec   Tom Ferguson   1975
         Tommy Puryear   1976

Fastest team-roping
4.9 sec   Reg and Jerold
          Camarillo   1976
          Doyle Gellerman and
          Dennis Motes   1980

Most saddle-bronc-riding titles
6   Casey Tibbs

Most bareback-riding titles
5   Joe Alexander

Most bull-riding titles
7   Jim Shoulders

Most calf roping titles
8   Dean Oliver

Most steer-wrestling titles
6   Homer Pettigrew

Most team-roping titles, individual
4   Jim Rodrigues, Jr.

Most steer-roping titles
6   Everett Shaw

Most All-Around Cowboy championships
6   Larry Mahan
    Tom Ferguson
    Jim Shoulders

Most world championships, any event
16   Jim Shoulders

Youngest world champion
Jim Rodriguez, Jr.   1959,
    team roping, age 18

Oldest world champion
Ike Rude   1953, steer roping, age 59

ABC Sports

Did you know ?

1. What was the most money ever paid for a bucking bronc?

2. Who was named the Girl's Rodeo Association Rookie of the Year in 1978?

3. What is the name of the bull that starred in the documentary, *The Great American Cowboy*?

4. Who is the only presidential cabinet member to be named the PRCA's Man of the Year?

5. What well-known movie actor competes in the rodeo ring?

6. Who was the first rodeo promoter to take rodeo overseas?

7. Who was the first All-Around Cowboy champion named by the RCA?

8. Where was the first National Finals Rodeo held?

Answers: 1. $12,500. Wayne Vold, of Calgary, paid the amount for "Peace River," a 13-year-old gelding; **2.** Carol Goostree; **3.** "Oscar," now retired at the PRCA Hall of Champions after 300 rides, only 11 of which lasted the full 8 seconds; **4.** Malcolm Baldridge, secretary of commerce under the Reagan administration; **5.** James Caan; **6.** Tex Austin; **7.** Earl Thode, in 1929; **8.** Dallas, Texas.

Key Words

added money   the purse put up by the rodeo committee, to which entry fees paid by contestants are added to make up the total prize money.

arena director   the person responsible for seeing that the rodeo goes smoothly and according to the rules. The director supervises all jobs and details within the rodeo arena itself, such as loading the chutes and keeping the arena clear.

association saddle   any saddle built to PRCA specifications and design; used in saddle bronc riding.

average   in rodeos with more than one round, the term used for the competition; expressed in the *average* times or scores for all the rounds.

bareback riding   an event in which a rider must stay on a bucking horse without saddle or reins for a minimum of eight seconds.

barrier   a rope stretched across the front end of the box from which the roper or steer wrestler emerges when the barrier flag drops.

breaking the barrier   riding through the barrier before it is released; a penalty of 10 seconds is added to the rider's time.

bull riding   an event in which a rider must stay on a bull for a minimum of eight seconds

bull rope   a flat-braided length of manila rope about one and a half inches thick, looped around the neck of bull for the rider to hold in a bull-riding contest. A weighted bell causes the rope to drop off the bull's neck at the end of the ride.

calf roping   a timed contest in which a calf gets a head start on a mounted rider, who must then cast a rope around the calf's neck, dismount, and secure three of the calf's feet with pigging string.

contract acts   any act that is retained on a contract by the rodeo committee to perform in the arena. Contract acts—for example, announcers, clowns, timers, pickup men, and trick riders—do not compete for prize money.

day money   the prize money paid to the winners of a performance or a round in bronc riding. In certain situations, day money is paid to all bull riders with qualified rides for the day.

entry fees   the money paid to the rodeo secretary by a contestant before he or she competes in an event at a rodeo. The size of the fee varies with the size of the rodeo, ranging from $30 to $200. Contestants must pay a separate entry fee for each event they enter.

fishing   an expression commonly used when the roper has thrown at an animal but has missed and then, by accident or by flipping the rope, turns it into a legal catch.

flank or flank strap   a sheepskin-lined strap with a self-holding buckle that is passed around the flank of a bronc or bull; in an effort to get rid of the flank strap, the animal bucks higher and harder.

go-round   see *round.*

ground money   when the purse and entry fees for an event are split equally among all entrants in that event, because all the contestants entered in that event failed to qualify.

hazer   a person who rides along beside a steer, on the opposite side of the steer wrestler. The hazer's job is to keep the steer running in a straight line and close to the contestant's horse.

honda   the eye at one end of a rope. The other end of the rope is passed through it to form a loop.

hooey   a wrap and a closing half hitch (around any three feet of the calf); used in calf roping.

jackpot   an event for which no purse is put up by the rodeo committee; winners split all or part of the entry fees.

lap-and-tap   a type of start in which the steer or calf is released from the chute without a head start on the roper or steer wrestler. Lap-and-tap starts are used only in special situations, but never as a first-start procedure.

mount money   paid when someone is riding, roping, or steer wrestling as an exhibition; mount money is never paid in competition riding.

no time   a signal by the field flagman indicating that the contestant is to receive no official time for the run; called when an animal is not caught or thrown legitimately.

pickup man   a mounted cowboy who helps the rider off a bronc after a ride. The pickup man then removes the flank strap from the bronc and leads the bronc out of the arena.

pigging string   a small line of rope used to tie a calf's legs in calf roping. It is six feet long and a half-inch thick. The rider carries it in the mouth with the tail tucked in the jeans.

prize money   the total purse, or money paid to the winners of the various events in a rodeo. The purse, put up by the rodeo committee, consists of entry fees from contestants.

pulling leather   holding on to any part of the saddle. A saddle bronc rider who "pulls leather" is disqualified if he does it before the eight-second ride is completed.

reride   another ride in the same round, given to a bronc or bull rider when the first ride is unsatisfactory for any of several reasons: the rider being hit ("fouled") on the chutes; or a horse failing to buck hard enough to give the rider a fair chance of winning.

rigging   the leather handle (like that of a suitcase) held by riders in bareback riding.

round   in a rodeo, the period during which contestants compete on a bronc or a bull. The number of rounds in a rodeo may vary from one, in a small one-day contest, to seven or more in large rodeos.

saddle bronc riding   rodeo's oldest event; in it, a cowboy must stay atop a bucking horse for at least eight seconds. The horse is saddled, and the rider holds onto a soft-woven bronc rein attached to the horse's halter.

score   the distance (usually 8 to 15 feet) from the chute to the score line; it serves as the head start for the steer or calf in roping contests.

steer wrestling   a two-person, timed event in which one rider keeps the steer running straight while the other jumps from the horse's back and twists the steer by the horns until its feet and head are free and pointing in the same direction; also called "bulldogging."

team roping   a two-person, timed event in which a steer is roped by two riders; one ropes the front legs and the other, the hind legs.

ABC Sports

14   SKIING

Anyone who has strapped on a pair of skis some winter morning for the very first time planning to schuss down a snow-capped peak that afternoon is in for a rude awakening: it may take all the unformed talent of that intrepid novice just to make it to the liftline. Once the basic skills have been mastered, though, skiing offers fun and excitement second to none. And, for the champion-caliber skier, the challenge of setting a new mark for downhill, or slalom, or cross-country, or ski jumping, is irresistible. The skier who wins a gold medal at a Winter Olympics or who takes a World Cup knows that the triumph was achieved with no small expense of hard work, not a little luck, and a generous measure of persistence and courage.

The remains of prehistoric artifacts that are definitely skis have been found in Finland, Norway, and Sweden; a rock wall carving in Norway that clearly shows a person on skis is known to be some 4,000 years old. For nearly all of that time—all, in fact, but the last 130 years—skis are thought to have been used solely for utilitarian purposes. If you lived in a region where snow blanketed the ground all or most of the time, you used skis to travel, to forage, and to hunt. They were, in short, the only effective means of transportation.

Since the Bronze and Stone ages, skis have found other applications. The first mention of skis in connection with warfare occurs in a contemporary account of the Norwegian Civil War: in 1200, soldiers loyal to King Sverre carried out a reconnaissance mission using skis to reach a ski-less, and thus snowbound, enemy force. In the same conflict, six years later, King Haakon's infant son, Haakon Haakonson, was carried in midwinter by two skiing scouts to safety across the mountains of Norway, a rescue commemorated today by the Birkebeinerrennet ("birch-leg race," so named because the "Birchlegs" of King Haakon wore birch bark on their legs to protect them from the cold), a 35-mile race that follows the route taken by Haakon's scouts nearly eight centuries ago.

Despite the antiquity of skiing, basic ski design altered little for thousands of years. (The Ovrebo Ski, found in a Norwegian bog and thought to be 2,500 years old, bears a striking resemblance to today's skis.) In 1721, a ski company in the Norwegian army was created and equipped with skis that had a leather strap around the heel, in addition to the toe strap long in use. Ski design generally varied from one country, region, even town, to another. A common eighteenth-century design was a long ski (of 9 to 12 feet) on one foot and a shorter one (of 6 to 7 feet) on the other; the long one was used for gliding while the shorter one was used, as on a child's scooter today, for propulsion. Fur was sometimes attached to the underside of the shorter ski to increase traction.

Skiing came to the New World in the person of John A. ("Snowshoe") Thomson (born Jon Thoresen Rue in Telemark, Norway, in 1827), who in 1856 used ski-like "snowshoes" to deliver mail between Placerville, California, on one side of the Sierra Nevada, and Genoa, Nevada, 90 miles away on the other, setting off a "snowshoeing" craze among the local gold miners that lasted 20 years—until the gold rush ended.

In Scandinavia, skiing, always a part of everyday life, continued as before, until, in the midnineteenth century, a Norwegian named Sondre Norheim invented a toe-and-heel binding that improved control, a ski having a tip shorter than its tail and a side camber, and, made possible by these innovations, slalom skiing, and the Telemark and parallel turns.

National Ski Hall of Fame

"Snowshoe" Thomson, the Norwegian immigrant who brought skiing to the New World, is shown here in a formal, indoor, pose.

Improvements in bindings, skis, and technique followed, all building upon Norheim's efforts. As equipment and technique advanced, so did the popularity of skiing as a sport. In the United States, the first jumping competition was held in 1887, at Red Wing, Minnesota, and in 1904 the National Ski Association was formed. Abroad, the first Holmenkollen meet, involving jumping and cross-country—the Nordic events—was held in 1892, and continues to be a principal Nordic ski competition today. Alpine—or downhill—skiing was slower to take hold, but by World War I all but the most difficult alpine peaks had been skied, and in 1928 the first Arlberg-Kandahar race, the alpine equivalent of the Holmenkollen, was organized by Sir Arnold Lunn and the great skiing teacher, theorist, practitioner, and popularizer, Hannes Schneider.

Today, skiers by the million head for the mountains of Switzerland, Austria, France, New England, and the western United States to participate in the sport of skiing as competitors and as spectators. Millions more follow the sport on television, especially during the quadrennial Olympic Winter Games. Names like Kidd, Killy, Stenmark, and Mahre are known to sports enthusiasts around the world. Skiing has come a long way since its origins in the early days of human civilization. How far it may go in the years to come will be determined by the skill, persistence, luck, stamina, and courage of skiers yet unborn.

Great Moments

1860 Sondre Norheim, of Norway, jumps 30.5 meters in the first officially measured ski jump.

1868 Norheim leads a group of skiers from Telemark to Christiania (present-day Oslo), in an early example of recreational skiing.

1888 Fridtjof Nansen, of Norway, skies across southern Greenland from east to west, a trek that takes 40 days and covers some 800 miles. This feat, and a book Nansen writes about it, create enormous interest in skiing throughout Europe.

1892 The first Holmenkollen competition, featuring jumping and cross-country events, is held, at Holmenkollen, Norway. It remains one of the principal Nordic ski competitions.

1904 The National Ski Association is formed by, and is at first largely restricted to, clubs of Norwegian-American immigrants.

1905 Mathias Zdarsky, an Austrian proponent of the single-pole skiing technique, sets the first slalom course.

1909 December 7: the Dartmouth Outing Club, first of several such clubs devoted principally or exclusively to skiing, is formed, in Hanover, New Hampshire.

1920 Hannes Schneider begins codifying his skiing technique, which is based on a turn called the stem christiania, in a system of instruction known as the Arlberg Technique. The old Telemark method of turning is abandoned, and Schneider's method becomes the first truly alpine skiing technique.

1924 The first Olympic Winter games are held, in Chamonix, France, and include jumping and cross-country racing. Also that year, the Federation Internationale de Ski is formed, to set the rules for competitive skiing, compile seeding lists, select sites for World Championships, and approve race courses and jumping hills for international competition.

1928 The first Arlberg-Kandahar race is held, at St. Anton, Austria. Organized by Sir Arnold Lunn and Hannes Schneider, it is the alpine equivalent of the Nordic Holmenkollen.

1932 The first rope tow is constructed by Alex Foster at Shawbridge, Quebec, Canada. The first rope tow in the United States, at Woodstock, Vermont, follows two years later.

1936 The FIS officially recognizes downhill and slalom racing as world-championship events. The rotational method of Toni Seelos gains wide attention as he uses it to beat the slalom gold-medalist by five seconds.

1939 Toni Matt takes the Headwall of Tuckerman's Ravine straight down as he wins the third, and final, running of the American Inferno race on Mount Washington in record time.

1948 Gretchen Fraser becomes the first American medalist in the Olympic Winter Games when she takes a gold in slalom and a silver in alpine combined at the fifth Winter Games, at St. Moritz, Switzerland.

1956 Austria's Toni Sailer, at the Olympic Winter Games at Cortina d'Ampezzo, Italy, wins the downhill, the slalom, and the giant slalom events for the Winter Games' only grand slam.

1964 Billy Kidd and Jimmy Heuga become the first American medalists in the Olympic Winter Games as they win, respectively, a silver and a bronze at the ninth Winter Games, at Innsbruck, Austria.

1975 Annemarie Moser-Proell, of Austria, wins her fifth consecutive World Cup; she will win it yet again in 1979.

1978 Ingemar Stenmark, of Sweden, wins his third consecutive World Cup.

1981 Phil Mahre becomes the first American to win the World Cup.

The Setup

Competitive skiing is governed internationally by the Federation Internationale de Ski (FIS), based in Switzerland. The FIS sponsors the major international competitions for all skiing events. In the United States, the United States Ski Association governs the sport, and members of the U.S. Ski Team represent the country at the Winter Olympics.

FEDERATION INTERNATIONALE
  DE SKI (FIS)
Eifaustrasse, 19 Postfach
CH-3000 Berne, Switzerland
Gian-Franco Kasper, sec. gen.

U.S. SKI TEAM
P.O. Box 100
Park City, UT 84060
(801) 649-9090
Inez Aimee, exec. dir.

UNITED STATES SKI ASSOCIATION
3000 Pearl St., Suite 200
Boulder, CO 80301
(303) 499-7902
E. A. Hammerle, pres. of bd. of gov.

The Basics

ALPINE EVENTS

ABC Sports

Monty Calvert/*Ski Racing*

Downhill

Object   To achieve the fastest time skiing down a designated course.

The course   The total vertical drop of a course must not be less than 800 meters for men and not less than 450 meters for women. A course must have no uphill or level terrain. The course is from one to five miles long. Control points are marked along the way.

Equipment   Skis made of metal or fiberglass; release bindings that hold the toe and heel on the ski; lightweight poles for balance; and heavy plastic or leather boots that reach just past the ankles.

Officials   A race is supervised by many officials, including referees at the start and finish, timers (electronic and manual), and a maintenance crew.

Rule 1   The start   A racer begins the race on signal, breaking an electronic beam at the starting gate. Competitors then follow at one-minute intervals.

Rule 2   The flags   Clearly visible red flags are direction flags, marking the skier's course. Yellow flags are posted to mark danger areas on the course. Blue flags are control gates; the skier must pass between them.

Rule 3   Control gates   Control gates, blue flags along the course, are set at least 26 feet apart. The skier must pass through all the controls by crossing the line between the inner poles of the flags with both feet.

Rule 4   Assistance   A skier is not permitted to receive assistance of any kind while skiing the course.

Rule 5   The finish   A finish time is recorded when the racer's feet have crossed the finish line. A skier must complete the course on at least one ski.

Slalom

Object   To achieve the fastest time skiing a strictly controlled course, passing through a series of gates in the proper sequence and making many short, quick turns. A racer makes two runs.

The course   The course must have a vertical drop of between 140 and 200 meters for men and 120 and 180 meters for women. The course is marked by 50 to 75 gates in men's competitions and 40 to 55 gates in women's. Gates are narrow, at least 11 feet wide, and are set in pairs with alternating colored flags.

Equipment   Same as downhill.

Officials   Same as downhill.

Rule 1   The start   A racer's time begins as soon as the signal to start is given.

Rule 2   The gates   A racer must take the gates in proper sequence. The gates are laid out in various combinations; racers usually encounter at least two flushes, three hairpins, and both open and closed gates.

Rule 3   Missing a gate   A racer who misses or overshoots a gate may go back and go through it; but that will add time. Penalty seconds are added to a skier's time for failure to take a gate properly or for missing a gate entirely.

Rule 4   The finish   A finish time is recorded when the racer's feet have crossed the finish line.

Giant Slalom

Object   To achieve the fastest combined time on two runs down a fast, open course, passing through wide gates.

The course   The course must have a vertical drop of 250 to 400 meters in the men's event and of 250 to 350 in the women's. The number of gates is determined according to a formula based on the hill's vertical drop (for example, a course with a 300-meter drop would have 40 to 50 gates).

Equipment   Same as downhill.

Officials   Same as downhill.

Rule 1   The start   A racer's time begins when the signal to start is given.

Rule 2   The gates   Gates are wider than those for slalom; the distance from one gate to the next is between 40 and 80 meters.

Rule 3   Missing a gate   Same as for slalom.

Rule 4   The finish   Same as for slalom.

NORDIC EVENTS

ABC Sports

ABC Sports

Cross-Country

Object   To race a course of designated length over natural terrain in the shortest elapsed time.

The course   Races are run over distances of 15, 30, and 50 kilometers for men, and 5, 10, and 20 kilometers for women. Courses are laid out so approximately one-third is flat, one-third is uphill, and one-third is downhill. The course is three to four meters wide, with two sets of parallel tracks laid in the packed snow.

Equipment   Cross-country skiers use narrow, long skis made of a combination of fiberglass, wood, and epoxy resins; lightweight toe bindings; extremely light, long poles made of carbon fiber; and light racing boots.

Rule 1   The start   Skiers start one at a time at 30-second intervals.

Rule 2   The course   Skiers must follow the course and pass all control posts.

Rule 3   Broken equipment   A broken ski or binding may be replaced, but a skier must finish the race with at least one of the original skis. There is no limit on the number of broken poles that may be replaced.

Rule 4   Stops during the race   A skier may stop to adjust his or her skis or bindings, wax his skis, take refreshments, and receive information about himself and his fellow competitors as long as the skier does not receive assistance.

Rule 5   The winner   The winner is the skier who, when all the competitors are in, has completed the course in the shortest elapsed time.

Ski Jumping

Object   To score the most points, based on the distance jumped and the form demonstrated, by jumping off a specially constructed jump and landing smoothly on skis.

The ski jump   Jumps are 70 and 90 meters and consist of approach and takeoff areas, a transition area, and a flat area where the skier decelerates and stops.

Equipment   Skis are from 240 to 255 centimeters long and half as wide as alpine skis. They are made of a combination of wood, fiberglass, and epoxy, and have five or six narrow grooves on the bottom. Jumping ski boots, similar to older model alpine leather boots, have a flexible sole and a high back. A cable heel-spring binding allows the heel to move freely up and down. Protective helmets are required.

Officials Five judges evaluate a jumper's form; distance measurers visually gauge the distance covered by the jumper, and the chief measurer decides any disputes and reports the distance to the official scorer.

Rule 1 The jump A skier is allowed one trial jump and then two jumps, which are scored and counted for the meet.

Rule 2 Scoring the distance Distance points are calculated from a table which awards 60 points to a jump that reaches the table point. Points will vary up and down from 60, depending on whether the jump was beyond or short of the table point.

Rule 3 Scoring the form A perfect jump earns 20 points. Each of five judges may award up to 20 points for each jump; the highest and the lowest score is dropped, and the three remaining scores are added to the distance points, which yields the total score of the jump.

Rule 4 Falling If a jumper falls, a judge may award only a maximum of 10 points, thereby usually eliminating that skier from competition with skiers of similar ability who do not fall.

Rule 5 The winner The winner is the skier with the most points after two jumps.

Nordic Combined

Object To score the most total points earned from a 15-kilometer, cross-country ski race and a ski-jumping competition.

The course Same as for cross-country, except that the distance is run at only 15 kilometers and may have slightly less uphill terrain.

The ski jump Same as for regular ski jump, except that only the 70-meter jump is used.

Officials Same as for regular cross-country and ski jumping.

Rule 1 Cross-country race The same rules apply as for regular cross-country ski competition.

Rule 2 Scoring the race Skiers' times are converted into points based on special tables, with the maximum 220 points going to the winner of the race. The scores of the other skiers are proportionately less, based on the number of additional seconds it took to complete the course.

Rule 3 Scoring the jump Three jumps are scored, and the skier's best two-out-of-three scores are used.

Rule 4 Scoring the distance Distance points are awarded, based on the longest standing jump of each round, regardless of the location of the table point. The jumper with the longest jump of the round earns the maximum 60 points; all other skiers earn proportionately fewer points, based on the table.

Rule 5 Scoring the form Same as for regular ski jumping.

Rule 6 The winner Final jumping points are added to the cross-country points; the skier with the most points wins the event.

How to watch

World Wide Ski Corp.

with Billy Kidd

Skiing is a viewer's smorgasbord. It offers the spectator everything from the speed and technique required on a slalom course to the stamina it takes to win a 30-mile cross-country race over rough terrain to the thrill of seeing a man swoop through the air from a 90-meter ski jump. They all show a single human pitting himself against the clock, nature, fear, or all three.

"The object in skiing is to push to the absolute edge and still maintain control," says Billy Kidd, who in 1964, with Jimmy Heuga, became one of the first Americans to earn an Olympic medal in skiing. The form of this challenge varies from alpine to Nordic skiing. Kidd discusses the technique and the strategy common to each:

ALPINE EVENTS

The first thing an alpine skier looks for is good skiing conditions, which means blue ice, according to Kidd. "This makes it so that each skier is skiing basically the same course and has the same conditions. With soft, mushy snow, the skiers who go first have an advantage over the others, who find themselves skiing in ruts down the mountain." With really good skiers, however, this can occasionally work well, Kidd adds. They simply get inside the ruts established by the first skiers and fly as though on rails.

Conditions also affect how a slalom skier approaches a course. "If the course is steep and icy," Kidd says, "you will see wider, earlier turns. If it is soft and mushy, you'll see skiers go straighter at the gates."

"There are no trial runs in slalom or giant slalom," Kidd says. "This means that skiers must look at the course, memorize how it is set up, and notice where it is steeper, where it is likely to get rutty, or where the snow is likely to change texture. A sunny spot, for instance, would have softer snow than a cooler, shadier part of the course."

Trial runs are permitted in downhill courses, so the skier has a chance to see where riskier spots are in advance.

Strategies used during the race depend somewhat on whether the race is amateur, as most are, or professional. In the professional slalom races, skiers race side by side 12 times, going through an elimination process that eventually produces the winner. In amateur racing, each skier is permitted two runs on the course. Some skiers go all out on both runs while others concentrate their efforts on one or the other, according to Kidd.

"Jean-Claude Killy, for instance, liked to go all out on the first run and then take it easy on the second—others like to save themselves for the second run."

Once skiers have taken conditions and the course into account, their strategies probably won't differ substantially from each other's. But their individual styles will.

For example, the 1981 World Cup champion, Phil Mahre, will not ski a course the same way 1980 World Cup champion Ingemar Stenmark will. "The basic difference is that Stenmark is more cautious than Mahre. His turns will be a shade wider and he will start to turn sooner than Mahre will. Mahre skis straighter at the gates and goes straight when he can. Mahre's style requires precise timing; Stenmark's allows a bit of room for error."

In downhill, the strategy is simple: go as fast as possible no matter what the conditions. In the 1976 Olympics, skiers were faced with a thick fog that limited their visibility. "Fog can't stop you," Kidd says. "You spend several days before the race skiing the course and memorizing it. And when it's time, you have to push yourself." Downhill skiers attain speeds of up to 90 miles per hour—a big difference from slalom, which averages 20 miles per hour and giant slalom, which averages 40.

Another rule alpine skiers try to follow is to get the most out of the start. It helps to be seeded among the first 15 skiers, to avoid running a bumpy course caused by the runs of those ahead. In the start, most skiers now use the one perfected by Killy, in which the skier leans way out over the tips of his skis, using the arm muscles to keep from breaking the electric eye at the top of the course before it's time to go.

Also, since skiers lose time when they are in the air, they reduce the lift from a mogul by jumping *before* they hit it, timing the maneuver so that their skis hit the downhill side of the mogul, which gives them a little push.

NORDIC EVENTS

The most spectacular of the Nordic events is the ski jumping competition. Jumpers are scored on the basis of form, distance, and courage. Good form is when the jumper leans at just the right angle on his takeoff, and does not move once in the air. "If he leans too far forward, his skis will dive," says Kidd. "It's bad form to get in the air and start waving the arms around." When jumpers need to stabilize themselves in the air, he adds, they can do it by moving their fingers in ways that are all but imperceptible to the judges and spectators. Jumpers must land with the Telemark landing, but once they have done so, they may come to a stop any way they choose.

According to Kidd, it is more difficult for spectators to watch such other Nordic events as the long-distance, cross-country races, events that require more than just strength and good physical shape. "They give the impression of requiring only stamina," he observes, "but there is a lot of technique involved. The skier has to know when to kick and how to keep his stride smooth and consistent under varying ground conditions."

Main Events

WINTER OLYMPICS

The Winter Olympics, held every four years at varying locations, have been known to help make a skier's name a household word. The Olympics feature both Nordic and alpine events, Nordic events comprising several cross-country races of different lengths, ski jumping, the biathlon, and two relays, and alpine events including the downhill, the slalom, and the giant slalom.

1980 ALPINE EVENTS

	Men	Women
Downhill	Leonard Stock, Austria	Annemarie Moser-Proell, Austria
Slalom	Ingemar Stenmark, Sweden	Hanni Wentzel, Liechtenstein
Giant slalom	Ingemar Stenmark, Sweden	Hanni Wentzel, Liechtenstein

1980 NORDIC EVENTS

	Men	Women
70-meter jump	Anton Innauer, Austria	—
90-meter jump	Jouko Tormanen, Finland	—

Cross-country	Men	Women
50 km	Nikolai Zimyatov, USSR	—
30 km	Nikolai Zimyatov, USSR	—
15 km	Thomas Wassberg, Sweden	—
10 km	—	Barbara Petzold, GDR*
5 km	—	Raisa Smetanina, USSR
Combined	Ulrich Wehling, GDR	—

German Democratic Republic (East Germany)

1976 ALPINE EVENTS

	Men	Women
Downhill	Franz Klammer, Austria	Rosi Mittermaier, FRG*
Slalom	Piero Gros, Italy	Rosi Mittermaier, FRG
Giant slalom	Heini Hemmi, Switzerland	Kathy Kreiner, Canada

1976 NORDIC EVENTS

	Men	Women
70-meter jump	Hans-Georg Aschenbach, GDR	—
90-meter jump	Karl Schnabl, Austria	—

Cross-country	Men	Women
50 km	Ivar Formo, Italy	—
30 km	Sergey Saveliev, USSR	—
15 km	Nikolai Bjuokov, USSR	—
10 km	—	Raisa Smetanina, USSR
5 km	—	Helena Tukalo, Finland
Combined	Ulrich Wehling, GDR	—

Federal Republic of Germany (West Germany)

1974 ALPINE EVENTS

	Men	Women
Downhill	David Zwilling, Austria	Annemarie Moser-Proell, Austria
Slalom	Gustavo Thoeni, Italy	Hanni Wenzel, Liechtenstein
Giant slalom	Gustavo Thoeni, Italy	Fabienne Serrat, France
Combined	Franz Klammer, Austria	Fabienne Serrat, France

1974 NORDIC EVENTS

	Men	Women
70-meter jump	Hans-Georg Aschenbach, GDR	—
90-meter jump	Hans-Georg Aschenbach, GDR	—

Cross-country	Men	Women
50 km	Gerhard Grimmer, GDR	—
30 km	Thomas Magnusson, Sweden	—
15 km	Magne Myrmo, Norway	—
10 km	—	Galina Koulakova, USSR
5 km	—	Galina Koulakova, USSR
Combined	Ulrich Wehling, GDR	—

1972 ALPINE EVENTS

	Men	Women
Downhill	Bernhard Russi, Switzerland	Marie Therese Nadig, Switzerland
Slalom	Francisco Fernandez Ochoa, Spain	Barbara Cochran, USA
Giant slalom	Gustavo Thoeni, Italy	Marie Therese Nadig, Switzerland

1972 NORDIC EVENTS

	Men	Women
70-meter jump	Yukio Kasaya, Japan	—
90-meter jump	Wojciech Fortuna, Poland	—

Cross-country	Men	Women
50 km	Paal Tyldum, Norway	—
30 km	Vyacheslav Vedenin, USSR	—
15 km	Sven-Ake Lundback, Sweden	—
10 km	—	Galina Koulakov, USSR
5 km	—	Galina Koulakov, USSR
Combined	Ulrich Wehling, GDR	—

FIS WORLD CHAMPIONSHIPS

Second only to the Winter Olympics in importance, the World Championships are held every four years, in between Olympic years, in varying locations.

1978 ALPINE EVENTS

	Men	Women
Downhill	Josef Walcher, Austria	Annemarie Moser-Proell, Austria
Slalom	Ingemar Stenmark, Sweden	Lea Soelkner, Austria
Giant slalom	Ingemar Stenmark, Sweden	Maria Epple, West Germany
Combined	Andreas Wenzel, Liechtenstein	Annemarie Moser-Proell, Austria

1978 NORDIC EVENTS

	Men	Women
70-meter jump	Mathias Buse, GDR	—
90-meter jump	Tapio Raeisaenen, Finland	—

Cross-country	Men	Women
50 km	Sven-Ake Lundback, Sweden	—
30 km	Sergey Saveliev, USSR	—
20 km	—	Zinaida Amosova, USSR
15 km	Josef Luszczek, Poland	—
10 km	—	Zinaida Amosova, USSR
5 km	—	Helena Takalo, Finland
Combined	Konrad Winkler, GDR	—

WORLD CUP

In World Cup competition, which made its debut in 1967, skiers earn points in nine meets held internationally. Each racer's top scores in the three alpine events make up the total. A maximum of 25 points is possible for first place. The World Cup races, designated at the start of the ski season, usually extend from January to March. Locations vary.

WORLD CUP WINNERS

Year	Men	Points
1981	Phil Mahre, USA	266
1980	Andreas Wenzel, Liechtenstein	204
1979	Peter Luescher, Switzerland	186
1978	Ingemar Stenmark, Sweden	150
1977	Ingemar Stenmark, Sweden	339
1976	Ingemar Stenmark, Sweden	249
1975	Gustavo Thoeni, Italy	250
1974	Piero Gros, Italy	181
1973	Gustavo Thoeni, Italy	166
1972	Gustavo Thoeni, Italy	154
1971	Gustavo Thoeni, Italy	144
1970	Karl Schranz, Austria	148

WORLD CUP WINNERS

Year	Women	Points
1981	Marie Therese Nadig, Switzerland	289
1980	Hanni Wenzel, Liechtenstein	311
1979	Annemarie Moser-Proell, Austria	243
1978	Hanni Wenzel, Liechtenstein	154
1977	Lise-Marie Morerod, Switzerland	319
1976	Rosi Mittermaier, FRG	281
1975	Annemarie Proell, Austria	305
1974	Annemarie Proell, Austria	268
1973	Annemarie Proell, Austria	297
1972	Annemarie Proell, Austria	269
1971	Annemarie Proell, Austria	210
1970	Michelle Jacot, France	180

NORDIC WORLD CUP

The Nordic World Cup is a new addition to the international racing circuit. Like the Alpine World Cup, it consists of a series of races and events at the end of which the overall winner is named. Men's events began in 1974 and women's competition in 1979.

NORDIC WORLD CUP WINNERS

Year	Men	Points
1981	Alexander Zavjalov, USSR	139
1980	Juha Mieto, Finland	134
1979	Oddvar Braa, Norway	117
1978	Sven-Ake Lundback, Sweden	124
1977	Thomas Wassberg, Sweden	113
1976	Juha Mieto, Finland	133
1975	Oddvar Braa, Norway	143
1974	Ivar Formo, Norway	113

Year	Women	Points
1981	Raisa Smetanina, USSR	178
1980	Not held	
1979	Galina Koulakova, USSR	123

All-Time Greats

Nancy Greene
(May 11, 1943–)

Ski Racing

Nancy Greene, an Olympic gold medalist and two-time World Cup winner, is recognized as the greatest woman competitor in North American skiing history. The Canadian skier won an Olympic gold medal in 1968 in the giant slalom event and took first overall in the World Cup championships the same year. In 1966, Greene won 17 major races in the United States and Canada, including the U.S. Nationals, the Roch Cup, and the Dominion Championships.

Jean-Claude Killy
(Aug. 30, 1943–)

Ski Racing

From 1967, when he took the World Cup with the maximum number of points possible, to his retirement after winning the world pro skiing championship over the American skier Spider Sabich in 1973, Jean-Claude Killy was the superstar of skiing. He won the World Cup two consecutive years and took three gold medals in the 1968 Olympic alpine events. The French skier's innovative starting position, in which he leaned far out over the starting gate without moving his skis past the breaking point, is an example of his superb technique. He was capable of devoting himself entirely to winning—even to the point of leaving all care of his equipment to another person. This ability allowed him to take the World Pro Skiing title after being out of competition for four years.

Phil Mahre
(June 10, 1957–)

Ski Racing

In 1981, Phil Mahre did something no other American skier had done: take first overall in World Cup competition. Even before he did so, however, Mahre was already considered the best American skier ever, with seven World Cup medals (for individual events), an Olympic silver, and an FIS World Championship combined medal to his credit. Three times injuries threatened Mahre's career. He made a remarkable comeback from a broken ankle suffered at the 1979 World Cup races, to win a third place overall in 1980. He won a silver medal at the 1980 Olympics in the slalom event, the only American skier to win a medal at Lake Placid. His twin brother Steve is also a member of the U.S. Ski Team and a world-class competitor in alpine events.

Annemarie Moser-Proell
(Mar. 27, 1953–)

Jerry Leblond/Ski Racing

The Austrian skier Annemarie Moser-Proell is the winningest skier, male or female, in the history of the alpine event. The year 1980 was the highlight of her career; that year, she won an Olympic gold medal in the downhill event. In the 1972 Olympics at Sapporo, Japan, she won silver medals in the downhill and giant slalom events. Moser-Proell missed the 1976 Olympics in Innsbruck, however, because of retirement for the season. She was World Cup champion from 1971 to 1975, and again in 1979. Since her first World Cup title in 1971, Moser-Proell has never placed lower than second in any World Cup competition she entered.

Ingemar Stenmark
(Mar. 18, 1956–)

Mark Gabriel/*Ski Racing*

Sweden's Ingemar Stenmark, a slalom specialist, is sometimes called "Comeback" Stenmark because of his amazing ability to follow a mediocre first run with a championship-winning second run. The three-time World Cup champion (1976–78) won his first Olympic gold at Lake Placid, making up a .32-second deficit with a stunning second run on the giant slalom course. Three days later, he won another gold medal in the slalom competition. In 1977, he won his World Cup title with a record 339 points. Stenmark won a bronze medal in the 1976 Winter Olympics at Innsbruck. Between 1976 and 1980, he was named *Ski Racing's* International Alpine Skier of the Year five consecutive times.

Wallace ("Buddy") Werner
(1937–Apr. 2, 1964)

SKI Magazine

"Buddy" Werner began his career as a ski jumper but quickly switched to downhill events, becoming the youngest skier to win a major international event when, at the age of 17, he took first in the 1954 Holmenkollen downhill. An injury put him out of the running for the 1954 FIS World Championships, but he continued to race until he was recognized as the champion downhill skier. Yet another injury prevented him from competing in the 1960 Olympics. He continued to race but began to devote much of his efforts to developing a training program for young American skiers. He was killed in an avalanche in Switzerland in 1964.

For the Record

Fastest speed, downhill
124.412 mph   Steve McKinney, USA
                        1978

Fastest average speed, downhill
63.894 mph   Franz Klammer, Austria
                        1976

Longest jump
176 m   Toni Innauer, Austria   1976

Most Olympic gold medals, men
4   Sixten Jernberg, Sweden
        1956–64

Most Olympic gold medals, women
4   Galina Koulakova, USSR
        1972–76

Most world titles, men's alpine
7   Toni Sailer, Austria   1956–58

Most world titles, women's alpine
12   Christel Cranz, Sweden
        1934–39

Most world titles, men's Nordic
8   Sixten Jernberg, Sweden
        1956–64

Most world titles, women's Nordic
9   Galina Koulakova, USSR
        1968–78

Did you know ?

1. The first buckle boots, the first stretch pants, and the first polyethylene base were all introduced in the same year. What year was it?

2. Who was the first American male skier to win a major European race?

3. Only one skier in the history of the Olympics has won gold medals in both Nordic and alpine events. Who was he?

4. In 1961, a French skier achieved the unprecedented feat of winning every major race he entered. Who was he?

5. What Winter Olympics living quarters were earmarked for use as a prison after the Winter Games?

6. In 1970, a Japanese skier skied down Mount Everest, starting from an altitude of 26,200 feet. Name the skier and the film made of his exploit.

Answers: 1. 1955, a year also marked by the death of the great Hannes Schneider; **2.** Buddy Werner, who in 1958 came in first in the Nordic Combined at the Lauberhorn. The following year, he became the first American male to win a major European downhill when he took first at the Hahnenkamm in Kitzbuehel, Austria; **3.** Birger Ruud, who in 1936 won both the downhill and the jumping competitions; **4.** Guy Perrillat; **5.** The Olympic Village at Lake Placid, site of the XIIIth Winter Olympiad in 1980; **6.** The skier's name was Yuichiro Miura; the film was entitled, appropriately, *The Man Who Skied Down Everest.*

Key Words

Arlberg technique   a skiing technique requiring the skier to crouch over the skis and make turns by stemming one ski and turning the body in the direction of the turn.

base   a layer of hard-packed snow covering bare ground; it protects the bottoms of skis from damage by rocks and dirt.

binding   the device that fastens the ski boot to the ski; it will release the boot from the ski in the event of a bad fall.

closed gate   in slalom events, a gate whose poles are set in a line parallel to the course.

control flags   flags erected along a downhill or a slalom course, indicating a gate or warning a skier of danger.

diagonal stride   the most common walklike ski-touring stride, in which the diagonally opposite arm and leg swing forward and back in unison.

double poling   a touring movement in which both arms swing forward and backward in unison, pushing on the poles; may be done with or without a leg kick.

edges   strips of metal, usually made of hardened steel, running on the edges of ski bottoms.

fall line   the most direct line from a given point on a hill to the end of a course.

flush   a series of three or more closed gates.

frozen granular   a snow condition in which the surface consists of crunchy particles of frozen snow.

gate   pairs of flags on poles set in a snakelike pattern through and around which skiers must pass in slalom and giant slalom races.

hairpin   a series of two closed gates.

inrun   in ski jumping, the ramp from which the jumper makes his or her approach.

kick   the push-off phase of the touring stride, which drives the skier forward.

mogul   a bump on the trail formed by the repeated turning of skiers.

open gate   in slalom events, a gate whose poles are set in a line perpendicular to the course.

outrun   in ski jumping, the flat area where the skier decelerates and stops.

packed powder   considered the perfect skiing condition: the snow has a firmly packed down base but a light, fluffy surface.

powder   a light, dry, fluffy snow surface.

schuss   to ski freely downhill at high speed without turning; a skier cannot maintain control easily at such speeds.

snowplow   a stemming of both skis which enables the skier to ski downhill slowly, to slow down, or to stop; usually the first movement learned by beginners.

stem christie   an advanced stem turn in which the ski is stemmed only slightly and the other ski is immediately brought alongside so that most of the turn is completed with the skis parallel; also known as a "stem christiania."

stem turn   an elementary turn in which the tail of one ski is pushed out so the turn is started from a half-V position.

stride   the basic touring movement.

table point   in ski jumping, the point on the landing hill midway between the norm point and the critical point; it is the farthest point at which a jumper should land.

tacking   a diagonal-stride touring turn used when the skier is changing directions on an uphill traverse.

touring   cross-country skiing through woods and across fields, as distinguished from downhill skiing.

transition area   in ski jumping, the area where the landing is steepest.

traverse   movement by a skier diagonally across a slope.

tuck   a skiing position in which the skier crouches forward and holds the ski poles under the arms and parallel to the ground; downhill skiers use it to minimize wind resistance.

wedeln   a series of parallel turns in which the tails of the skis are moved from side to side while heading straight down a slope.

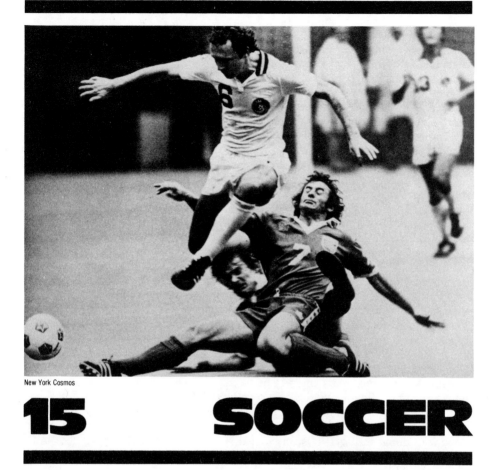

New York Cosmos

15 SOCCER

Soccer, by far the leading international sport, demands both individual and team effort. From the individual, it demands speed, skill, and endurance. The game is widely believed to be the ancestor of American football; in fact, outside the United States, soccer is *called* football. The object of the game is simply to move a round leather ball down the field into the opponent's goal. It is the accomplishing of that objective that makes soccer so exciting.

The early development of soccer is difficult to trace. Several countries claim to have invented it. Some evidence, however, has been unearthed of a similar game played in China before the time of Christ; it was called *tsu chu,* or "kick ball." There is also evidence of games similar to soccer being played in Japan and in ancient Greece and Rome. The game's best-traced lineage is found in England, dating from at least the third century A.D. Soccer apparently was a religious ceremony enacted on Shrove Tuesday. Entire towns engaged in a kind of group sport, with goals placed at either end of the town, or even outside the town. Rules were nonexistent, and injuries were numerous.

During the fourteenth century, football, as it was then known, gained a foothold among the English people; but it was outlawed by rulers, who felt that the game interfered with the practice of archery (on which the country's defense depended). Despite statutes outlawing the game, football grew in popularity. During a match in 1823, a player for Rugby College, named William Webb Ellis, ran with the ball—

and "rugby" was born. In 1848, students at Cambridge University drafted the first formal rules of the game. In an effort to deemphasize violence, they forbade the use of hands. "Football" had begun.

There was some confusion about the word *football*. Did it refer to the old style of play, using no hands, or to the new "rugby" style, in which use of hands was allowed? The old style was known as "association football," or "assoc football," for short. Eventually the shortened version became soccer, a name sometimes credited to Charles W. Brown. According to this version, Brown, a player for Oxford, was asked by a friend if he was playing "rugger" that day. "No," Brown replied, "I'm playing soccer," apparently in a wordplay on *assoc* (pronounced "a-sock") football.

With the formation, on October 26, 1863, of the Football Association (FA) by representatives of 11 clubs meeting in London, the game of soccer was effectively organized. In 1870, Charles W. Alcock, a leading player for and organizer of the FA, proposed formal contests, including a cup competition. In 1865, it was legalized as a professional sport in England, although players apparently received money before then. During this period, the game was primarily one of offense, of attack, with each side having eight forwards and three defenders. Subsequently, soccer developed more of a balance between offense and defense.

By the turn of the century, soccer was firmly entrenched in the sporting life of almost every country except the United States, and in 1904, the International Federation of Football Associations (IFFA) was founded to oversee the sport. The IFFA, with more than 140 member countries, is still the major international sanctioning body for soccer. The foremost international competition is the World Cup, first held in 1930 and known formally as the Jules Rimet Trophy. The competition is held every four years, midway between Olympic years. In the competition, 16 teams meet and play a round robin to determine the world champion.

The popularization of soccer in the United States parallels only slightly the growth of the sport in Europe. Although it is widely thought that soccer made its American debut in the 1960s, organized soccer teams were playing here in the 1880s. Representatives met in Newark in 1884 and established the American Football Association (AFA). Two years later, the first recorded soccer match was played, in Central Park. Americans participated in their first international soccer match in 1886, when New Jersey's best players formed a team to represent the AFA and traveled to Canada for a three-game series. The next year, the American and Canadian teams met again, this time in the United States.

In the late nineteenth century, soccer organizations sprang up around the country, especially in New England and in St. Louis, which, for a long time, were bastions of the sport. The United States Football Association, formed in 1913, soon affiliated itself with the IFFA. To avoid confusion with the quite different sport of American football, the association later changed its name to the United States Soccer Football Association.

Although crowds at North American Soccer League games today average 16,000, soccer is by no means a national sport as yet. Many people in soccer are looking to indoor soccer, with its fast-paced action and similarity to ice hockey, to stimulate enthusiasm for the sport. Indoor soccer, with its six-man teams, requires players to serve time in the penalty box for certain fouls; it also employs a kick-in rather than a throw-in for out-of-bounds balls.

Theories abound as to why soccer is not followed as fanatically in the United States as it is in other countries. One theory holds that soccer lacks the intricate tactics and plays that fascinate American football fans, and the play-after-play violence that galvanizes them. Another theory blames the weak American support on a lack of American superstars and poor management. Other countries, however, began playing without benefit of native-son stars or backers, and the game thrived.

Whatever the explanation, the number of soccer leagues is growing. Possibly more significant, children are increasingly playing and following the sport. If the sports pundits can be believed, soccer may be America's next national pastime.

Great Moments

1960 The International Soccer League (ISL) begins playing at New York's Polo Grounds. The summer league draws players from Europe and South America, as well as large crowds, but lasts only six seasons.

1967 The National Professional Soccer League (NPSL) is established and begins recruiting American and foreign players for its 12 teams. The United Soccer Association (USA) is formed by importing entire foreign clubs for its franchise cities.

1968 It becomes clear that, while the United States is ready for professional soccer, it is not ready for two competing soccer leagues. The NPSL and the USA merge and form the North American Soccer League (NASL), consisting of 17 clubs in 2 conferences.

1969 Of 17 initial NASL franchises, 12 fold after the first season; only Atlanta, Baltimore, Dallas, Kansas City, and St. Louis play another season.

1970 The Rochester Lancers and the Washington Darts join the NASL; the Baltimore Bays leave the league.

1971 The Dallas Tornado plays three overtime matches in playoff action, going on to capture the crown. The New York Cosmos join the league and quickly move to the top.

1972 The NASL, attempting to foster greater interest in the sport, adopts rules requiring each club to carry a certain number of American players on its roster.

1973 Rookie Kyle Rote, Jr., playing for Dallas, leads the NASL in scoring, thus stimulating American interest in a sport until now dominated by foreign athletes.

1974 The NASL makes its presence felt on the West Coast, with the addition of franchises in Los Angeles, San Jose, Seattle, and Vancouver. For the first time, attendance surpasses the 1 million mark.

1975 The New York Cosmos sign Brazil's legendary soccer star, Pelé, whose presence lends credibility to the sport in the United States and increases its popularity.

1977 The Major Indoor Soccer League (MISL) is officially formed on November 10, with six teams: Cincinnati, Cleveland, Houston, New York, Philadelphia, and Pittsburgh.

1979 The NASL changes its alignment, shifting some franchises to other cities, dropping some franchises, and rearranging its 21 teams in 5 divisions.

The Setup

NORTH AMERICAN SOCCER LEAGUE

The North American Soccer League was reorganized after the 1980 season to include 21 teams in 5 divisions. Each team plays a 32-game regular season; 15 teams will make the playoffs. The team with the most points receives a bye in the first round. The final two teams compete in a single-game championship known as the Soccer Bowl.

NASL

Eastern Division	Central Division	Southern Division
Detroit Express	Chicago Sting	Atlanta Chiefs
Montreal Manic	Dallas Tornado	Fort Lauderdale Strikers
New York Cosmos	Minnesota Kicks	Jacksonville Tea Men
Toronto Blizzard	Tulsa Roughnecks	Tampa Bay Rowdies

Western Division	Northwest Division
California Surf	Calgary Boomers
Los Angeles Aztecs	Edmonton Drillers
San Diego Sockers	Portland Timbers
San Jose Earthquakes	Seattle Sounders
	Vancouver Whitecaps

ATLANTA CHIEFS
P.O. Box 5015
Atlanta, GA 30302
(404) 577-5425
Richard A. Cecil, pres.
(games played at Atlanta–Fulton County Stadium)

CALGARY BOOMERS
3715 Edmonton Trail NE
Calgary, Alberta T2E 3P3
(403) 203-3103
Rudi Schiffer, gen. mgr.
(games played at McMahon Stadium)

CALIFORNIA SURF
P.O. Box 7910
Newport Beach, CA 92660
(714) 545-0551
Bill Dawson, pres. and gen. mgr.
(games played at Anaheim Stadium)

CHICAGO STING
333 N. Michigan Ave., Suite 1525
Chicago, IL 60601
(312) 558-5425
Lee B. Stern, pres.
(games played at Wrigley Field or Comiskey Park)

DALLAS TORNADO
6116 North Central Expy., Suite 333
Dallas, TX 75206
(214) 750-0900
Kent Kramer, gen. mgr.
(games played at Texas Stadium)

DETROIT EXPRESS
1200 Featherstone Rd.
Pontiac, MI 48057
(313) 338-9100
Duncan Hill, gen. mgr.
(games played at Pontiac Silverdome)

EDMONTON DRILLERS
10735 107th Ave., Suite 200
Edmonton, Alberta T5H 0W6
(403) 428-8989
Joe Petrone, gen. mgr.
(games played at Commonwealth Stadium)

FORT LAUDERDALE STRIKERS
1350 N.E. 56th St.
Fort Lauderdale, FL 33334
(305) 491-5140
Bob Lemieux, gen. mgr.
(games played at Lockhart Stadium)

JACKSONVILLE TEA MEN
1245 E. Adams St.
Jacksonville, FL 32202
(904) 354-2380
Dick Kravitz, gen. mgr.
(games played at the Gator Bowl)

LOS ANGELES AZTECS
7362 Santa Monica Blvd.
Los Angeles, CA 90046
(213) 851-9161
Marvin Milkes, vice-pres. and gen. mgr.
(games played at Los Angeles Memorial
  Coliseum)

MINNESOTA KICKS
7200 France Ave. S, Suite 128
Minneapolis, MN 55435
(612) 831-8871
Freddie Goodwin, pres.
(games played at Metropolitan Stadium)

MONTREAL MANIC
5199 E. rue Sherbrooke
Village Olympique, Tour D
Montreal H1T 3X1
(514) 252-1350
Roger Sansom, gen. mgr.
(games played at Olympic Stadium)

NEW YORK COSMOS
75 Rockefeller Plaza
New York, NY 10019
(212) 265-7315
Krikor Yepremian, vice-pres. and gen. mgr.
(games played at Giants Stadium)

PORTLAND TIMBERS
910 S.W. 18th Ave.
Portland, OR 97205
(503) 226-4628
Peter D. Warner, gen. mgr.
(games played at Portland Civic Stadium)

SAN DIEGO SOCKERS
9449 Friars Rd.
San Diego, CA 92108
(714) 280-4625
Fred Whitacre, pres. and gen. mgr.
(games played at San Diego/Jack Murphy
  Stadium)

SAN JOSE EARTHQUAKES
800 Charcot Ave., Suite 100
San Jose, CA 95131
(408) 998-5425
John L. Carbray, exec. vice-pres. and
  gen. mgr.
(games played at Spartan Stadium)

SEATTLE SOUNDERS
419 Occidental Ave. S
Seattle, WA 98104
(206) 628-3551
John E. Daley, pres. and gen. mgr.
(games played at the Kingdome)

TAMPA BAY ROWDIES
1410 N. Westshore Blvd., Suite 802
Tampa, FL 33607
(813) 870-1122
Charles Serednesky, Jr., exec. vice-pres.
  and gen. mgr.
(games played at Tampa Stadium)

TORONTO BLIZZARD
Exhibition Place
Toronto, Ontario M6K 3C3
(416) 977-4625
Clive Toye, pres.
(games played at Exhibition Stadium)

TULSA ROUGHNECKS
P.O. Box 35190
Tulsa, OK 74135
(918) 494-4625
Noel Lemon, gen. mgr.
(games played at Skelly Stadium)

VANCOUVER WHITECAPS
3683 E. Hastings St.
Vancouver, B.C. V5K 2B1
(604) 291-8811
Tony Waiters, gen. mgr.
(games played at Empire Stadium)

New York Cosmos

MAJOR INDOOR SOCCER LEAGUE

The Major Indoor Soccer League (MISL) has undergone realignment and changes in structure every year since its inception in 1977. It is currently divided into two divisions of seven teams each. Each team plays its divisional opponents five times during the season, as well as facing teams from the opposing division during the regular season. The top four teams from each division qualify for the playoffs. They meet in a best-of-three quarterfinals, with winners advancing to the semifinals for another best-of-three series. The winner of the championship series must take a best-of-five series.

MISL

Eastern Division	Western Division
Baltimore Blast	Chicago Horizons
Buffalo Stallions	Denver Avalanche
Cleveland Force	Kansas City Comets
New Jersey	Memphis Americans
New York Arrows	Phoenix Inferno
Philadelphia Fever	St. Louis Steamers
Pittsburgh Spirit	Wichita Wings

MAJOR INDOOR SOCCER LEAGUE
One Bala Cynwyd Plaza, Suite 415
Bala Cynwyd, PA 19004
(215) 667-8020
Earl Foreman, commissioner

BALTIMORE BLAST
201 W. Baltimore St.
Baltimore, MD 21201
(301) 528-0100
Mitch Burke, gen. mgr.
(games played at the Civic Center)

BUFFALO STALLIONS
Memorial Auditorium
Buffalo, NY 14202
(716) 845-6200
Sal DeRosa, gen. mgr.
(games played at Memorial Auditorium)

CHICAGO HORIZONS
780 W. Oakton
Des Plaines, IL 60018
(312) 439-2680
Jim Walker, gen. mgr.
(games played at Rosemont Horizon)

CLEVELAND FORCE
34555 Chagrin Blvd.
Moreland Hills, OH 44022
(216) 247-4740
Tim Pearson, gen. mgr.
(games played at Richfield Coliseum)

DENVER AVALANCHE
8000 E. Prentice St.
Bldg. D, Suite 7
Englewood, CO 80111
(303) 741-4625
Ron Maierhofer, gen. mgr.
(games played at McNichols Arena)

KANSAS CITY COMETS
Kemper Arena
1800 Genesse St.
Kansas City, MO 64102
(816) 421-7770
Tom Leiweke, gen. mgr.
(games played at Kemper Arena)

MEMPHIS AMERICANS
2500 Mt. Moriah
Perimeter Office Park D-316
Memphis, TN 38115
(901) 795-7113
Greg Hicks, gen. mgr.
(games played at Mid-South Coliseum)

NEW JERSEY
(team being formed during summer 1981)
The Meadowlands
East Rutherford, NJ 07073
Ed Tepper, mng. partner
(games played at Brendan Byrne Arena)

NEW YORK ARROWS
Hangar 6, Mitchell Field
Garden City, NY 11530
(516) 692-7769
Rich Altomare, gen. mgr.
(games played at Nassau Coliseum)

PHILADELPHIA FEVER
230 S. 15th St.
Philadelphia, PA 19103
(215) 546-5600
Mike Sauers, gen. mgr.
(games played at the Spectrum)

ST. LOUIS STEAMERS
212 N. Kirkwood
St. Louis, MO 63122
(314) 821-1111
Mike Sanger, gen. mgr.
(games played at the Checkerdome)

PHOENIX INFERNO
Civic Arena
Pittsburgh, PA 15219
(412) 434-8911
Chris Wright, gen. mgr.
(games played at Civic Arena)

WICHITA WINGS
114 S. Broadway
Wichita, KS 67202
(316) 262-3545
Bill Kentling, gen mgr.
(games played at Kansas Coliseum)

The Basics

NASL

Object of the game   To score the most points by getting the ball past the opponent's goal.

The Field   Soccer is played on a grassy field, approximately 120 yards long by 75 yards wide, as shown in diagram.

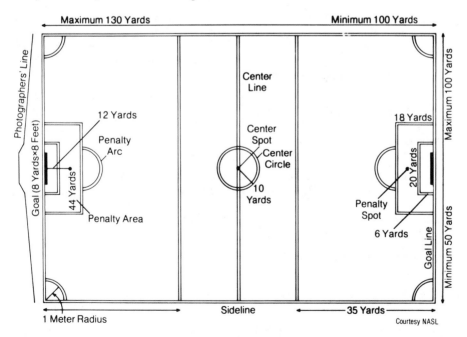

Courtesy NASL

Ball   Made of leather, 27 to 28 inches in circumference and weighing 14 to 16 ounces.

Players   Each team consists of 11 players, one of whom must be the goalkeeper. A maximum of 3 substitutes may be used.

Officials   One referee is appointed for each match. He is responsible for control of the game and for all final decisions. Two linesmen assist the referee by indicating offsides, when the ball is out of play, and which team is entitled to a corner kick or a throw-in.

Duration of game   A game consists of 2 periods, each one 45 minutes.

Rule 1   Start of play   The flip of a coin decides which team will kick off. Each team must stay on its own half of the field, and the defending players must be at least 10 yards from the ball until it is kicked.

Rule 2   Ball in or out of play   The ball is out of play when (1) it has completely crossed the goal line, or touch line, whether it is on the ground or in the air; or (2) the game has been stopped by the referee.

Rule 3   Scoring   A goal is scored when the entire ball has crossed the goal line between the goal posts and under the cross bar. A goal may not be scored directly from a kickoff.

Rule 4   Throw-in   When the ball crosses the touchline, it is put back in play from the spot where it went out, by a player from the team opposing the team that last touched it.

Rule 5   Penalty kick   A penalty kick is awarded to an opponent, to penalize fouls or misconduct. It is a direct kick taken at the penalty mark.

Rule 6   Offside   A player is offside if the player is nearer the opponents' goal line than the ball, unless that player is in his own half of the field of play, or unless at least two of his opponents are nearer to their own goal line than he is. A player is declared offside and penalized if, at the moment the ball touches, or is played by, one of his team, he is, in the opinion of the referee, interfering with play or with an opponent or is seeking to gain advantage by being in that position. **Note:** The new "blue line" concept allows an attacking player to come within 35 yards of his opponents' goal without being offside.

Rule 7   Free kick   A free kick, direct or indirect, may be awarded upon a penalty by opponent. A direct kick is one from which a goal can be scored directly; an indirect kick must be touched by a player other than the kicker before it can result in a goal.

MISL—INDOOR SOCCER

Object of the game   To score the most points by getting the ball past the opponent's goal.

Ball   Made of leather, 27 to 28 inches in circumference and weighing 14 to 16 ounces.

The field   The field is approximately 200 feet long and 85 feet wide, covered with artificial turf. Dasher boards, topped with clear plastic, surround the field.

Players   A goalkeeper and five field players per team are usually on the field together; 16 players may dress for a match.

Referee   One referee is on the field; this referee has total jurisdiction. An alternate supervises the clock, penalty box, and team benches; keeps a record of the game; and assists the referee.

Duration   The game is played in four 15-minute quarters, with two 3-minute intervals between the first and second quarters and between the third and fourth quarters.

Rule 1   Play   The visiting team kicks off at the start of the first and third quarters; the home team at the start of the second and fourth quarters. Play resumes (when the ball leaves the playing area) with a kick-in at the touchline where the ball left the playing area.

Rule 2   Substitution   Players enter and leave the game during play. An un-limited number of substitutions may be made during a match.

Rule 3   Scoring   Goals are scored when the ball is completely past the goal line.

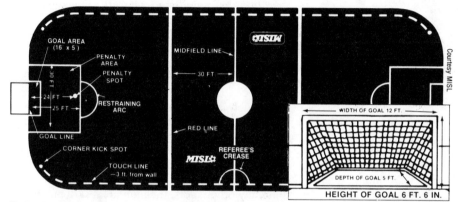

Rule 4   Penalties   A team plays with less than a full complement if the referee cites a player or a team for ungentlemanly conduct, delay of the game, or violent conduct, or when a penalty kick is awarded.

Rule 5   Minor infractions   The penalty for a minor infraction is an indirect kick, from which a goal cannot be scored directly.

Rule 6   Major infractions   The penalty for a major infraction is a direct kick for the opponent, from which a goal can be scored and—depending on the severity of the infraction—serving time in the penalty box.

Rule 7   Delay of game   A two-minute penalty may be called; if a player deliberately puts the ball over the perimeter and out of play; if a field player returns a kick back to his goalkeeper, and the goalkeeper handles the ball; if the defending players line up closer than 10 feet for direct and indirect kicks; or if a goalkeeper fails to give up the ball within 5 seconds.

Rule 8   Penalty kick   A kick is awarded to players when a defender intentionally commits an offense against an attacker in the penalty area. The penalty kick is taken from the penalty spot; all players except the designated kicker and the goalkeeper must stay outside the penalty area and arc.

Rule 9   Red-line violation   Occurs when a forward pass crosses both red lines in the air without being touched by another player. Play is resumed by awarding the opposing team possession and an indirect kick from the first red line.

Rule 10   Corner kicks   Corner kicks are taken when the ball has left the playing area between the two flags on the goal line and was last touched by a member of the defending team.

How to watch

New York Cosmos

with Ricky Davis

Because outdoor soccer differs so much from most other American sports—and because, unlike many sports, its rules have not been adapted to television broadcasting—watching soccer on TV demands careful attention by uninitiated viewers. Once viewers learn how to watch, though, they can look forward to seeing increasingly exciting soccer on American television.

"Soccer is at a bit of a disadvantage on television," says New York Cosmos midfielder Ricky Davis. "Because the playing field is so much larger than, say, that of football, there are fewer cameras covering the players. A player with great influence on a play may, at the moment, be 40 yards from the ball. The camera can't follow him and at the same time let viewers watch the player with the ball. In such cases, however, viewers *can* tell when a pass is a good one—first, if it is successful, and second, if it puts the player's team in an advantageous position."

In soccer, perhaps more than in any other sport, the individual skill and judgment of a player determine the outcome of the game, Davis says. Because there are no time-outs, the coach has little influence over the conduct of the game, once it begins. The players are left on their own; they must rely on individual initiative and communication with other members of their team. This style of play enables the viewer at home to see and appreciate all kinds of skills and styles among the players.

According to Davis, the most important skills of a forward are dribbling and shooting. The player must be able to cushion a caught ball—that is, relax his muscles so the ball will drop to the ground and not bounce, then retain possession until he gets a chance to shoot. The ability to feint (fake out another player by appearing to move in one direction, then moving in another) is just as important in soccer as it is in some other sports.

Of course, forwards must also be able to shoot. The best can use almost any part of their body to shoot—the instep of a foot, a heel, shin, knee, hip, or head. A forward's skill lies not only in how he shoots—how he strikes the ball, how hard the ball is propelled, and so forth—but also in his ability to maneuver himself into a position where he is open to take a shot—by, for instance, taking long runs or faking, whether he's trying to get control of the ball or is simply trying to create open space for a later opportunity.

When observing the midfielders, Davis feels, viewers should keep in mind that they are "like the quarterbacks in a football game; they are the ones who set the pace of a game, who decide how fast the game will be played, who determine how this will be done. If a team can win the game at midfield, it will do so by scoring. The thing to watch is not only the way they control the game, but also the choices they make in passes—whether backward or forward, to the right or the left side—and how well they control both themselves and the midfield." The ability to dribble well is a requirement for midfielders and forwards alike, Davis points out. Because of the one-on-one nature of soccer, each midfielder also has to defend himself and his teammates, as well as advance the ball toward the goal.

When watching the defense, the most important thing to remember is that each player is, for the most part, relying on instinctive reactions and individual skills. In American soccer, few set plays are agreed on beforehand by the entire team. Thus, the viewer is, in a sense, watching a series of two-player battles occurring simultaneously. "It's a lot like a guard covering a guard in basketball," Davis explains. "You see the forward dribbling and faking, trying to beat the defender; meanwhile, the defender is trying to get the forward to go a particular way—going into a tackle, contesting possession of the ball, using whatever skills the defending player has to keep that forward from getting the ball."

If the contest between defenders and midfielders makes for exciting soccer, so do the movements of the goalkeeper, who often has to make spectacular saves, hurling himself from one side of a goal to the other, trying to tip the ball wide of the goal, or lunging to keep a forward from taking a shot.

Although American soccer players use far fewer set plays than do football players, for example, soccer players do have favorite maneuvers that distinguish one team from another. Corner kicks, free kicks, running plays—all can vary, depending on the skills and preferences of individual teams. The Cosmos, for instance, use a corner kick in which one player kicks the ball to another on the near post who, in turn, deflects it with his head to a waiting player behind him. Other teams will maneuver their corners differently.

It is this potential variety that makes soccer one of the most unpredictable—and thus exciting—sports to watch. Because it can be played well by a great variety of athletes, with a wide range of physiques and styles, soccer constantly offers the viewer the chance to see something new.

Some things remain constant, though, Davis says. There are certain skills that distinguish the great player from the merely adequate. "The game requires a great deal of sensitivity and awareness of what is happening with other people. That's one of the reasons Pelé was a great player: at any given moment, he was aware of what was going on all over the field. He was a master of all the necessary skills; he could stop the ball with any part of his body, and do it with ease; he could make phenomenal passes at great distances and with great accuracy. Pelé knew what player was making a run without ever looking at him. He could sense when the other team was going to make a pass somewhere, and he would move to intercept it. "Pelé could remember when his right fullback had made a long run two or three times in a row, and would therefore be winded for the moment. He wouldn't send the player out on another run because that would wear him out; he would make the run himself, or make sure the ball got to someone who *could* make the run. Pelé could exploit a lot of little situations like that. It was almost as though he had a computer in his head. That kind of sensitivity can't be learned the way passing or dribbling can. But it's what makes a great soccer player."

Davis believes that, although most players can't be a Pelé, or play for the Cosmos, they can learn to improve their game by watching the professionals. The amateur who plays for recreation, for the fun of it, cannot, of course, perform like a pro; that player can, nevertheless, keep in the back of his mind the *way* a professional performs, and try to emulate it. "Watch a player take a diving header, hurling himself into the air and heading the ball into the corner. You probably won't be able to do that yourself, but you can remember that he did it, and some of how he did it. And the next time you play, lunge forward and hit the ball with your head. It may go into the goal, or it may go wide; but at least you will be learning more about the game—learning by watching, then doing."

Depending on whom they are watching, casual players will pick up different pointers. International matches—those played, for the most part, by Europeans and South Americans who have been refining their game for years—are more "efficient." That is, there's more emphasis on set plays and on technique. Because they are newer to the sport, Americans teams tend to be more exuberant and enthusiastic, less technical, more willing to experiment.

As soccer becomes more popular in the United States, attracting more athletes and better coaches, the game should become more complex. It should combine the best of Old World technical expertise with American persistence and determination—creating, for the spectator, a continuing source of excitement.

Main Events

NASL

SOCCER BOWL

Year	Score
1980	New York 3, Fort Lauderdale 0
1979	Vancouver 2, Tampa Bay 1
1978	New York 3, Tampa Bay 1
1977	New York 2, Seattle 1
1976	Toronto 3, Minnesota 0
1975	Tampa Bay 2, Portland 0

NASL MOST VALUABLE PLAYER
(chosen by a vote of NASL players)

Year	Winner
1980	Roger Davis, Seattle Sounders
1979	Johan Cruyff, Los Angeles Aztecs
1978	Mike Flanagan, New England Tea Men
1977	Franz Beckenbauer, New York Cosmos
1976	Pelé, New York Cosmos
1975	Steven David, Miami Toros

NASL LEADING SCORER

Year	Winner
1980	Giorgio Chinaglia, New York Cosmos
1979	Oscar Fabbiani, Tampa Bay Rowdies
1978	Giorgio Chinaglia, New York Cosmos
1977	Steven David, Los Angeles Aztecs
1976	Giorgio Chinaglia, New York Cosmos
1975	Steven David, Miami Toros

NASL GOAL OF THE YEAR
(chosen by ABC Sports)

Year	Winner
1980	Johan Cruyff, Washington Diplomats, July 16, against Seattle
1979	Oscar Fabbiani, Tampa Bay Rowdies, June 20, against Houston
1978	Giorgio Chinaglia, New York Cosmos, July 31, against Tampa Bay

MISL

1981 CHAMPIONSHIP GAME

New York 6, St. Louis 5

1980 CHAMPIONSHIP GAME

New York 7, Houston 4

1979 CHAMPIONSHIP SERIES

New York 14, Philadelphia 7
New York 9, Philadelphia 5

New York Arrows won best-of-three series, 2–0

MISL MOST VALUABLE PLAYER AWARD
(chosen by a panel of sportswriters)

1981	Steve Zungul, New York
1980	Steve Zungul, New York
1979	Steve Zungul, New York

MISL MOST VALUABLE PLAYER IN PLAYOFFS AWARD
(chosen by a panel of sportswriters covering the playoffs)

1981	Steve Zungul, New York
1980	Steve Zungul, New York
1979	Shep Messing, New York

MISL VELVET TOUCH AWARD
(awarded to player with the greatest number of points for the season)

1981	Steve Zungul, New York, 152
1980	Steve Zungul, New York, 136
1979	Fred Gregurev, Philadelphia, 74

ABC Sports

ABC Sports

All-Time Greats

Franz Beckenbauer
(Sept. 11, 1945–)

New York Cosmos

A skillful sweeper, Beckenbauer led the West Germans to the European Championship in 1972 and the World Cup in 1974 before being lured away by the North American Soccer League's New York Cosmos in 1977. Although the versatile Beckenbauer has played many positions during his soccer career, he clearly prefers that of sweeper, making it both an offensive and defensive position. In 1977, Beckenbauer played his first season in the United States, and was voted Most Valuable Player by the NASL.

Giorgio Chinaglia
(Jan. 24, 1947–)

New York Cosmos

Giorgio Chinaglia grew up and learned to play soccer in Wales. The Italian-born star probably would have made his career in Great Britain had it not been for a personality conflict with a coach early in Chinaglia's career. Chinaglia returned to Italy in the late 1960s, and there began his rise to international recognition. Arriving in the United States in the summer of 1976, he immediately left his mark on the NASL by finishing the season as the league's leading scorer even though he had missed the first month. Chinaglia has since led the NASL twice in season scoring.

Johan Cruyff
(Apr. 25, 1947–)

NASL Photo

A hard-shooting forward with great speed and control, Cruyff can score from almost any position. Almost singlehandedly, he has made Holland a world-class competitor; the team won the European Cup and went on to the World Cup finals. In 1973, Cruyff went to Spain and joined a losing Barcelona club; in a matter of months, the club had won the Spanish League championship. Moving to the United States in 1979, he was picked for all-star teams in each of his first two seasons.

Pelé (Edson Arantes do Nascimento)
(Oct. 23, 1940–)

Pelé, considered by many the greatest player in the history of soccer, was an international superstar whose popularity spanned two playing careers and several continents. He first gained international prominence in the World Cup finals of 1958, scoring two goals in his native Brazil's victory over Sweden. He was a passer with an uncanny sense of timing and a kicker with strength and precision. When Pelé joined the New York Cosmos in June 1975, professional soccer broke into the American sports consciousness. Although his career was often interrupted by injuries, Pelé, who retired in 1978, has had a tremendous impact on the game. His playing brought fans to games, hope to investors, and credibility to soccer as a major American sport.

Kyle Rote, Jr.
(Dec. 25, 1950–)

Rote, the son of All-Pro running back Kyle Rote, began his career, not surprisingly, as a football player. In 1968, he transferred from Oklahoma State to the University of the South, to gain more time for study and to play soccer for fun. A few years later, he was the NASL's leading scorer. Rote in his rookie year with the Dallas Tornado, was something of a pioneer of the sport, in that he was the first American-born soccer star in the United States. Although he had an impressive career in soccer, Rote may be better known for his victories on television's "Superstars," a series of athletic events between the world's top professional athletes.

Steve Zungul
(July 28, 1954–)

Zungul, a member of indoor soccer's New York Arrows, is by far the leading player on the MISL scene. The all-time scoring leader in the new league, he holds records in almost every offensive category. Zungul is the only soccer player in North America to score more than 100 goals in a season (108 in the 1980–81 season). He was named Most Valuable Player in the MISL for three consecutive years. One of the few true stars of the fledgling sport, Zungul scored at least 1 goal in 83 of the 90 games he played during three seasons with the league.

For the Record

NORTH AMERICAN SOCCER LEAGUE (NASL)

Individual Player

Most total points, season
79 Giorgio Chinaglia 1978

Most total points, game
12 Giorgio Chinaglia Aug. 10, 1976

Most goals, season
34 Giorgio Chinaglia 1978

Most consecutive games scoring a goal
10 Steve David 1977

Earliest goal
0:21 Willie Mfum (vs Rochester) Aug. 2, 1971

Shortest time to score two goals
0:41 Jeff Bourne (vs Houston) July 29, 1978

Most assists, season
30 Alan Hinton 1978

Goalkeeper

Fewest goals allowed, season
8 Bob Rigby 1973

Most goals allowed, season
70 Mark Poole 1979

Most saves, game
22 Mike Winter (vs Rochester) May 27, 1973

Most minutes played, season
2,798 Alan Mayer 1978

Team

Most games won, season
24 New York 1978, 1979; Vancouver 1978

Fewest games won, season
2 Dallas 1968; Baltimore 1969

Most goals scored, season
88 New York 1978

Most goals allowed, season
109 Dallas 1968 (32 games)

Greatest margin of victory
10 San Jose (0) at Detroit (10) July 12, 1978

MAJOR INDOOR SOCCER LEAGUE (MISL)

Individual Player

Most goals, game
7 Gene Geimer (vs Houston) Jan. 7, 1979
Steve Zungul (vs Chicago) Mar. 8, 1981

Most goals, season
108 Steve Zungul 1981

Most consecutive games scoring a goal
26 Steve Zungul 1980–81

Most points, game
9 Kai Haaskivi Dec. 23, 1979
Vic Davidson Dec. 10, 1980

Most points season
152 Steve Zungul 1981

ABC Sports

Goalkeeper

Most saves, game
44 Mike Hewitt (vs New York)
    Feb. 29, 1980
    Frank Bucci   (vs St. Louis)
    Nov. 22, 1980

Most saves, season
786   Slobo Ilijevski   1980–81

Most consecutive shutouts, season
2   Mike Dowler   1980–81

Team

Most wins, season
35   New York   1980–81

Most consecutive wins, season
19   New York   1980–81

Most losses, season
29   San Francisco   1980–81

Did you know?

1. Name the only club of the five original NASL franchises still in the league.

2. Who was the first American to win the title of leading goalkeeper in the NASL?

3. Name four NASL players known professionally by a single name.

4. In an NASL shootout, which team kicks first?

5. Name the NASL Rookie of the Year who left professional soccer for an NFL kicking career.

6. What teams captured the first and only NPSL and USA titles in 1967?

7. When was the first soccer match under lights played? Where?

8. Who holds the record for the most goals scored in a World Cup final? How many goals were made?

9. What happened in a 1964 match in Lima, Peru, after the Peruvian team had a goal disallowed?

10. What international match holds the record for the highest soccer attendance?

Answers: 1. Dallas Tornado; **2.** Bob Rigby, Philadelphia Atoms, 1973; **3.** Pele, Marinho, Artur, Humberto; **4.** The visiting team kicks first; **5.** Chris Bahr; **6.** Oakland Clippers (NPSL) and Los Angeles Wolves (USA); **7.** 1878, at Bramall Lane, Sheffield, between two teams from the Sheffield Association; **8.** Just Fontaine of France, 13 goals, 1958 World Cup finals; **9.** A riot occurred that left 301 dead; it is the worst disaster in soccer history; **10.** 1950 World Cup final, Brazil vs Uruguay at Rio de Janeiro; the attendance was 199,850.

Key Words

center to pass the ball from a wide position on the field into the penalty area.

charging legally pushing an opponent off balance by shoulder-to-shoulder contact.

clear a throw or kick by the defender in an attempt to get the ball away from the goal area.

crease the area in front of the goal, usually guarded by the goalkeeper.

cross the same type of pass as a center.

defender usually a defensive player who helps the goalkeeper defend the goal.

dribble advance the ball past defenders by a series of short taps with one or both feet.

forward usually an offensive player whose responsibility it is to set up and score goals.

goalkeeper the last line of defense; the only player allowed to use his hands within the field of play, but who is limited to using the hands only within the penalty area.

half-volley kicking the ball just as it rebounds from the ground.

hands intentionally touching the ball with the hands or arms; illegal.

heading scoring, passing, or controlling the ball by making contact with the head.

linkman another name for a midfielder.

lob a high, light kick taken on the volley, which lifts the ball over the heads of the opponents.

marking guarding an opponent.

midfielder both an offensive and a defensive player, primarily responsible for linking the forwards and the defenders.

obstructing preventing an opponent from going around a player by standing in his path.

offside the situation in which a player is nearer the opponents' goal line than the ball and in which fewer than two opponents are between the player and the goal line.

overlap the attacking play of a defender, going down the touchline past his own winger.

pitch the field of play.

save the goalkeeper blocking an attempted goal by catching the ball or deflecting it away from the goal.

screen retaining possession and protecting the ball by keeping one's body between the ball and the opponent.

shootout   the procedure used after an overtime period to break a tie; in a one-on-one situation, teams take five turns, attempting to kick the ball past the opposing goalkeeper and into the net.

sliding tackle   attempting to take the ball away from an opponent by sliding on the ground.

striker   a central forward player with a major responsibility for scoring goals.

sweeper   a defender who roams in front of or behind the defender line, trying to pick up stray passes.

trap   controlling a ball passed close to a player by means of the feet, thighs, or chest.

volley   kicking the ball while it is in flight.

wall pass   a pass to a teammate followed by a first-time return pass on the other side of the opponent; also called a "give and go."

wing   an area of the field near the touchline.

winger   a right or left outside forward.

MISL Photo

ABC Sports

16 SWIMMING & DIVING

Swimming

Benjamin Franklin liked to dive and experiment with different strokes and highly unusual methods and equipment. Once, he propelled himself through the water using wood paddles on his hands and feet; another time, he held the end of a kite while floating on his back, and thus was towed to the other side of a pond.

Presumably, racing followed soon after prehistoric people began swimming although swimmers then were, very likely, quite slow. The earliest known races were held in 36 B.C., when the Japanese Emperor Sugiu organized a meet for his warriors. It wasn't until the nineteenth century, though, that swimming became organized. Swim competitions were held first in England, next in Australia, and then in other countries. By 1850, indoor swimming "tanks" were commonplace in Great Britain, and by 1869 there were some 300 swimming clubs. The clubs joined to form the Amateur Swimming Association, which sponsored national competitions and named champions. During this period, the British relied on the breaststroke; though not fast, it was dependable, and it got Matthew Webb across the English channel while allowing him to sip coffee and eat along the way. The crawl was the next stroke to be introduced.

The origin of the overhand stroke, used to pull a swimmer through the water more efficiently than the breaststroke, is unknown. American Indians and natives of the South Seas were seen using it in the nineteenth century. Such swimmers as John Arthur Trudgen, Frederick Cavill, and Alick Wickham are credited with introducing the stroke to the Western world. Trudgen began to teach a form of the crawl after visiting the South Seas, where he had seen it. Although the overhand stroke still used the frog kick that was part of the breaststroke, it helped English swimmers break all the records for the breaststroke and the sidestroke.

Cavill and his six sons refined the "Trudgen stroke" by adapting the flutter kick to it and combining the stroke with the overhand. Cavill built the first swimming tanks in Australia and began to teach the new stroke, which became known as the "Australian crawl." Essentially, the Australian crawl is the same stroke seen today in national and international competitions. Also seen in modern competitions are such offshoots of the breaststroke as the backstroke and butterfly.

Swimming, introduced into the Olympics in 1896, has been a major part since. The Olympics are where the crème de la crème compete. Johnny Weissmuller and Ethel Lackie were the stars in 1924; the next Games, it was Buster Crabbe and Eleanor Holm. During the 1950s and 60s, it was Australia's Dawn Fraser and Shane Gould, and the United States' Don Schollander and Debbie Meyer. Then in 1972, it was Mark Spitz who won an unprecedented seven gold medals.

Today's stars are Tracy Caulkins, Cynthia Woodhead, and Brian Goodell. Their speeds would make Weissmuller's look as though he were treading water. At the same time, the training required today for a swimmer to shave a mere one one-hundredth of a second off a world record is far more extensive and rigorous than it was in Weissmuller's day. Weissmuller swam competitively until he was in his 30s, and Duke Kahanamoku was still competing at the age of 45; today, it is not uncommon for a swimmer to reach the peak of a career at the age of 14, and to retire from competition swimming before reaching the age of 20.

Great Moments

1828   The first indoor pool is built, in England.

1837   England holds the first organized swim meet in the Western world.

1846   Australia holds the first swimming championships of modern times.

1850   The Australian C. W. Wallis introduces the single overarm sidestroke; it becomes the dominant stroke in competitions for the next 50 years.

1858   Jo Bennet, an Australian, wins the first international swim race, beating Charles Stedman, of England.

1869   The first federation of swim clubs is organized, in England, and draws up the rules for amateur competition.

1873   John Trudgen introduces the crawl-arms-frog-kick stroke. The stroke later becomes the scissor kick, then the scissor and flutter.

1875   Matthew Webb becomes the first person to swim the English Channel.

1878 The first recognized world record is set: E. T. ("Stivie") Jones swims 100 yards in 68.5 seconds.

1886 The Amateur Swimming Association is founded, in Great Britain.

1902 With a mark of 59.6 seconds, Freddy Lane, of Australia, becomes the first man to swim 100 yards in less than a minute.

1903 Sydney Cavill, the son of Frederick Cavill, introduces the modern crawl into the United States.

1908 The Federation Internationale de Natation Amateur is formed at the Olympics held in London that year.

1912 The first Olympic women's event is won by Fanny Durack, of Australia; Harry Hebner, of the United States, uses a back crawl (alternating arms) in the Olympics for the first time.

1920 Ethelda Bleibtrey, of the United States, wins every women's swimming event in the Olympics that year.

1924 Sybil Bauer becomes the first woman to break an existing men's world record (for the 400-meter backstroke).

1926 Gertrude Ederle becomes the first woman to swim the English Channel, and in the process, beats all men's records. Erick Rademacher incorporates the butterfly-arms stroke with the breaststroke.

1932 Kusuo Kitamura, at age 14, becomes the youngest male swimmer to win an Olympic gold medal.

1964 An electronic touch-pad system is used in an Olympics for the first time. Don Schollander becomes the first swimmer to win four Olympic gold medals in one Olympic Games.

1965 Freestylers are no longer required to make *hand*-touch turns.

1968 Debbie Meyer becomes the first woman to win three individual Olympic gold medals.

1972 Mark Spitz wins seven Olympic gold medals, the most ever won in one Olympic Games.

The Setup

THE SETUP

Competitive swimming, a totally amateur sport, is governed in the United States by United States Swimming, Inc., which is affiliated with the Federation Internationale de Natation Amateur (FINA), an international organization. It is linked to FINA through United States Aquatic Sports, Inc. United States

Swimming is responsible for the administration of swimming in the United States. Collegiate competition is governed by the National Collegiate Athletic Association, which sets rules for intercollegiate competition.

UNITED STATES SWIMMING, INC.
1750 E. Boulder St.
Colorado Springs, CO 80909
Ray Essick, exec. dir.

FEDERATION INTERNATIONALE
  DE NATATION AMATEUR
Vojovde Misica #19-1 11040
Belgrade, Yugoslavia
Ante Lambasa, pres.

The Basics

SWIMMING

Object   To swim a prescribed distance in as short a time as possible, using one or more of the four approved swimming strokes: crawl, breaststroke, backstroke, or butterfly.

The pool   International swim meets are held in 50-meter (55-yard) rectangular pools; high school and college meets are usually held in pools about 23 meters (25 yards) long. In both cases, the pool's swimming lanes are marked by tiles on the floor of the pool and by ropes and floats on the water. Courses set in 50-meter pools are called "long courses"; those set in the smaller pools are "short courses."

Equipment   Ropes and floats are used to divide the pool into lanes.

Attire   A lightweight, approved swimsuit; a bathing cap is optional. A swimmer may wear goggles to protect the eyes from chlorine.

Officials   The following officials are required at all swim meets: a referee, starter, and course clerk; three timers per lane; two lane-place judges or two across-the-board judges; two scorers; a recorder; and two stroke-and-turn judges.

    The referee is the final authority.

    The starter controls the contestants until the race begins, making sure the swimmers are in the proper lanes. The starter and the referee are the sole judges of a valid start.

    The clerk of the course supervises entries in each event.

    The timers clock each race in which no electronic timing equipment is used; at least three timers per lane are required. Race results are never determined by one timer alone.

    Lane-place judges determine the end of a race, as do across-the-board judges.

    Scorers compile team scores, based on the results recorded.

    The recorder keeps complete records of the race results.

    Stroke-and-turn judges make sure each swimmer executes turns and strokes properly.

Rule 1   ***The start***   For all strokes except the backstroke, swimmers step onto starting blocks when the referee calls them. When the starter says, "On your marks," the swimmers go into their starting positions. When they are motionless, the starter gives the signal for the start of the race. In the backstroke, swimmers get in the water first and hold the side of the pool with their hands, pressing their feet against the pool wall. When the starter gives the signal, they push themselves off and the race begins.

Rule 2   False start   A false start occurs when a swimmer starts before the signal. The swimmer who commits three false starts is disqualified.

Rule 3   Events   Swimming-meet events vary according to the level of competition. International and Olympic meets include: the 100-meter freestyle (in which any stroke may be used, but where the crawl is most often used because it is the fastest); the 200-meter freestyle; the 400-meter freestyle; the 800-meter freestyle (usually for women); the 1,500-meter freestyle (usually men); the 100-meter breaststroke; the 200-meter breaststroke; the 100-meter butterfly; the 200-meter butterfly; the 100-meter backstroke; the 200-meter backstroke; the 400-meter individual medley (in which a swimmer uses all four basic strokes, for 100 meters each); the 400-meter relay (women); the 800-meter relay (men); and the 400-meter medley relay.

Rule 4   Disqualification   A competitor may be disqualified from a race for: committing three false starts; swimming outside the proper lane; failing to appear for the start of a race when called; walking on the floor of the pool; or entering a race that is already in progress.

How to watch

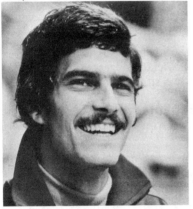

ABC Sports

with Mark Spitz

The most important factors in any swimming competition aren't style and strategy, they're speed, strength, and good mental preparation. So says Mark Spitz, the only swimmer in history to win seven gold medals in one Olympics (1972). He also won three gold medals in the 1968 Games, in Mexico City.

In swimming meets, as in track and field meets, athletes must be in peak physical and mental condition. This means that training methods and coaching are crucial, just as they are in track and field. "The swimmers who come from colleges with good coaches and facilities have the edge," says Spitz. "In the 1980–81 season, it was the University of Texas and Florida State. Texas won the NCAA championships, and the Florida swimmers did well."

To most spectators, "the only way to tell how a swimmer is doing in short races is whether the swimmer is in the lead. Tactics play a bigger part in the longer races." The most important thing for a swimmer to remember is, learn from mistakes. The second most important thing is to remember *what* you've learned, and apply it in the next race. "A case in point is my swimming in the Olympics. I made a lot of mistakes.

If I had to do it over again, I'd do it differently. For instance, in the hundred-meter freestyle, when I went out too fast. I was just lucky enough that I went out too fast, I at least had enough speed out in front to get in the lead far enough so that when I died, they had to cover more real estate to catch me. I was lucky the wall came up quick enough. If I'd gone out slower, I might have had a little more energy to bring it home a little quicker toward the end of the race.

"We're talking about pacing out a tenth of a second, but it could have made a difference of picking up an extra three- or four-tenths on the leg home, in which case the overall result would have been even faster."

According to Spitz, an important thing for a swimmer to do—and again, this is something the spectator won't be able to see—is review all his or her races before the next one comes up. "The mark of a champion is the ability to analyze what he did wrong even in a race he won. Most swimmers review what went wrong when they lose, but hardly anybody does it when they win. I always did it because I think it's the way to stay on top."

Physical training techniques for swimming have evolved since about 1970. Now we include weight training, something only the Europeans did before. This, Spitz says, has made a difference in the speed and strength of the American swimmer. "When I was training for the Olympics, we swam a lot. All we had then were rudimentary dry-land training exercises."

Swimmers, like track athletes, become specialists, Spitz says. "Usually, breaststrokers are not good freestylers because of the kind of muscle groups needed to develop the breaststroke. But backstrokers can be freestylers and butterfliers. A good freestyler is not necessarily a good butterfly swimmer or a good backstroker."

Some of the mistakes that can hurt a swimmer in a race can be picked up by the trained eye. "For instance, breathing excessively in the butterfly slows a swimmer down," Spitz says. "Breathing every other stroke is better. Also, a swimmer should avoid breathing off a turn; that's when there's a big wave caused by all the swimmers going down on the the first lap. It's better to push off from a turn underwater. That way, the swimmer can avoid the big swell."

Main Events

MAIN EVENTS

Olympics

MEN'S 100-METER FREESTYLE	MEN'S 200-METER FREESTYLE
1980 Jorg Woithe (50.40), GDR*	1980 Sergei Kopliakov (1:49.81), USSR
1976 Jim Montgomery (49.99), USA	1976 Bruce Furniss (1:50.29), USA
1972 Mark Spitz (51.2), USA	1972 Mark Spitz (1:52.8), USA
1968 Mike Wenden (52.2), Australia	1968 Mike Wenden (1:55.2), Australia

German Democratic Republic (East Germany).

MEN'S
400-METER FREESTYLE

1980	Vladimir Salnikov (3:51.31), USSR	
1976	Brian Goodell (3:51.93), USA	
1972	Brad Cooper (4:00.3), Australia	
1968	Mike Burton (4:09.0), USA	

MEN'S
1,500-METER FREESTYLE

1980	Vladimir Salnikov (14:58.27), USSR
1976	Brian Goodell (15:02.40), USA
1972	Mike Burton (15:52.6), USA
1968	Mike Burton (16:38.9), USA

MEN'S
100-METER BACKSTROKE

1980	Bengt Baron (56.53), Sweden
1976	John Naber (55.49), USA
1972	Roland Matthes (56.6), GDR
1968	Roland Matthes (58.7), GDR

MEN'S
200-METER BACKSTROKE

1980	Sandor Wladar (2:01.93), Hungary
1976	John Naber (1:59.19), USA
1972	Roland Matthes (2:02.8), GDR
1968	Roland Matthes (2:09.6), GDR

MEN'S
100-METER BREASTSTROKE

1980	Duncan Goodhew (1:03.34), UK
1976	John Hencken (1:03.11), USA
1972	Nobutaka Taguchi (1:04.9), Japan
1968	Don McKenzie (1:07.7), USA

MEN'S
200-METER BREASTSTROKE

1980	Robertas Zulpa (2:15.85), USSR
1976	David Wilkie (2:15.11), UK
1972	John Hencken (2:21.5), USA
1968	Felipe Munoz (2:28.7), Mexico

MEN'S
100-METER BUTTERFLY

1980	Par Arvidsson (54.92), Sweden
1976	Matt Vogel (54.35), USA
1972	Mark Spitz (54.3), USA
1968	Doug Russell (55.9), USA

MEN'S
200-METER BUTTERFLY

1980	Sergei Fesenko (1:59.76), USSR
1976	Mike Bruner (1:59.23), USA
1972	Mark Spitz (2:00.7), USA
1968	Carl Robie (2:08.7), USA

MEN'S
200-METER INDIVIDUAL MEDLEY

1976	(event not held)
1972	Gunnar Larsson (2:07.2), Sweden
1968	Charles Hickcox (2:12.0), USA

MEN'S
400-METER INDIVIDUAL MEDLEY

1980	Aleksandr Sidorenko (4:22.89), USSR
1976	Rod Strachan (4:23.68), USA
1972	Gunnar Larsson (4:32.0), Sweden
1968	Charles Hickcox (4:48.4), USA

MEN'S
400-METER MEDLEY RELAY

1980	Australia (3:45.7)
1976	USA (3:42.22)
1972	USA (3:48.2)
1968	USA (3:54.9)

MEN'S
800-METER FREESTYLE RELAY

1980	USSR (7:23.5)
1976	USA (7:23.22)
1972	USA (7:38.8)
1968	USA (7:52.3)

WOMEN'S
100-METER FREESTYLE

1980	Barbara Krause (54.79), GDR
1976	Kornelia Ender (55.65), GDR
1972	Sandra Neilson (58.6), USA
1968	Jan Henne (1:00.0), USA

WOMEN'S
200-METER FREESTYLE

1980	Barbara Krause (1:58.33), GDR
1976	Kornelia Ender (1:59.26), GDR
1972	Shane Gould (2:03.6), Australia
1968	Debbie Meyer (2:10.5), USA

WOMEN'S
400-METER FREESTYLE

1980	Ines Diers (4:08.76), GDR
1976	Petra Thumer (4:09.89), GDR
1972	Shane Gould (4:19.0), Australia
1968	Debbie Meyer (4:31.8), USA

WOMEN'S
800-METER FREESTYLE

1980	Michelle Ford (8:28.9), Australia
1976	Petra Thumer (8:37.14), GDR
1972	Keena Rothhammer (8:53.7), USA
1968	Debbie Meyer (9:24.0), USA

WOMEN'S
100-METER BACKSTROKE

1980	Rica Reinisch (1:00.86), GDR
1976	Ulrike Richter (1:01.83), GDR
1972	Melissa Belote (1:05.8), USA
1968	Kaye Hall (1:06.2), USA

WOMEN'S
200-METER BACKSTROKE

1980	Rica Reinisch (2:11.77), GDR
1976	Ulrike Richter (2:13.43), GDR
1972	Melissa Belote (2:19.2), USA
1968	Pokey Watson (2:24.8), USA

WOMEN'S
100-METER BREASTSTROKE

1980	Ute Geweniger (1:10.22), GDR
1976	Hannelore Anke (1:10.86), GDR
1972	Cathy Carr (1:13.6), USA
1968	Djurdjica Bjedov (1:15.8), Yugoslavia

WOMEN'S
200-METER BREASTSTROKE

1980	Lina Kachushite, (2:29.54), USSR
1976	Marina Koshevaia (2:33.35), USSR
1972	Beverly Whitfield (2:41.7), Australia
1968	Sharon Wichman (2:44.4), USA

WOMEN'S
100-METER BUTTERFLY

1980	Caren Metschuck (1:00.42), GDR
1976	Kornelia Ender (1:00.13), GDR
1972	Mayumi Aoki (1:03.3), Japan
1968	Lynn McClements (1:05.5), Australia

WOMEN'S
200-METER BUTTERFLY

1980	Ines Geissler (2:10.44), GDR*
1976	Andrea Pollack (2:11.41), GDR
1972	Karen Moe (2:15.6), USA
1968	Ada Kok (2:24.7), Netherlands

WOMEN'S
200-METER INDIVIDUAL MEDLEY

1976	(discontinued)
1972	Shane Gould (2:23.1), Australia
1968	Claudia Kolb (2:24.7), USA

WOMEN'S
400-METER MEDLEY RELAY

1980	GDR (4:06.67)
1976	GDR (4:07.95)
1972	USA (4:20.7)
1968	USA (4:28.3)

WOMEN'S
400-METER FREESTYLE RELAY

1980	GDR (3:42.71)
1976	USA (3:44.82)
1972	USA (3:55.2)
1968	USA (4:02.5)

WOMEN'S
400-METER INDIVIDUAL MEDLEY

1980	Petra Schneider (4:36.29), GDR
1976	Ulrike Tauber (4:42.27), GDR
1972	Gail Neall (5:03), Australia
1968	Claudia Kolb (5:08.5), USA

WORLD AQUATIC CHAMPIONSHIPS

MEN'S
100-METER FREESTYLE

1978	David McCagg (50.24)
1975	Andy Coan (51.25)
1973	James Montgomery (51.708)

MEN'S
200-METER FREESTYLE

1978	Bill Forrester (1:51.02)
1975	Tim Shaw (1:51.04)
1973	James Montgomery (1:53.027)

MEN'S
400-METER FREESTYLE

| 1978 | Vladimir Salnikov (3:51.94) |
| 1975 | Tim Shaw (3:54.88) |

MEN'S
400-METER FREESTYLE

1978	Vladimir Salnikov (3:51.94)
1975	Tim Shaw (3:54.88)
1973	Rick DeMont (3:58.188)

MEN'S
1,500-METER FREESTYLE

1978	Vladimir Salnikov (15:03.99)
1975	Tim Shaw (15:28.92)
1973	Stephen Holland (15:31.859)

MEN'S
100-METER BACKSTROKE

1978	Robert Jackson (56.36)
1975	Roland Matthes (58.15)
1973	Roland Matthes (57.477)

MEN'S
200-METER BACKSTROKE

1978	Jesse Vassallo (2:02.16)
1975	Zoltan Verraszto (2:05.05)
1973	Roland Matthes (2:01.878)

MEN'S
100-METER BREASTSTROKE

1978	Walter Kusch (1:03.56)
1975	David Wilkie (1:04.26)
1973	John Hencken (1:04.023)

MEN'S
200-METER BREASTSTROKE

1978 Nick Nevid (2:18.37)
1975 David Wilkie (2:18.23)
1973 David Wilkie (2:19.285)

MEN'S
100-METER BUTTERFLY

1978 Joe Bottom (54.3)
1975 Greg Jagenburg (55.63)
1973 Bruce Robertson (55.69)

MEN'S
200-METER BUTTERFLY

1978 Mike Bruner (1:59.38)
1975 Bill Forrester (2:01.95)
1973 Robin Backhaus (2:03.325)

MEN'S
200-METER INDIVIDUAL MEDLEY

1978 Graham Smith (2:03.65)
1975 Andra Hargitay (2:07.72)
1973 Gunnar Larsson (2:08.36)

MEN'S
400-METER INDIVIDUAL MEDLEY

1978 Jesse Vassallo (4:20.05)
1975 Andra Hargitay (4:32.57)
1973 Andra Hargitay (4:31.116)

MEN'S
400-METER MEDLEY RELAY

1978 USA (3:44.63)
1975 USA (3:49)
1973 USA (3:49.491)

MEN'S
400-METER FREESTYLE RELAY

1978 USA (3:19.74)
1975 USA (3:24.85)
1973 USA (3:27.183)

MEN'S
800-METER FREESTYLE RELAY

1978 USA (7:20.82)
1975 FRG* (7:39.44)
1973 USA (7:33.221)

WOMEN'S
100-METER FREESTYLE

1978 Barbara Krause (55.68)
1975 Kornelia Ender (56.5)
1973 Kornelia Ender (57.542)

WOMEN'S
200-METER FREESTYLE

1978 Cynthia Woodhead (1:58.53)
1975 Shirley Babashoff (2:02.5)
1973 Keena Rothhammer
       (2:04.999)

WOMEN'S
400-METER FREESTYLE

1978 Tracey Wickham (4:06.28)
1975 Shirley Babashoff (4:16.87)
1973 Heather Greenwood
       (4:20.287)

WOMEN'S
800-METER FREESTYLE

1978 Tracey Wickham (8:24.94)
1975 Jenny Turrall (8:44.75)
1973 Novella Calligaris (8:52.973)

WOMEN'S
100-METER BACKSTROKE

1978 Linda Jezek (1:02.55)
1975 Ulrike Richter (1:03.3)
1973 Ulrike Richter (1:05.427)

WOMEN'S
200-METER BACKSTROKE

1978 Linda Jezek (2:11.93)
1975 Birgit Treiber (2:15.46)
1973 Melissa Belote (2:20.552)

WOMEN'S
100-METER BREASTSTROKE

1978 Julie Bogdanova (1:10.31)
1975 Hannelore Anke (1:12.72)
1973 Renate Vogel (1:13.748)

*German Democratic Republic (East Germany).
*Federal Republic of Germany (West Germany).

WOMEN'S
200-METER BREASTSTROKE

1978   Lina Kachushite (2:31.42)
1975   Hannelore Anke (2:37.25)
1973   Renate Vogel (2:40.012)

WOMEN'S
200-METER INDIVIDUAL MEDLEY

1978   Tracy Caulkins (2:14.07)
1975   Kathy Heddy (2:19.80)
1973   Andrea Huebner (2:20.518)

WOMEN'S
100-METER BUTTERFLY

1978   Joan Pennington (1:00.2)
1975   Kornelia Ender (1:01.24)
1973   Kornelia Ender (1:02.539)

WOMEN'S
400-METER INDIVIDUAL MEDLEY

1978   Tracy Caulkins (4:40.83)
1975   Ulrike Tauber (4:52.76)
1973   Gudren Wegner (4:57.51)

WOMEN'S
200-METER BUTTERFLY

1978   Tracy Caulkins (2:09.87)
1975   Rosemarie Kother (2:13.82)
1973   Rosemarie Kother
        (2:13.766)

WOMEN'S
400-METER MEDLEY RELAY

1978   USA (4:14.55)
1975   GDR (4:14.74)
1973   GDR (4:16.844)

WOMEN'S
400-METER FREESTYLE RELAY

1978   USA (3:44.82)
1975   GDR (3:49.37)
1973   GDR (3:52.452)

NCAA Championships

50-YARD FREESTYLE

1981   Chris Kirchner (19.66)
1980   Andrew Coan (19.92)
1979   Ambrose Gaines (19.99)
1978   Andrew Coan (20.29)
1977   Joe Bottom (19.75)

500-YARD FREESTYLE

1981   Doug Towne (4:16.54)
1980   Brian Goodell (4:17.81)
1979   Brian Goodell (4:16.43)
1978   Brian Goodell (4:18.05)
1977   Tim Shaw (4:17.39)

100-YARD FREESTYLE

1981   Ambrose Gaines (42.38)
1980   Ambrose Gaines (43.36)
1979   Andrew Coan (43.42)
1978   Andrew Coan (44.1)
1977   David Fairbank (43.68)

1,650-YARD FREESTYLE

1981   Rafael Escalas (14.28.3)
1980   Brian Goodell (14.54.07)
1979   Brian Goodell (14:54.13)
1978   Brian Goodell (14:55.53)
1977   Keith Converse (14:57.3)

200-YARD FREESTYLE

1981   Ambrose Gaines (1:33.91)
1980   Ambrose Gaines (1:34.57)
1979   Andrew Coan (1:35.62)
1978   Bruce Furniss (1:37.02)
1977   Bruce Furniss (1:36.16)

100-YARD BACKSTROKE

1981   Clay Britt (49.08)
1980   Clay Britt (49.52)
1979   Carlos Berrocal (49.71)
1978   Robert Jackson (49.88)
1977   John Naber (49.36)

200-YARD BACKSTROKE

1981 Wade Flemons (1:46.30)
1980 James Fowler (1:47.76)
1979 Peter Rocca (1:46.21)
1978 Peter Rocca (1:47.48)
1977 John Naber (1:46.09)

100-YARD BREASTSTROKE

1981 Steve Lundquist (52.93)
√1980 Steve Lundquist (53.59)
1979 D. Graham Smith (54.91)
1978 Scott Spann (56.62)
1977 D. Graham Smith (55.1)

200-YARD SURFACE BREASTSTROKE

1981 Steve Lundquist (1:55.01)
1980 William Barrett (1:58.43)
1979 D. Graham Smith (2:00.37)
1978 D. Graham Smith (2:00.05)
1977 D. Graham Smith (2:00.05)
1976 David Wilkie (2:00.74)

100-YARD BUTTERFLY

1981 Scott Spann (47.22)
1980 Par Arvidsson (47.36)
1979 Par Arvidsson (47.76)
1978 Greg Jagenburg (48.77)
1977 Joe Bottom (47.77)

200-YARD BUTTERFLY

1981 Craig Beardsley (1:44.15)
1980 Par Arvidsson (1:44.43)
1979 Par Arvidsson (1:45.53)
1978 Greg Jagenburg (1:46.01)
1977 Michael Bruner (1:45.27)
1976 Steve Gregg (1:47.00)

400-YARD FREESTYLE RELAY

1981 Texas (2:54.84)
1980 Auburn (2:55.16)
1979 Tennessee (2:54.74)
1978 Tennessee (2:55.66)
1977 Southern Cal (2:55.28)

800-YARD FREESTYLE RELAY

1981 Florida (6:27.02)
1980 Auburn (6:28.07)
1979 Florida (6:28.01)
1978 Auburn (6:31.93)
1977 Southern Cal (6:28.01)

200-YARD INDIVIDUAL MEDLEY

1981 William Barrett (1:45.01)
1980 William Barrett (1:46.25)
1979 D. Graham Smith (1:48.44)
1978 Scott Spann (1:48.69)
1977 Scott Spann (1:48.69)

400-YARD INDIVIDUAL MEDLEY

1981 Jesse Vassallo (3:48.16)
1980 Brian Goodell (3:51.38)
1979 Brian Goodell (3:50.8)
1978 Brian Goodell (3:53.61)
1977 Rod Strachan (3:54.76)

400-YARD MEDLEY RELAY

1981 Texas (3:12.93)
1980 Texas (3:14.59)
1979 Cal–Berkeley (3:15.22)
1978 Cal–Berkeley (3:18.26)
1977 Indiana (3:17.14)

All-Time Greats

Clarence ("Buster") Crabbe
(Feb. 7, 1908–)

Buster Crabbe—along with Esther Williams and a few other swimming stars—became a movie star, playing such roles as Flash Gordon, Buck Rogers, Captain Gallant, and Tarzan of the Apes. Born in Hawaii, he moved with his family to California. As a student at the University of Southern California, Crabbe won a place on the U.S. Olympic team in 1928. At the Olympics, he won a gold medal in the 400-meter and a bronze in the 1,500-meter. Crabbe held 11 U.S. records, including the one-mile outdoors record.

Gertrude Ederle
(Oct. 23, 1906–)

The Olympic medalist Gertrude Ederle achieved worldwide fame when, in 1926, she became the first woman to swim the English Channel, covering the distance in 14 hours and 39 minutes and setting a world record at the same time (the men's record included). During her career, Ederle set nine world records. In the 1924 Olympics, she won bronze medals in the 100-meter freestyle and the 400-meter freestyle and shared the gold medal won by the American freestyle relay team.

Shane Gould
(Nov. 23, 1956–)

Shane Gould stopped swimming when she was only 16. In her short career, however, she set world records and was a five-time Olympic medalist. At the 1972 Games, she won gold medals in the 200-meter medley, the 400-meter freestyle, and the 200-meter freestyle, winning a bronze in the 100-meter freestyle and a silver in the 800-meter freestyle. Between 1971 and 1973, Gould, an Australian, set 11 world records and became the first woman to swim 1,500 meters in less than 17 minutes.

Photos courtesy International Swimming Hall of Fame

Don Schollander
(Apr. 30, 1946–)

Schollander became the first swimmer to win four gold medals at one Olympic Games, winning the 100-meter, the 400-meter (setting a new world record of 4 minutes 12.2 seconds), and taking golds in the 400-meter and 800-meter freestyle relays. Schollander did not repeat his success at the 1968 Mexico Games; he qualified only for the 200-meter freestyle event. But in it he broke his own world record, swimming the 200-meter course in 1 minute 54.3 seconds. At the 1967 Pan American Games, Schollander won the 200-meter event again and was a member of the American freestyle relay team, which set eight world records.

Mark Spitz
(Feb. 10, 1950–)

Mark Spitz became the first and only athlete to win seven gold medals at one Olympics. At the 1972 Games in Munich, he won gold medals in the 100-meter and 200-meter freestyle races, the 100-meter and 200-meter butterfly races, and in three United States team relay races. He was coached in college by James ("Doc") Counsilman and swam for four national championship teams at Indiana University. His confidence sometimes made Spitz unpopular with fellow swimmers in the early years of his career, but his achievements proved that he had good reason to feel self-assured. Spitz won five titles at the 1967 Pan American Games, as well as a bronze medal at the 1968 Olympics. His accomplishment at the 1972 Olympics, however, makes his other credentials pale by comparison. Spitz retired from competition after the 1972 Olympics and is now involved in business enterprises.

Johnny Weissmuller
(June 2, 1904–)

Most people today remember Weissmuller as Tarzan; but to those who followed swimming in the 1920s, he was the greatest swimmer who ever lived. During his competitive swimming career, the native Chicagoan won five Olympic gold medals and a bronze, and set 24 world records. Weissmuller's success was often attributed to his unique stroke, which involved a deep flutter kick, turning his head only when he wanted to breathe, and a "pull-push arm stroke." At the 1924 Games, Weissmuller, then 19, won gold medals in the 100- and 400-meter freestyle events. (He had been only 17 when he set his first world records, swimming 300 yards and 300 meters in 3:16.6 and 3:52.2, respectively.) Also that year, Weissmuller broke the one-minute barrier for 100 meters, swimming the distance in 58.6 seconds. Weissmuller set his last record in 1941 when he swam 440 yards in 4 minutes and 52 seconds. At the age of 36, he joined Billy Rose's World's Fair Aquacade. Later, after a stint selling bathing suits, he went into movies, playing Tarzan.

International Swimming Hall of Fame
1 Hall of Fame Dr.
Ft. Lauderdale, FL 33316
(305) 462-6536

Members of the Hall of Fame are:

1965
Buster Crabbe
C. M. ("Charlie") Daniels
Gertrude Ederle
Dawn Fraser
Beulah Gundling
Jamison Handy
Duke Kahanamoku
Adolph Kiefer
Robert J. H. Kiphuth
Kusuo Kitamura
Commodore Longfellow
Pat McCormick
Matt Mann
Pam Morris
R. Max Ritter
Murray Rose
Don Schollander
Matthew Webb
Johnny Weissmuller
Al White
Katherine Rawls

1966
Dave Armbruster
Bill Bachrach
Arne Borg
Ernst Brandsten
Steve Clark
Georgia Coleman
Ann Curtis
Pete Desjardins
Alan Ford
Alfred Hajos
Eleanor Holm
Ragnhild Hveger
Edward T. Kennedy
Helene Madison
Shelley Mann
Jack Medica
Wally O'Connor
Mike Peppe
Clarence Pinkston
Wally Ris
Soichi Sakamoto
Bill Smith
Joe Verdeur
Chris Von Saltza
Esther Williams

1967
Miller Anderson
Carl Bauer
Sybil Bauer
Sir Frank Beaurepaire
Ethelda Bleibtrey
Ma Braun
Teddy Cann
Jacques Yves Cousteau
Fanny Durack
Hironoshin Furuhashi
L. deB. Handley
Beth Kaufman
Al Neuschaefer
Martha Norelius
Betty Becker Pinkston
Paul Radmilovic
Aileen Riggin
Norman Ross
The Spence brothers

1968
Jeff Farrell
Benjamin Franklin
Zoltan de Halmay
Harry Hebner
George Hodgson
John Jarvis
Warren Kealoha
George Kojac
Sammy Lee
Hendrika Mastenbroek
Emil Rausch
E. Carroll Schaeffer
Dorothy Poynton
David Theile
Yoshiyuki Tsuruta

1969
Greta Andersen
Fred Cady
Donna de Varona
Vickie Draves
Stephen Hunyadfi
Barney Kieran
Ethel Lackie
Freddy Lane
Michael McDermott
James Nemeth
Al Patnik
Henry Taylor

1970
Walter Bathe
Cavill family
Florence Chadwick
Jack Cody
Willy den Ouden
Olga Dorfner
Claire Galligan
Richard R. Hough
Jimmy McLane
Henri Padou
Charlie Sava
Robert Webster

1971
George Corsan, Sr.
Ray Daughters
Dick Degener
Jennie Fletcher
Budd Goodwin
John Higgins
Martin Homonnay
Cor Kint
Konrads Kids
Helen Meany
Mike Troy
Bill Yorzyk

1972
Stan Brauninger
Andrew M. Charlton
Earl Clark
Lorraine Crapp
Ford Konno
Mario Majoni
Erich Rademacher
Sharon Stouder
Helen Wainwright

1973
Greta Brandsten
Bruce Harlan
Jon Henricks
Walter Laufer
John Marshall
Eva & Ilona Novak
Yoshi Oyakawa
Jan Stender
Nel Van Vliet

1974
Bert Cummins
Charlotte Epstein
Harold Fern
Ellen Fullard-Leo
William Henry
Annette Kellerman
Fred Luehring
John Trudgen
Alick Wickham

1975
George Breen
David Browning
Karen Harup
Claudia Kolb
Ingrid Kramer
Frank McKinney
Keo Nakama
Tom Robinson
Mina Wylie

1976
Catie Ball
Joaquin Capilla
Forbes Carlile
James Counsilman
Marjorie Gestring
Dezso Gyarmati
Charles Hickcox
Ada Kok
Charles McCaffree

Carl Robie
Sylvia Ruuska
Roy Saari
Charles Silvia
Eva Szekely
Alberto Zorrilla

1977
Mike Burton
Sherman Chavoor
Peter Daland
Shane Gould
George Haines
Alex Jany
Chet Jastremski
Debbie Meyer
Galina Prozumenshikova
Mickey Riley
Mark Spitz

1978
Istvan Barany
Lynn Burke
Cathy Ferguson
Peter Fick
Ralph Flanagan
Valerie Gyenge
Oliver Halassy
Micki King
Masaji Kiyokawa
Walt Schlueter
Gary Tobian
Kay Vilen

1979
Kay Curtis
John Devitt
Kaye Hall
Jan Henne
Harold Henning
Gunnar Larsson
Hideko Maehata
Paula Jean Myers
Dick Smith
Harold ("Dutch") Smith
Allen Stack
Don Talbot
Michael Wenden

1980
Kevin Berry
Marie Braun
Robert Clotworthy
Thomas K. Cureton, Jr.
Juno Stover Irwin
Mary Kok
Lance Larson
Hakan Malmrot
Alban Minville
Phil Moriarty
Karen Muir
Heidi O'Rourke
Clarke Scholes
Elaine Tanner
George Wilkinson

For the Record

Men's 100-meter freestyle
49.44   Jonty Skinner   1976

Men's 200-meter freestyle
1:49.16   Ambrose Gaines   1980

Men's 400-meter freestyle
3:50.49   Peter Szmidt   1980

Men's 800-meter freestyle
7:65.49   Vladimir Salnikov   1979

Men's 1,500-meter freestyle
14:58.27   Vladimir Salnikov   1980

Men's 100-meter backstroke
55.49   John Naber   1976

Men's 200-meter backstroke
1:59.19   John Naber   1976

Men's 100-meter breaststroke
1:02.86   Gerald Moerken   1977

Men's 200-meter breaststroke
2:15.11   David Wilkie   1976

Men's 100-meter butterfly
54.15   Par Arvidsson   1980

Men's 200-meter butterfly
1:58.21   Craig Beardsley   1980

Men's 200-meter individual medley
2:03.24   William M. Barrett   1980

Men's 400-meter individual medley
4:20.05   Jesse Vassallo   1978

Men's 400-meter freestyle relay
3:19.74   USA national team   1978

Men's 800-meter freestyle relay
7:20.82   USA national team   1978

Men's 400-meter medley relay
3:42.22   USA national team   1976

Women's 100-meter freestyle
54.79   Barbara Krause   1980

Women's 200-meter freestyle
1:58.23   Cynthia Woodhead   1979

Women's 400-meter freestyle
4:06.28   Tracey Wickham   1978

Women's 800-meter freestyle
8:24.62   Tracey Wickham   1978

Women's 1,500-meter freestyle
16:04.49   Kimberly Linehan   1979

Women's 100-meter backstroke
1:00.86   Rica Reinisch   1980

Women's 200-meter backstroke
2:11.77   Rica Reinisch   1980

Women's 100-meter breaststroke
1:09.52   Ute Geweniger   1980

Women's 200-meter breaststroke
2:28.36   Lina Kachushite   1979

Women's 100-meter butterfly
59.26   Mary T. Meagher   1980

Women's 200-meter butterfly
2:06.37   Mary T. Meagher   1980

Women's 200-meter individual medley
2:13.00   Petra Schneider   1980

Women's 400-meter individual medley
4:36.29   Petra Schneider   1980

Women's 400-meter freestyle relay
3:42.71   GDR national team   1980

Women's 400-meter medley relay
4:06.67   GDR national team   1980

Did you know ?

1. Who is the youngest person to swim the English Channel? The oldest?

2. Although it is said there are no ties in swimming, two women did it in the 1950s. Their medals, for first and second places simultaneously, were half gold and half silver. Who were they?

3. Who invented the grease suit and wore it when she swam from Albany to New York City?

4. Who is the only man to win two Olympic golds in the 200-meter breaststroke?

5. What Australian swimmer, during his brief career in the 1920s, held records for every event from the 220-yard to the mile, records that stood for 15 years?

6. Who holds the record for the most unsuccessful attempts to cross the English Channel?

7. Who holds the world record for long-distance swimming?

Answers: 1. David Morgan, at age 13, swam the Channel; James ("Doc") Counsilman swam it when he was 58; **2.** Marge Hulton Dolan and Evelyn Kawamoto; **3.** Lottie Mae Schoemmel, carrying a letter in her bathing cap from Governor Al Smith to Mayor Jimmy Walker; **4.** Yoshiyuki Tsuruta; **5.** Barney Kieran amazed the swimming world with his speed over long distances before his death at 19; **6.** Jabey Wolffe; **7.** John Sigmund swam nonstop from St. Louis to the mouth of the Mississippi, a distance of 292 miles in 89 hours and 42 minutes.

Key Words

aggregate time   the time achieved by four swimmers.

backstroke   in competition swimming, an upside-down crawl, with the swimmer using a flutter kick; the arms are alternately extended past the head and pulled to the hips. The elementary backstroke combines the frog kick and the double-arm pull, from past the shoulders to the hips.

breaststroke   a swim stroke done in the prone position, combining the frog kick and the double-arm pull, downward and to the side.

butterfly stroke   a stroke performed in the prone position, combining the dolphin kick and the double-overarm pull. The arms and face come out of the water upon recovery.

composite time   in a relay event, the time achieved by four swimmers.

crawl   a stroke that is done in the prone position, combining the flutter kick with alternate arm pulls.

dolphin kick   a kick in which the legs are moved up and down together; used in the butterfly.

flip turn   a turn made by a swimmer at the edge of the pool, comprised of a half-forward somersault and a half-twist underwater before a push with the feet against the pool wall.

flutter kick   a kick in which the legs are alternately moved past each other; used in the backstroke and the crawl.

freestyle   a competition in which a swimmer may use any recognized stroke; the crawl is most commonly used. The terms *freestyle* and *crawl* are often used interchangeably.

frog kick   a kick used with the breaststroke and the elementary backstroke. The knees are brought up almost level with the hips, the feet are kicked out; and the legs are pulled together—all in one continuous movement.

lane   a narrow strip running the length of the pool, within which a swimmer must keep throughout a race.

leg   a section of a relay.

long course   a pool at least 50 yards long.

scissor   a kicking motion in which the top of the instep of one foot and the bottom of the other kick alternately, providing propulsion.

short course   a pool at least 25 yards long but not more than 50 yards long.

split time   the time required to complete half the distance in a long event.

trudgen stroke   a crawl done with a scissor kick.

Diving

Although there is evidence suggesting that diving was performed in ancient Greece and Rome, little is known of how diving was done before the nineteenth century. By then the swan dive, first known as the Swedish swallow, already existed. What other prenineteenth-century forms existed—beyond the formless tumble into the water—is unknown.

In the early nineteenth century, gymnastics was popular in Germany and Sweden; during the summer months, enthusiasts practiced on beaches and in the water. Eventually trapezes, springboards, and flying rings were erected near or in the water, and the fancy dive, as it was originally called, had its beginning. Gradually the trapeze and rings were discarded, the platform and the springboard were perfected, and diving emerged as a distinct sport.

The progression from gymnastics to diving is logical enough, since both sports call for many of the same movements. A comparable degree of control, coordination, and grace is also required.

As a competitive sport, diving began in England during the 1880s, a result of arguments among various swim clubs all of which claimed to have the best divers. In 1889, in Scotland, the first diving championship took place, an event that included dives from poolside and from a height of approximately six feet. Six years later, the National Graceful Diving Competition—later renamed the Plain Diving Championship—began under the auspices of the Royal Life Saving Society. Open worldwide, but only to men, this competition consisted of standing and running dives from heights of 15 and 33 feet and took place at Highgate Ponds, England.

Then, in 1901, the Amateur Diving Association was formed, the first official organization in the world devoted exclusively to diving. Shortly after the advent of the association, diving entered a period of growth and innovation. Inclusion in the Olympic Games also helped diving gain stature as a sport. The year 1904 was the first in which diving was an official Olympic event; in 1908, the first table of tariffs, giving a value to each dive based on difficulty, was used. The principle on which these tables were based is still used, though they were greatly simplified in 1924.

Women's diving became an Olympic sport in 1912; but it wasn't until 1956 that restrictions limiting the types of dives women could perform were lifted. In fact, diving was long considered unsuitable for women; even in 1912, when it became an Olympic competition, many questioned the wisdom of women's participation.

Europeans dominated the initial Olympic diving competitions, particularly Germans and Swedes. German divers generally triumphed in springboard competitions and Swedish divers dominated plain and fancy high diving. World War I interrupted competition by European nations; with the resumption of the Olympics in 1920, the United States achieved a preeminence it has only occasionally relinquished since. At Antwerp that year, the United States swept all six springboard medals in the men's and women's events. The United States won 9 of the 10 men's platform gold medals and all the men's gold springboard medals from that Olympics through 1964. American women have also done well in springboard, winning the gold medal from 1920 through 1948, and both springboard and high diving in 1952 and 1956.

To a large extent, the history of diving in this century is one of U.S. diving. The development of the modern diving board and diving techniques dates only from about 1900. Ernst Brandsten, a member of the Swedish diving team in 1908, is credited both with the development of the first modern diving board and with organizing the sport in the United States. Called the "father of the dive," he emigrated to this country shortly before World War I and became the coach at Stanford University; there he developed teaching fundamentals and worked on standardizing equipment.

Fred Cady, another great American coach, influenced the sport by stressing grace and poise in diving. The ideas and teaching methods of Brandsten and Cady helped produce U.S. diving champions, thereby influencing the development of diving throughout the world.

In early Olympic competitions, dives were simple movements; today, diving involves intricate combinations of twists and multiple somersaults. It has been said that divers in early Olympics spoiled their chances of winning by attempting a forward double somersault, that no diver could possibly control so many spins without risking serious injury. Today, more than 110 different springboard and platform dives are performed, with each dive made up of one or more basic diving combinations: forward dives, backward, reverse, inward, twisting, and armstand. New techniques and dives are constantly being developed. Competitive diving, a sport scarcely a century old, is now a highlight of every Summer Olympics, as well as of numerous other international aquatic competitions.

Great Moments

1893 The Amateur Swimming Association holds the first "plunging" championship, in England.

1895 The Royal Life Saving Society holds its first "Graceful Diving Competition."

1901 The Amateur Diving Association, the world's first official diving organization, is formed.

1904 Diving becomes an Olympic event when the men's plunge and springboard are included. Plunging, an event in which competitors make a standing, head-first, horizontal dive and then drift, motionless and without breathing, for the greatest possible distance in a maximum of 60 seconds, is not subsequently repeated as an Olympic event, and is discontinued from all organized competition in 1947.

1907 The first United States diving meet is held, at the University of Pennsylvania.

1908 The Federation Internationale de Natation Amateur is founded. Men's plain diving is added to Olympic events, and a tariff table, giving a value to each dive and based on difficulty, is used in judging for the first time.

1908 Men's plain diving is added to Olympic events, and a tariff table, giving a value to each dive and based on difficulty, is used in judging for the first time.

1912 Platform diving becomes an Olympic sport for women. Men's fancy diving is added to the schedule of events. Germany wins first, second, and third places in the men's springboard diving competition.

1920 Women's springboard competition is included in the Olympics. The United States becomes a major competitor, sweeping all six springboard medals in the women's and men's divisions. Ernst Brandsten's wood diving board is used in the Olympics for the first time.

1928   Highboard diving for women becomes an Olympic event; women, however, are restricted from performing some types of dives, a restriction that continues until 1956.

1929   Dives are divided into five categories: forward, backward, reverse, inward, and twisting—with an additional category, the armstand, for platform diving.

1933   Frank Parrington sets the English amateur record for a plunging dive.

1937   Plunging championships end as a competitive sport.

1952   An aluminum diving board designed by Norman Buck—the first standardized board—becomes the official Olympic Games board.

1956   Pat McCormick becomes the first diver to win four Olympic gold medals in the springboard and platform events.

1964   For the first time, an indoor pool is used for swimming and diving events at the Olympics.

1976   Italy's Klaus Dibiasi, "The Blond Angel," takes his third successive Olympic gold medal in platform diving, the only diver in history to do so.

The Setup

Competitive diving in the United States is organized in much the same way as competitive swimming. It is governed by United States Diving, Inc., an organization comparable to United States Swimming, Inc., and recognized by the U.S. Olympic Committee as the national governing body for diving in the United States. Competitions are open to all American divers. Collegiate competition is overseen by the NCAA, the AIAW, and other organizations that govern collegiate sports.

U.S. DIVING, INC.
P.O. Box 1811
Indianapolis, IN 46206
(317) 872-2900
Bill Flesher, exec. dir.

The Basics

Diving

Object   To execute dives from one or more approved groups of dives as nearly perfect as possible. Dives are made from springboards or from rigid, high-dive platforms.

Diving area   Diving pools are usually deeper than, and are kept separate from, regular competition pools. The high-dive platform and the springboard are at heights ranging from 1 meter to 10 meters from the surface of the water. Usually, the water's surface is mechanically agitated to help divers judge better the distance between them and the water.

Officials   The judging panel consists of a referee and five to seven judges (seven, in international competitions), who are stationed on either side of the diving board or together on one side of the board. When the referee signals at the end of each dive, all judges give their marks for the dive. Two secretaries record the results.

Rule 1   Preliminaries   Preliminaries are held when more than 16 competitors are entered in the diving event. In the springboard preliminaries, men must execute 11 dives and women, 10; the rules for platform preliminaries require men to execute 10 dives and women, 8. Once the diver has selected the dives for the preliminary contest, that diver must perform the same dives in the finals. Eight divers are chosen from the preliminaries to compete in the finals.

Rule 2   Dives   Divers perform dives from six groups: forward, backward, reverse, inward, twist, and armstand.

Rule 3   Events   Both platform and springboard diving events consist of required dives and voluntary dives chosen from the six groups. Required dives for the springboard competitions are a forward, backward, reverse, and inward dives, as well as a forward dive with a half-twist. These may be performed straight, piked, or with a tuck (*see* "Key Words"). Platform divers must perform four voluntary dives above a certain level of difficulty and six more of any degree of difficulty. Each dive must be from a separate group. Requirements for men and women differ. For instance, in the springboard competition, men must perform six voluntary dives in addition to the five required, whereas women must perform five. In the platform competition, men must perform six voluntary dives after the first four; women must perform four.

Rule 4   Notice of dives to be executed   Each diver must submit to the diving secretaries a written description of the dives he or she intends to use, before the events.

Rule 5   Starting positions   Divers may start from a backward, forward, or armstand position. Forward dives are started either from a standstill or by running.

Rule 6   Scoring   Judges mark each dive in points and half-points, from 1 to 10. The highest and lowest scores are eliminated and the remainder are totalled and multiplied according to the degree of difficulty, to obtain a score for the dive. The "degree of difficulty" is established using a table that awards points to each position. The diver with the most points wins.

Rule 7   Execution   Judges base their marks on the following parts of a dive: the start, the flight, and the entry. (a) *start.* Divers starting from a standstill must stand perfectly straight, with the arms straight at the sides or straight above the head. Divers starting by running must run smoothly and without hesitation before leaving the board. The diver must take at least four steps—including the takeoff, which can be done from one or both feet. Judges look for boldness and confidence in the takeoff. In an armstand start, the diver must hold a steady balance before leaving the board. (b) *flight.* The diver may use the pike position (bent at the hips), the tuck (curled up, with the knees against the chest), or the straight position. In the pike, the diver must have both feet together, with the toes pointed. In the tuck, the entire body must be bunched, with the hands on the lower part of the legs and the toes pointed. In the straight position, the diver must not bend the knees, and the feet must be together. (c) *entry.* The body must be vertical or near vertical when the diver enters the water. The toes must be pointed. The dive is considered complete when the entire body is submerged.

How to watch

with Dr. Sammy Lee

According to Dr. Sammy Lee, two-time Olympic champion and a former Olympic coach, a good diver does not make waves. In fact, he barely makes a ripple in executing a perfect dive and entry. "In my days, we were happy just to get in the water straight up and down. We made a kind of *ker-plunk* sound. Nowadays, you hear a sound something like *schwouitt*—almost like a sheet ripping." This sound, plus the angle of the diver's body at takeoff and entry, are good clues to how good the dive was. "The perfect dive is practically at a ninety-degree angle," Lee says.

Basically, judges and spectators alike should look for smoothness of execution and control when gauging a dive. These qualities must be present in each phase of the dive: the takeoff, the positioning in the air, and the entry into the water. "The sign of a good takeoff is a diver's body that is almost at attention. When the diver leaves the board, his arms are straight over his shoulder, lined up with his head. It will look like he is almost perpendicular to the board; but actually, he is leaning a bit forward. The important thing to remember is that the head is in line with the back and torso—and the chin must be on the chest. If the diver's chin is off the chest, the diver will go too far out from the tower, or when the diver is doing a straight dive, it looks like a pelican heading toward the water—ugly."

Control in the air during the dive is easy to spot, Lee says. During this part of the dive, the athlete must be so "computerized" that he can allow for variables such as getting a few feet higher than planned during his takeoff. In recent years, a precision approach has been developed for the more difficult dives. "These kids now count their somersaults as they are spinning. In fact, they're watching the water *and* the tower—for example, when they do a back two-and-a-half somersault. They jump up, see the sky, see the water, tower, water, sky, water, tower; then they kick and press back, and look for the water. I never did that," Lee says. "I was terrified. I said, the hell with it and closed my eyes until the somersaults were over. Then I looked for the entry."

According to Lee, new techniques have made the final phase of the dive—the entry—smoother than ever. For instance, divers now use a flat-hand entry in which the diver's hands are parallel to the water instead of perpendicular to it. "This pushes the surface down and out of the way. When the body is perfectly straight, there's almost no splash."

Divers pay a price, however. Because this type of entry increases the impact on the diver's shoulders and back, divers suffer shoulder and back problems much earlier in their careers than their predecessors did.

When it comes to scoring, Lee says, spectators at a diving meet may see what they think is a perfect dive by the first contestant. But the judges may not think it was perfect. "They may be a little afraid to give the first diver a perfect score, and then get a diver who makes a better one. But this doesn't always hold true. Jennifer Chandler, for instance, was the first diver in the 1976 games at Montreal, and she won the contest. For divers, going first is a psychological disadvantage. It helps them to go after others. It gives them something to aim for."

During a meet, Lee says, "divers tend to get tired emotionally rather than physically. The diver just has to psych himself up every time, for every dive. He's got to do that ten times on the tower and eleven on the springboard for men."

What goes into a diver's preparation for that kind of competition? "Repetition, just repetition. You have to think: each dive I go for the perfect dive; I have to psych myself up and tell myself that each practice dive is a championship dive."

Main Events

Olympic Diving Championships

MEN'S SPRINGBOARD

1980	Aleksandr Portnov, USSR
1976	Phil Boggs, USA
1972	Vladimir Basin, USSR
1968	Bernie Wrightson, USA
1964	Kenneth R. Sitzberger, USA
1960	Gary Tobian, USA
1956	Bob Clotworthy, USA
1952	David Browning, USA
1948	Bruce Harlan, USA

MEN'S PLATFORM

1980	Falk Hoffman, GDR*
1976	Klaus Dibiasi, Italy
1972	Klaus Dibiasi, Italy
1968	Klaus Dibiasi, Italy
1964	Robert Webster, USA
1960	Robert Webster, USA
1956	Joaquin Capilla, Mexico
1952	Sammy Lee, USA
1948	Sammy Lee, USA

WOMEN'S SPRINGBOARD

1980	Irina Kalinina, USSR
1976	Jenni Chandler, USA
1972	Micki King, USA
1968	Sue Gossick, USA
1964	Ingrid Engle-Kramer, Germany
1960	Ingrid Kramer, Germany
1956	Patricia McCormick, USA
1952	Patricia McCormick, USA
1948	Vickie Draves, USA

WOMEN'S PLATFORM

1980	Martina Jaschke, USSR
1976	Elena Vaytsekhouskaya, USSR
1972	Ulrika Knape, Sweden
1968	Milena Duchkova, Czechoslovakia
1964	Lesley Bush, USA
1960	Ingrid Kramer, Germany
1956	Patricia McCormick, USA
1952	Patricia McCormick, USA
1948	Vickie Draves, USA

World Diving Championships

MEN'S SPRINGBOARD

1978	Phil Boggs, USA
1975	Phil Boggs, USA
1973	Phil Boggs, USA

German Democratic Republic (East Germany).

WOMEN'S SPRINGBOARD

1978	Irina Kalinina, USSR
1975	Irina Kalinina, USSR
1973	Christine Kohler, GDR

WOMEN'S PLATFORM

1978	Irina Kalinina, USSR
1975	Janet Ely, USA
1973	Ulrika Knape, Sweden

MEN'S PLATFORM

1978	Greg Louganis, USA
1975	Klaus Dibiasi, Italy
1973	Klaus Dibiasi, Italy

U.S. Diving Champions (Indoors)

MEN'S 1-METER

1980	Greg Louganis
1979	Greg Louganis
1978	Greg Louganis
1977	Robert Cragg
1976	Tim Moore
1975	Tim Moore
1974	Tim Moore
1973	Tim Moore
1972	Don Dunfield
1971	Craig Lincoln

WOMEN'S 3-METER

1980	Carrie Finneran
1979	Carrie Finneran
1978	Jennifer Chandler
1977	Cynthia Potter McIngvale
1976	Jennifer Chandler
1975	Carrie Irish
1974	Jennifer Chandler
1973	Cynthia Potter
1972	Cynthia Potter
1971	Micki King

WOMEN'S 1-METER

1980	Karen Gorham
1979	Cynthia Potter
1978	Julie Bachman
1977	Cynthia Potter
1976	Cynthia Potter
1975	Jennifer Chandler
1974	Christine Loock
1973	Cynthia Potter
1972	Micki King
1971	Cynthia Potter

MEN'S PLATFORM

1980	Bruce Kimball
1979	Kent Vosler
1978	Greg Louganis
1977	Kent Vosler
1976	Tim Moore
1975	Tim Moore
1974	Steve McFarland
1973	Steve McFarland
1972	Dick Rydze
1971	Dick Rydze

MEN'S 3-METER

1980	Greg Louganis
1979	Greg Louganis
1978	Jim Kennedy
1977	Phil Boggs
1976	Tim Moore
1975	Phil Boggs
1974	Phil Boggs
1973	Phil Boggs
1972	Phil Boggs
1971	Mike Finneran

WOMEN'S PLATFORM

1980	Christine Loock
1979	Barb Weinstein
1978	Melissa Briley
1977	Melissa Briley
1976	Melissa Briley
1975	Carrie Irish
1974	Janet Ely
1973	Debbie Lipman
1972	Ulrika Knape
1971	Micki King

U.S. Diving Champions (Outdoors)

MEN'S 1-METER

1980	Greg Louganis
1979	Greg Louganis
1978	Greg Louganis
1977	Scott Reich
1976	Jim Kennedy
1975	Tim Moore
1974	Tim Moore
1973	Mike Finneran
1972	Don Dunfield
1971	Mike Brown

WOMEN'S 3-METER

1980	Chris Seufert
1979	Michele Hain
1978	Jennifer Chandler
1977	Christine Loock
1976	Cynthia Potter
1975	Cynthia Potter
1974	Christine Loock
1973	Carrie Irish
1972	Cynthia Potter
1971	Cynthia Potter

WOMEN'S 1-METER

1980	Kelly McCormick
1979	Kelly McCormick
1978	Cynthia Potter
1977	Jennifer Chandler
1976	Cynthia Potter McIngvale
1975	Cynthia Potter McIngvale
1974	Cynthia Potter
1973	Cynthia Potter
1972	Cynthia Potter
1971	Cynthia Potter

MEN'S PLATFORM

1980	Greg Louganis
1979	Greg Louganis
1978	Greg Louganis
1977	Phil Boggs
1976	Kent Vosler
1975	Kent Vosler
1974	Keith Russell
1973	Tim Moore
1972	Rick Earley
1971	Dick Rydze

MEN'S 3-METER

1980	Greg Louganis
1979	Greg Louganis
1978	Jim Kennedy
1977	Phil Boggs
1976	Jim Kennedy
1975	Phil Boggs
1974	Keith Russell
1973	Phil Boggs
1972	Mike Finneran
1971	Jim Henry

WOMEN'S PLATFORM

1980	Barb Weinstein
1979	Kit Salness
1978	Melissa Briley
1977	Christine Loock
1976	Barb Weinstein
1975	Janet Ely
1974	Terri York
1973	Deborah Keplar
1972	Janet Ely
1971	Cynthia Potter

Pan American Games

MEN'S SPRINGBOARD

1979	Greg Louganis (627.84)
1975	Tim Moore (579.75)
1971	Michael Finneran (551.57)
1967	Bernie Wrightson (166.95)
1963	Tom Dinsley (154.40)
1959	Gary Tobian (161.40)
1955	Joaquin Capilla (175.76)
1951	Joaquin Capilla (201.716)

WOMEN'S SPRINGBOARD

1979	Denise Christiensen (477.96)
1975	Denise Chandler (427.62)
1971	Elizabeth Carruthers (435.24)
1967	Sue Gossick (150.41)
1963	Barbara McAlister (144.31)
1959	Paula Meyers Pope (139.23)
1955	Pat McCormick (142.42)
1951	Mary Cunningham (131.93)

MEN'S PLATFORM		WOMEN'S PLATFORM	
1979	Greg Louganis (592.71)	1979	Barb Weinstein (402.21)
1975	Carlo Giron (532.83)	1975	Janet Nutter (162.00)
1971	Rick Earley (479.09)	1971	Nancy Robertson (375.12)
1967	Winn Young (154.93)	1967	Lesley Bush (108.20)
1963	Robert Webster (164.12)	1963	Linda Cooper (100.35)
1959	Alvaro Gaxiola (168.77)	1959	Paula Meyers Pope (97.13)
1955	Joaquin Capilla (172.33)	1955	Pat McCormick (94.05)
1951	Joaquin Capilla (159.966)	1951	Pat McCormick (65.71)

NCAA DIVING CHAMPIONSHIPS

MEN'S 1-METER		MEN'S 3-METER	
1980	Greg Louganis (557.20)	1980	Greg Louganis (608.10)
1979	Greg Louganis (513.75)	1979	Matthew Chelich (527.85)
1978	Wayne Chester (485.10)	1978	Chris Snode (543.18)
1977	Matthew Chelich (503.13)	1977	Brian Bungum (542.40)
1976	James Kennedy (514.29)	1976	Brian Bungum (542.19)
1975	Tim Moore (502.71)	1975	Tim Moore (590.61)
1974	Tim Moore (494.25)	1974	Richard McAlister (516.41)
1973	Tim Moore (487.90)	1973	Tim Moore (539.61)
1972	Todd Smith (503.25)	1972	Craig Lincoln (545.94)
1971	Mike Finneran (520.98)	1971	Phil Boggs (552.93)

All-Time Greats

Micki King
(July 26, 1944–)

In the 1968 Olympics, Micki King was on her way to a gold medal when she hit the board while doing a reverse one-and-a-half somersault and broke her arm. In 1972, King was back, having made a long recovery. This time she got an Olympic gold medal in springboard diving. She has won the AAU National Diving title nine times and was springboard Diver of the Year in 1965, 1969, and 1972 and for platform in 1969. King, the first woman coach at the U.S. Air Force Academy, is the first woman to compete in the Military International Sports Council Games.

Sammy Lee
(Aug. 1, 1920–)

Lee won his first AAU title in 1942 while he was a student at Occidental College, winning both the platform and the springboard events. He quit competition diving to enter medical school at the University of Southern California, but returned for outdoor meets in 1946 and for the 1948 Olympics. At the Olympics, Lee took his first gold medal, in the platform competition, as well as a bronze in the springboard event. At the 1952 Olympics in Helsinki, the 32-year-old Lee became the first man to take back-to-back gold medals in the platform event. (The next diver to accomplish the achievement of successive gold medals was Lee's pupil, Bob Webster, who won in 1960 and 1964.) Dr. Lee now divides his time between medical practice and coaching divers, many of whom have been highly successful.

Greg Louganis
(Jan. 29, 1960–)

Currently considered one of the best divers in the world, Louganis may be the best springboard diver in diving history. He has won 16 U.S. national championships, a gold medal at the 1978 World Championships, and two gold medals at the 1979 Pan American Games and World Cup. The three-time NCCA titleholder won a silver medal at the 1976 Olympics and was expected to take a gold in 1980; but his hopes were dashed by the U.S. boycott of the 1980 Olympics. Louganis, who began as a platform diver, developed into a premier springboard diver, with the reverse one-and-a-half layout off the three-meter board his best dive. In 1980, he took titles in five of six events at the U.S. Indoor and Outdoor championships.

Pat Keller McCormick
(May 12, 1930–)

Pat McCormick was the first diver, man or woman, to take Olympic gold medals in both the springboard and the platform events at two Olympics. She did it in 1956, climaxing a diving career that included 77 national championships and gold medals in 2 Pan American Games. McCormick began diving competitively in 1947, when she took second in the National Platform diving event. She missed qualifying for the 1948 Olympic team by one point, but made it in 1952 when she took her first double championship. During the next four years, McCormick dominated diving competition in the United States and won platform and springboard gold medals at the 1955 Pan American Games, to add to the two she won at the 1951 Games.

Photos courtesy International Swimming Hall of Fame

Hall of Fame

Divers in the International Swimming Hall of Fame are:

1965	**1969**	**1975**	**1979**
Pat McCormick	Vickie Draves	David Browning	Paula Jean Myers Pope
	Al Patnik	Ingrid Kramer	Harold ("Dutch") Smith
1966			
Georgia Coleman	**1970**	**1976**	
Pete Desjardins	Bob Webster	Joaquin Capilla	**1980**
		Marjorie Gestring	Robert Clotworthy
1967	**1971**		Juno Stover Irwin
Miller Anderson	Dick Degener	**1977**	
Betty Becker Pinkston	**1972**	Mickey Riley	
1968	Earl Clark		**1981**
		1978	Helen Crlenkovich
Sammy Lee	**1973**	Micki King	Klaus Dibiasi
Dorothy Poynton	Bruce Harlan	Gary Tobian	Marshall Wayne

For the Record

Most Olympic gold medals, women
4   Pat McCormick, USA   1952, 1956

Most Olympic gold medals, men
3   Klaus Dibiasi, Italy   1968, 1972, 1976

Best NCAA score recorded (since 1953)—1-meter
557.20   Greg Louganis, Miami 1980

Best NCAA score recorded (since 1953)—3-meter
608.10   Greg Louganis, Miami 1980

Most individual NCAA titles, career
6 (1- and 3-meter)   Bruce Harlan, Ohio State 1948, 1949, 1950

ABC Sports

Did you know ?

1. Who is the youngest woman diver to win an Olympic gold medal?

2. What country won every men's springboard gold medal from 1920 to 1968?

3. What unprecedented dive did Michael Finneran perform during the 1972 U.S. Olympic Trials?

4. What diver has won back-to-back gold medals in Olympic springboard competition?

5. In 1960, the tradition of American women divers winning one of the two Olympic events was broken by a 17-year-old. Who was she, and what country did she represent?

Answers: 1. Marjorie Gestring, of the United States, won the gold medal for springboard diving during the 1936 Olympic Games. At the time, she was 13 years and 9 months old. **2.** The United States won every men's springboard gold medal from 1920 through 1968, and all the silver medals until 1968; **3.** Michael Finneran performed a perfect backward one-and-a-half somersault, two-and-a-half twist free dive from a 10-meter board. All 7 judges gave him an unprecedented perfect score of 10; **4.** No diver has accomplished successive Olympic wins in the springboard event; **5.** Ingrid Kramer, of Germany.

Key Words

armstand   one of three starting positions for dives; the diver is balanced in a handstand.

back dive   any dive that starts with the diver facing away from the water.

cannonball   a feet-first jump into the water, with the body in the tuck position.

forward dive   a dive that starts with the diver facing the water.

free dive   a condition whereby a diver may use any position for a dive.

inward dive   a dive that starts with the diver facing the diving board and in which the diver jumps up and away from the board, rotating forward toward the board and entering the water feet or head first.

platform   a rigid board used by divers, 20.5 feet long and 6.5 feet wide and covered with material designed to provide traction.

reverse dive   a dive in which a diver begins in forward position, rotates backwards and enters the water head first facing inward, or feet first facing outward; also called a gainer.

springboard a flat board of steel or aluminum, 16 feet long and 20 inches wide, that is designed to flex and thereby to give a diver height in a dive.

swan dive a dive in which the legs are extended to the rear and the back is arched, with the arms out and up as the diver turns toward the water.

tuck a diving position in which the diver holds the knees against the chest.

twist a move that makes a dive more complicated. It can be done from a forward or a backward starting position. In performing a twist, divers make one-half to two and one-half spins about the long axis of the body.

ABC Sports

17   TENNIS

Tennis is one of the few games that owes its existence to a single person; its inventor was Major Walter C. Wingfield, an officer in the British army during the late nineteenth century.

Wingfield was an avid devotee of the garden parties then so popular in Britain, and, being a conscientious host, he set about to invent a game that could be played by his lawn-party guests. In 1873, after careful study and experiment, he introduced the game of "tennis-on-the-lawn." Although the major insisted that his game, which he patented under the name *sphairistike* (Greek for "to play"), had been played by the ancient Greeks, a more reliable explanation is that Wingfield simply adapted the rules of court tennis, an indoor game akin to racquetball, to the outdoors.

In any event, *sphairistike* soon became a popular amusement at the better British social gatherings, where young men played the game quickly and young women, as befitted the times, sedately. Their elders found enough action in the game to hold their interest as spectators.

While remaining popular with the elite in Britain, lawn tennis also made early inroads in the New World. A guest at one of Major Wingfield's parties took the game home with him to Bermuda, where Mary Ewing Outerbridge, a vacationing American, found it fascinating. She returned to America with tennis balls and rackets—which were briefly confiscated by mystified customs officials—and received permission from the Staten Island Cricket and Baseball Club to create a tennis court on the edge of the club's cricket field. Although few of Outerbridge's women friends were taken by the game, which seemed to them unladylike, her brothers played enthusiastically. In a short time, tennis was the fashionable game in Newport, Boston, Philadelphia, and other bastions of Eastern high society; by 1879, it had spread to the West Coast.

With the game only a few years old, problems often arose because of differences in rules. In 1881, one of Mary's brothers solved that problem by organizing the United States Lawn Tennis Association (now the U.S. Tennis Association), which remains the governing body of amateur tennis in this country.

The association held its first championship games, for men, the year it was formed; women's championships followed six years later. For decades afterward, those amateur championships *were* tennis. Players did not begin to turn pro until 1926, and "open" tournaments, in which amateurs and professionals could compete against each other, did not become prevalent until the late 1960s. By that time, tennis had become one of the most popular sports, both participant and spectator, in the world, with hundreds of thousands of men and women avidly rooting for their favorite players or competing themselves.

Great Moments

1881	The U.S. Lawn Tennis Association is formed; equipment and rules are standardized. In August, the first national championship is played, in Newport, Rhode Island.
1887	The first national women's championship matches are held at the Philadelphia Cricket Club. Ellen F. Hansell wins.
1900	Dwight F. Davis puts up a cup for play between the United States and England. The Davis Cup, later open to players from all countries, helps bring worldwide attention to tennis.
1915	The national championship moves to Forest Hills, New York.
1921	The women's championship moves from Philadelphia to Forest Hills.
1923	Hazel Hotchkiss Wightman donates the Wightman Cup, a championship series for women's teams throughout the world.
1926	The first professional tennis games are played after Charles Pyle offers Suzanne Lenglen, the best-known player of her day, $50,000 to tour the United States. Although tennis has not been a popular spectator sport, Lenglen accepts, on the condition that she receive a share of the profits. The tour is a smashing success and makes Lenglen rich.
1927	The U.S. Professional Lawn Tennis Association is formed.
1937–38	Don Budge becomes the first tennis player to achieve the Grand Slam by winning Wimbledon, the United States, the French, and the Australian opens in the same season.

1953	Eighteen-year-old Maureen ("Little Mo") Connolly becomes the first woman to win the tennis Grand Slam.
1962	Rod Laver wins the Grand Slam, and seven years later becomes the only player to win it twice.
1968	Rules for the Wimbledon tournament are changed to allow professionals and amateurs to compete for the first time.
1970	Margaret Smith Court becomes the second woman to win the Grand Slam.
1973	Billie Jean King, at age 35, easily defeats 55-year-old Bobby Riggs in a highly promoted "Battle of the Sexes." (Riggs had boasted that he could beat any woman under any circumstances.)
1979	Tracy Austin, at age 16 years and 9 months, becomes the youngest woman to win the U.S. Open singles championship.
1980	Bjorn Borg wins the Wimbledon singles championship for a fifth consecutive year, a modern record.
1981	John McEnroe ends Bjorn Borg's Wimbledon streak by beating Borg in a close match.

The Setup

Unlike most sports, tennis has never been permanently adapted to a team structure; the few attempts to develop tennis teams and leagues on a grand scale, such as the World Team Tennis experiment of the 1960s, have been largely unsuccessful.

On the professional level, tennis remains a sport of individuals who compete for prize money in tournaments sponsored by various companies and corporations. Each series of sponsored tournaments is known as a circuit, and players may compete on various of these circuits. In "open" tournaments, such as the U.S. Open and Wimbledon, amateur players may compete with professionals and, so long as they decline any prize money, they do not compromise their amateur standing.

Rules for major tournament competition are established by the Men's and Women's International Professional Tennis Councils. Seeding and matchups for tournaments are established on the basis of points earned by each player the previous week. The points are determined by computer and are awarded on the basis of performance, with consideration being given to the amount of prize money at stake in the particular tournament, the number of rounds the player advances, the number of players competing, the size of the crowd the tournament draws, and the rating of the player a person defeats. A player's eligibility for each tournament and the order of play within a tournament depend on the player's weekly computer ranking.

Among the most important circuits in professional tennis are the Grand Prix (men) and the Colgate Series (women). The Grand Prix has more than 95 tournaments and offers more than $14 million in prize money. Its events are divided into three classes: Grand Slam events (Wimbledon, U.S. Open, French Open,

Australian Open), Group I (28 tournaments, each offering at least $175,000 in prize money), and Group II (63 tournaments with prize money ranging from $50,000 to $125,000).

The Colgate Series offers competition in approximately 40 professional women's tournaments throughout the world and the annual $250,000 Colgate Series Championships. The series is divided into five classifications, beginning with the Grand Slam events (with prizes of at least $250,000) through "A" tournaments (offering prize money of at least $50,000). The Colgate Series also offers a year-end bonus pool of more than $800,000, divided among the top 50 singles players and top 25 doubles teams in the year's final point standings.

Within professional tennis, two organizations were formed in the early 1970s to unify players, improve player input into professional tennis decision making, and lobby for more professional standards in the game. These are the Association of Tennis Professionals (ATP), formed in 1972, which includes the 200 top-ranked professional men players, and the Women's Tennis Association (WTA), founded in 1973 to improve the status and protect the rights of women competitors.

Besides the sponsored circuits, other championships and important events in which tennis players compete are the Ambre Solaire Nations Cup (the official ATP championships), the Davis Cup (international singles and doubles competition for men), the Wightman Cup (between U.S. and British women), the Federation Cup (international women's competition), and various national open and professional tournaments in nations throughout the world.

The following associations are involved in the organization of tennis:

ASSOCIATION OF TENNIS
  PROFESSIONALS
319 Country Club
Garland, TX 75040
(214) 494-5991
Robert A. Briner, exec. dir.

U.S. TENNIS ASSOCIATION
51 East 42nd St.
New York, NY 10017
(212) 949-9112
Don Conway, exec. dir.

WOMEN'S TENNIS ASSOCIATION
1604 Union St.
San Francisco, CA 94123
(415) 673-2018
Jerry Diamond, exec. vice-pres.

The Basics

Object of the game   To hit a ball over a net so that it lands within the court and in such a way that one's opponent is unable to return it, thus scoring points until the game, the set, and the match have been won.

The court *(see diagram)*   Inner sideline boundaries apply in singles matches; outer-sideline boundaries apply in doubles matches.

The ball   Tennis balls must be white, yellow, or orange, weigh between 2 and 2.06 ounces and be from 2.5 to 2.62 inches in diameter.

Equipment   The only equipment a player needs is a strung racket with a metal or wooden frame, weighing between 13 and 14 ounces, and rubber-soled shoes.

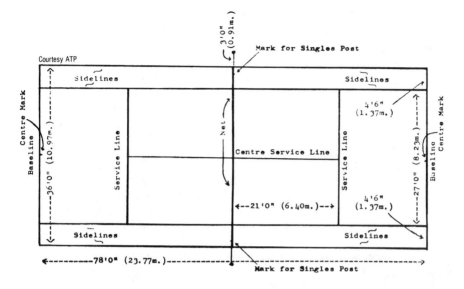

Courtesy ATP

Officials   Officials present at tournament games are the umpire, several linesmen, a net-cord judge, and a foot-fault judge.

Length of game   Play is continuous until a winner is determined. The first player to win a minimum of six games by at least a two-game margin, wins the set. A men's match is the best of five sets; matches in which women participate are best of three. A tie-break system operates when the score reaches a six-game tie or an eight-game tie in any set but the match-deciding set. The first player to win seven points, provided he leads by a margin of two, wins the game and the set.

Singles and doubles   Except for the order of service and the side boundaries, the rules for singles matches also apply to doubles and mixed doubles.

Start of play   Choice of serving and sides is decided by throwing a racket into the air and allowing one of the players to call "rough" or "smooth" (the two opposite sides of the racket).

Rule 1   Service   The server must serve with both feet behind the baseline, from alternate courts, and hit the ball into the opponent's diagonally opposite forecourt without hitting the net. The player may not walk or run while serving. A server breaking a rule may repeat the serve without penalty; if the second serve is also faulty (a "double fault"), the receiver wins a point.

   Doubles service: The pair to serve in the first game decides who shall serve; the second pair does the same for the second game. The next two beginning-game serves are by the person in the pair who did not serve the first time around. That order is maintained throughout the rest of the set.

Rule 2   Changing Ends   Players change ends at the end of the first and third games and any subsequent alternate games in each set.

Rule 3   Loss of points   Points are lost to the opponent if a player: (1) does not return the ball before it touches the ground twice on his or her side of the net; (2) hits the ball into the net; (3) hits the ball twice; (4) hits the net with body or racket; (5) is hit by the ball; (6) deliberately interferes with an opponent.

Rule 4   Returns   To be good, a return must bounce within the court after crossing the net. A ball may touch the net or cross outside the post so long as it lands in the correct court. A player may pass the racket over the net after hitting a ball so long as that player does not hit the ball before it crosses the net.

Rule 5   Scoring   A player with 4 points before an opponent has 3, wins a game; a player who wins 6 games before an opponent wins 5, wins a set; a player who wins 3 out of 5 or 2 out of 3 sets first, wins the match.

A player begins the game with a score of 0 ("love"). The first point is worth a score of 15, so that a player who wins one point before an opponent will bring the game to a score of 15–love. A second point brings the score to 30, a third point to 40.

After a player scores 40, his next point wins the game, unless his opponent also has 40, which ties the game at 40–all. A score of 40–all is called "deuce." The first point after gives the "advantage" to the player who earns it. If that player also wins the next point, he wins the game. If not, the score becomes deuce again, and this continues until someone wins. Once a game reaches deuce, a player must score two consecutive points to win.

How to watch

Courtesy ProServ, Inc.

with Dick Stockton

In tennis, as in many other sports, the most daring or spectacular moves are not always the most effective. In fact, says tennis pro Dick Stockton, five-time U.S. Davis Cup team member and former U.S. Indoor champion, "the really great players don't try to do anything too fancy. They play good, solid, consistent tennis. That's what wins for them in very tight situations."

Stockton says the differences between the top-ranked players in the world and those of slightly lower caliber is the way they play the important points, and games, of the match. He defines the important points as those in which a player is serving at 15–30, 30–all, or 30–40. The big games are those in which the player is serving at 3–all, 3–4, and 4–all. "If you watch closely the games that can really swing a set one way or another, all of a sudden the top player will concentrate a little better and rely on what he does best." The less experienced player might try a crazy shot, but the best players will not depend on a low-percentage shot for an important point. They will try their best shots and hope their opponent will respond with a weaker one.

It is thus crucial that tennis players have a very good idea of their opponents' strengths and weaknesses. Good players will always have in the back of their minds an idea of what an opponent is likely to do in any given situation, and at some point they will try to outguess the opponent, maneuvering him or her into attempting a low-percentage shot. That ability, says Stockton, is one of the reasons Bjorn Borg, among others, is a champion.

"If you watch Borg closely," he says, "you'll see that sooner or later he'll force his opponent to play with a style that's not his own. If he's playing against a big server, a person who likes to serve and volley, for example, his return of the serve and his passing shots will be so good that sooner or later he'll force that person to play from the back court a little bit.

"Or if he's playing someone who likes to play from the baseline—and there's no one in the world who can beat Borg from the baseline—sooner or later that player will have to attack a little bit more and play a game that he's not accustomed to playing. Borg always has that hidden ability, and sooner or later in every match he'll pull his opponent out of his normal playing style. That's a tremendous advantage for him."

Because of the speed with which tennis is played, responses to another player's shots must be almost automatic reflexes, Stockton adds. "If, for instance, you're lining up to hit a shot and you start thinking about one, two, or maybe even three different possibilities of what you want to do with the ball, you're probably going to miss the shot, because you don't have enough time to think about all those different opportunities. So much of the time you just have to go with what you do best and let the other player try to beat you with what he does best."

Another mark of a good tennis player is the ability to play in all kinds of conditions and on all types of surfaces. Although it is not readily apparent to someone watching tennis on television, each type of court has its own unique characteristics, and players must develop different skills to play on them.

When playing on grass, for instance, players must get used to a very fast game—because the grass is cut short the ball stays low and skids. As the tournament progresses, and the courts get worn and hard, the game gets even faster. That, says Stockton, is why matches played on grass courts, such as Wimbledon, are basically "serve-and-volley" games. "Even Borg, who likes to play from the back court, will serve and volley some on the grass," Stockton says. "He never does that on any other surface."

Clay courts, on the other hand, are very slow, and players have to learn to slide into the ball and hit it at the same time, a way of playing tennis dramatically different from play on grass. It is hard to serve and volley consistently, and it is also difficult to change direction quickly on a clay court. It is thus a slower game than tennis on grass, and it's usually played much closer to the baseline.

Indoor tennis, which takes place on a specially designed, synthetic court, is, as Stockton sees it, the most enjoyable and the most exciting to watch. "The courts are a medium speed and the footing is good, so you can play from the back court, or from the net, or however you want to play," he explains. "You generally get a play on almost every ball. If you hit a really good shot, it will be a winner and you'll be rewarded for it. So, in my opinion, that's the best surface for tennis."

Another obvious advantage of indoor tennis is the lack of weather variables. Because tennis is played all over the world at all times of the year, a good player must be able to adjust to rainy cold (as in England), intense heat (as in Australia), energy-draining humidity (as in the eastern United States), and high-velocity winds (as in the western United States).

The differences in tennis come not only with individual players, different style courts, or different weather conditions. Each type of game—women's or men's singles or doubles, or mixed doubles—has its own unique qualities.

Men's singles, for example, may be a boring game for the spectator unless the very top players are in the match, because men play more of a "serve-and-volley" game. Two opponents who are both strong servers, for instance, will find it very difficult to get the ball into play. There is a serve, and at most a return and a volley, and then the point is over. That, as Stockton points out, "is not very exciting to watch." Women's singles, on the other hand, involves more of a baseline game with longer rallies, and so can be much more exciting for the spectator.

According to Stockton, men's doubles is much more exciting for most spectators. Because the camera is usually located behind the court, he says, viewers get an excellent chance to see all the unusual angles and shots that develop in a doubles game.

"The players on a team must almost have ESP with each other," he says. "They have to know who will pick up which shot 90 percent of the time so that they don't both go for it, or both let it go and miss the shot. Also, players have to have quick reflexes and play both offensive and defensive shots. A viewer can get to see how two players will position themselves and take away most of the court area, and how they will virtually say to the other team, 'We'll give you such and such a shot, because it's such a difficult shot that if you make it, you can have it.' It's that kind of game in doubles."

Mixed doubles is basically the same kind of game, says Stockton, except that there's also an "ego factor" involved. Women enjoy it because they love to watch the women hold their own against the big, powerful male players, and the men love to watch it because they like to watch the men try to intimidate the women, he says.

"If I'm playing mixed doubles, it's important for me to try to intimidate the woman on the other side and make her feel that I'm going to overpower her. At the same time, I have to reassure my partner to make sure she doesn't feel intimidated by the other man. It's the same job for the man on the other side. It's a great psychological game; mixed doubles has produced some of the best tennis I've ever seen," Stockton says.

Because mixed doubles is the "orphan" of professional tennis, however, coming in last both in prize money and in the minds of promoters, most tournaments will continue to feature same-sex doubles and singles tennis most prominently. Stockton has developed his own vision of the best singles match from a spectators point of view.

"For sheer excitement, the best match would be a player with a not necessarily overpowering serve, but a good serve and a good volley, against a player who plays mostly from the back court," he says. "That way, people would see the struggle of one player who prefers to come to the net, and he's trying to get to the net and set himself up to win the point at the net, while the other guy is trying to keep him from the net and make him play from the back court. Meanwhile, the net player is trying to bring the baseline player to the net because that's not where he feels at home.

"In this kind of match, as opposed to a match between two baseline players (who can have some long rallies, but there's only so much of that you can watch), spectators get to see all the shots hit, offensive and defensive shots, and a lot of running. Unfortunately, it doesn't usually work out that way."

Nevertheless, careful observers will see most strategies and most types of shots in the course of a tournament. And it helps to keep in mind that the truly great players get that way by accepting their weaknesses, emphasizing their strengths, and not sweating the small stuff.

Main Events

WIMBLEDON

Men's Singles

Year	Winner	Year	Winner
1981	John McEnroe	1978	Bjorn Borg
1980	Bjorn Borg	1977	Bjorn Borg
1979	Bjorn Borg	1976	Bjorn Borg

1975	Arthur Ashe	1972	Stan Smith
1974	Jimmy Connors	1971	John Newcombe
1973	Jan Kodes		

Women's Singles

Year	Winner	Year	Winner
1981	Chris Evert Lloyd	1975	Billie Jean King
1980	Evonne Goolagong	1974	Chris Evert
1979	Martina Navratilova	1973	Billie Jean King
1978	Martina Navratilova	1972	Billie Jean King
1977	Virginia Wade	1971	Evonne Goolagong
1976	Chris Evert		

AUSTRALIAN OPEN

Men's Singles

Year	Winner	Year	Winner
1980	Guillermo Vilas	1975	John Newcombe
1979	Guillermo Vilas	1974	Jimmy Connors
1978	Guillermo Vilas	1973	John Newcombe
1977	Vitas Gerulaitis	1972	Ken Rosewall
1976	Mark Edmondson	1971	Ken Rosewall

Women's Singles

Year	Winner	Year	Winner
1980	Barbara Jordan	1975	Evonne Goolagong
1979	Chris O'Neil	1974	Evonne Goolagong
1978	Evonne Goolagong	1973	Margaret Smith Court
1977	Kerry Reid	1972	Virginia Wade
1976	Evonne Goolagong	1971	Margaret Smith Court

FRENCH OPEN

Men's Singles

Year	Winner	Year	Winner
1980	Bjorn Borg	1975	Bjorn Borg
1979	Bjorn Borg	1974	Bjorn Borg
1978	Bjorn Borg	1973	Ilie Nastase
1977	Guillermo Vilas	1972	Andres Gimeno
1976	Adriano Panatta	1971	Jan Kodes

Women's Singles

Year	Winner	Year	Winner
1980	Chris Evert Lloyd	1975	Chris Evert
1979	Chris Evert Lloyd	1974	Chris Evert
1978	Virginia Ruzici	1973	Margaret Smith Court
1977	Mima Jausovec	1972	Billie Jean King
1976	Sue Barker	1971	Evonne Goolagong

U.S. OPEN

Men's Singles

Year	Winner	Year	Winner
1980	John McEnroe	1975	Manuel Orantes
1979	John McEnroe	1974	Jimmy Connors
1978	Jimmy Connors	1973	John Newcombe
1977	Guillermo Vilas	1972	Ilie Nastase
1976	Jimmy Connors	1971	Stan Smith

Women's Singles

Year	Winner	Year	Winner
1980	Chris Evert Lloyd	1975	Chris Evert
1979	Tracy Austin	1974	Billie Jean King
1978	Chris Evert	1973	Margaret Smith Court
1977	Chris Evert	1972	Billie Jean King
1976	Chris Evert	1971	Billie Jean King

All-Time Greats

Arthur Ashe
(July 10, 1943–)

ProServ, Inc.

The first black to play on the U.S. Davis Cup team (1963) and the first amateur to win the U.S. Open (1968), Ashe defeated Jimmy Connors in 1975 when Connors was acknowledged to be at the height of his career. Ashe was also the first American tennis player to earn more than $100,000 in a year (1972). At the top of his game in 1978, Ashe was forced out of competitive tennis when he suffered a mild heart attack and then had open-heart surgery. He began a stint as captain-coach of the U.S. Davis Cup team in 1981.

Bjorn Borg
(June 6, 1956–)

ABC Sports

Known for his incredible ability to keep plugging away at a seemingly hopeless match until he finds a way to win it, Bjorn Borg is widely considered the finest player in the world. He reached the quarterfinals at Wimbledon at the age of 15 and won that title in 1976, 77, 78, 79, and 80. He has won the French Open five times since 1974 and has a host of other titles to his credit. Borg, who married the Romanian tour player Mariana Simionescu, led Sweden to a Davis Cup win in 1975.

Maureen ("Little Mo") Connolly Brinker
(Sept. 17, 1934–June 21, 1969)

Maureen Connolly was the first woman to win the Grand Slam of tennis, taking the French, U.S., Australian, and Wimbledon titles in 1953. She won both the U.S. and Wimbledon titles three times while still a teenager, and she won all singles and doubles matches on winning Wightman Cup teams from 1951 to 1954. Her tennis career ended in 1954 when she broke a leg in a fall from a horse. She died of cancer at the age of 35.

Margaret Smith Court
(Aug. 6, 1942–)

Margaret Smith Court is the only woman besides Maureen Connolly to win the tennis Grand Slam in singles, taking all big-four titles in 1970. With fellow Australian Ken Fletcher, she also took the Grand Slam in mixed doubles in 1963. Court, who was the youngest player ever to win the Australian Open, was inducted into the International Tennis Hall of Fame in 1979.

Althea Gibson Darben
(Aug. 25, 1927–)

Althea Gibson was the first black player to win the Wimbledon and the U.S. championships, which she did in both 1957 and 1958. Those same years she was a member of the Wightman Cup team, and in 1958 she became a professional player. From 1952 to 1958 she was ranked in the top 10 six times.

Richard A. ("Pancho") Gonzales
(May 9, 1928–)

Pancho Gonzales won his first U.S. Championship in 1947 when he was 20 years old. He turned professional two years later, and thus, although he is regarded by many as one of the best tennis players ever, was unable to compete in many of tennis's main events, which at that time were restricted to amateurs. Famous for both his footwork and his strong serve, Gonzales dominated professional tennis from the time he entered it until the mid-1960s.

Billie Jean King
(Nov. 22, 1943–)

ABC Sports

King is famous in tennis annals not only for her talent, dedication, and string of championships, but also for her strenuous efforts to improve the status of women professionals and to bring tennis into the forefront of the national consciousness. A prime force behind the organization of the Women's Tennis Association, as well as the ill-fated World Team Tennis league, King was the first woman athlete in any sport to win more than $100,000 in a single season. She has ranked number one in the world four times and has consistently ranked in the top ten for the last eighteen years. The record holder for most Wimbledon wins and most Federation Cup wins, she is the only woman to win the U.S. singles championships on clay, grass, carpet, and hard courts. Despite three knee operations, King continues to be active in professional tennis.

Rod Laver
(Aug. 9, 1938–)

ABC Sports

Rod Laver is the only tennis player to win the Grand Slam twice (1962 and 1969). He is also a four-time Wimbledon winner (1961, 1962, 1968, 1969), and victor in the Australian championship three times (1960, 1962, 1969). In 1970, he joined World Championship Tennis, playing for the San Diego Friars in 1976, 1977, and 1978. For his. contributions to tennis, and to Australia, he was inducted into the Order of the British Empire.

Chris Evert Lloyd
(Dec. 21, 1954–)

Cheryl Traendly/WTA

The child wonder of tennis in the early 1970s, Evert has become the undisputed queen of the sport. She holds records for the longest winning streak and the most singles wins on one surface (clay), and she has been ranked number one in U.S. tennis more years than any other women. Evert has won more money in the history of professional tennis than any other woman. Among her many titles are multiple wins at Wimbledon (singles and doubles), the French Open (singles and doubles), the Colgate Series, the Virginia Slims Championships, the Italian Open (singles and doubles), and the U.S. Clay Court Championships (singles and doubles). She was on the Wightman Cup Team in 1971–72, 1975, and 1977–80. Famous for a hard-driving style that energized the entire game of women's tennis, Evert was the first woman to earn more than one million dollars in professional tennis. She has been named Female Athlete of the Year by The Associated Press and Sportswoman of the Year by *Sports Illustrated* magazine; she was ranked number one player of the 1970s by *Tennis* magazine.

Helen Wills Moody
(Oct. 6, 1905–)

Tennis Hall of Fame

Considered one of the best players ever, male or female, Moody won Wimbledon singles titles eight times, never losing a single set between 1927 and 1932. She also won the Wimbledon doubles title three times, the U.S. Singles title seven, and the French Singles title four. Because of disputes with authorities, Moody was barred from U.S. competition in 1933.

John Newcombe
(May 23, 1944–)

ABC Sports

The winner of 23 Grand Prix titles in singles and doubles, Newcombe, a founder of the Association of Tennis Professionals, won the first of his six Wimbledon titles in 1967. A longtime Davis and World Cup player for Australia, Newcombe is easing himself out of competition and into broadcasting and commentary, winning the JAKS award as Broadcaster of the Year in 1978.

William ("Big Bill") Tilden III
(Feb. 10, 1893–June 5, 1953)

USTA Photo

Tilden won the U.S. Singles title seven times. In 1920, he began a record string of Davis Cup wins, continuing to capture the trophy for the next seven years. Tilden gained professional status in 1931 and, despite amputation of part of a finger in 1922, excelled at tennis until his death.

HALL OF FAME

International Tennis Hall of Fame
194 Bellevue Ave.
Newport, RI 02840
(401) 846-4567

Members of the International Tennis Hall of Fame are:

1955	1956	1957
Oliver Campbell	May Sutton Bundy	Mary K. Browne
Joseph S. Clark	William J. Clothier	Maurice E. McLoughlin
James Dwight	Dwight Filley Davis	Hazel Hotchkiss Wightman
Richard D. Sears	William A. Larned	Richard N. Williams II
Henry W. Slocum, Jr.	Holcombe Ward	
Malcolm D. Whitman	Beals O. Wright	
Robert D. Wrenn		

1958
William ("Little Bill") Johnston
Molla Bjurstedt Mallory
R. Lindley Murray
Helen Wills Moody Roark
William ("Big Bill") Tilden III
Maud Barger Wallach

1961
Fred B. Alexander
Malcolm G. Chace
Harold H. Hackett
Francis T. Hunter
Vincent Richards

1962
John H. Doeg
Helen Hull Jacobs
Ellsworth Vines

1963
Wilmer L. Allison
Sarah Palfrey Danzig
Julian S. Myrick
John Van Ryn

1964
George T. Adee
Don Budge
George M. Lott, Jr.
Alice Marble
Francis X. Shields
Sidney B. Wood, Jr.

1965
Pauline Betz Addie
Ellen Hansell Allerdice
W. Donald McNeill
James H. Van Allen
Watson Washburn

1966
Joseph R. Hunt
Frank A. Parker
Theodore R. Pell
Frederick R. ("Ted") Schroeder, Jr.

1967
Louise Brough Clapp
Margaret Osborne DuPont
Robert L. ("Bobby") Riggs
William F. Talbert

1968
Maureen Connolly Brinker
Allison Danzig
Richard A. ("Pancho") Gonzales
John A. Kramer
Eleonora R. Sears

1969
Karl H. Behr
Charles S. Garland
Doris Hart
Arthur Larsen
Marie Wagner

1970
Clarence J. ("Peck") Griffin
Shirley Fry Irvin
Perry T. Jones
Marion ("Tony") Trabert

1971
Althea Gibson Darben
Elizabeth H. Moore
Arthur C. Nielsen
Elias Victor Seixas

1972
Bryan M. ("Bitsy") Grant, Jr.
Gardner Mulloy
Elizabeth Ryan

1973
Darlene R. Hard
Gene Mako
Alistair Martin

1974
Juliette Atkinson
Robert Falkenburg
Fred H. Hovey
Bertha Townsend Toulmin

1975
Lawrence A. Baker
Fred Perry
Ellen Roosevelt

1976
Jean Borotra
Jacques ("Toto") Brugnon
Mabel Cahill
Henri Cochet
Jean-Rene Lacoste
Richard Savitt

1977
Manuel Alonso
Norman Brookes
Budge Patty
Betty Nuthall Shoemaker
Gottfried von Kramm

1978
Maria Bueno
Pierre Etchebaster
Kathleen McKane Godfree
Harry Hopman
Suzanne Lenglen
Anthony Wilding

1979
Margaret Smith Court
John H. Crawford
Gladys Heldman
Al Laney
Raphael Osuna
Frank Sedgman

1980
H. Laurence Doherty
Reginald Doherty
Gustav V of Sweden
Lewis Hoad
Ken Rosewall

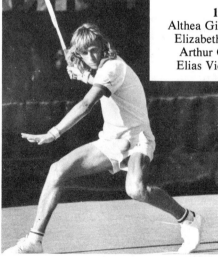
ABC Sports

For the Record

Grand Slam
2   Rod Laver, 1962 and 1969
     Don Budge, 1938

Longest match, singles
126 games   Roger Taylor vs Wieslaw Gasiorek, Kings Cup, Warsaw, 1966

Fastest serve
163.6 mph   Bill Tilden, 1931

Longest championship career
50 years   Alphonso Smith, 1924–74—from National Boy's Championship to
            National 65-and-Over Championship

Grand Slam (Wimbledon and U.S., French and Australian opens)
1   Maureen Connolly, 1953
     Margaret Smith Court, 1970

Most singles titles, Big Four
24   Margaret Smith Court

Most singles titles, overall
62   Margaret Smith Court

Youngest winner of Big Four singles titles
Wimbledon   Charlotte Dod (15), 1887
United States   Tracy Austin (16), 1979
France   Christine Truman (18), 1959
Australia   Margaret Smith Court (17), 1960

Longest winning streak, tournament singles
56 matches   Chris Evert   1964

Most singles matches, one surface
125   Chris Evert   August 1973–May 1979
       (clay courts)

Fastest serve
126 mph   Beth Jassoy, U.S. National Fast Serve Championships, 1979

Longest match, tournament singles
62 games   Kathy Blake vs Elena Subirats, Locust Valley, NY, 1966

Longest tournament doubles
81 games   Nancy Richey and Carole Graebner vs
            Justina Bricka and Carol Hanks, South Orange, NJ, 1964

Longest set, singles
36 games   Billie Jean King vs Christine Truman, Wightman Cup, 1963

Longest set, doubles
64 games   Richey & Graebner vs Hanks & Bricka, South Orange, NJ, 1964

1. For some monarchs, the game of tennis has been decidedly unlucky. What four European kings lost their lives because of a passion for tennis?

2. Although tennis expertise often seems to run in families, only two brothers have been inducted into the International Hall of Fame. Who were they?

3. Tennis has one of the most unusual scoring systems in sports. How did the term *love* come to mean a score of zero in tennis?

4. Wimbledon was the first international tennis tournament, and no player's career is complete without at least one Wimbledon title. Yet one of the legendary greats of the game never won a tournament there. Who?

5. What player went to great lengths to keep his Wimbledon victory a secret?

6. In the 1970s an ophthalmologist, considered a superb player but never a star, became the center of a sports controversy that reached international proportions. How did this talented but obscure player create such a ruckus?

Answers: 1. Henry I of Castile, Louis X of France, and Philip I of Spain all died of colds caught while playing tennis. In addition, James I of Scotland, assassinated in 1437, died because he couldn't escape through a passageway he had ordered blocked to prevent the escape of tennis balls; **2.** Laurence and Reginald Doherty were both added to the Hall of Fame's roster in 1980; **3.** *Love* is probably derived from *l'oeuf,* French for "egg." *L'oeuf* became the French equivalent of "duck egg" (zero in English cricket) and the American "goose egg"; **4.** "Pancho" Gonzales, one of the best players in the history of tennis, became a professional before he could win Wimbledon. By 1968, when the rules were changed to allow pros to compete, Gonzales was past his prime; **5.** In 1893, Joshua Pim, an English physician, entered Wimbledon under an assumed name, fearing his medical practice would suffer if it were known he was competing, "Mr. X." won the title that year. **6.** In 1976, Dr. Richard Raskin underwent a sex-change operation and renamed herself Renee Richards. Although many female athletes objected strenuously to Dr. Richard's participation as a woman, she remained on the tennis circuit for the next two years.

ace   *see* service ace.

advantage   the first point scored after deuce. If the same player wins the next point, he wins the game. If the other player takes the next point, the score goes back to deuce.

all   used in scoring to denote an even score; for example, if each player has 30 points, the score is 30–all.

backhand   a stroke from the left side of a right-handed player or from the right side of a left-handed player.

base lines   the lines defining the boundaries of the court parallel to the net.

championship match   a match played by the last two players left in an elimination tournament.

deuce   score tied at 40 points-all. Once deuce is reached, a player must win two consecutive points to win the game.

double fault   two consecutive faults by the server, resulting in loss of the point.

doubles   games played by two teams of two persons each.

elimination tournament   the most common type of tournament, in which individual players are eliminated as soon as they lose a single round.

fault   a rule violation in which a serve does not fall within the bounds of the proper service court or the player steps out of the legal area from which he may serve (foot fault).

forecourt   the area of the court in front of the service line.

forehand   a stroke from the right side of a right-handed player or from the left side of a left-handed player.

game   the unit of a set won by a player who wins four points before his or her opponent wins three, or two points more than an opponent with three or more points.

ground stroke   stroke hit after one bounce close to the net.

half-court line   the line dividing the area between service lines into left and right service courts.

let   a serve that lands in the correct service court after (1) hitting the net or (2) being served before the opponent is ready.

linesmen   fourteen officials stationed at each sideline, both base lines, and each center line, and one with his or her hand on the net, each of whom may signal to the umpire that balls are "good" or "out."

lob   a high, soft shot.

love   a score of zero. Each player starts out with a score of love.

match   the unit of play won by the player who wins two out of three (for women, or, by prearrangement, for men) or three out of five (men only) sets.

mixed doubles   games in which two teams, each composed of a man and a woman, compete.

open   a tournament in which amateurs can compete with professionals without losing their amateur standing so long as they do not accept prize money.

overhead smash   a stroke used to hit down hard on the ball.

passing shot   a difficult shot landing to one side of and beyond the opponent.

quarterfinals   the first four matches played by the last eight players left in an elimination tournament.

rally   a series of shots hit back and forth over the net until the point is decided; also, practice of the same before a game.

round robin   a tournament in which each player meets against each other player at least once, with a won-lost record determining standing.

seeding   arranging the order of an elimination tournament so that the best players get easier opponents in the earlier rounds and do not meet against each other until later in the tournament.

semifinals   two matches played by the last four players left in an elimination tournament.

serve   the stroke that puts the ball into play.

service ace   a hard-hit or well-positioned serve that the opponent is unable to return.

service break   the case of a player's winning a game that the opponent served.

service courts   the two left and two right boxes formed by the intersections of the net, service lines, and half-court line.

service ace   a hard-hit or well-positioned serve that the opponent is unable to touch with the racket.

service break   the case of a player's winning a game that the opponent served. wins five, or two games more than the opponent who has won five or more games.

umpire   the official who sits at the end of the net and records and calls out the score.

volley   a ball hit before it has bounced.

ABC Sports

18   TRACK & FIELD

As anyone who has ever taken even a cursory glance at a playground can attest, running, jumping, and throwing things all seem to be innate urges in human beings. And, as prehistoric people were doubtless aware, skill and speed in these activities went a long way to guaranteeing, or at least increasing, one's chances for survival.

Although formal competition in running, jumping, and throwing (now called athletics, or track and field) is thought to have originated in Greece, similar sports, and similar competitions, have sprung up independently in many other cultures. Ancient Irish lore, for example, mentions games held at County Meath in the eighteenth century B.C., and the initiation rites of hundreds of cultures required that young men demonstrate their prowess in running (for both speed and endurance), leaping high or far, and throwing with force and accuracy.

The first "modern" contest, however, was the Greek Olympiad of 776 B.C., an event that, like its immediate successors during the next 52 years, consisted of a single 200-yard sprint. Subsequent Olympiads included longer and more complex races and field events, such as high and long jumping and the throwing of the discus, javelin, and hammer. From the time the Romans held their own Olympics until they banned them in A.D. 392, the games consisted of a relatively elaborate set of tests including the pentathlon, and such nontrack-and-field events as boxing, chariot racing, and wrestling. Track-and-field events similar to those of ancient times still form the core of the modern Olympic games. Most of these sports are held at the collegiate level as well, and thousands of athletes participate in them noncompetitively, for the pleasure they afford.

For many, the major attraction of track and field is the absence of any obstacle to achievement—other than one's own strength, skill, and endurance. In track and field, no one is trying to block or impede your performance; the essence of competition is in the attempt to master one's own body and force it to perform better, and better, and better. Thus competitors are usually as interested in breaking their own records as in breaking those of others.

Most Olympics and other track-and-field competitions are the occasion for a good deal of record-breaking. Improved nutrition, an increased understanding of how the body works, and improvements in technology (better tracks, rubber-soled shoes, fiberglass poles, and so on) have resulted in consistently improved performances, so much so that records which made many stars of yesterday seem almost superhuman are now routinely broken at high school and college track meets.

The quest for even greater speed, endurance, and distance continues, and the prize, whether an Olympic gold medal, a place in the record book, or the like, still goes to the person who can throw the farthest, leap the highest, or be the first to cross the finish line.

Great Moments

1849 The Royal Military Academy at Woolwich, England, sponsors the first recorded amateur athletic meet.

1876 The Intercollegiate Association of America is formed and holds the first of its annual championship series.

1888 The Amateur Athletic Union is organized.

1890 John H. Owen breaks the 10-second barrier for the 100-yard dash, running it in 9.8 seconds.

1893 The first intercollegiate relay races are held between Princeton University and the University of Pennsylvania. Princeton wins.

1895 The first international track meet is held as New York plays London. New York wins.

1897 The first Boston Marathon is held.

1901 In Colorado Springs, Colorado, Candiras De Foya, a Ute Indian, runs the 100-yard dash in 9 seconds flat, setting a new record so incredible the track world decides to ignore it. That same year, the Harvard relay team sets a new mile record of 3:21.2.

1912 Jim Thorpe, a Sac and Fox Indian, wins gold medals in the Olympic pentathlon and decathlon. Later, a Boston paper reveals that Thorpe had once played minor league baseball, and he is forced to return his medals.

1913 The International Amateur Athletic Federation is founded, in Berlin.

1929   Eric Krenz throws the discus 163 feet 8.75 inches. He thus becomes the first person ever to exceed 160 feet.

1931   Nineteen-year-old Babe Didrikson breaks the world record for 80-meter hurdles.

1936   The success of Jesse Owens at the Olympics in Berlin cheers millions as it deflates the vaunted Nazi claim of Aryan superiority.

1941   Al Blozis sets a world indoor shotput record of 56 feet 4.5 inches.

1952   American Bob Mathias becomes the first man to win back-to-back gold medals in the grueling Olympic decathlon.

1956   Milton Campbell becomes the first black to win the Olympic decathlon as he defeats Rafer Johnson, another black contender.

1960   Sprinter Wilma Rudolph captures three gold medals at the Rome Olympics, becoming the first American woman to win three gold medals in one year.

1968   Bob Beamon takes the gold medal in Mexico City with a long jump of 29 feet 2.5 inches. Beamon's jump, often called "the perfect leap," becomes the standard against which all others are measured. That year, Bob Seagren pole vaults 17 feet 9 inches, setting his third world record.

1972   Nina Kuscsik becomes the first woman to officially complete the Boston Marathon, coming in before some 400 men.

1980   The Athletics Congress of the U.S.A. takes over governance of track and field from the AAU.

1981   On July 11, Edwin Moses wins his sixty-fifth consecutive race in the 400-meter hurdles, with a time of 47.99.

The
Setup

The most important track-and-field events today take place in the realm of amateur athletics, either in a college setting, in the Olympics, or in various national and international contests. Although some events, chiefly exhibitions and marathons, are sponsored by one or the other of several independent athletic organizations, most track and field today is under the aegis of either the Athletics Congress of the U.S.A. (ACUSA) or the intercollegiate associations.

All Olympic competition is governed by the International Amateur Athletic Federation (IAAF), which is closely allied with the World Olympic Committee. The American representative of the IAAF has in the past been the Amateur Athletic Union, which is closely tied to the U.S. Olympic Committee. In 1980, however, governance of track-and-field events passed from the AAU to ACUSA, which conducts all national amateur track-and-field meets in the United States, sanctioning champions, establishing records, and granting eligibility to compete in the Olympic Games.

On the collegiate level, competitions in track and field are organized by the National Collegiate Athletic Association (NCAA), the National Association of Intercollegiate Athletics (NAIA), and the Association for Intercollegiate Athletics for Women (AIAW).

ASSOCIATION FOR
  INTERCOLLEGIATE ATHLETICS
  FOR WOMEN
1201 16th St. NW
Washington, DC 20036
Ann Uhlir, dir.

NATIONAL ASSOCIATION OF
  INTERCOLLEGIATE ATHLETICS
1221 Baltimore St.
Kansas City, MO 64105
(816) 842-5050
Harry Fritz, exec. dir.

ATHLETICS CONGRESS OF THE
  U.S.A.
3400 W. 86th St.
Indianapolis, IN 46268
(317) 297-2900
Ollan C. Cassell, exec. dir.

NATIONAL COLLEGIATE
  ATHLETIC ASSOCIATION
P.O. Box 1906
Shawnee Mission, KS 66222
(913) 384-3220
Walter Byers, exec. dir.

The Basics

TRACK EVENTS

Object   To cross the finish line in the least time.

The track   Tracks may be indoors or outdoors, and they may vary in length, configuration, and construction. All lanes must be of uniform size and all races must end at the same point. Inclinations may not exceed a specified maximum in the lateral, throwing, or running direction.

Competitors   The number of competitors varies. All competitors wear numbers on the front and back of their shirts. Competitors draw lots to determine their positions at the starting line.

Officials   Numerous officials are required at track meets, including: finish judges, photo-finish panel, inspectors, referee, starter, recall starter, timers, lap scorers, and wind-gauge operators.

Events   Many different events comprise a track meet, including: running races of varying distances, races requiring runners to jump over obstacles, and race walking.

Rule 1   The start   All competitors must be situated behind the starting line before the race begins. Except in time-handicap races, the start occurs when a starter's pistol is fired. Commands of the starter are "on your mark" and "set," followed by the firing of the pistol. If any competitor moves after the command "set," but before the start, the race may not begin. A competitor commits a false start by touching the starting line or the ground in front of it before the shot; two false starts result in disqualification. If an official decides that the start was not fair, the racers may be recalled.

Rule 2   Direction of run   All racers run counterclockwise.

Rule 3   Markers   No competitor may place a marker on the field.

Rule 4   Obstructing   No competitor may jostle or otherwise interfere with another so as to impede his or her progress.

Rule 5   Aid   No competitor may receive aid or advice (pacing, coaching, and so on) during a race.

Rule 6   Fouls   A referee may disqualify any competitor who, in the referee's judgment, commits a foul during the final heat of a race.

Rule 7   Timing   The head timer announces lap times to competitors.

Rule 8   Leaving the track or field   No contestant who has left the track or field during the competition may return to it, either to rejoin the event or to aid another competitor.

Rule 9   The finish   All competitors must run the full distance. Competitors are ranked in the order in which they cross the finish line (with the torso, not the head or limbs). The winner is the first person to cross.

FIELD EVENTS

Javelin Throw

The javelin, a spearlike instrument, is thrown from behind an arc, and it must land in the marked sector of the arc. Although it must land tip first, it does not have to remain stuck in the ground. Competitors are judged on their approach, the way they hold and throw the javelin, the way the javelin lands, and on distance it is thrown.

Shot Put

A spherical piece of solid metal weighing 16 pounds is thrown by a person standing within a marked circle. Each competitor gets 6 throws (3 if more than 8 are competing, with the best 8 getting 3 more tries) to throw the shot the farthest. The shot must land within a marked segment of the field. The person with the best throw wins.

Discus Throw

A flat disk weighing at least two kilograms (one kilogram for women) is thrown from within a marked circle. Competitors get six throws (three if eliminations are being held) to throw the discus the farthest and have it land within a marked sector. A thrower may not touch or leave the circle while throwing or while the discus is in motion. Competitors must begin their throws from stationary positions. The person who throws the discus the farthest wins.

ABC Sports Photos

Hammer Throw

A spherical piece of metal weighing at least 16 pounds is attached to a handle with a piece of wire. A gloved competitor swings this "hammer" from within a circle (as with the discus event, the circle is enclosed by a mesh cage, for safety reasons) and throws it toward a marked segment of the field. Throwers may not rest the hammer on the ground (except during practice swings) or touch any part of the circle. As in other events, throwers may be eliminated after three trials, and the person who in six tries achieves the greatest distance, wins.

High Jump

Jumpers get a running start (in as much space as they need) to approach and jump over a crossbar. After each distance is cleared by all competitors, the bar is raised, until only one person is able to clear it; that person is the winner. Participants may decide whether to try any jump; they are eliminated after three failures. They must not have both feet on the ground before jumping, touch the ground before clearing the bar, or knock the bar down.

Pole Vault

Competitors use a fiberglass pole to boost them over a crossbar after an unlimited run-up. Competitors must not knock the bar off with their bodies or their poles, and they may not move their upper hand higher (or move their lower hand higher than the upper one) after they have left the ground. After three consecutive failures, an entrant is eliminated. The winner is the person who clears the highest crossbar.

Long Jump

Formerly called the broad jump, this event consists of competitors jumping from a takeoff board into a landing area filled with sand. Jumpers have six tries (although in large matches there may be some elimination after three). Jumpers have unlimited space in which to run up to the takeoff line but may not touch or cross the line before jumping. The person who jumps the farthest wins.

ABC Sports Photos

Triple Jump

Also known as the hop-step-and-jump, the triple jump uses the same landing board and takeoff area as the long jump (but, in international competition, with a 13-meter space between them). Competitors take three leaps, landing first on the takeoff foot (the hop), then on the other foot (the step), and finally on both feet (the jump). The winner is the entrant with the longest distance in six tries.

The Pentathlon

A two-day series of five events, scored by a point system. The first day's events are the 100-meter hurdles, the shot put, and the high jump. On the second day, competitors complete the long jump and the 200-meter dash. The entrant with the highest combined score for all events wins.

The Decathlon

A 10-event test of all-round athletic skill that lasts two days. On the first day, participants compete in the 100-meter dash, the 400-meter dash, the high jump, the long jump, and the shot put. On the second day, they enter the 110-meter hurdles, the discus throw, the pole vault, the javelin throw, and the 1,500-meter run. The competitor with the highest combined score for all events wins.

How to watch

with Tom Jordan

Watching a track-and-field event is a little like watching a horse race: the end result is obvious, but it is nearly impossible for an onlooker to detect all the thinking, training, and strategy that go into it. The key, according to Tom Jordan, assistant publisher of *Track and Field News* magazine and an experienced observer of track-and-field meets, is what you know about the racers beforehand—their backgrounds and records.

"There are infinite subtleties within each event," Jordan says. "If you are reasonably well informed before you start you will be able to get more enjoyment out of it." Meet programs, sports magazines, and newspaper sections are all good sources of information.

Each track-and-field event requires its own kind of strategy, technique, and physical strength, according to Jordan. Strategy enters more into the running events, while technique is almost all of the other events. In every case, the athlete's personality affects his approach as well as the track-and-field event he excels at.

The sprinter, for instance, is a lot like a boxer, according to Jordan. "Sprinters are great psych-out artists," he says. "Boxers hope that what is said and done before they step into the ring gives them a mental edge. It's the same with sprinters. They will often attempt to assert their dominance before they even get to the block—once a sprinter has done that he may have a mental edge over his opponent, who may not get off to as fast a start."

Distance runners, on the other hand, "are usually more humble people, and are not out to psych *out* their opponents as much as they want to psych themselves *up* for a long race," according to Jordan. For them, strategy means knowing how to pace themselves and when to pour on that extra energy needed to win the race.

"For instance, Steve Scott, who is America's best miler, ran a very fast race in May 1981. The pace was quite slow and he was back in the pack about 10 yards or so, but because it was slow and he is so strong and so fast, he ended up running an extremely fast last lap and won by 20 yards. He could tell by his own kind of internal computer that he didn't need to worry about being behind."

In both sprints and long-distance races smooth running is "absolutely paramount," Jordan observes. "You have to be the most efficient you can be. You can tell the caliber of runners just by how smooth they are."

Technique matters more than strategy in field events. "So much depends on the athlete's timing, footwork, and mental state on the day of the competition," says Jordan. "If any one factor is off, he will perform below his maximum potential." Often the event happens so fast that it is difficult to tell how an athlete will do until he has completed the event, but Jordan lists the following points an onlooker can watch for.

High Jump The technique most commonly used for clearing high jumps, today, according to Jordan, is the flop, in which the athlete goes over the jump back first. "If his plant leg is six inches off or if he fails to torque his body at exactly the right point in the air, or if he fails to flip his calves up into the air, he will miss."

Pole Vault "This is probably the most gymnastic of all track-and-field events. It requires a great deal of speed, a lot of strength and, most of all, agility. The athlete must know when to push away from the pole and curl his body around the bar without knocking it off."

Triple Jump "The technique for this event is very difficult to master. It is more artificial than the long jump. You have to run and hop on the same leg, switch legs, and jump into the pit. If the athlete fails to hop on the same leg or to switch legs before making the leap, he misses the jump."

Long Jump "This is more classic. It's been done since the days of ancient Greece. You look for speed, a build-up of momentum, and the ability to jump far."

Shot Put "The bigger and stronger the athlete is, the better."

Discus Throw/Hammer Throw "In both the discus throw and the hammer throw, speed is important. The ability to build momentum and throw at just the right moment makes the difference."

Javelin Throw Jordan calls this a classic event requiring a combination of strength and coordination. "You will find thin men who are very good at it and stocky ones who are good at it—just as there are some thin baseball players who have a tremendous arm and some very stocky ones who do as well."

In events such as the men's decathlon or the women's pentathlon, training is the key. Once at the competition, the decathlon or pentathlon competitor must go all out on each event. Over the years, there have been changes in training techniques that have led to changes in the outcomes. For instance, Jordan points out, Bruce Jenner trained hard at the running events, something decathlon competitors had not done before.

"At the 1976 Olympics, he was tired when he finished the 1,500-meter, the last of the ten events, but he wasn't on his knees like some of the others.

Finally, an important way for the spectator to tell how an athlete will do is by noticing where he's from and who his coach is. "An excellent coach can get more out of an athlete than can a merely adequate coach working with the same athlete," Jordan says.

Main Events

OLYMPICS

Men's
100-METER DASH

Year	Winner	Country	Time
1980	Allan Wells	UK	10.25 sec
1976	Hasely Crawford	Trinidad and Tobago	10.06 sec
1972	Valery Borzov	USSR	10.14 sec
1968	Jim Hines	USA	9.90 sec

200-METER DASH

Year	Winner	Country	Time
1980	Pietro Mennea	Italy	20.19 sec
1976	Don Quarrie	Jamaica	20.23 sec
1972	Valery Borzov	USSR	20.00 sec
1968	Tommie Smith	USA	19.80 sec

400-METER DASH

Year	Winner	Country	Time
1980	Viktor Markin	USSR	44.60 sec
1976	Alberto Juantorena	Cuba	44.26 sec
1972	Vincent Matthews	USA	44.66 sec
1968	Lee Evans	USA	43.80 sec

800-METER RUN

Year	Winner	Country	Time
1980	Steve Ovett	UK	1 min 45.40 sec
1976	Alberto Juantorena	Cuba	1 min 43.40 sec
1972	Dave Wottle	USA	1 min 45.90 sec
1968	Ralph Doubell	Australia	1 min 44.30 sec

1,500-METER RUN

Year	Winner	Country	Time
1980	Sebastian Coe	UK	3 min 38.40 sec
1976	John Walker	New Zealand	3 min 39.17 sec
1972	Pekka Vasala	Finland	3 min 36.30 sec
1968	Kipchoge Keino	Kenya	3 min 34.90 sec

5,000-METER RUN

Year	Winner	Country	Time
1980	Miruts Yifter	Ethiopia	13 min 21 sec
1976	Lasse Viren	Finland	13 min 24.76 sec
1972	Lasse Viren	Finland	13 min 26.4 sec
1968	Mohammed Gammoudi	Tunisia	14 min .05 sec

ABC Sports

10,000-METER RUN

Year	Winner	Country	Time
1980	Miruts Yifter	Ethiopia	27 min 42.7 sec
1976	Lasse Viren	Finland	27 min 40.38 sec
1972	Lasse Viren	Finland	27 min 38.4 sec
1968	Naftali Temu	Kenya	29 min 27.4 sec

MARATHON

Year	Winner	Country	Time
1980	Waldemar Cierpinski	GDR	2 hr 11 min 3 sec
1976	Waldemar Cierpinski	GDR	2 hr 9 min 55 sec
1972	Frank Shorter	USA	2 hr 12 min 19.8 sec
1968	Mamo Wolde	Ethiopia	2 hr 20 min 26.4 sec

3,000-METER STEEPLECHASE

Year	Winner	Country	Time
1980	Bronislaw Malinowski	Poland	8 min 9.7 sec
1976	Anders Garderud	Sweden	8 min 8.02 sec
1972	Kipchoge Keino	Kenya	8 min 23 sec
1968	Amos Biwott	Kenya	8 min 51 sec

400-METER RELAY

Year	Winner	Country	Time
1980	National Team	USSR	38.26 sec
1976	National Team	USA	38.33 sec
1972	National Team	USA	38.19 sec
1968	National Team	USA	38.2 sec

1,600-METER RELAY

Year	Winner	Country	Time
1980	National Team	USSR	3 min 1.1 sec
1976	National Team	USA	2 min 58.65 sec
1972	National Team	Kenya	2 min 59.8 sec
1968	National Team	USA	2 min 56.1 sec

110-METER HURDLES

Year	Winner	Country	Time
1980	Thomas Munkelt	GDR	13.39 sec
1976	Guy Drut	France	13.30 sec
1972	Rodney Milburn	USA	13.24 sec
1968	Willie Davenport	USA	13.30 sec

400-METER HURDLES

Year	Winner	Country	Time
1980	Volker Beck	GDR	48.70 sec
1976	Edwin Moses	USA	47.64 sec

| 1972 | John Akii-Bua | Uganda | 47.80 sec |
| 1968 | David Hemery | UK | 48.10 sec |

20,000-METER WALK

Year	Winner	Country	Time
1980	Maurizio Damiliano	Italy	1 hr 23 min 35.5 sec
1976	Daniel Bautista	Mexico	1 hr 24 min 40.6 sec
1972	Peter Frenkel	GDR	1 hr 26 min 42.4 sec
1968	Vladimir Golubnichy	USSR	1 hr 33 min 58.4 sec

RUNNING HIGH JUMP

Year	Winner	Country	Distance
1980	Gerd Wessig	GDR	7 ft 8.25 in
1976	Jacek Wszola	Poland	7 ft 4.5 in
1972	Yuri Tarmak	USSR	7 ft 3.75 in
1968	Dick Fosbury	USA	7 ft 4.25 in

RUNNING HIGH JUMP

Year	Winner	Country	Distance
1980	Gerd Wessig	GDR	7 ft 8.25 in
1976	Jacek Wszola	Poland	7 ft 4.5 in
1972	Yuri Tarmak	USSR	7 ft 3.75 in
1968	Dick Fosbury	USA	7 ft 4.25 in

LONG JUMP

Year	Winner	Country	Distance
1980	Lutz Dombrowski	Poland	28 ft .25 in
1976	Arnie Robinson	USA	27 ft 4.5 in
1972	Randy Williams	USA	27 ft .5 in
1968	Bob Beamon	USA	29 ft 2.5 in

TRIPLE JUMP

Year	Winner	Country	Distance
1980	Jaak Uudmae	USSR	56 ft 11.125 in
1976	Viktor Saneyev	USSR	56 ft 8.75 in
1972	Viktor Saneyev	USSR	56 ft 11 in
1968	Viktor Saneyev	USSR	57 ft .75 in

POLE VAULT

Year	Winner	Country	Distance
1980	Wladyslaw Kozakiewicz	Poland	18 ft 11.5 in
1976	Tadeusz Slusarski	Poland	18 ft 11.5 in
1972	Wolfgang Nordwig	GDR	18 ft .5 in
1968	Bob Seagren	USA	17 ft 8.5 in

SHOT PUT

Year	Winner	Country	Distance
1980	Vladimir Kiselyov	USSR	70 ft .5 in
1976	Udo Beyer	GDR	69 ft .75 in
1972	Wladyslaw Komar	Poland	69 ft 6 in
1968	Randy Matson	USA	67 ft 4.75 in

DISCUS THROW

Year	Winner	Country	Distance
1980	Viktor Rashchupkin	USSR	218 ft 8 in
1976	Mac Wilkins	USA	221 ft 5 in
1972	Ludvik Danek	Czechoslovakia	211 ft 3 in
1968	Al Oerter	USA	212 ft 6 in

JAVELIN THROW

Year	Winner	Country	Distance
1980	Dainus Kula	USSR	299 ft 2.375 in
1976	Miklos Nemeth	Hungary	310 ft 4 in
1972	Klaus Wolfermann	FRG	296 ft 10 in
1968	Janis Lusis	USSR	295 ft 7 in

HAMMER THROW

Year	Winner	Country	Distance
1980	Yuri Sedykh	USSR	268 ft 4.5 in
1976	Yuri Sedykh	USSR	254 ft 4 in
1972	Anatoly Bondarchuk	USSR	247 ft 8.5 in
1968	Gyula Zsivotzky	Hungary	240 ft 8 in

DECATHLON

Year	Winner	Country	Points
1980	Daley Thompson	UK	8,495
1976	Bruce Jenner	USA	8,618
1972	Nikolai Avilov	USSR	8,454
1968	Bill Toomey	USA	8,193

WOMEN'S

100-METER RUN

Year	Winner	Country	Time
1980	Lyudmila Kondratyeva	USSR	11.06 sec
1976	Annegret Richter	FRG	11.08 sec
1972	Renate Stecher	GDR	11.07 sec
1968	Wyomia Tyus	USA	11 sec

200-METER RUN

Year	Winner	Country	Time
1980	Barbara Wockel	GDR	22.03 sec
1976	Baerbel Ecker	GDR	22.37 sec
1972	Renate Stecher	GDR	22.4 sec
1968	Irena Szewinska	Poland	22.5 sec

400-METER RUN

Year	Winner	Country	Time
1980	Marita Koch	GDR	48.88 sec
1976	Irena Szewinska	Poland	49.29 sec
1972	Monika Zehrt	GDR	51.08 sec
1968	Colette Besson	France	52 sec

800-METER RUN

Year	Winner	Country	Time
1980	Nadezhda Olizarenk	USSR	1 min 53.5 sec
1976	Tatyana Kazankina	USSR	1 min 54.94 sec
1972	Hildegard Flack	FRG	1 min 58.6 sec
1968	Madeline Manning	USA	2 min 0.9 sec

1,500-METER RUN

Year	Winner	Country	Time
1980	Tatyana Kazankina	USSR	3 min 56.6 sec
1976	Tatyana Kazankina	USSR	4 min 5.48 sec
1972	Ludmila Bragina	USSR	4 min 1.4 sec

400-METER RELAY

Year	Winner	Country	Time
1980	National Team	GDR	41.6 sec
1976	National Team	GDR	42.55 sec
1972	National Team	FRG	42.81 sec
1968	National Team	USA	42.8 sec

1,600-METER RELAY

Year	Winner	Country	Time
1980	National Team	USSR	3 min 20.02 sec
1976	National Team	GDR	3 min 19.22 sec
1972	National Team	GDR	3 min 0.23 sec

100-METER HURDLES

Year	Winner	Country	Time
1980	Vera Komisova	USSR	12.56 sec
1976	Johanna Schaller	GDR	12.77 sec

1972	Annelie Ehrhardt	GDR	12.59 sec
1968	Maureen Caird (80 meters)	Australia	10.30 sec

HIGH JUMP

Year	Winner	Country	Distance
1980	Sara Simeoni	Italy	6 ft 5.5 in
1976	Rosemarie Ackerman	GDR	6 ft 4 in
1972	Ulrike Meyfarth	FRG	6 ft 3.625 in
1968	Miloslava Rezkova	Czechoslovakia	5 ft 11.75 in

LONG JUMP

Year	Winner	Country	Distance
1980	Tatyana Kolpakova	USSR	23 ft 2 in
1976	Angela Voigt	GDR	23 ft .5 in
1972	Heidemarie Rosendahl	FRG	22 ft 3 in
1968	Viorica Ciscopoleanu	Romania	22 ft 3 in

SHOT PUT

Year	Winner	Country	Distance
1980	Ilona Sluplanek	GDR	73 ft 6 in
1976	Ivanka Christova	Bulgaria	69 ft 5 in
1972	Nadezhda Chizhova	USSR	69 ft
1968	Margitta Gummer	GDR	64 ft 4 in

DISCUS THROW

Year	Winner	Country	Distance
1980	Evelin Jahl	GDR	229 ft 6.5 in
1976	Evelin Schlaak	GDR	226 ft 4 in
1972	Faina Melnik	USSR	218 ft 7 in
1968	Lia Manoliu	Romania	191 ft 2.5 in

JAVELIN THROW

Year	Winner	Country	Distance
1980	Maria Colon	Cuba	224 ft 5 in
1976	Ruth Fuchs	GDR	216 ft 4 in
1972	Ruth Fuchs	GDR	209 ft 7 in
1968	Angela Nemeth	Hungary	198 ft

PENTATHLON

Year	Winner	Country	Points
1980	Nadyezhda Tkachenko	USSR	5,083
1976	Siegrun Siegl	GDR	4,745
1972	Mary Peters	UK	4,801
1968	Ingrid Becker	FRG	5,098

BOSTON MARATHON

Year	Winner	Year	Winner
1981	Toshihiko Seko	1976	Jack Fultz
1980	Bill Rodgers	1975	Bill Rodgers
1979	Bill Rodgers	1974	Neil Cusack
1978	Bill Rodgers	1973	Jon Anderson
1977	Jerome Drayton	1972	Olav Suomalainen

AAU CROSS-COUNTRY CHAMPIONS (10,000-METER)

Year	Winner		Year	Winner	
1980	John Sinclair	USA	1975	Greg Fredericks	USA
1979	Alberto Salazar	USA	1974	John Ngeno	Kenya
1978	Greg Meyer	USA	1973	Frank Shorter	USA
1977	Nick Rose	USA	1972	Frank Shorter	USA
1976	Rick Rojas	USA	1971	Frank Shorter	USA

All-Time Greats

Harrison Dillard
(July 8, 1923–)

National Track and Field Hall of Fame

Dillard is the only person ever to win Olympic gold medals in both sprints and hurdles. While still in college, in 1947–48, he took both the AAU and NCAA hurdling titles, setting records of 13.6 seconds for high hurdles and 22.3 for low. By 1948 he had won 52 consecutive hurdling races before an unexpected loss dissuaded him from trying the hurdles in the Olympics. He instead joined the games for the 100-meter sprint, which he made in 10.3 seconds, tying Jim Thorpe's record and winning the gold medal. In 1952 he returned to the Olympics, winning one gold medal for the high hurdles and another as a member of the U.S. 400-meter relay National Team.

Bruce Jenner
(May 28, 1949–)

ABC Sports

If the winner of the grueling Olympic decathlon is truly the world's greatest athlete, then Bruce Jenner is the crème de la crème. Jenner took the Olympic world by storm when, in Montreal in 1976, he not only returned to the United States with a decathlon trophy that had eluded it since 1968, but he did so by achieving the highest score ever, a whopping 8,618 points. Jenner, who also competed with the U.S. team in the 1972 Olympic Games in Munich, finished out his winning year by being named AP Male Athlete of the Year and *Sport* magazine's Track and Field Performer of the Year, as well as carrying home the James E. Sullivan Trophy for Outstanding

Amateur Athlete of the Year. Now a professional, he is active on the lecture circuit, has written several books, and lends his services as a sports commentator.

Robert B. Mathias
(Nov. 17, 1930–)

U.S. Olympic Training Center

Bob Mathias won the California State High School discus and shot put championships in 1947, when he was a junior, and went on to an illustrious field-event career. In 1948, when he was only 17 years old, he took the gold medal for the decathlon at the London Olympic Games. After the games were over he won four national decathlon championships in a row before returning for an unprecedented second Olympic win in 1952–doing all of this while he was also playing football for Stanford University. In 1966 he retired from athletics to enter politics and served as a representative from California's 18th District.

Jesse Owens
(Sept. 12, 1913–Mar. 31, 1980)

National Track and Field Hall of Fame

James Cleveland (J. C. and later "Jesse") Owens tied the world record for the 100-yard dash (10 seconds flat) when he was still in junior high school. In 1933 he was a triple winner in the National Intercollegiate Championships, and in 1935 he set or equaled six track records in a single day. Owen's greatest triumph—both athletic and moral—came when he won four gold medals at the 1936 Olympics in Berlin, tying one record, setting another two, and running anchor on the record-breaking U.S. 400-meter relay team. This stellar performance caused Adolf Hitler, who was presiding over the ceremonies, to walk out of the Olympic Stadium rather than present a medal to a non-Aryan (Owens was black). Owens became a hero to many in the world for dealing the Nazi master race theory a humiliating blow. He left competition in 1937, pursuing business enterprises, exhibition performances, and public service.

Wilma Rudolph
(June 23, 1940–)

A childhood illness temporarily left her with the use of only one leg when she was just eight years old, but Wilma Rudolph went on to become a great sprinter and the first American woman to win three Olympic gold medals in one year. Three years after her illness she was playing backyard basketball, and by the time she was a sophomore she had broken the state girl's high school basketball scoring record. At the 1960 Olympics, when she was 20 years old, she ran the 100-meter dash in 11 seconds (because the wind was at her back she didn't get to set a record), and the 200-meter sprint in 24 seconds; she also served as anchor on the U.S. 400-meter relay team. Her performances earned her three gold medals plus The AP Award for U.S. Female Athlete of the Year and the UPI Athlete of the Year Award.

Jim Thorpe
(May 28, 1888–Mar. 28, 1953)

Pro Football Hall of Fame

Many believe that Jim Thorpe was the finest all-round athlete of all time. A Sac and Fox Indian from Oklahoma, Thorpe played football at the now-defunct Carlisle Indian School under "Pop" Warner, and put the school on the athletic map. At the same time he was firmly entrenching himself as a track star. Thorpe is the only person in Olympic history to win both the pentathlon and decathlon, which he did in Stockholm in 1912. After his spectacular performance, a Boston newspaper created a scandal by revealing that Thorpe had played semiprofessional baseball in 1911 (a charge Thorpe admitted) and insisting that Thorpe had thereby forfeited amateur standing. Thorpe was forced to surrender his medals. After the incident, he went on to play professional baseball and football, enjoying successful careers in both. In 1920 he was elected the first president of the NFL's forerunner, the AFPA, a job for which he was not well equipped and in which he was unhappy. He was replaced the next year and his career took a downward turn. At the end of his life Thorpe was earning a meager living as a sometime movie extra. He died in obscurity in 1953.

Mildred ("Babe") Didrikson Zaharias
(June 26, 1914–Sept. 27, 1956)

LPGA Photo

America's greatest female athlete, Babe Didrikson made her mark in many fields, including basketball (she was an All-American while still in high school) and golf (she was the best woman golfer of her time). She made her first national appearances as a track star, however, in the 1932 AAU National Track and Field Tournament, where she entered eight out of ten events and won five. Later that year she entered the Olympic Games, held in Los Angeles, and won two gold medals, setting a new world record for the javelin throw and a new U.S. record for the 80-meter hurdles. She also set a record in the high jump, but it was disallowed because of a technicality. After her triumph in the Olympics, Didrikson became a professional track-and-field performer, touring the country giving exhibitions, until she took up professional golf in 1935. She married the champion wrestler George Zaharias in 1938, and died of cancer in 1955.

ABC Sports

TRACK AND FIELD HALL OF FAME

Citizens Savings Hall of Fame Athletic Museum
9800 S. Sepulveda Blvd.
Los Angeles, CA 90045
(213) 670-7556
W. R. ("Bill") Schroeder, dir.

Members of the Track and Field Hall of Fame are:

Harry Adams
Platt Adams
Daniel Ahearn
David Albritton
Frank Anderson
Horace ("Ash") Ashenfelter III
Richard Attlesey
Robert Backus
Raymond Barbutti
Lee Barnes
Weems Baskin
Robert Beamon
Gregory Bell
Albert C. Blozis
William Bonthron
Johnny Borican
Ralph H. Boston
Donald ("Tarzan") Bragg
Emil Breikrutz
George Bresnahan
Herman Brix
Earlene Brown
Emmett Brunswon
T. Edward Burke
Michael Butler
Lee Q. Calhoun
Milton Campbell
Kenneth Carpenter
Sabin Carr
Walter Christie
Mack Clark
Roy B. Cochran
Boyd Comstock
Thomas Conneff
Harold Connolly
Olga Fikotova Connolly
Lillian Copeland
Tom Courtney
Ralph Craig
Dean B. Cromwell
Glenn Cunningham
William B. Curtis
Willie Davenport
Alice Coachman Davis
Glenn ("Jeep") Davis
Harold ("Hal") Davis
Jack Davis
Ron Delany
Clarence DeMar

John Deni
Harrison Dillard
Gilbert Dodds
Dorothy Dodson
J. Kenneth Dohery
James Donahue
Henry F. Dreyer
Charles Dumas
Clarence Dussault
Edith McGuire Duvall
Benjamin Eastman
Millard ("Bill") Easton
Clarence ("Hec") Edmundson
James ("Jumbo") Elliot
Norwood ("Barney") Ewell
Ray C. Ewry
Edward Farrell
Stephen Farrell
Barbara Ferrell
Daniel J. Ferris
Robert Fetzer
Keane Fitzpatrick
John J. Flanagan
M. W. Ford
Ivan Fuqua
Matthew Geis
John Gibson
Harry L. Gill
Fortune Gordien
Edward Gordon
Alex Grant
George R. Gray
Charles Edward Greene
Louis Gregory
George Griffin
Archie Hahn
Evelyn Hall
Brutus Hamilton
Edward Hamm
J. Flint Hanner
James B. Haralson
Glen Hardin
E. C. ("Billy") Hayes
Robert L. Hayes
Ward Haylett
William Hayward
Oscar Hedlund
Franklin ("Bud") Held
Ralph Higgins

Frank Hill
Harry Hillman
Harry Hinkel
George Horine
Clarence Houser
Lawrence Houston
Charles ("Chuck") Hoyt
William DeHart Hubbard
Ward Hutsell
John Jacobs
Chester Jenkins
Cornelius Johnson
Leo T. Johnson
Rafer Johnson
Hayes W. Jones
John Paul Jones
Thomas Jones
Payton Jordan
Frances Kaszubski
Thomas Keane
Jim Kelley
John A. Kelley
John J. Kelley
Abel Kiviat
Alvin C. Kraenzlein
Mabel Landry
Mike Larabee
Marjorie Larney
Donald Lash
Henry Laskau
James D. Lightbody
Leland P. Lingle
Clyde B. Littlefield
Hilmer Lodge
Dallas Long
Leslie MacMitchell
John J. ("Jack") Magee
Ralph Mann
Medline Jackson Manning
Robert Bruce Mathias
Randel Matson
Peter McArdle
Joseph P. McCluskey
Mildred McDaniel
Patrick J. ("Babe") McDonald
Matthew McGrath
Harry McMillian
Earle Meadows
James E. ("Ted") Meredith

Ralph Metcalfe	Joie ("Chesty") Ray	Bartholomew J. Sullivan
William Mihalo	George Rhoden	James E. Sullivan
Rodney Milburn	Gregory J. Rice	Elizabeth ("Betty") Robinson Swartz
Billy Mills	Alma Richards	F. Morgan Taylor
J. S. Mitchell	Robert E. Richards	Robert L. ("Dink") Templeton
John Moakley	George L. Rider	John C. Thomas
Bernice H. Moore	Lawson N. ("Robbie") Robertson	Wilbur Thompson
Charles J. Moore, Jr.	Thomas P. Rosandich	Earl Thomson
Glenn Morris	Ralph Rose	Eddie Tolan
Ronald Morris	Jack Rourke	Bill Toomey
Bobby Joe Morrow	Wilma Rudolph	Fred Tootell
Jesse Mortensen	Michael Ryan	Jack ("Baby Jack") Torrance
Loren Murchison	Patrick Ryan	Forrest ("Speck") Towns
Michael C. Murphy	Jack Ryder	Wyomia Tyus
Laurence E. ("Lon") Myers	James Ryun	Emil Von Elling
Jean Shiley Newhouse	Karl Schlademan	Stella Walsh
William Nieder	Fred Schmertz	Cornelius ("Dutch") Warmerdam
Winton E. Noah	Jackson Scholz	Bernard J. Wefers
Parry O'Brien	Harry Schulte	Willye White
Alfred Oerter	Bob Seagren	Malvin Whitfield
George Orton	Melvin W. Sheppard	A. Heath Whittle
Harold M. Osborn	Martin Sheridan	Alex Wilson
James Cleveland ("Jesse") Owens	Jay Silvester	Fred Wilt
Charles W. Paddock	Arthur Smith	Fred Wolcott
Melvin Patton	Larry Snyder	John ("Long John") Woodruff
Eulace Peacock	Arnold Sowell	Frank Wykoff
Joseph Pipal	Amos Alonzo Stagg	Chuan-Kwang Yang
Anthony Plansky	Andrew Stanfield	Mildred ("Babe") Didrikson Zaharias
William ("Bill") Plant	Heriwentha Mae Faggls Starr	Ronald L. Zinn
Archie Post	Lester Steers	
Myer Prinstein	Helen Stephens	
Dale Ranson	Curtis C. Stone	

For the Record

WORLD

Men

Event	Competitor	Record	Year
100-meter dash	Jim Hines, USA	0:09.95	1968
110-meter hurdles	Renaldo Nehemiah, USA	0:13.00	1980
200-meter dash	Pietro Mennea, Italy	0:19.72	1979
400-meter dash	Lee Evans, USA	0:43.86	1969
400-meter hurdles	Edwin Moses, USA	0:47.13	1980
800-meter run	Sebastian Coe, UK	1:41.72	1981
1,000-meter run	Sebastian Coe, UK	2:12.18	1981
1,500-meter run	Steve Ovett, UK	3:31.40	1980
1-mile run	Steve Ovett, UK	3:48.80	1980
2,000-meter run	John Walker, New Zealand	4:51.40	1976
3,000-meter run	Henry Rono, Kenya	7:32.10	1978
3,000-meter steeplechase	Henry Rono, Kenya	8:05.40	1978

Event	Competitor	Record	Year
5,000-meter run	Henry Rono, Kenya	13:08.40	1978
10,000-meter run	Henry Rono, Kenya	27:22.40	1978
20,000-meter walk	Domingo Colin, Mexico	1:20:59	1979
25,000-meter run	Bill Rodgers, USA	1:14:12	1979
30,000-meter run	Jim Adler, UK	1:31:31	1970
30,000-meter walk	Jose Marin, Spain	2:08:00	1979
50,000-meter walk	Raul Gonzales, Mexico	3:41:39	1979
1-hour run	Jos Hermans, The Netherlands	13 mi 24 yd	1976
2-hour walk	Jose Marin, Spain	17 mi 881 yd	1979
High jump	Gerd Wessig, GDR*	7 ft 8.75 in	1980
Long jump	Bob Beamon, USA	29 ft 2.5 in	1968
Triple jump	Joao Oliveira, Brazil	58 ft 8.25 in	1975
Pole vault	Vladimir Polyakov, USSR	19 ft 0.75 in	1981
Shot put	Udo Beyer, GDR	72 ft 8 in	1978
Discus throw	Wolfgang Schmidt, GDR	233 ft 5 in	1978
Javelin throw	Ferenc Paragi, Hungary	317 ft 4 in	1980
Hammer throw	Yuri Sedyky, USSR	268 ft 4 in	1980
Decathlon	Guido Kratschmer, FRG*	8,649 points	1980

Women

Event	Competitor	Record	Year
100-meter run	Lyudmila Kondratyeva, USSR	0:10.87	1980
200-meter run	Marita Koch, GDR	0:21.71	1979
400-meter run	Marita Koch, GDR	0:48.89	1979
1,500-meter run	Tatyana Kazankina, USSR	3:55	1980
1-mile run	Mary Decker, USA	4:21.7	1980
3,000-meter run	Lyudmila Bragina, USSR	8:27.1	1976
100-meter hurdles	Grazyna Rabsztyn, Poland	0:12.36	1980
400-meter hurdles	Karin Rossley, GDR	0:54.28	1980
High jump	Sara Simeoni, Italy	6 ft 7 in	1978
Long jump	Vilma Bardauskiene, USSR	23 ft 3.25 in	1978
Shot put	Ilona Slupianek, GDR	73 ft 4.25 in	1980
Discus throw	Maria Vergova, Bulgaria	235 ft 7 in	1980
Javelin throw	Tatyana Biryulina, USSR	229 ft 11 in	1980
Pentathlon	Nadezhda Tkachenko, USSR	5,083 points	1980

*German Democratic Republic (East Germany)
*Federal Republic of Germany (West Germany)

Did you know ?

1. In the 1968 Olympics in Mexico City, two American gold and bronze medalists in track events shocked the U.S. Olympic Committee by raising their fists in a "Black Power" salute. Who were they?

2. Besides Jesse Owens, what two American blacks also won gold medals for track in the 1936 Olympics?

3. The only individual medal winners for the United States at the 1972 Olympics in Munich were two women named Kathy. Who were they and what did they win?

4. Who is the only American to win the Olympic pole vault event more than once?

5. For what countries did runners Emil Zatopek, Herb McKinley, and Abebe Bikila win gold medals?

6. What track star had his name entered in the record book the most times in one day?

7. What record-setting hurdler lost his chance to qualify for the Olympic hurdling team, but went on to win a gold medal in the 100-meter dash? When did this happen?

8. Who was Horace Ashenfelter, and what is his claim to athletic fame?

9. What track star won the most medals in the history of the Olympics?

Answers: 1. Tommie Smith and John Carlos; **2.** Archie Williams and John Woodruff, for the 400- and 800-meter events; **3.** Kathy Hammond won the 400-meters and Kathy Schmidt won the javelin throw; **4.** Bob Richards, in 1952 and 1956; **5.** Czechoslovakia, Jamaica, and Ethiopia, respectively; **6.** Jesse Owens set or equaled six records on May 25, 1935; **7.** Although Harrison Dillard held the world's record in hurdling in 1948, he failed to make the Olympic team, and barely managed to win the third spot on the 100-meter dash team. He won the gold medal in that event; **8.** Horace Ashenfelter, an F.B.I. agent as of 1952, was the only American ever to win the 3,000-meter steeplechase. At a high point in the Cold War, he defeated the Soviet Union's entry, who held the world record and who was considered a shoo-in for the gold medal. Ashenfelter had run the event fewer than ten times before the 1952 Olympics; **9.** Finnish Paavo Nurmi won a total of nine gold and three silver medals in the 1920, 1924, and 1928 Olympic Games.

Key Words

anchor man   last runner in a relay race, who runs the "anchor leg,"or last leg, of the race.

baton   a hollow cylinder of wood, metal, or plastic that is carried and exchanged by relay-race runners.

(in the) blocks   the equipment a sprinter uses to get the fastest start possible, consisting of angled pedals placed behind the starting line, "in the blocks" refers to a sprinter who is ready for the gun.

championship meets   official meets of a sponsoring organization, such as the NCAA or AAU, to establish its own annual champions.

cross-country   distance running, usually two to six miles, over varying terrain rather than a track.

dual meets   track meets between different schools or countries that emphasize the team's score.

exchange   the transferring of the baton in a relay race from one runner to another in the designated exchange zone.

heats   preliminary rounds in track events.

high hurdles   barriers 3 feet 6 inches high placed over a straightaway 120 yards long.

invitational meets   commercial meets to which the promoter invites individual participants and in which individual or relay events are emphasized.

kick   to pour on a burst of speed near the finish line.

low hurdles   barriers 2 feet 6 inches high placed over a 220-yard (200-meter) straightaway.

middle-distance races   races of distances between a half-mile and 1 mile.

multiple team meets   competition between several teams from different areas, countries, or schools with emphasis on the team score.

oval   an elliptical-shaped track, used for races of more than 200 yards. Outdoor ovals are 440 yards (400 meters) around. Indoor arena tracks are shorter.

relays   running events in which usually four teammates each run part (a leg) of a race, passing the baton to the next teammate upon the completion of a leg.

sprint   a race of up to 220 yards (200 meters).

sprint medley   a four-person relay race in which the distance run by each runner varies.

sprint relay   relay races in which the runners complete 110 yards each in one race and 220 yards in another race.

steeplechase   a race in which the runner must clear obstacles.

straightaway   straight tracks used for races of 200 meters or less.

ABC Sports